AF531196

ROADWORKS

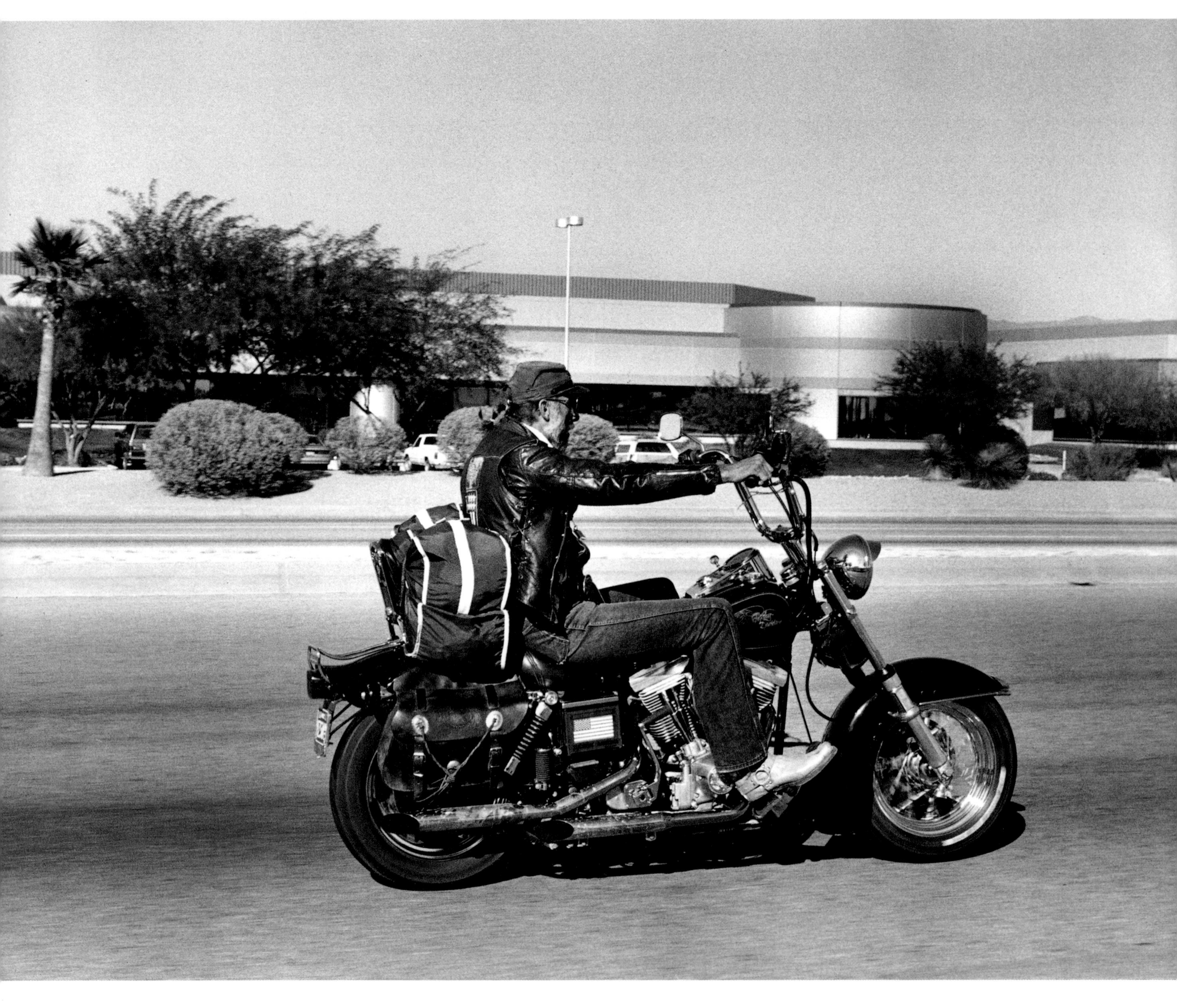

ROADWORKS

LINDA McCARTNEY

A BULFINCH PRESS BOOK / LITTLE, BROWN AND COMPANY

BOSTON · NEW YORK · TORONTO · LONDON

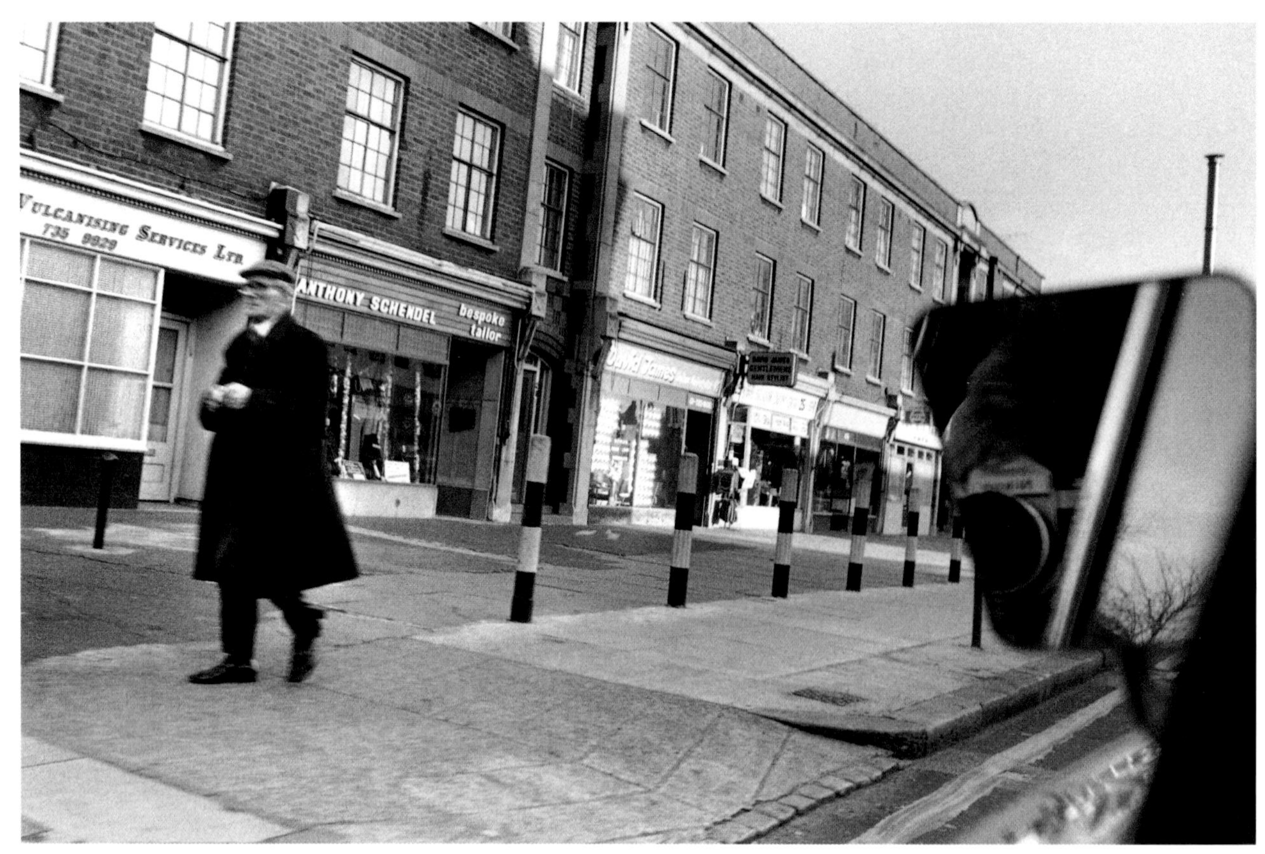

Fear crawled in through my open window
and strangled me with my own hands.

IN THE FIFTIES THEY HAD THE BEST CARS – the Ford Thunderbird, Cadillacs, the Chevy Bel Air, Oldsmobile 88s, Pontiacs – marvelous chrome streamlining and great fins! So I was in love with cars, horses, and then, when I was fourteen or fifteen, boys. I grew up in the suburb of Scarsdale. It was great fun, but a blinkered kind of existence. My father was friendly with – so I grew up around – some of the New York painters, and I often visited the Museum of Modern Art. Mostly I went there in the sixties, but I can still remember the Family of Man exhibit – the first photographs that had a real impact on me.

After graduating from high school I traveled through Europe for two months, visiting the usual tourist sites and most of the art museums. With my Box Brownie I took photographs of two girls in front of Heidelberg University. I remember being quite pleased with the results, though at the time it never occurred to me to be a photographer. Instead I took art history at the University of Arizona. After finishing my studies I attended just two nights of a class run by Hazel Archer. I had no technical training, but almost without knowing it I was becoming a photographer.

Most of my photographs are in black and white. One reason for this, I think, is that my earlier influences were black-and-white television: *Felix the Cat, Hopalong Cassidy* – you know the sort of thing; and films: *On the Waterfront, La Strada, Lonely Are the Brave, The Bicycle Thief, The Seventh Seal* – they were all black and white. And I almost floated out of the cinema after I first saw *La Dolce Vita.*

Photography was an interest at first, then a passion. By chance I was even able to make some money photographing musicians. But I always photographed *for myself,* and I've never stopped. Later, as well as photographing on the street, I began to take pictures from inside cars. I was traveling a lot, so there were plenty of opportunities. I made so many that an assistant of mine once said, "Linda, you've gotta get out of the car." Well, some of the photographs here are from cars, some aren't. They are like stills from a kind of personal road movie recording a slice of my life.

LINDA McCARTNEY

Magic Robin three-wheel XCM 597N smiles at me.

Drive

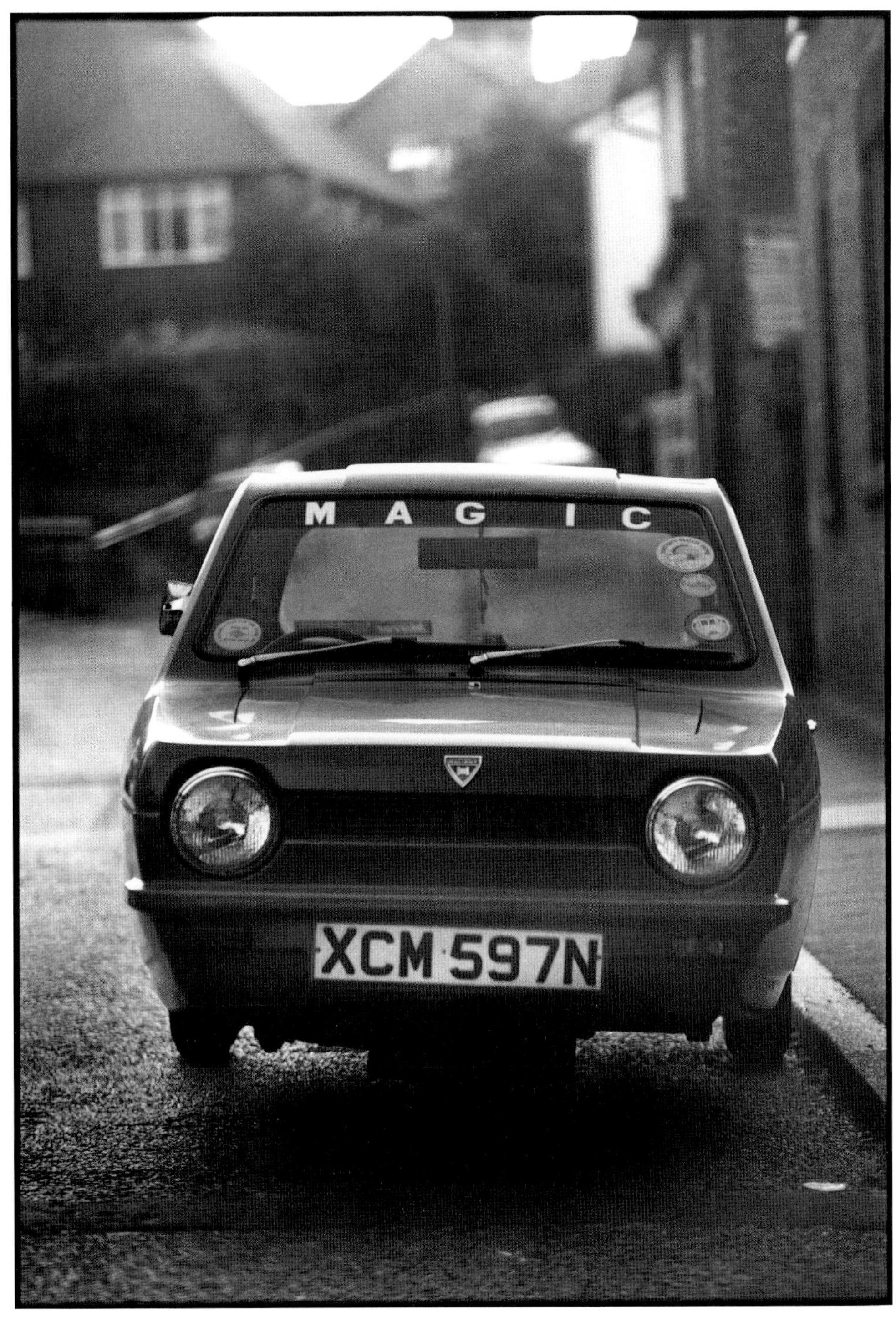
MAGIC
XCM 597N

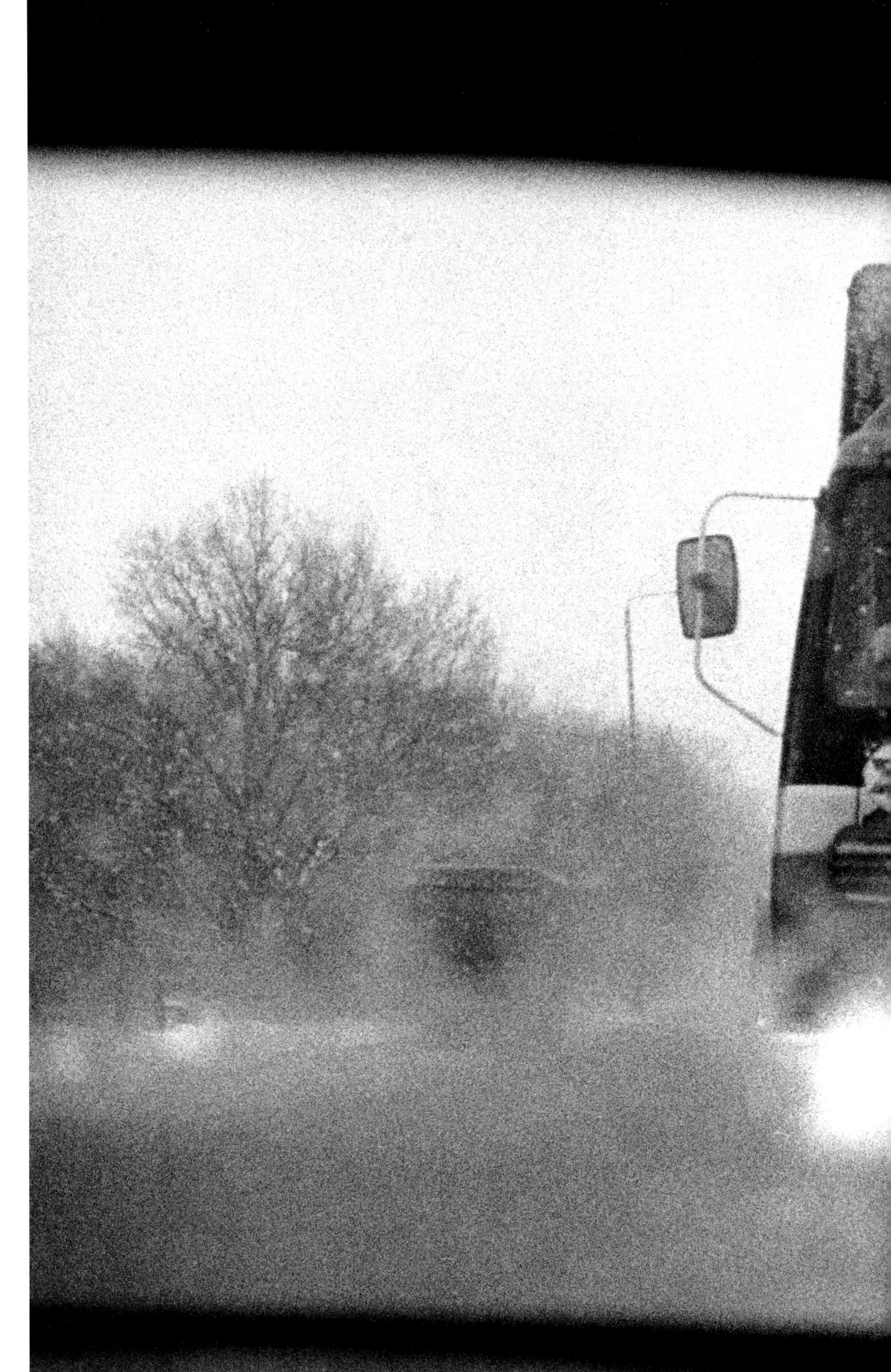

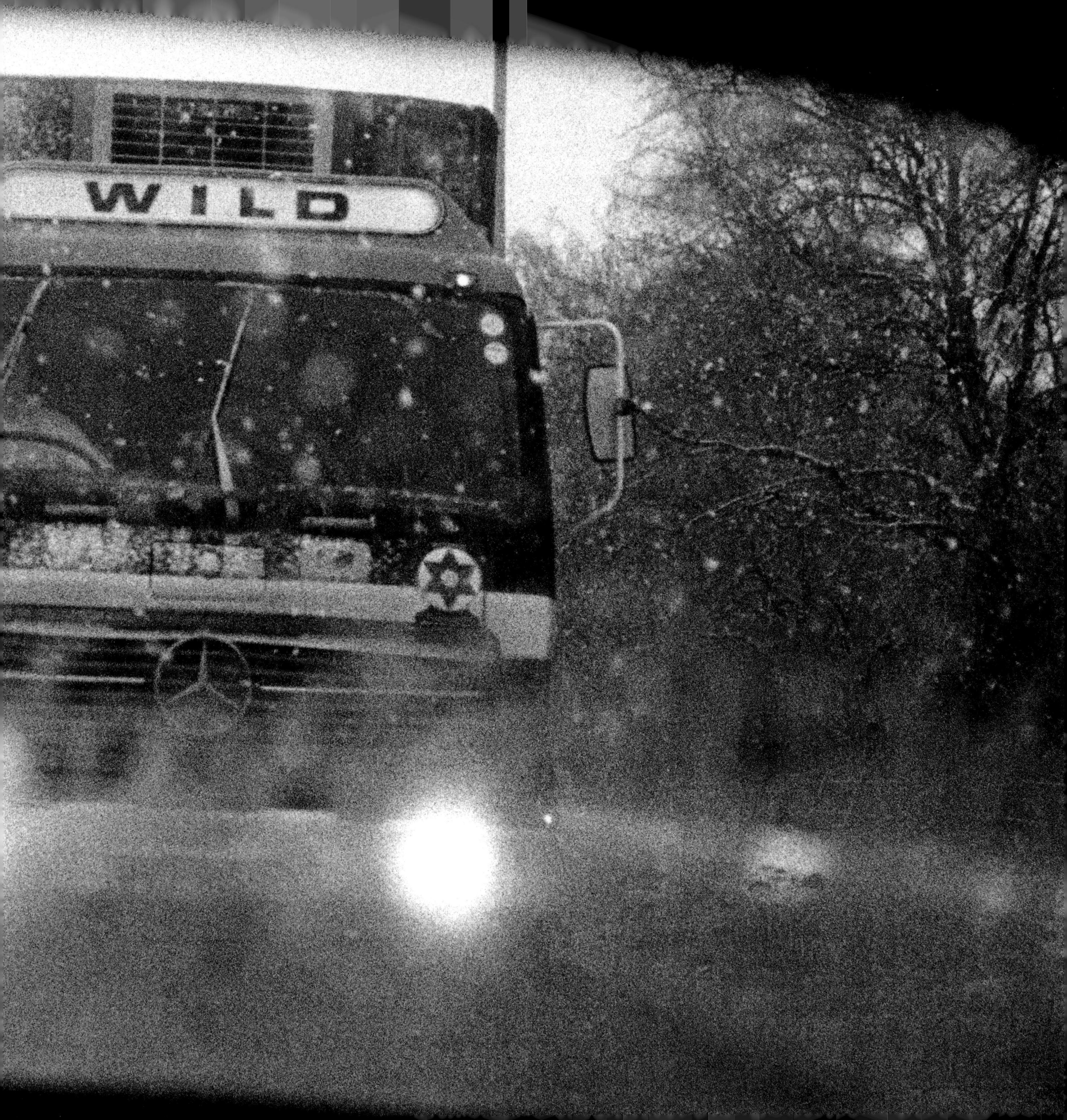
WILD

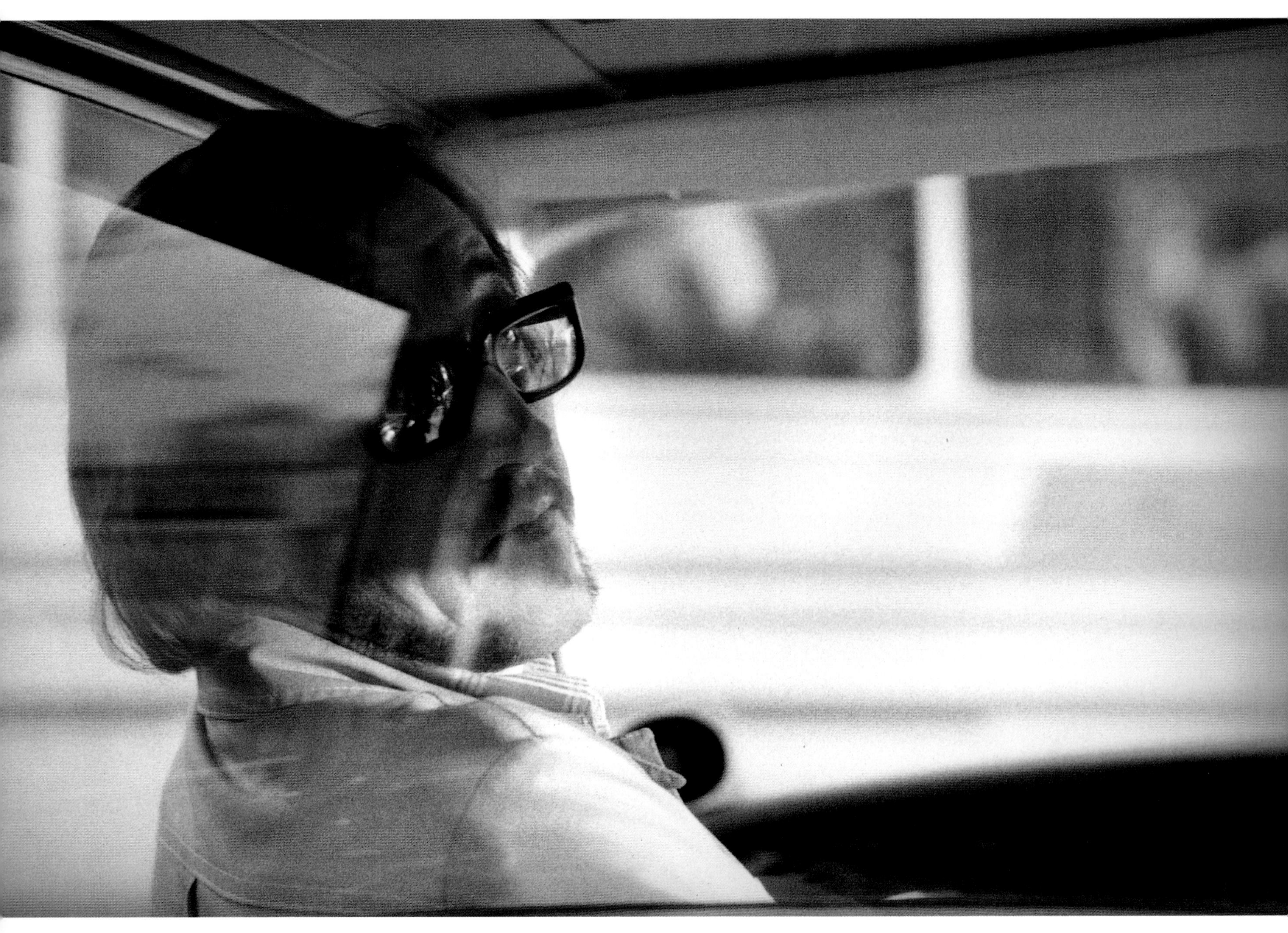

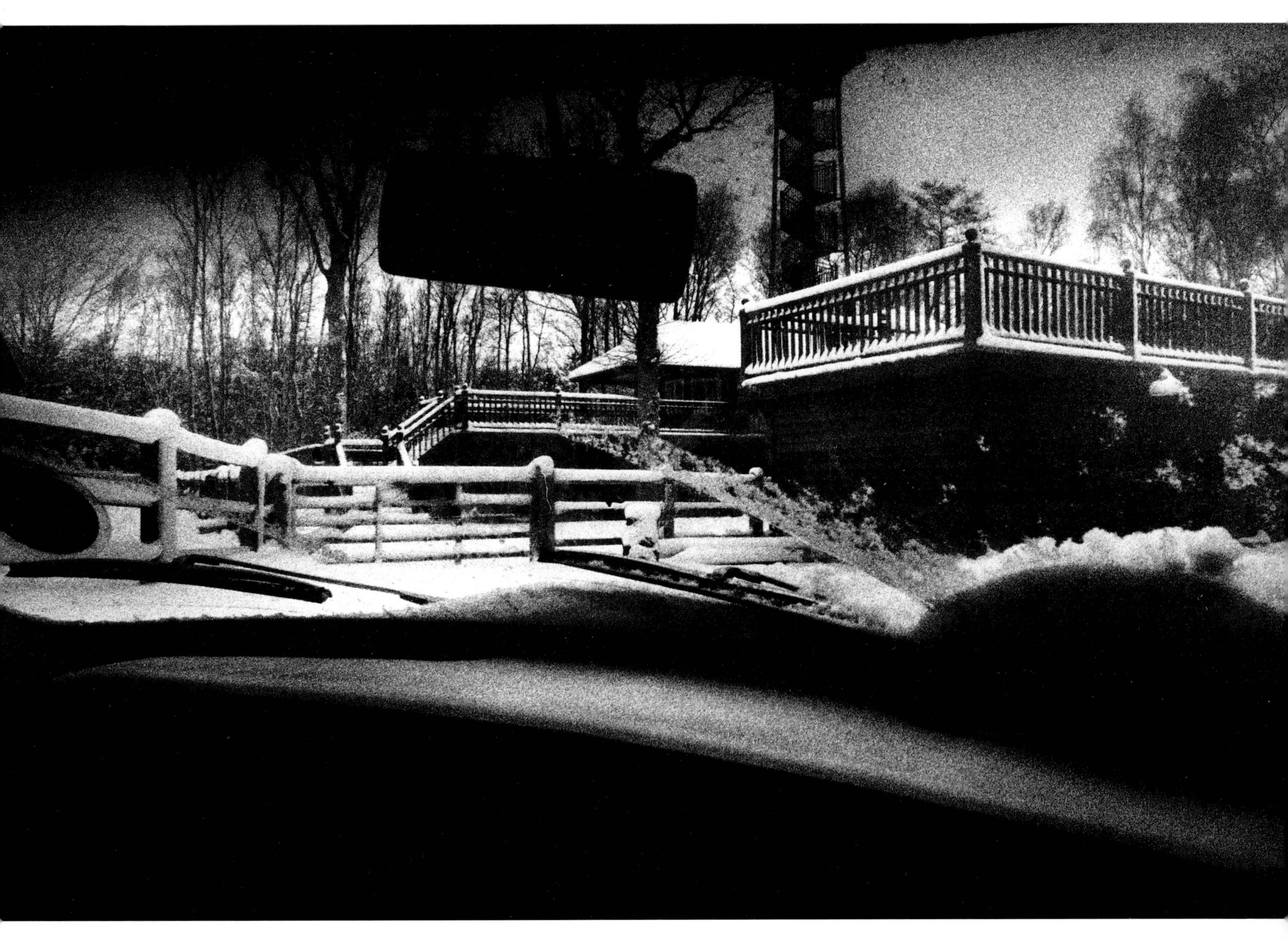

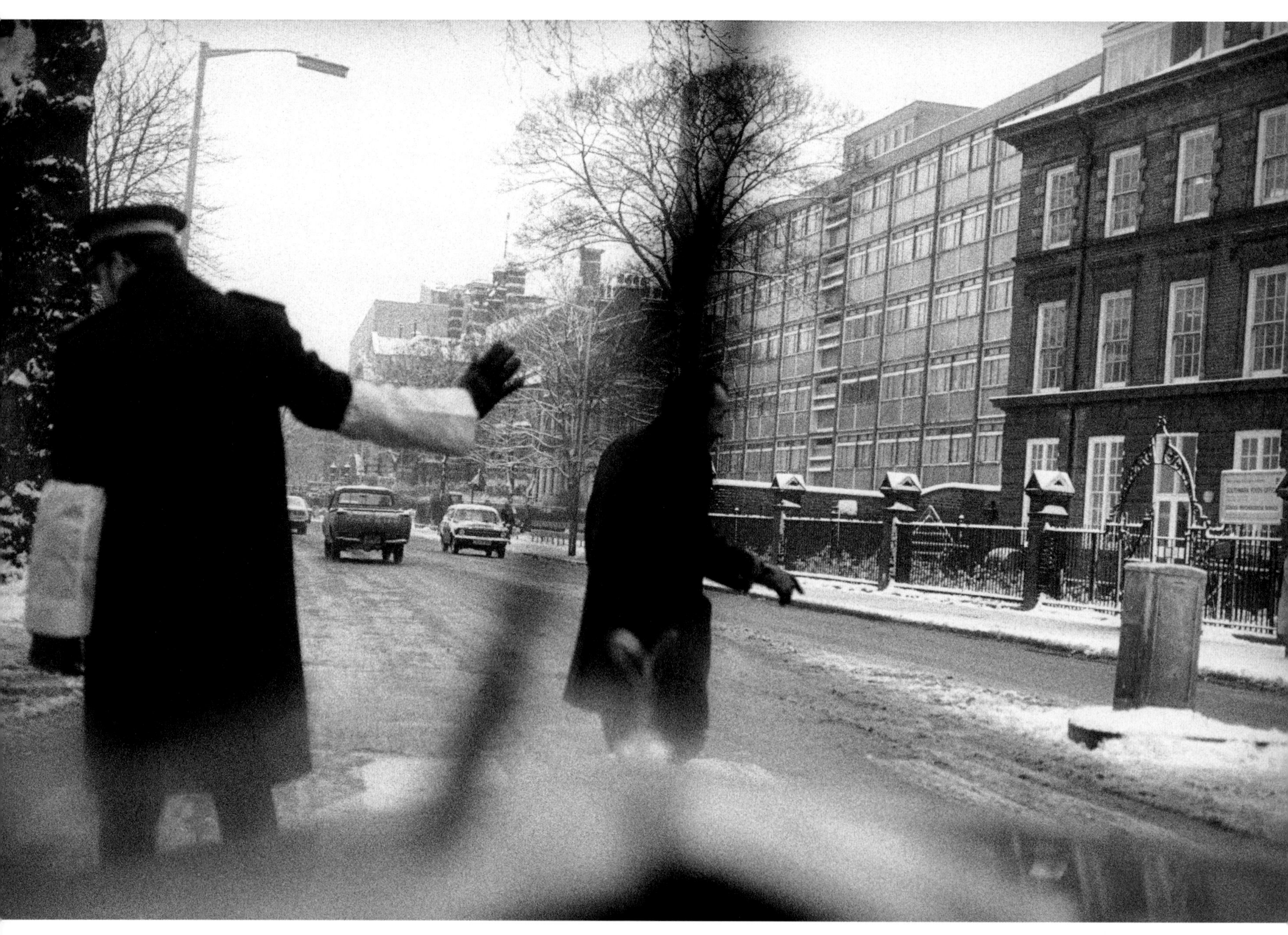

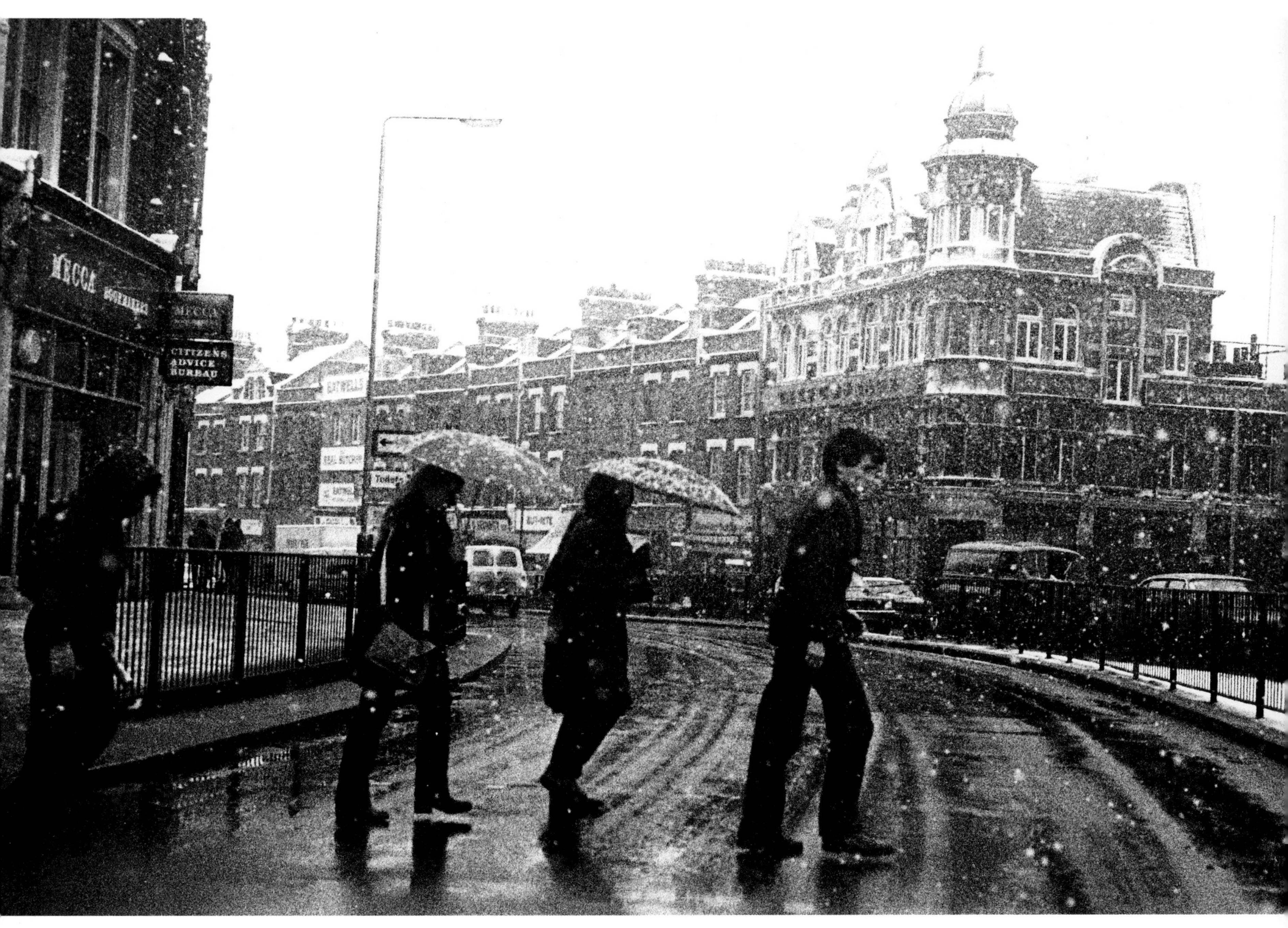
MECCA
CITIZENS
ADVICE
BUREAU

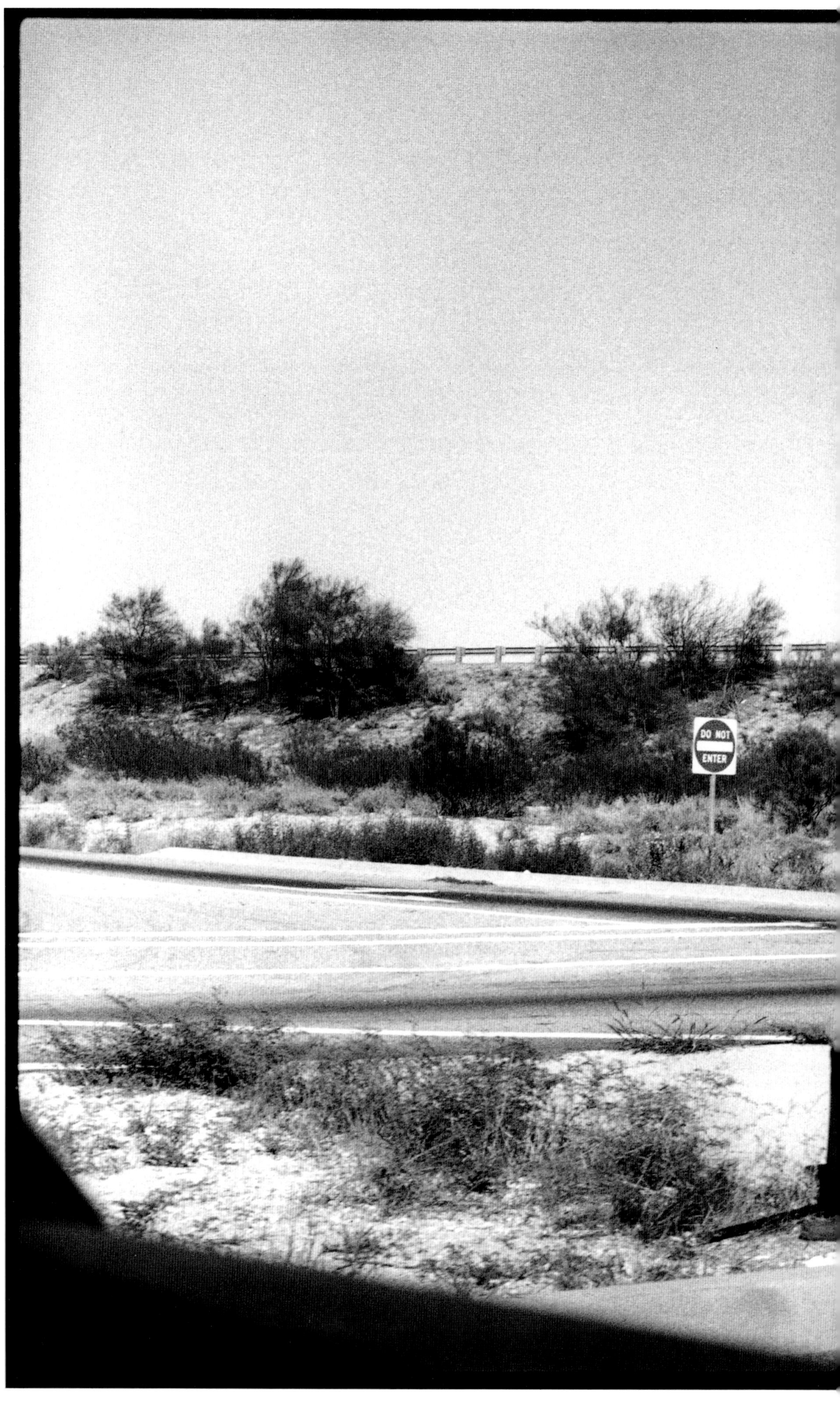
DO NOT
ENTER

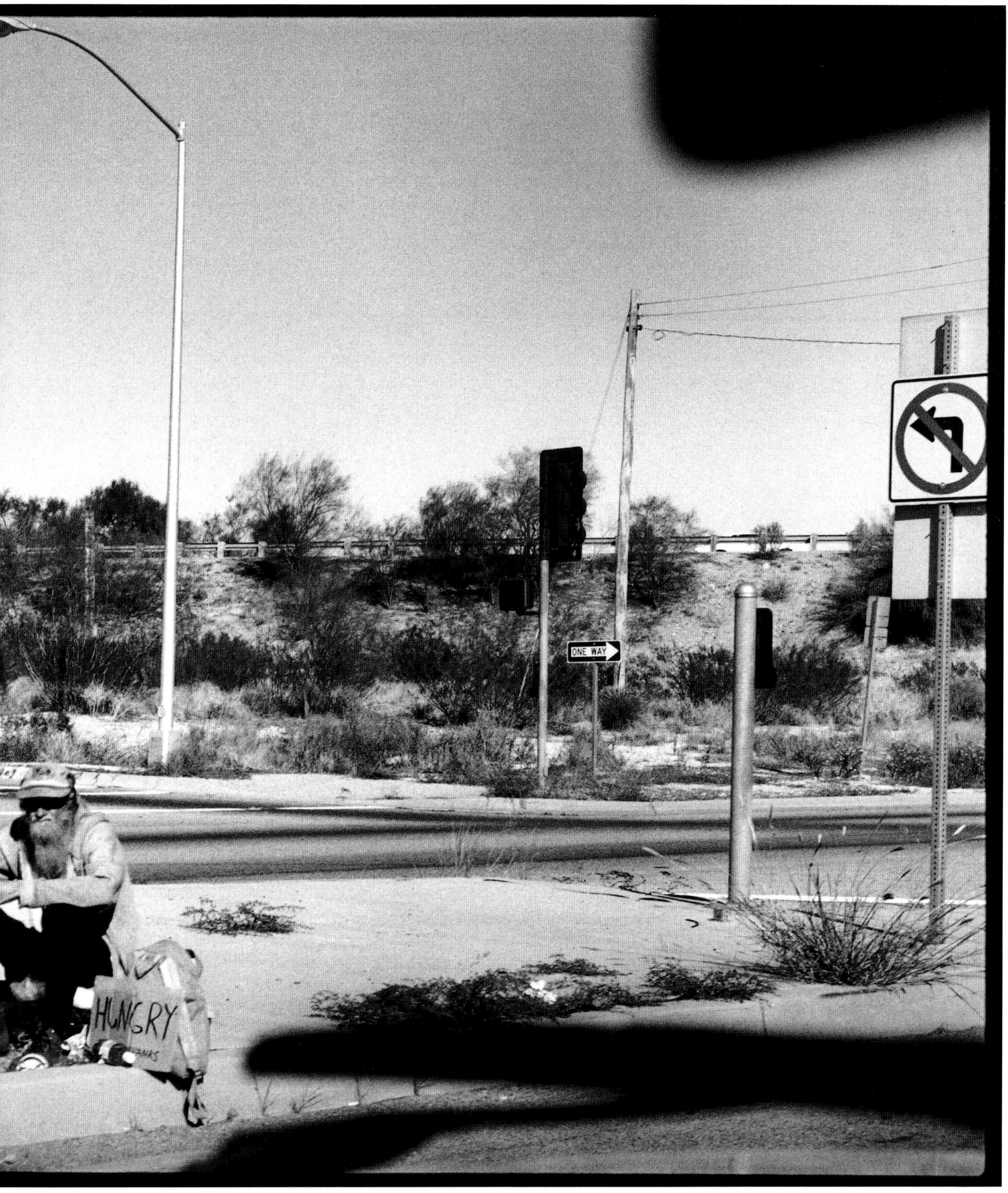
ONE WAY
HUNGRY

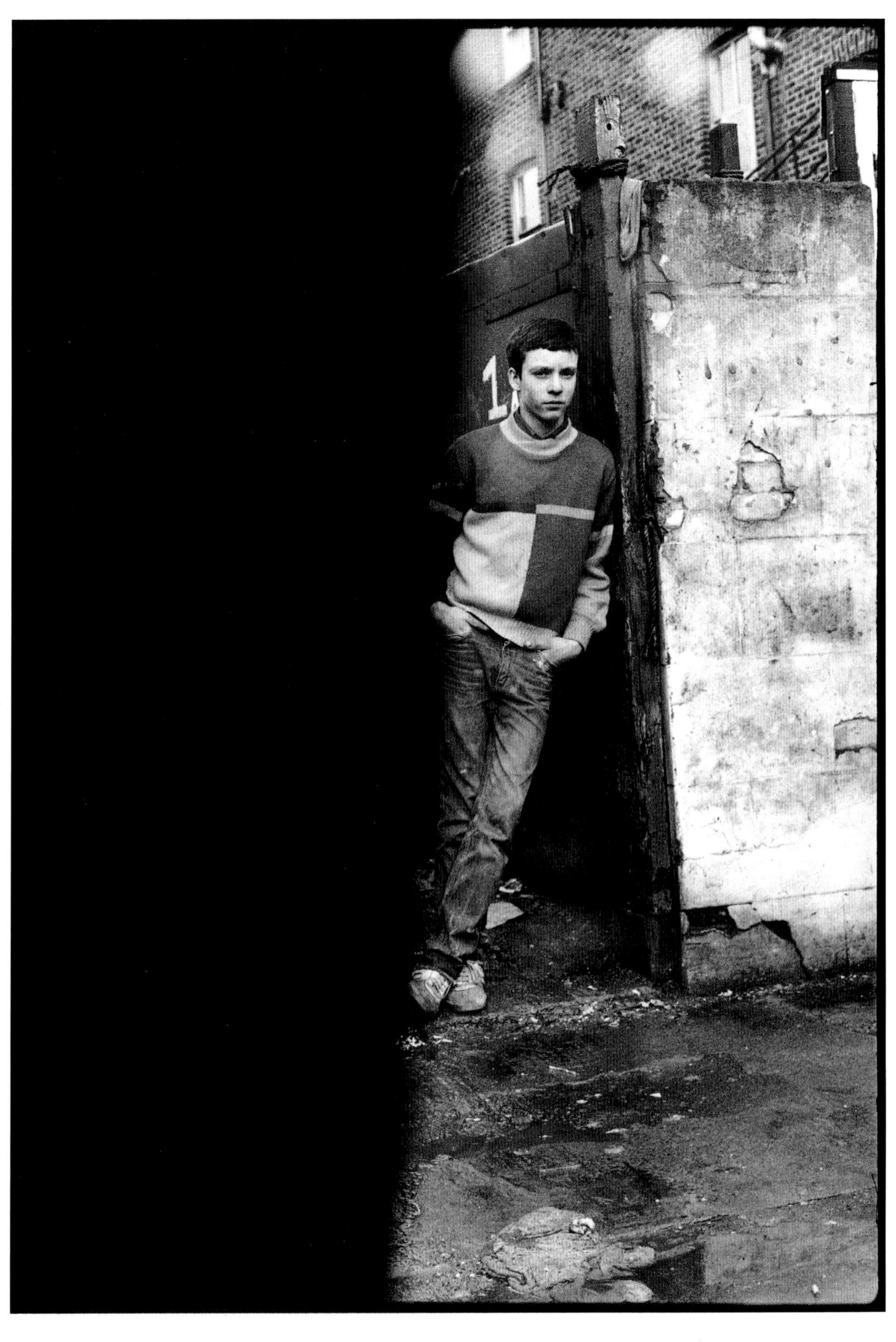

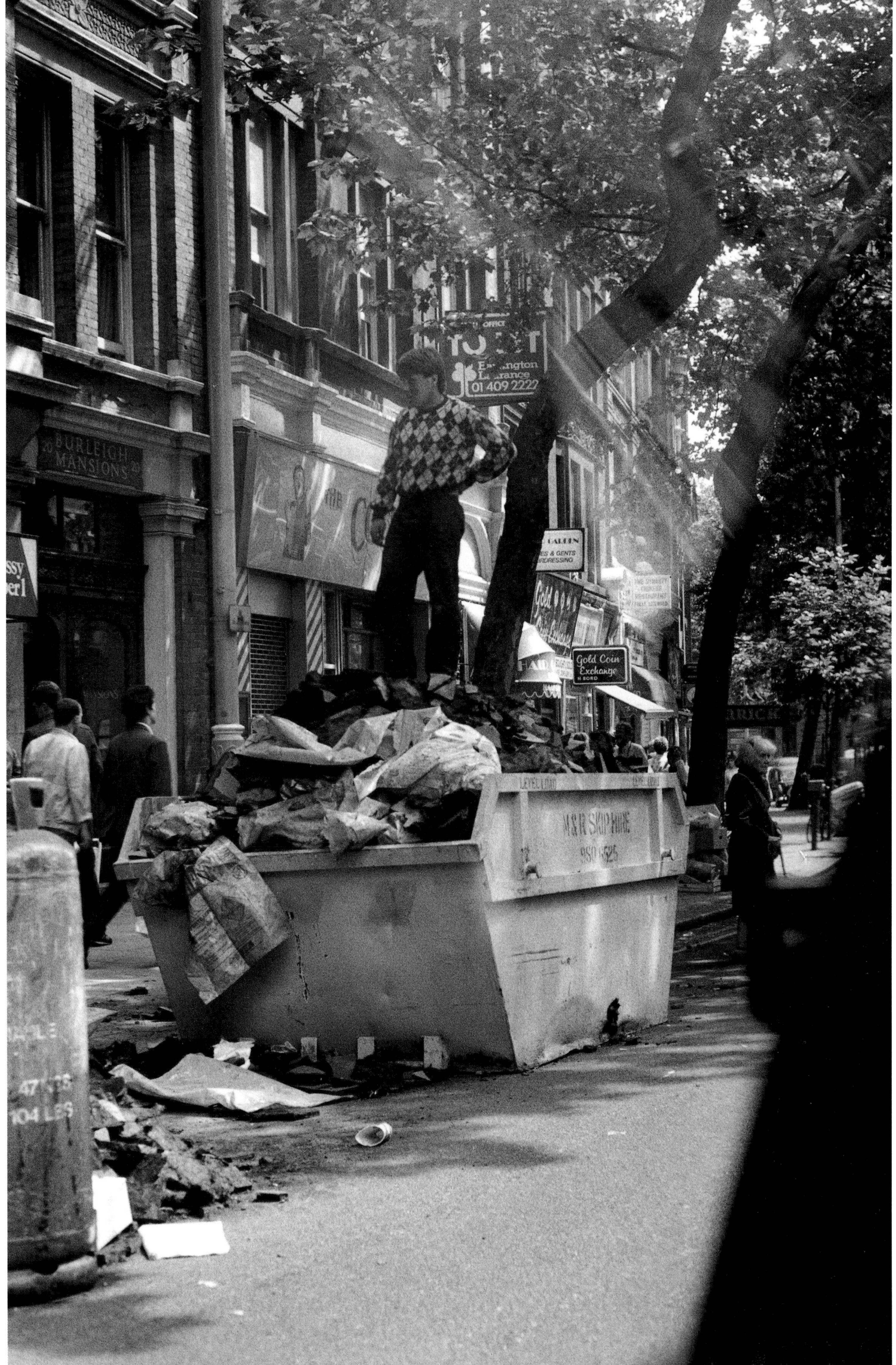
BURLEIGH MANSIONS
01 409 2222
Gold Coin Exchange
M&R SKIP HIRE

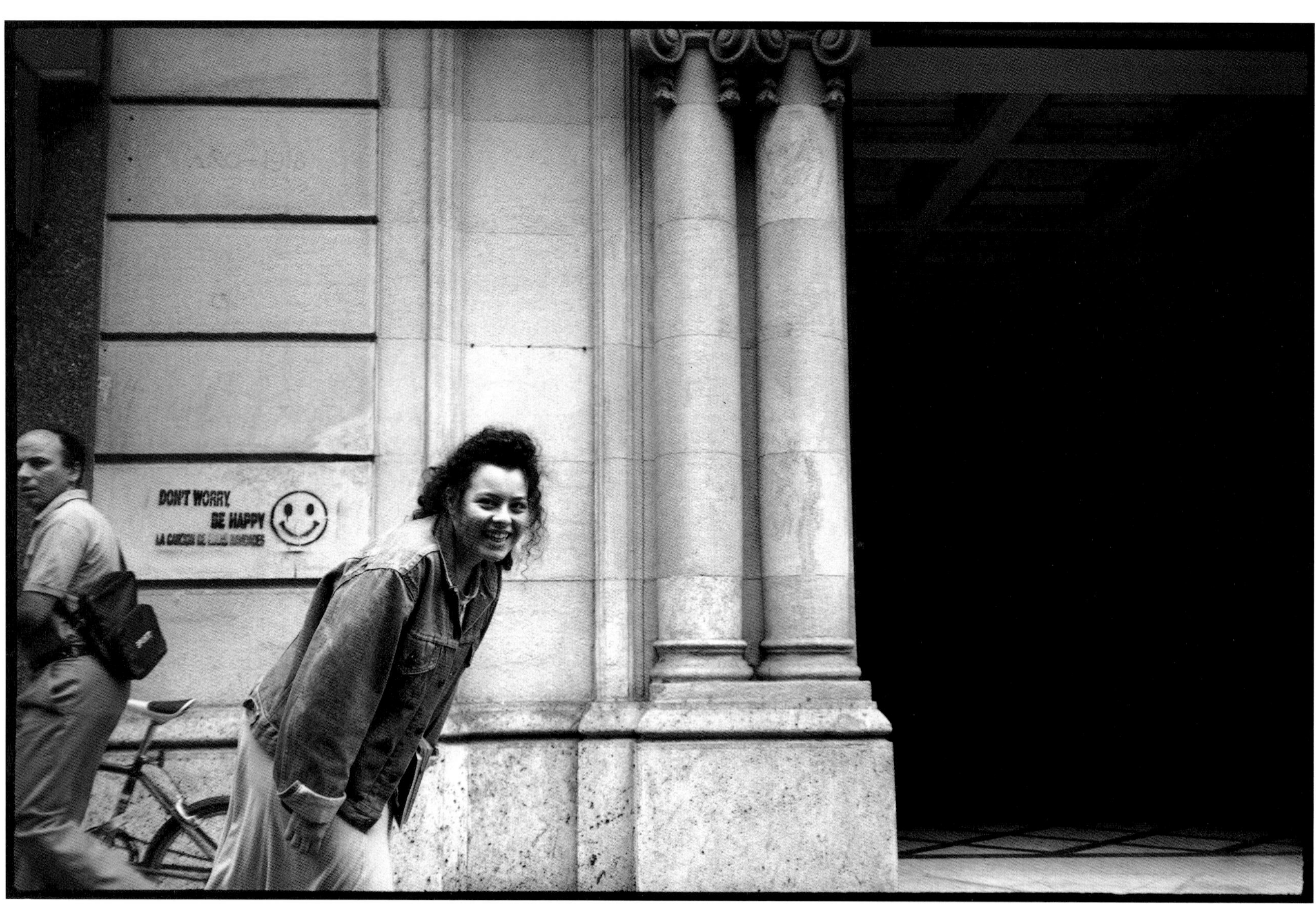
DON'T WORRY,
BE HAPPY

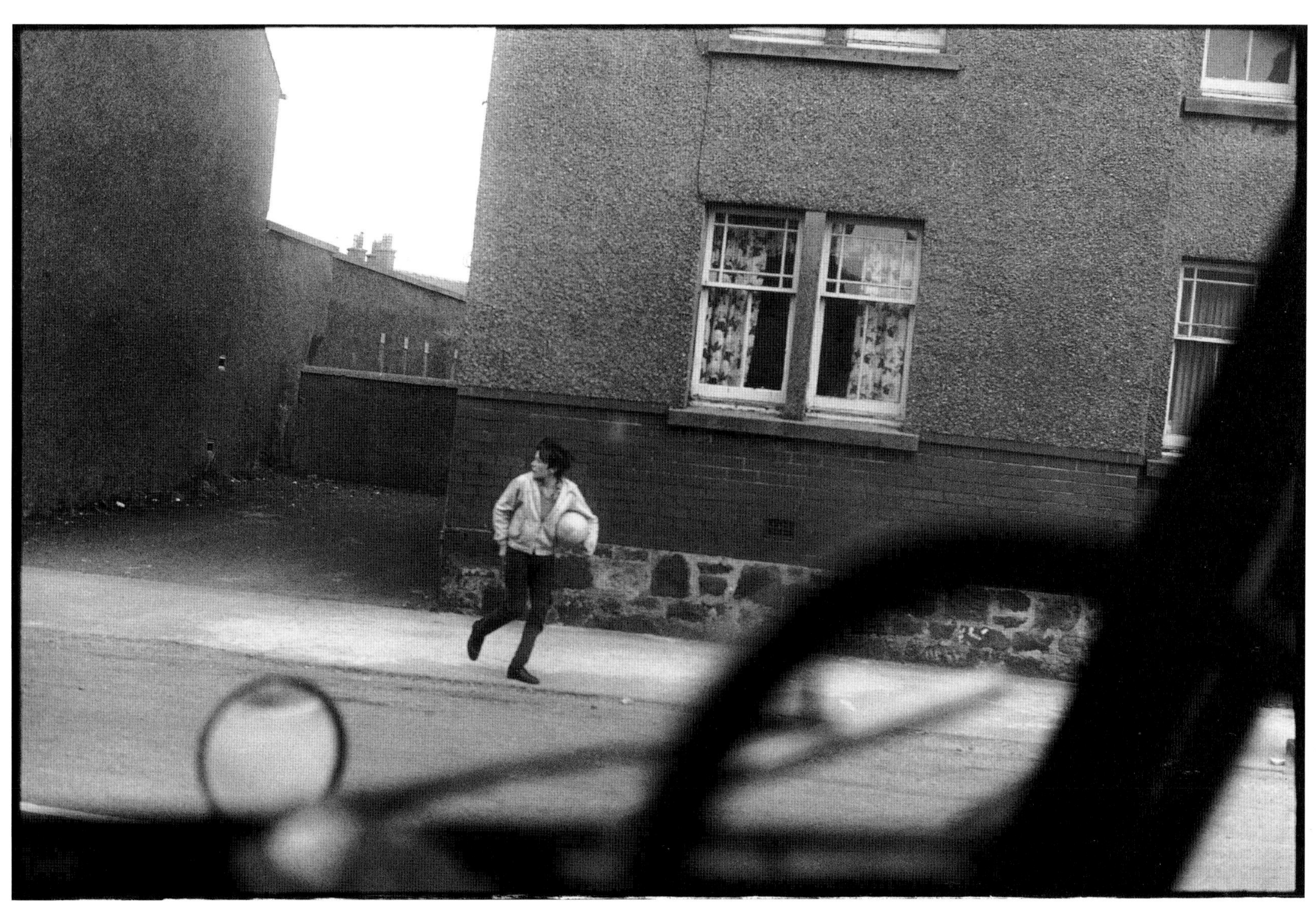

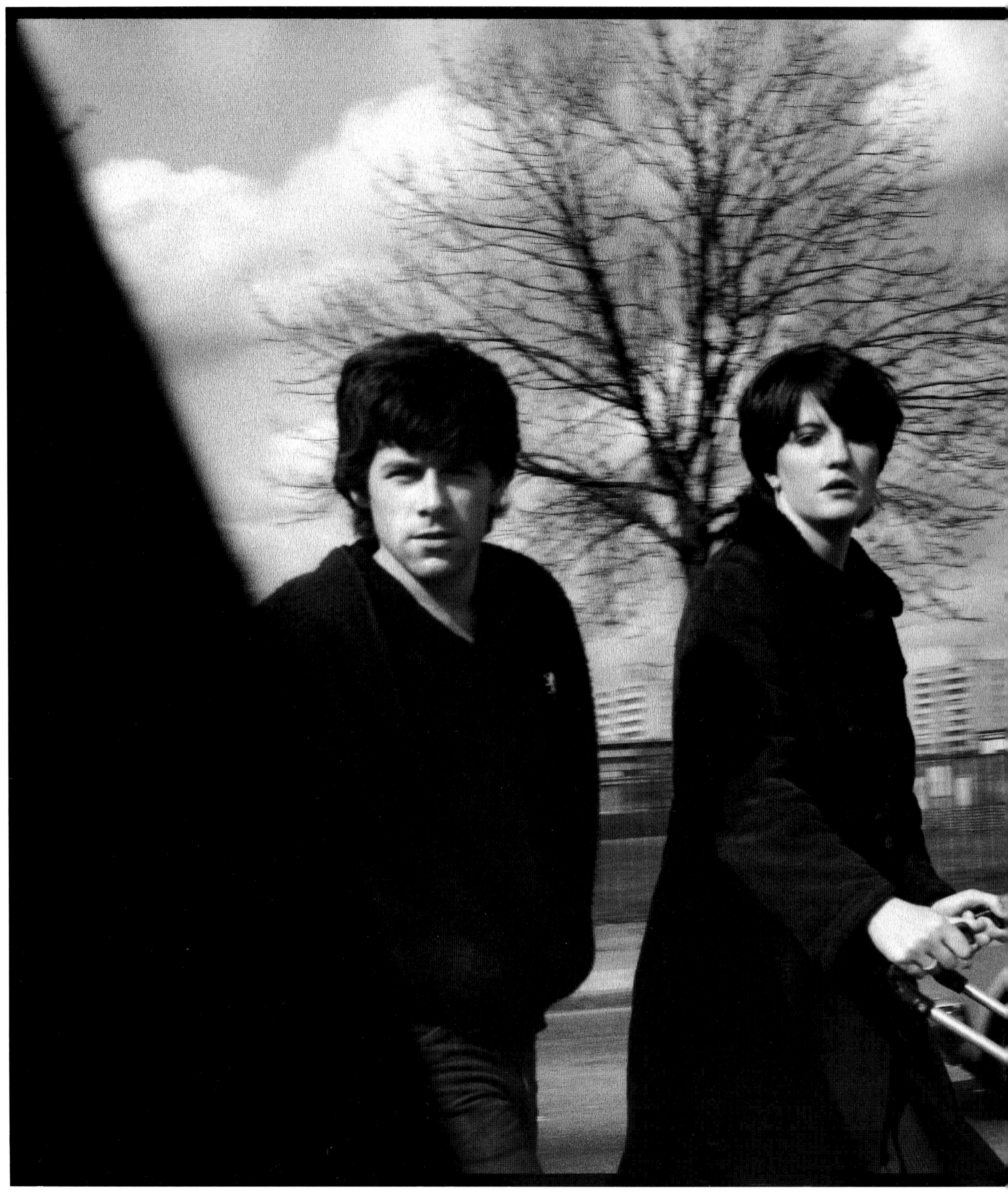

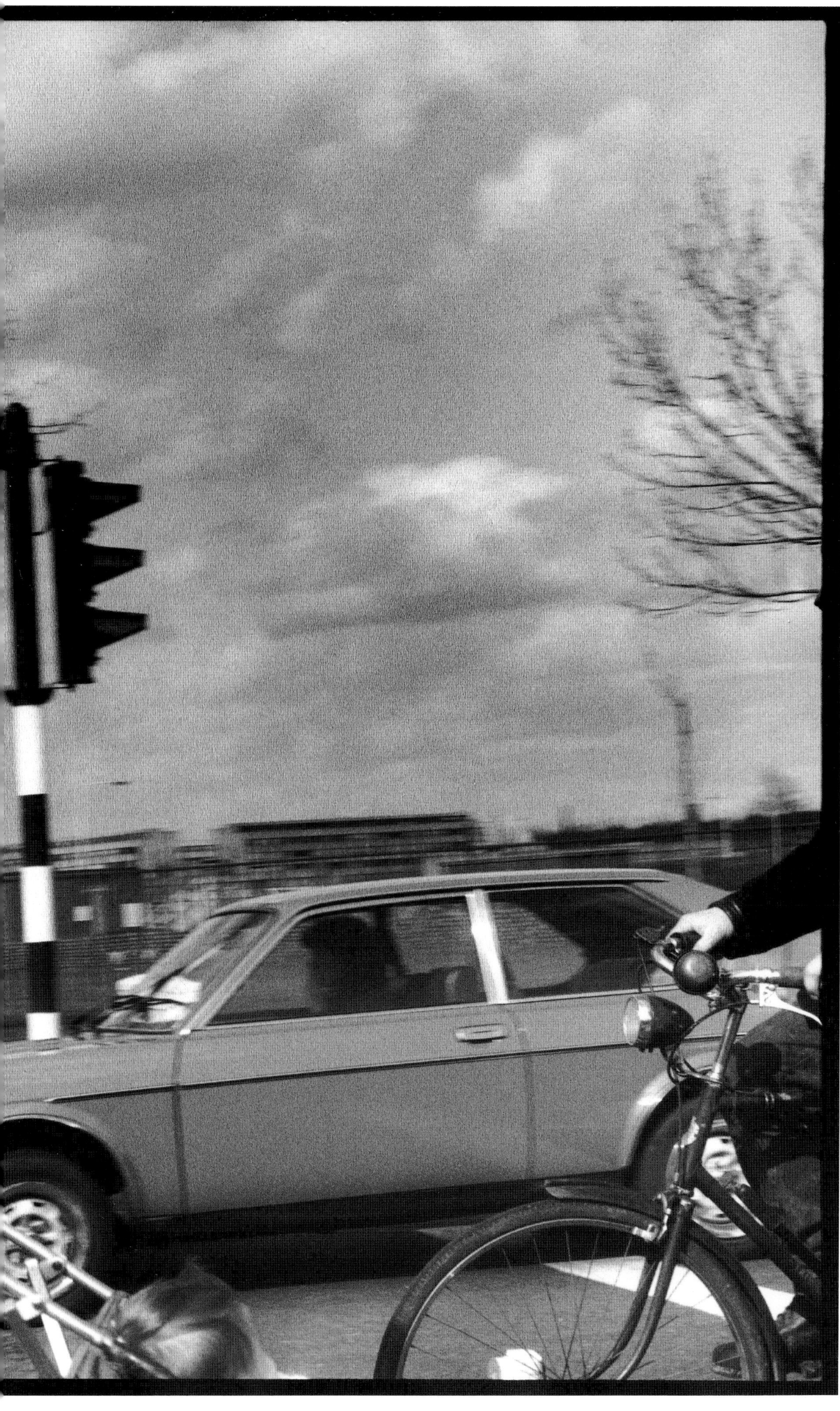

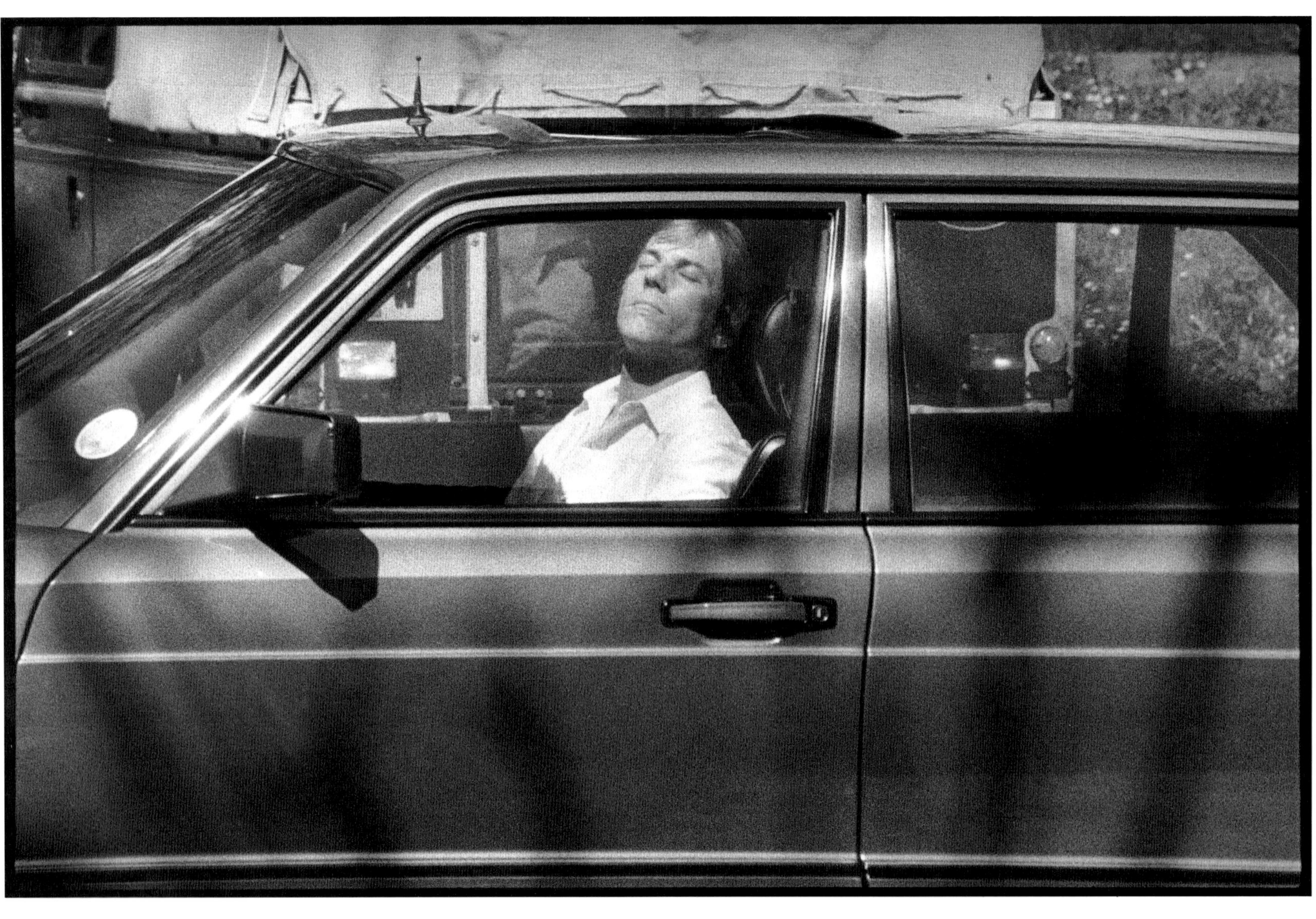

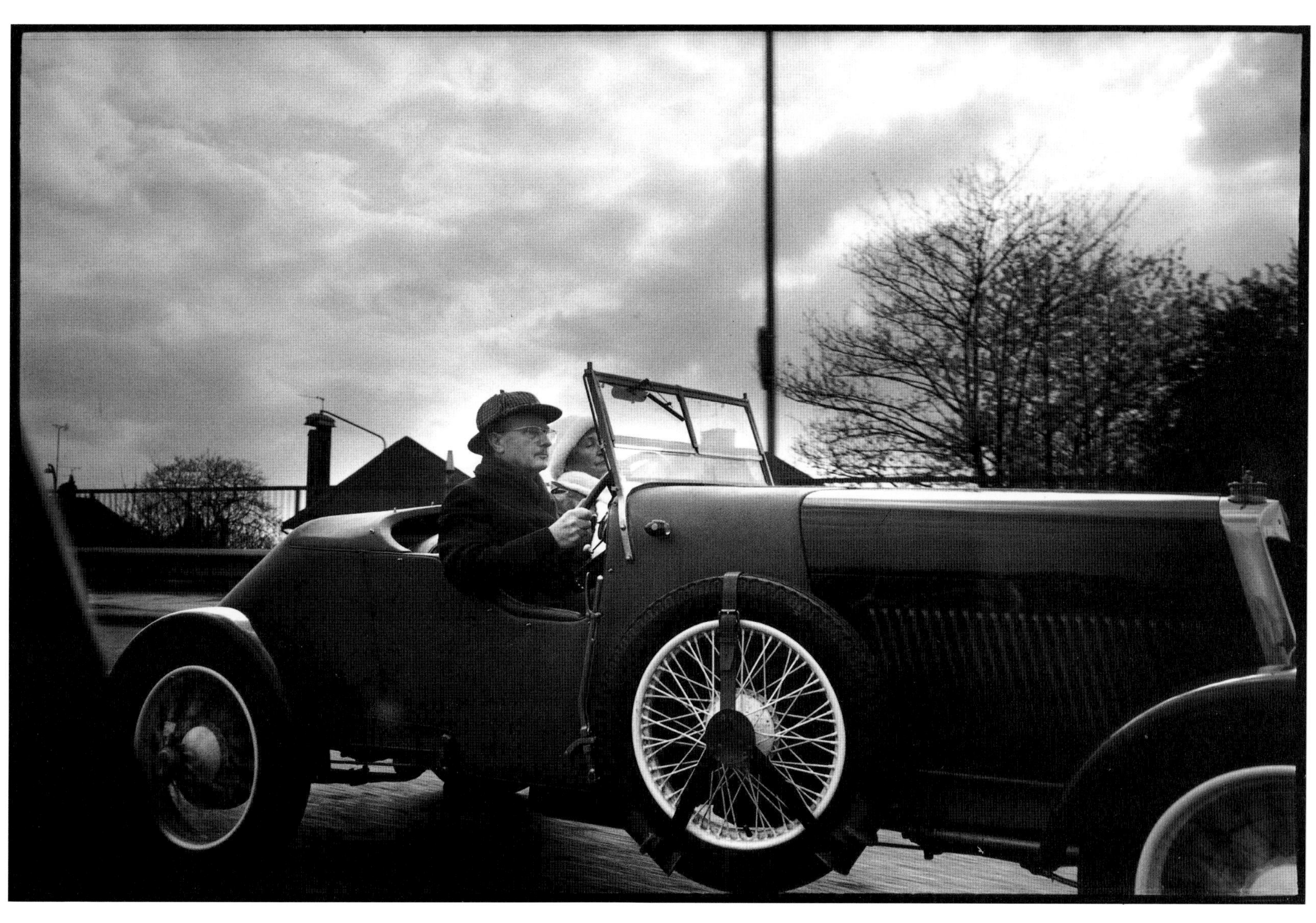

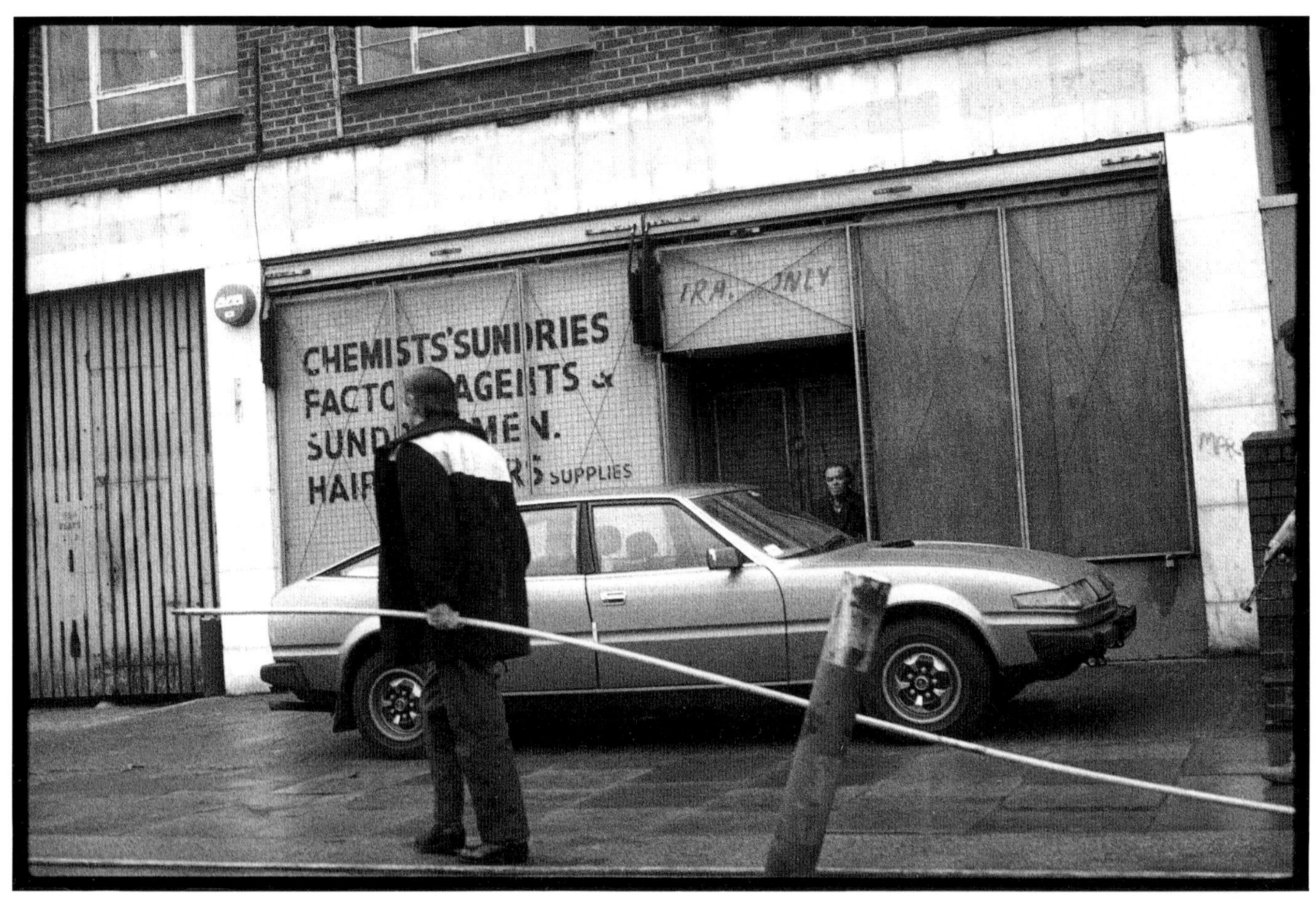
CHEMISTS'SUNDRIES
AGENTS &
MEN.
SUPPLIES

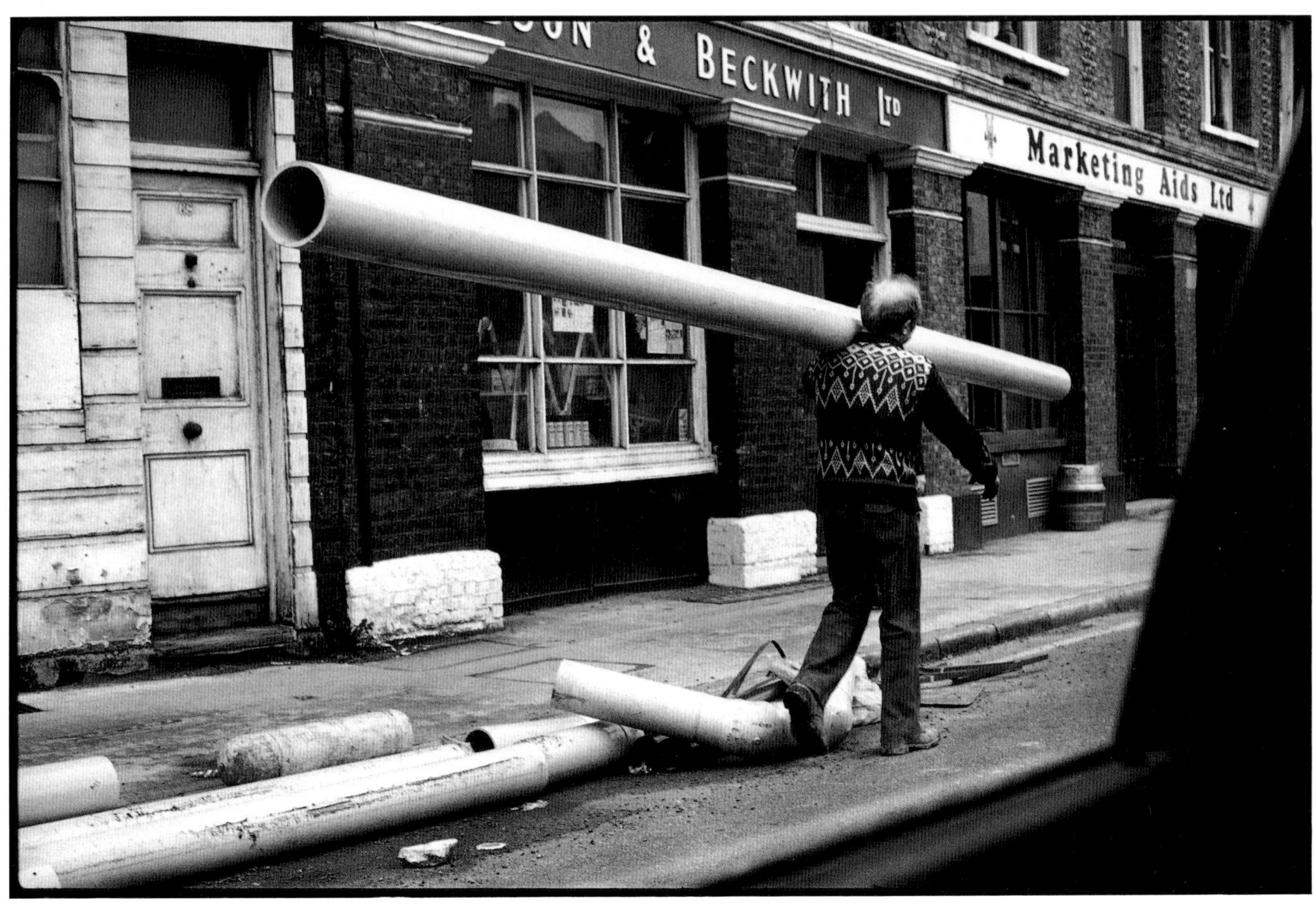
& BECKWITH Ltd
Marketing Aids Ltd

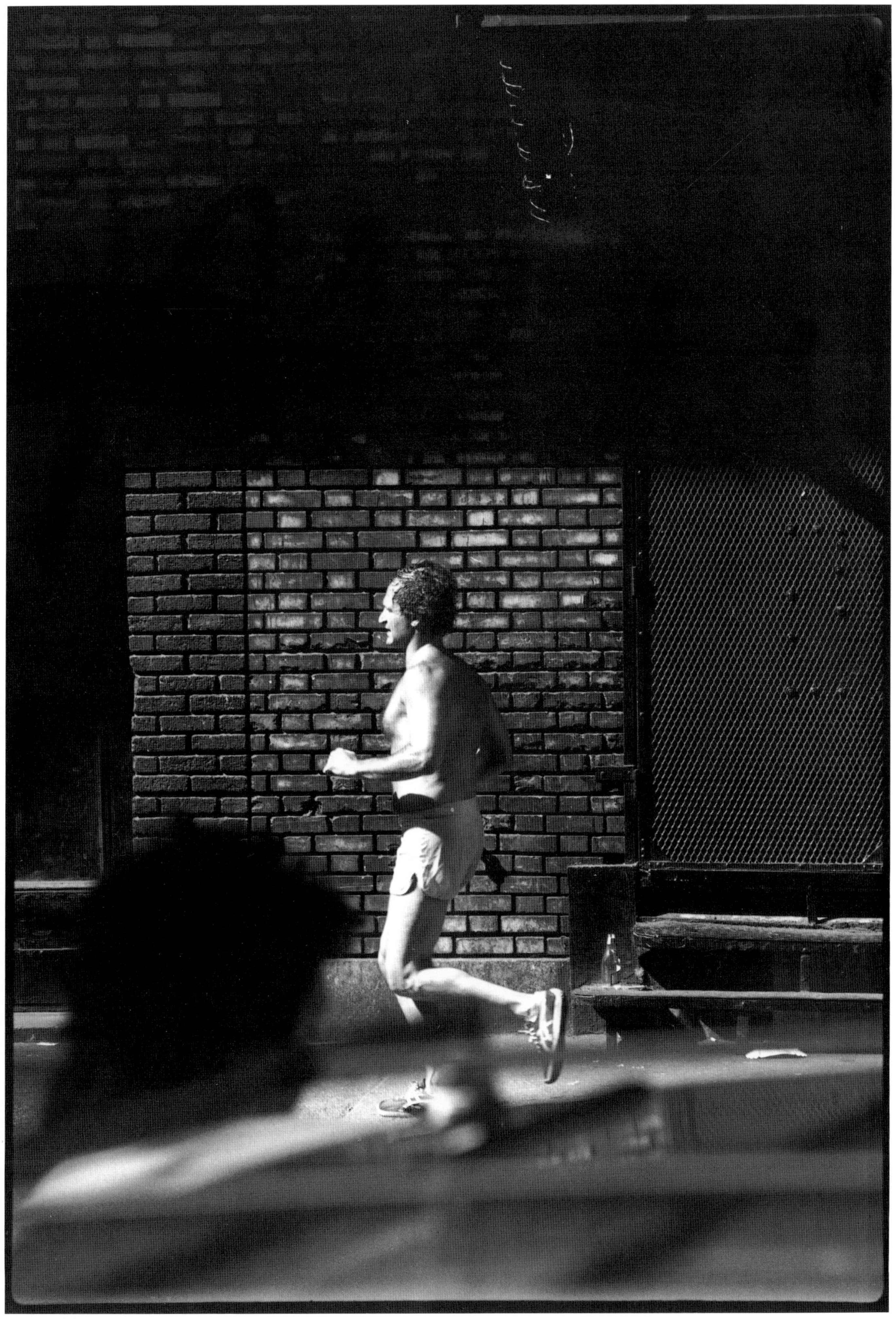

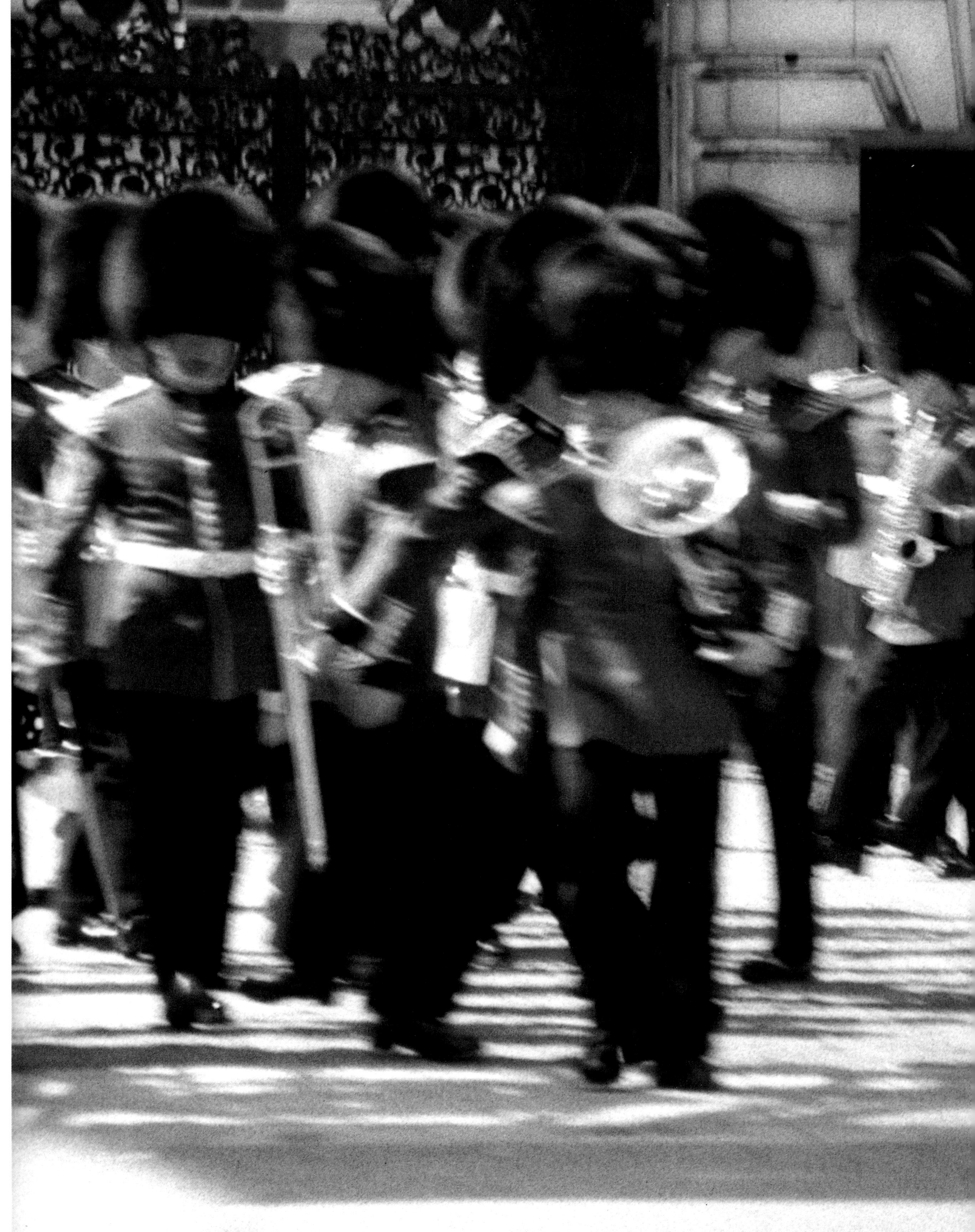

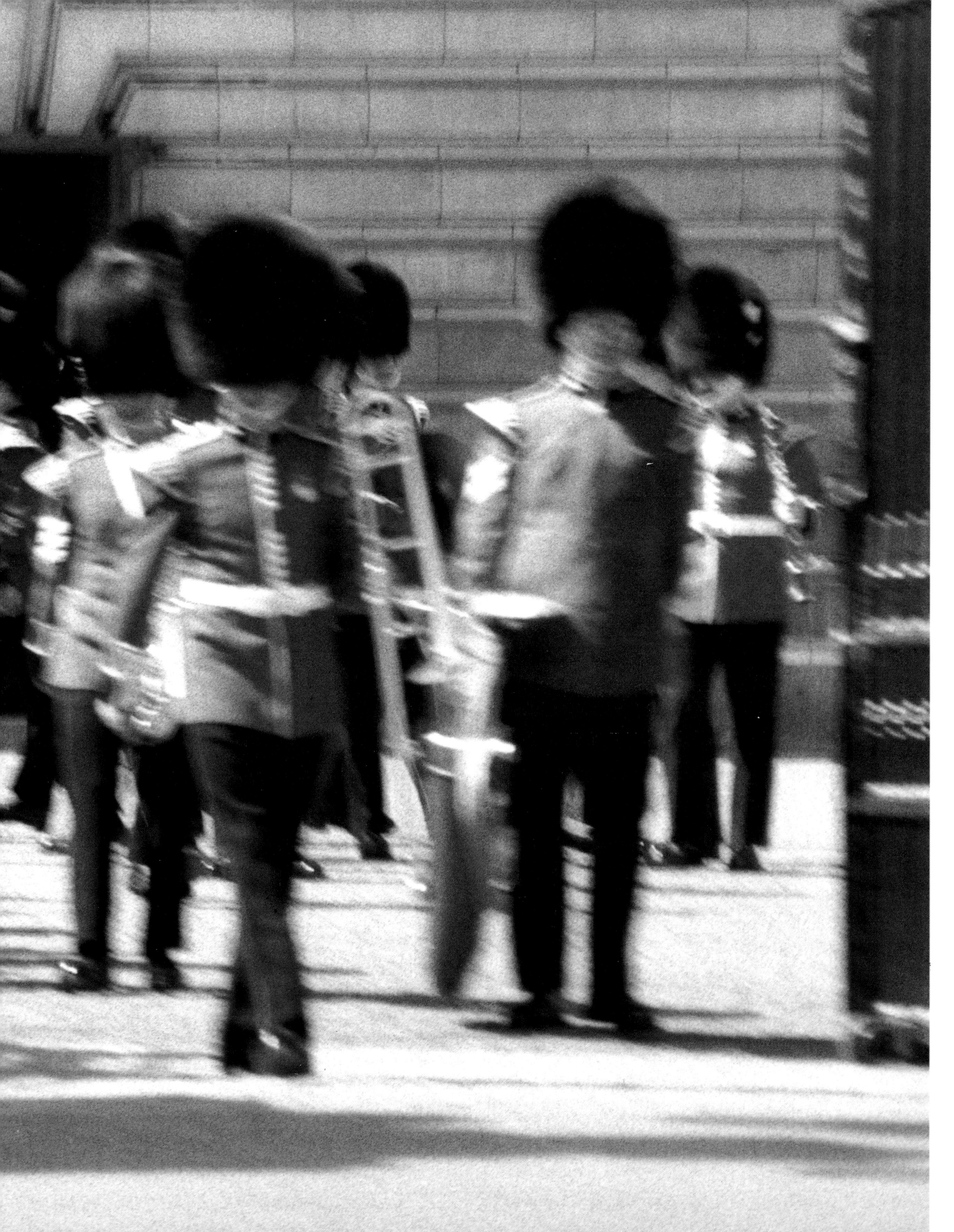

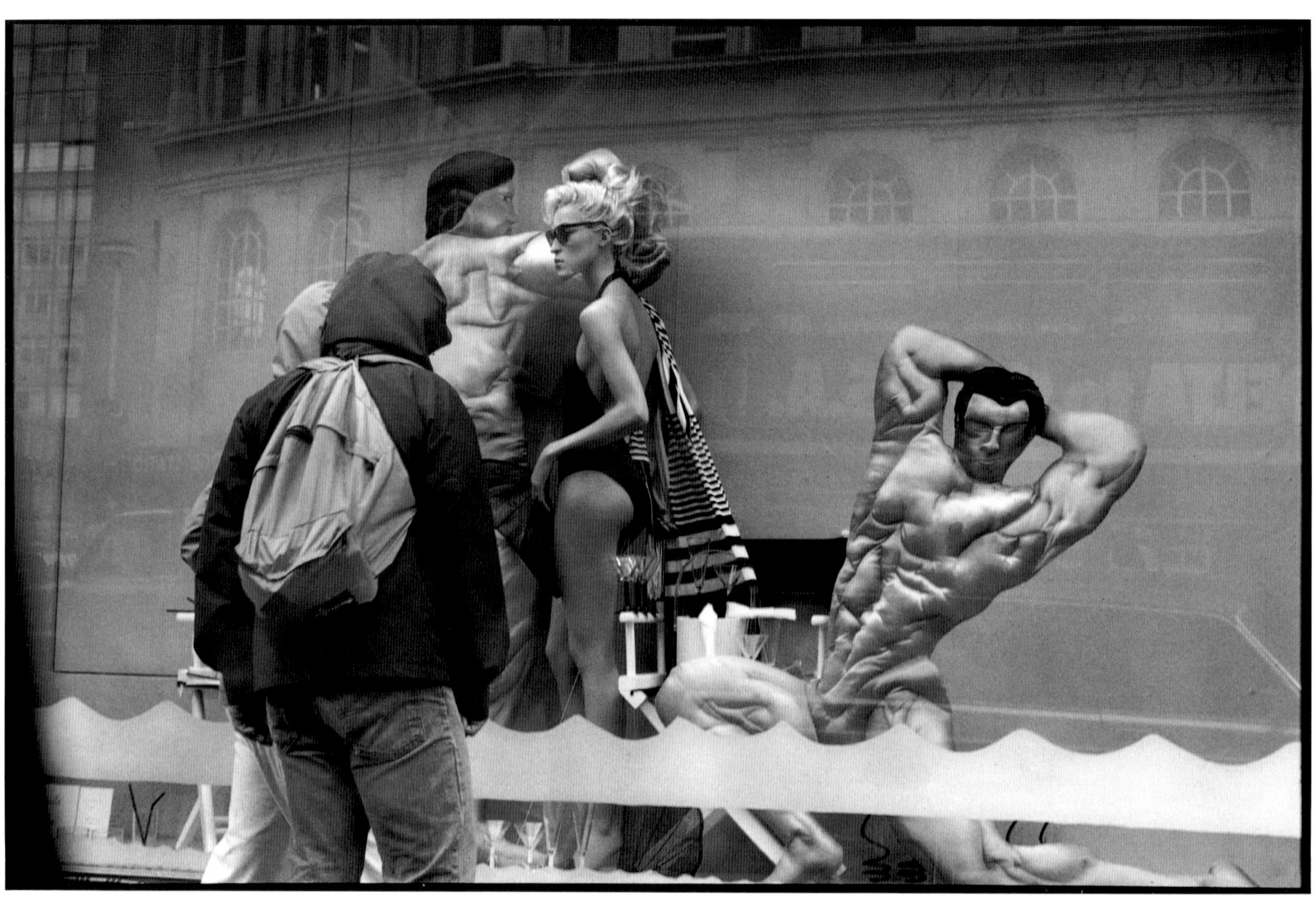

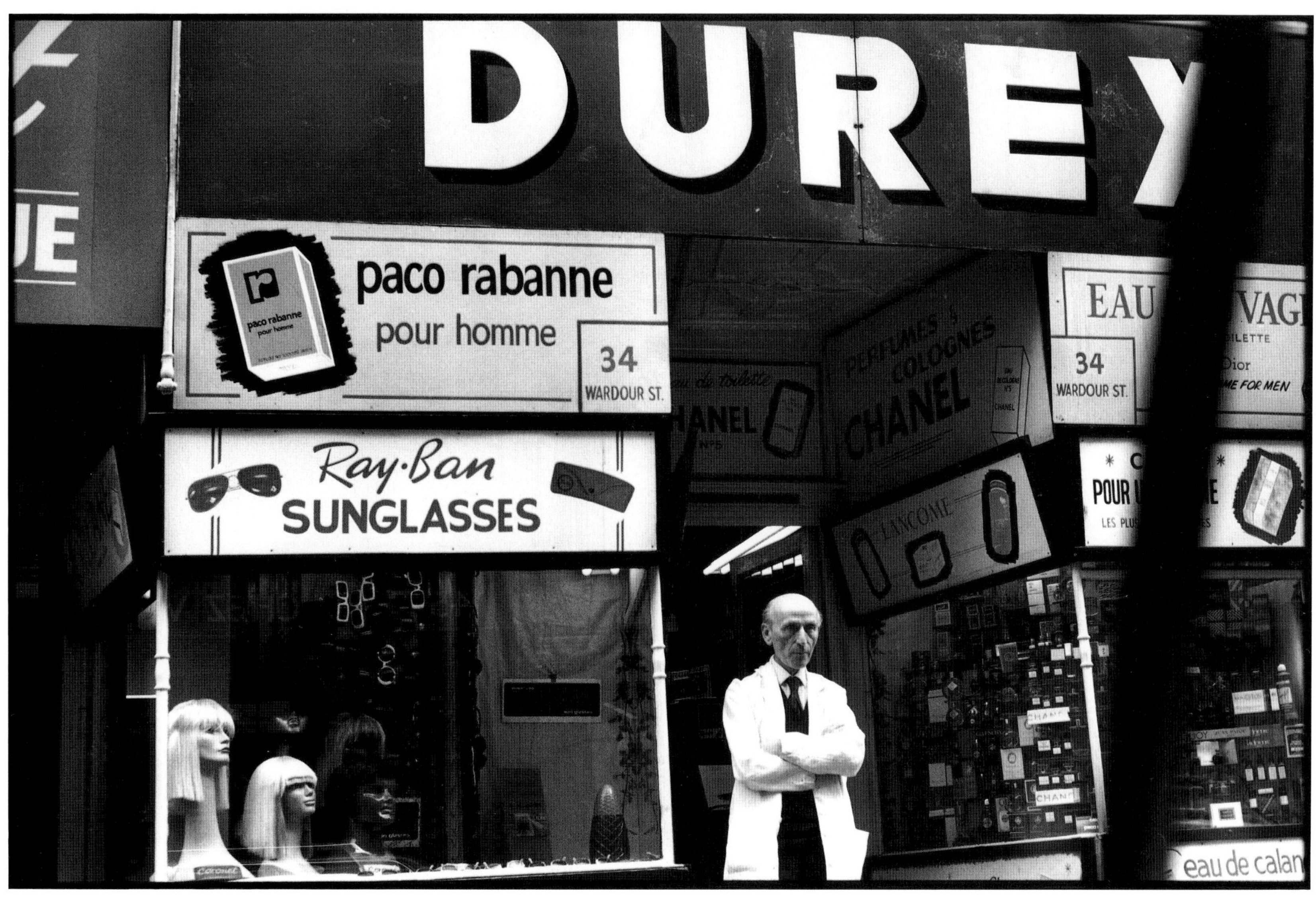
DUREY
paco rabanne
pour homme
34
WARDOUR ST.
Ray-Ban
SUNGLASSES
PERFUMES &
COLOGNES
CHANEL
EAU
34
WARDOUR ST.
LANCOME
POUR
eau de calan

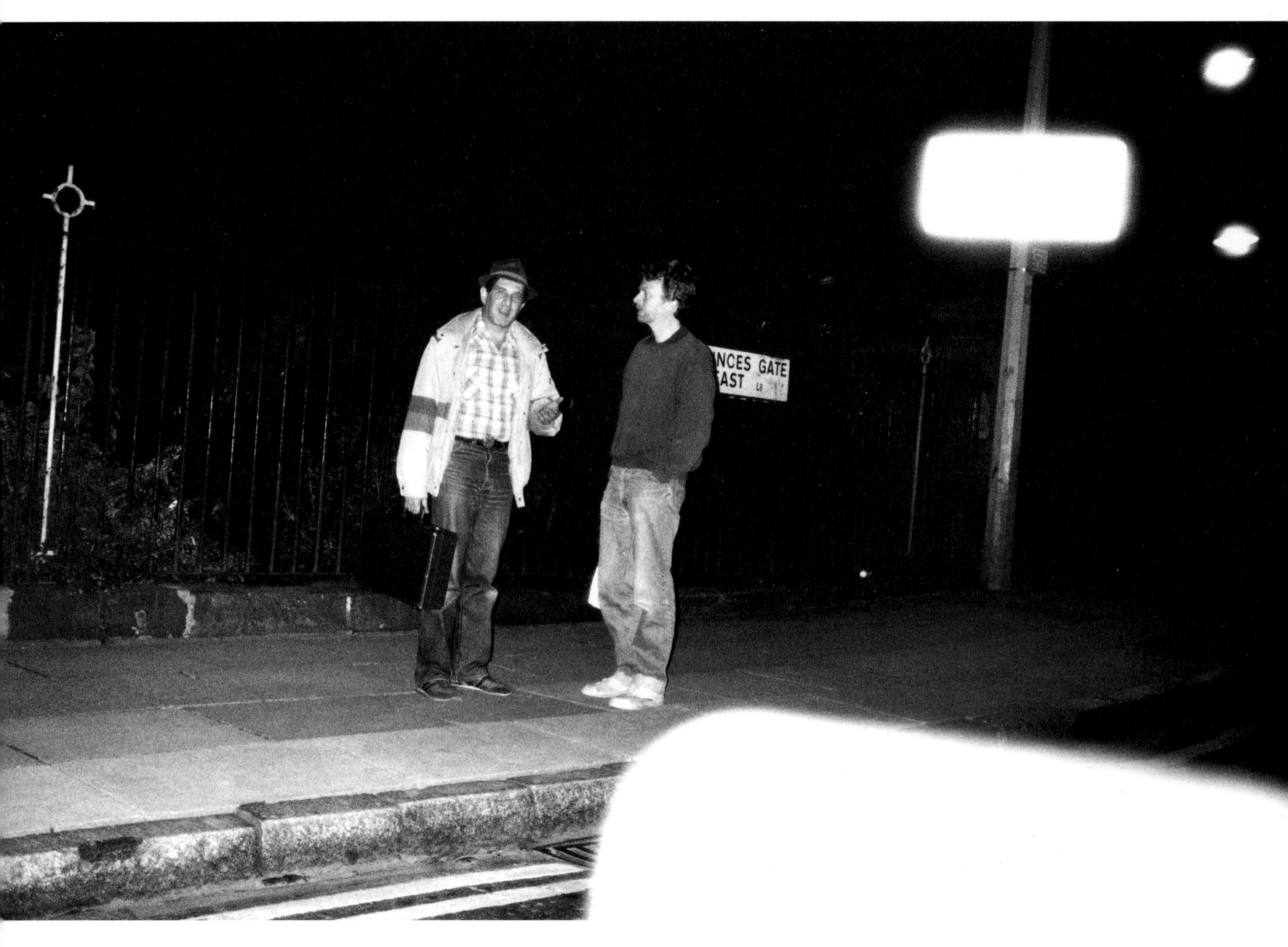
NCES GATE
EAST L8

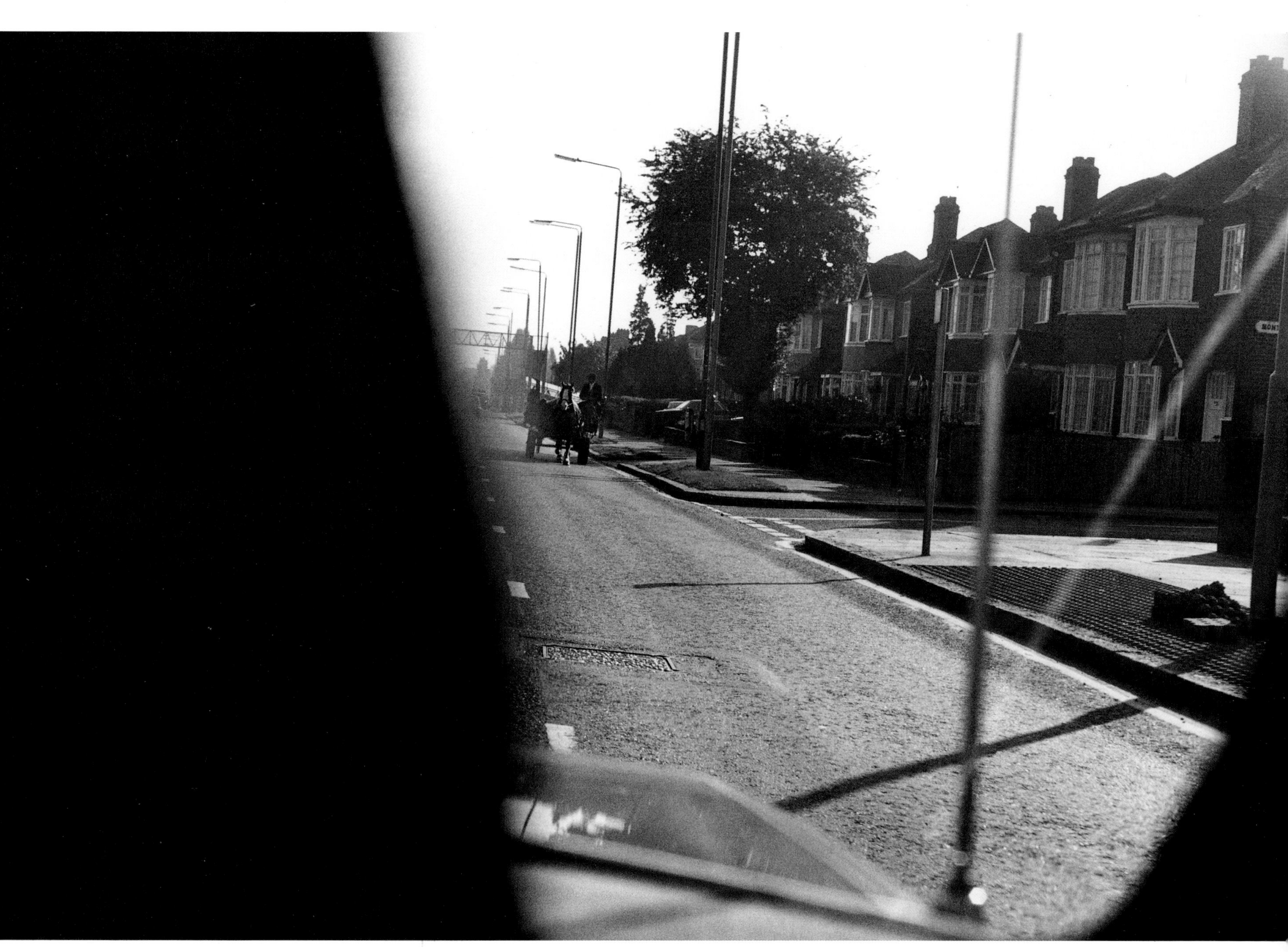

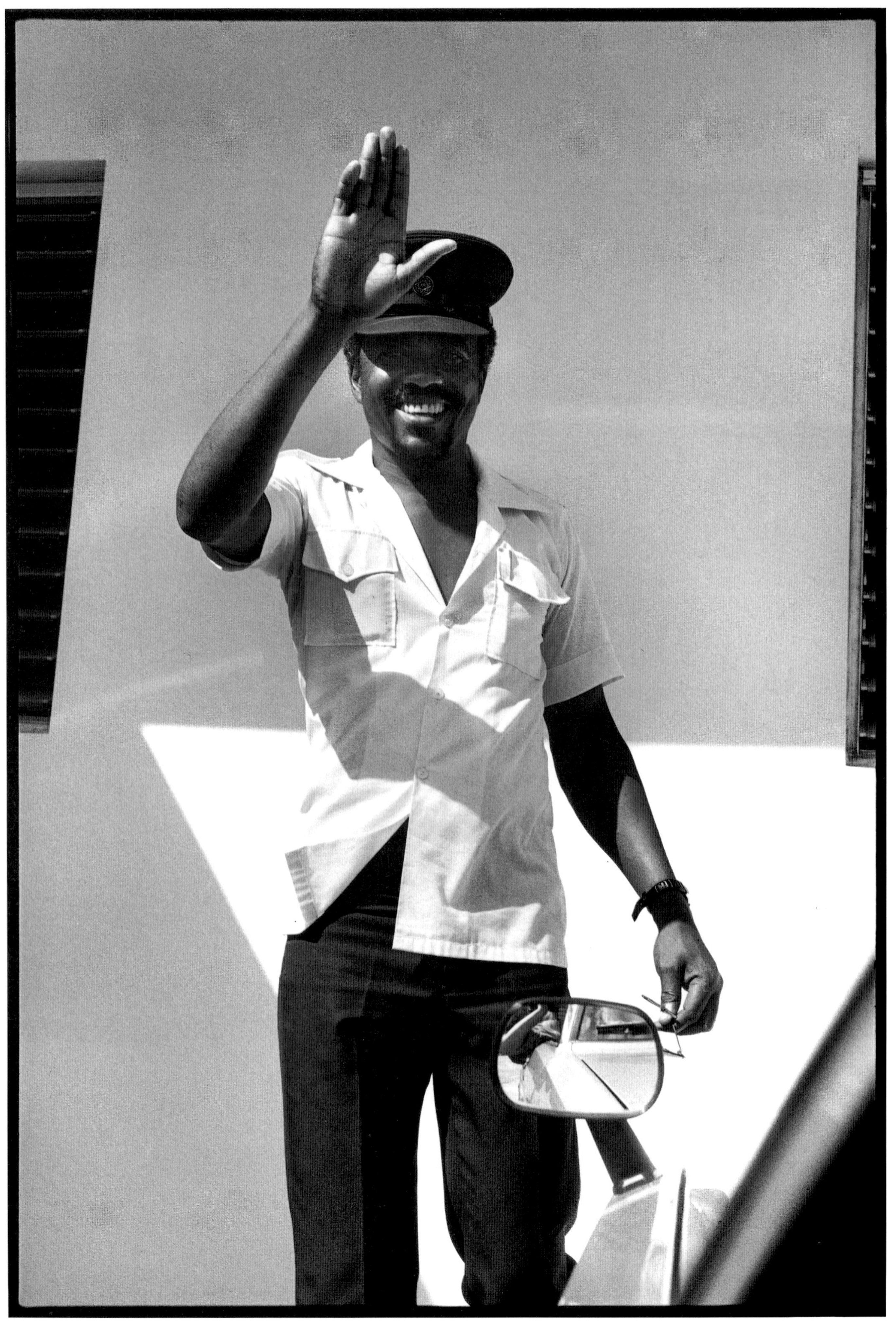

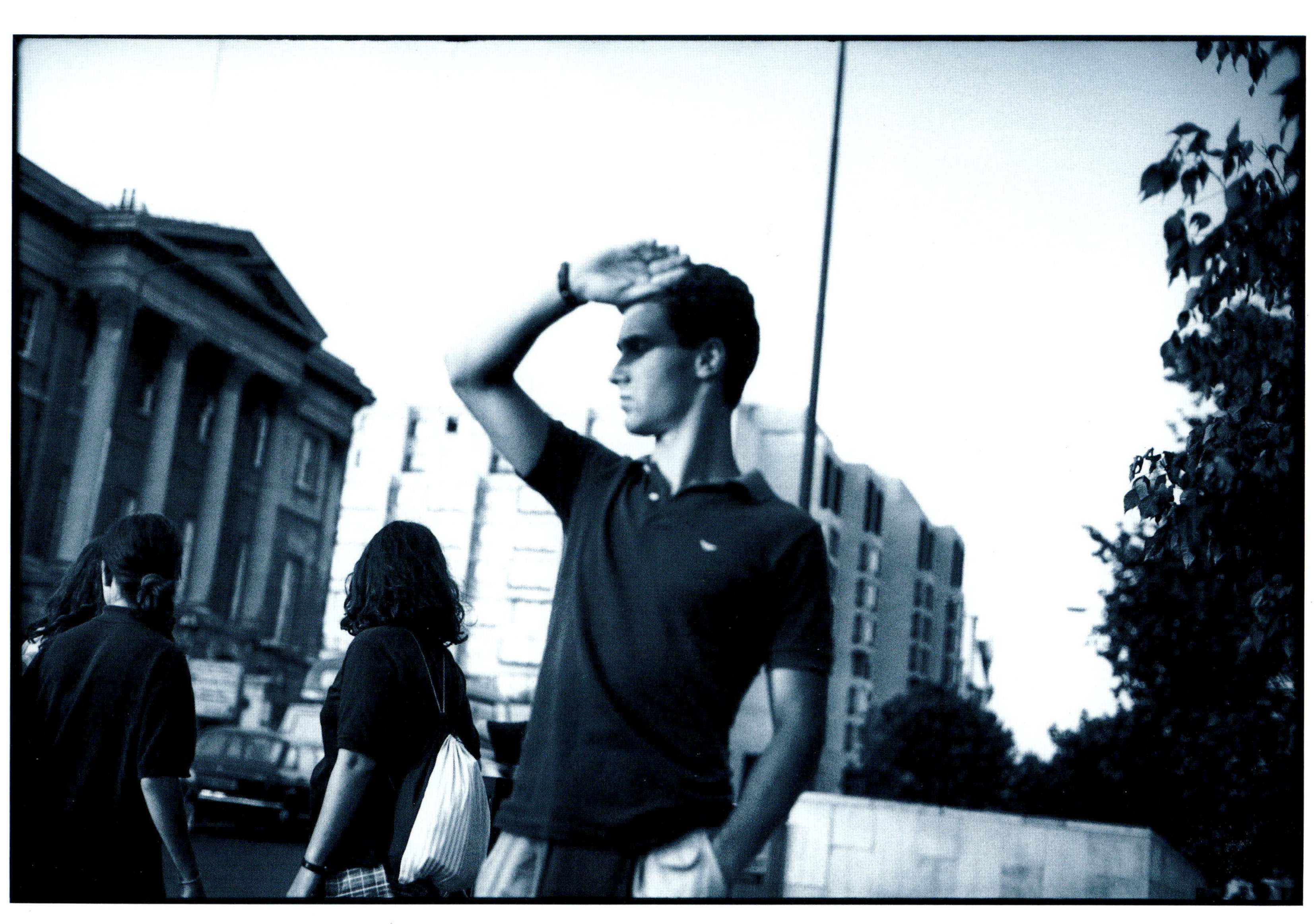

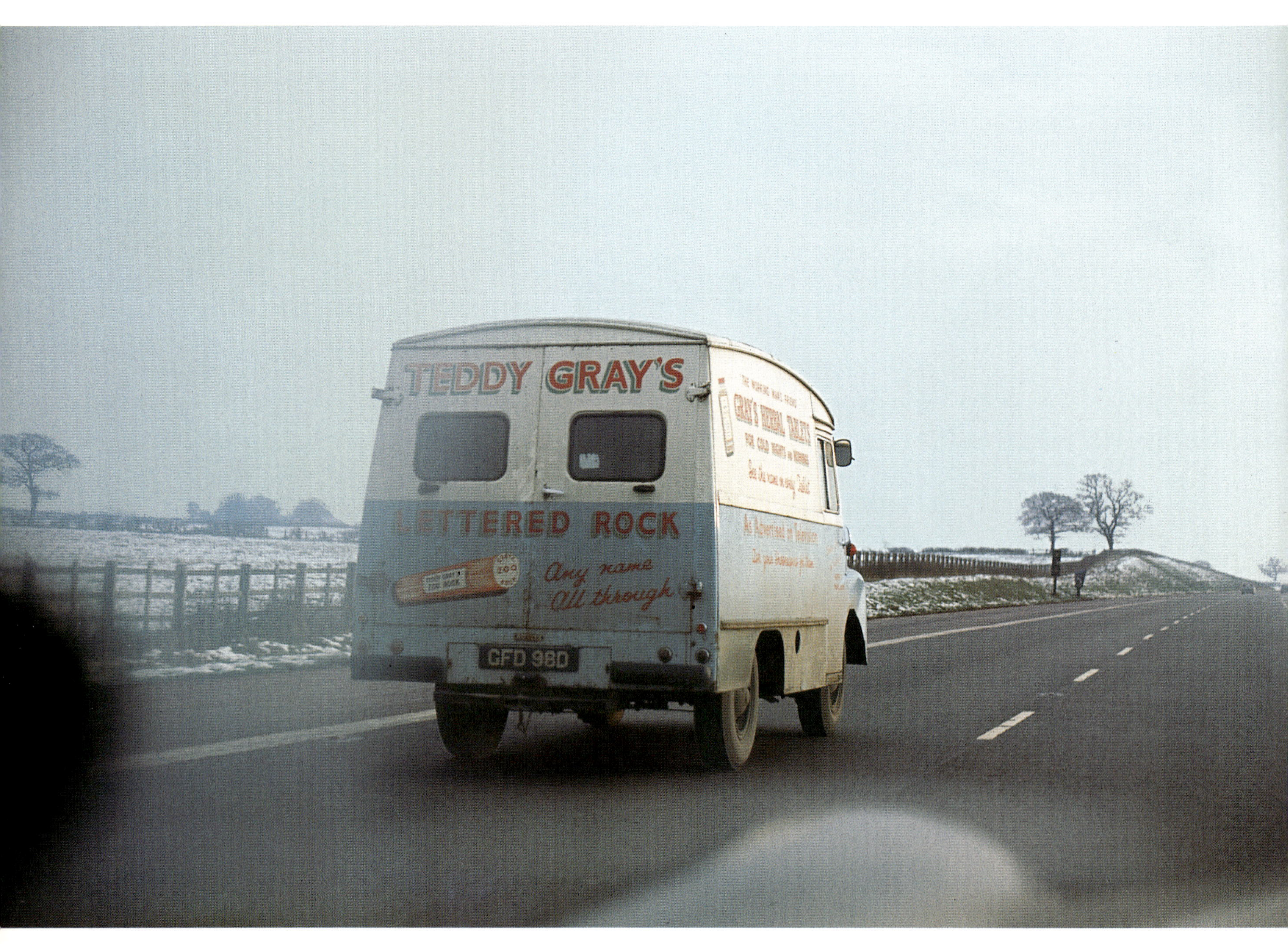
TEDDY GRAY'S
LETTERED ROCK
Any name
All through
GFD 98D

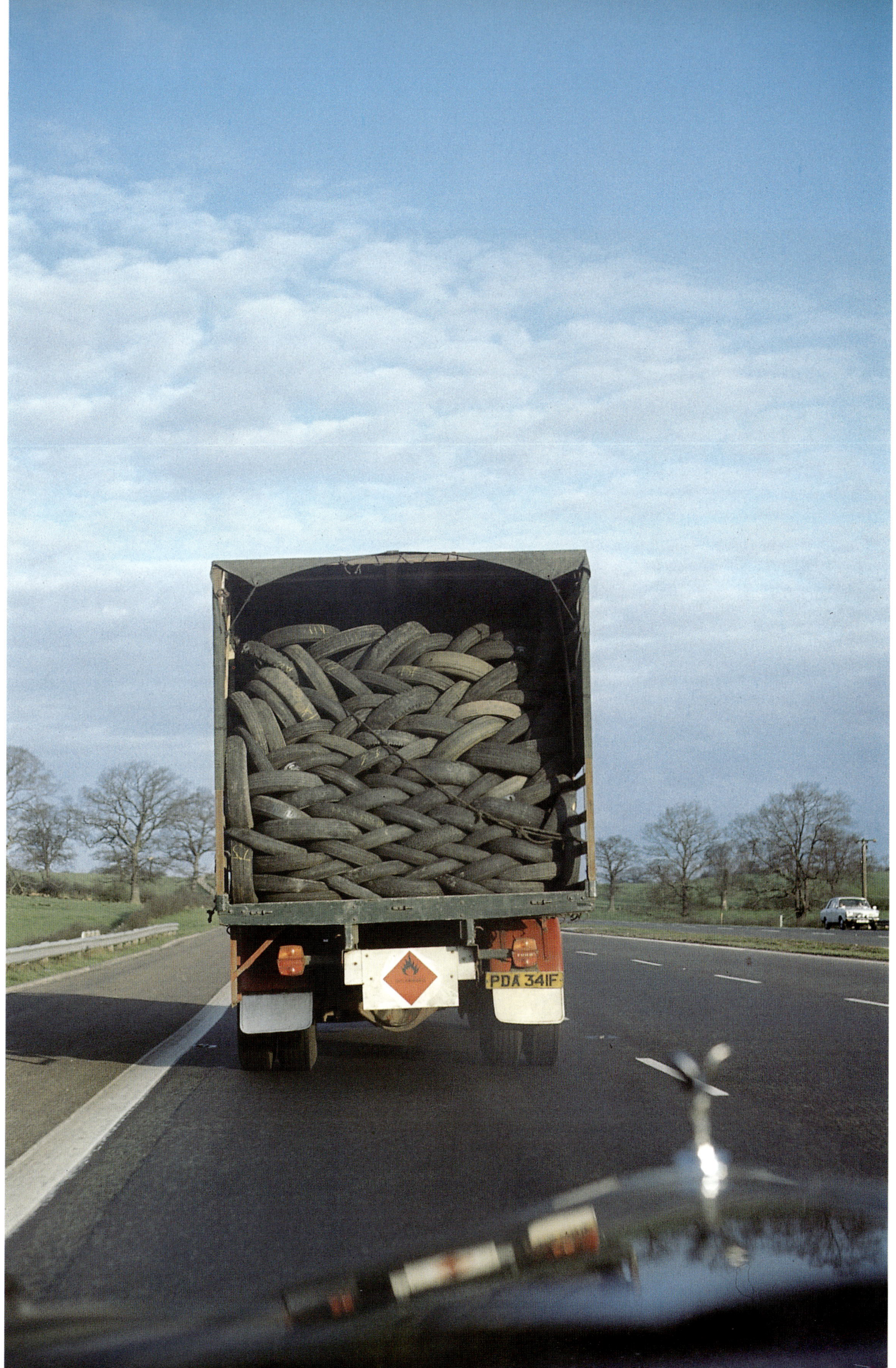
PDA 341F

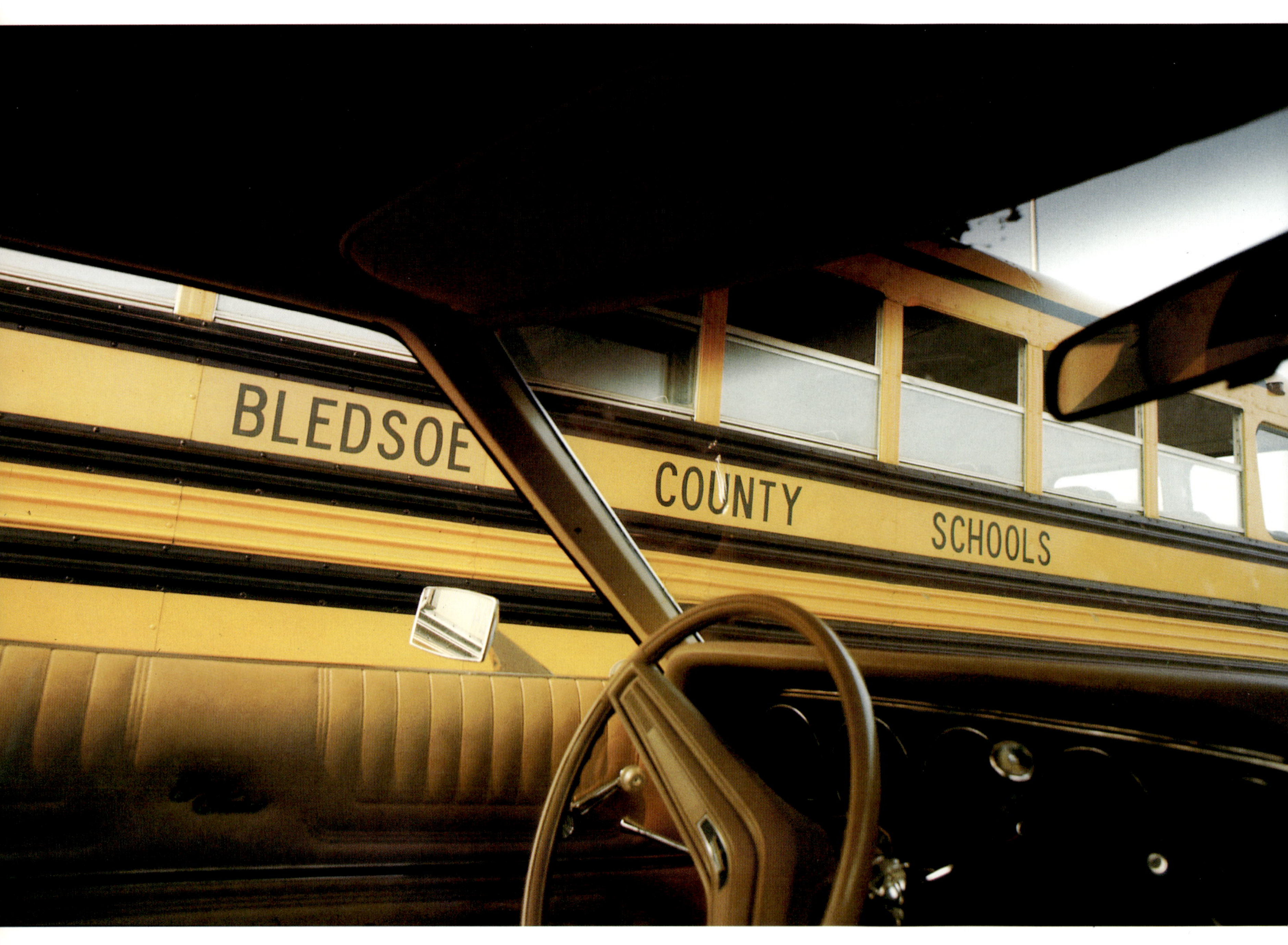
BLEDSOE
COUNTY
SCHOOLS

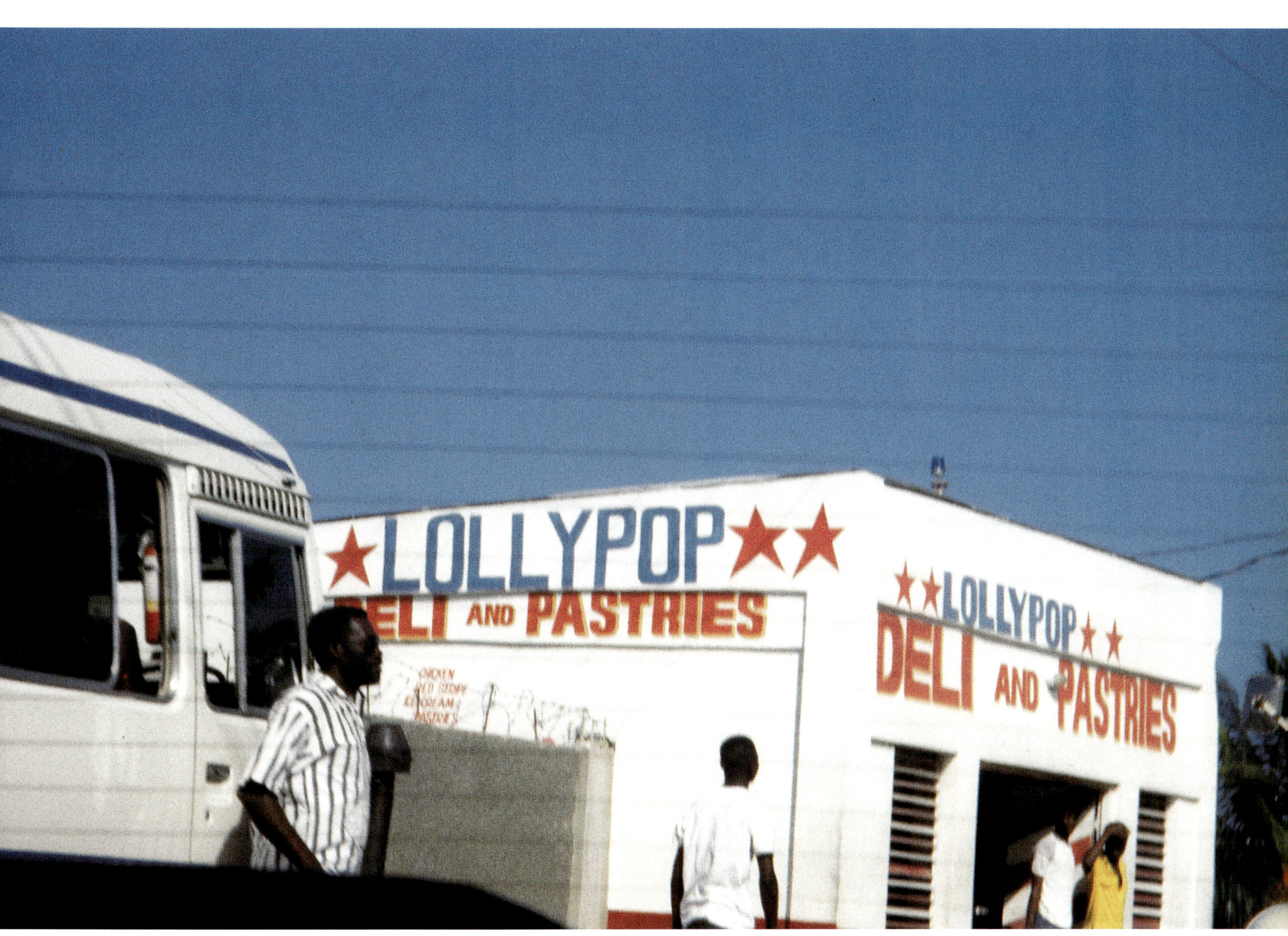
LOLLYPOP
DELI AND PASTRIES
LOLLYPOP
DELI AND PASTRIES

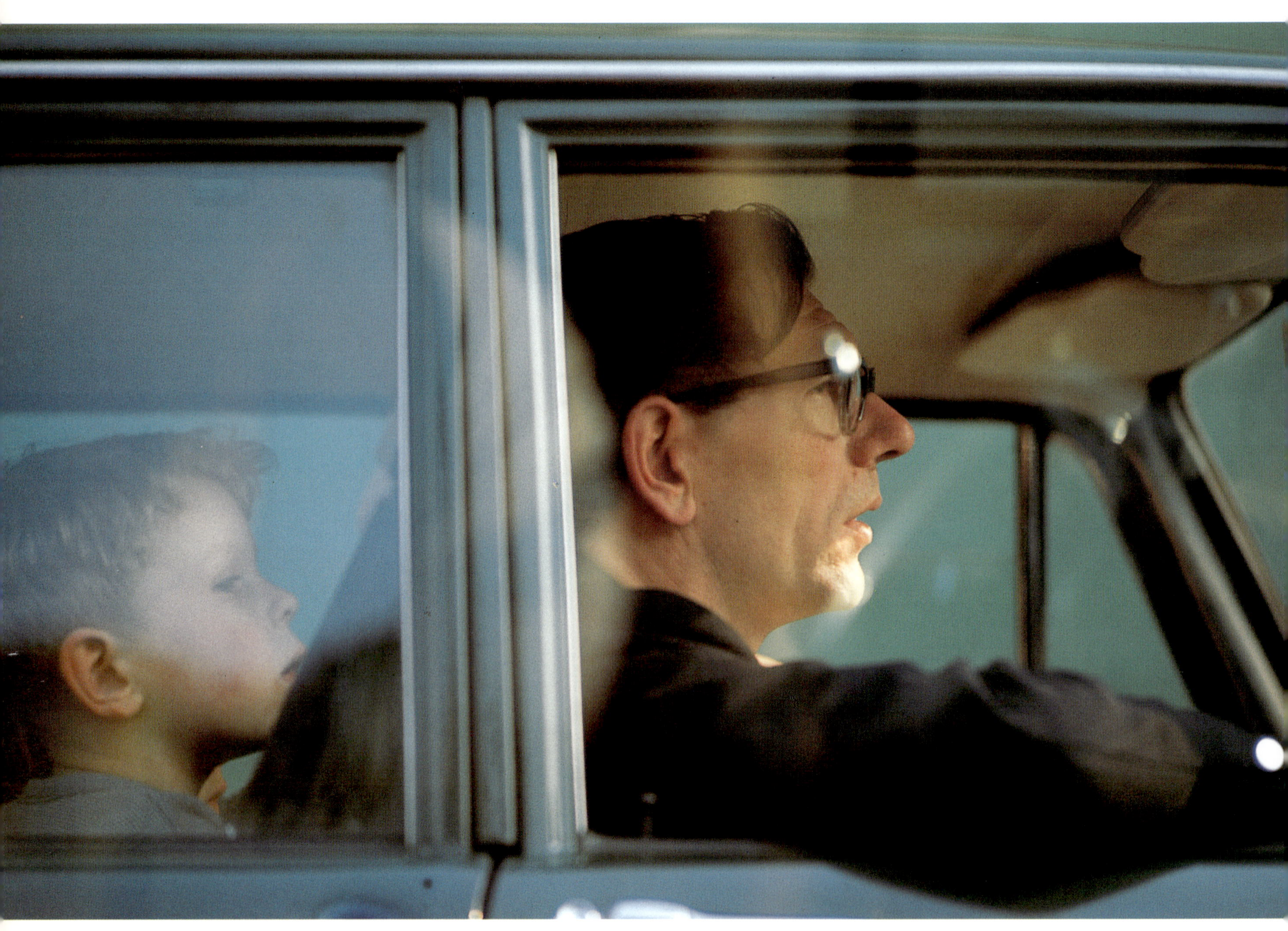

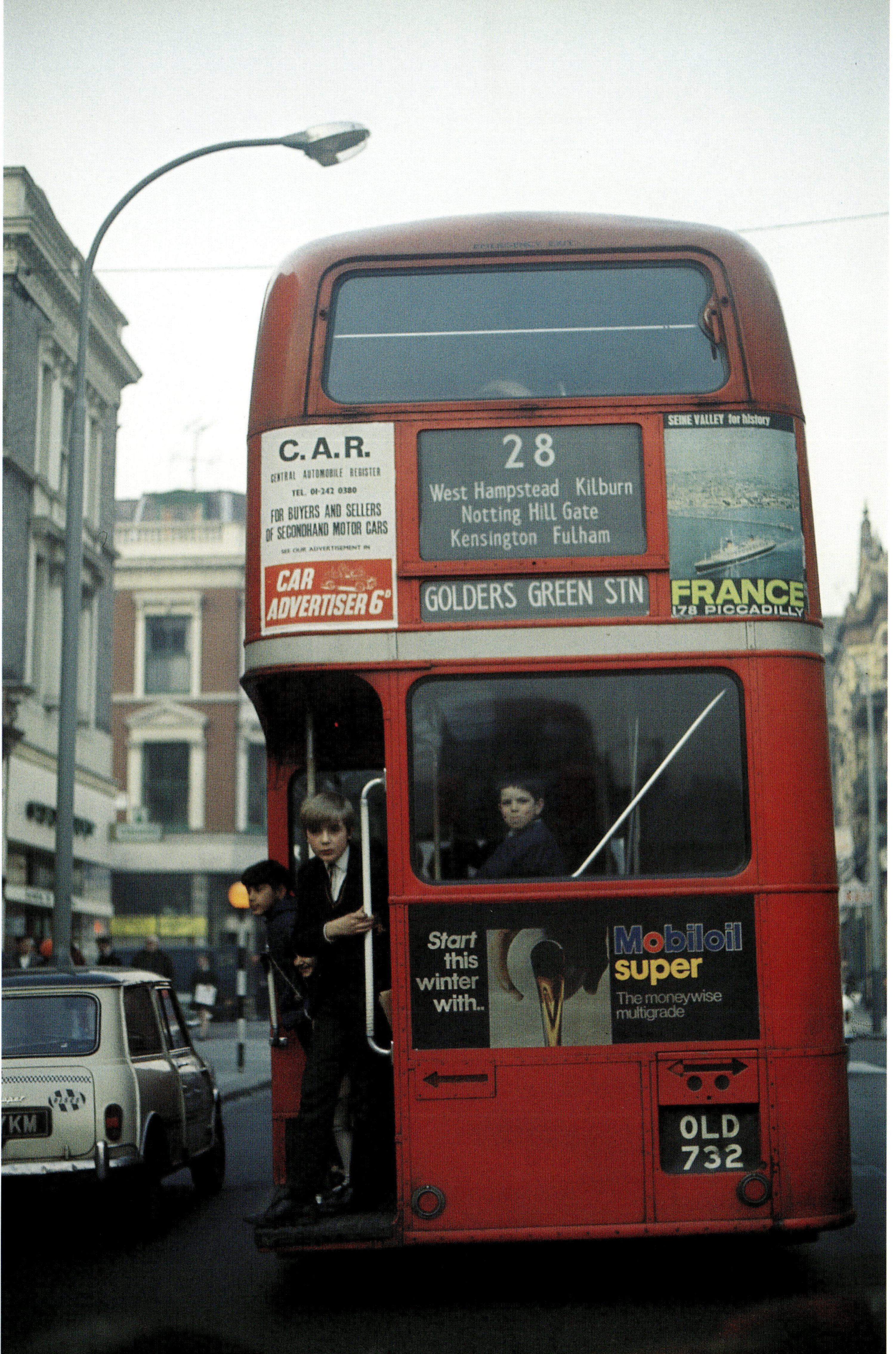
C.A.R.
CENTRAL AUTOMOBILE REGISTER
TEL. 01-242 0380
FOR BUYERS AND SELLERS OF SECONDHAND MOTOR CARS
SEE OUR ADVERTISEMENT IN
CAR ADVERTISER 6d
28
West Hampstead Kilburn
Notting Hill Gate
Kensington Fulham
GOLDERS GREEN STN
SEINE VALLEY for history
FRANCE
178 PICCADILLY
Start this winter with..
Mobiloil super
The moneywise multigrade
OLD 732

Blinkered conditioned soul from past escapes through my lens to see out.

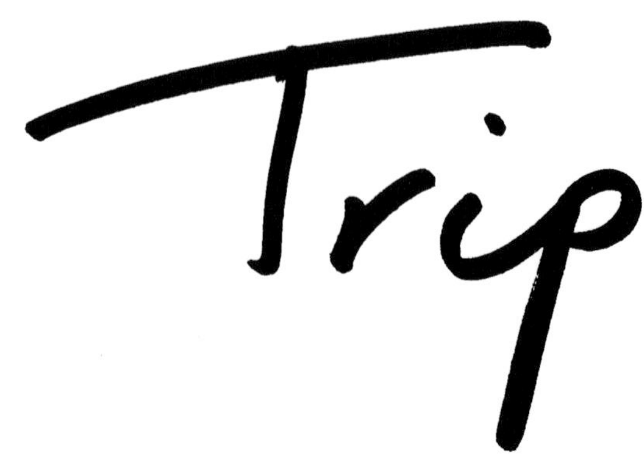

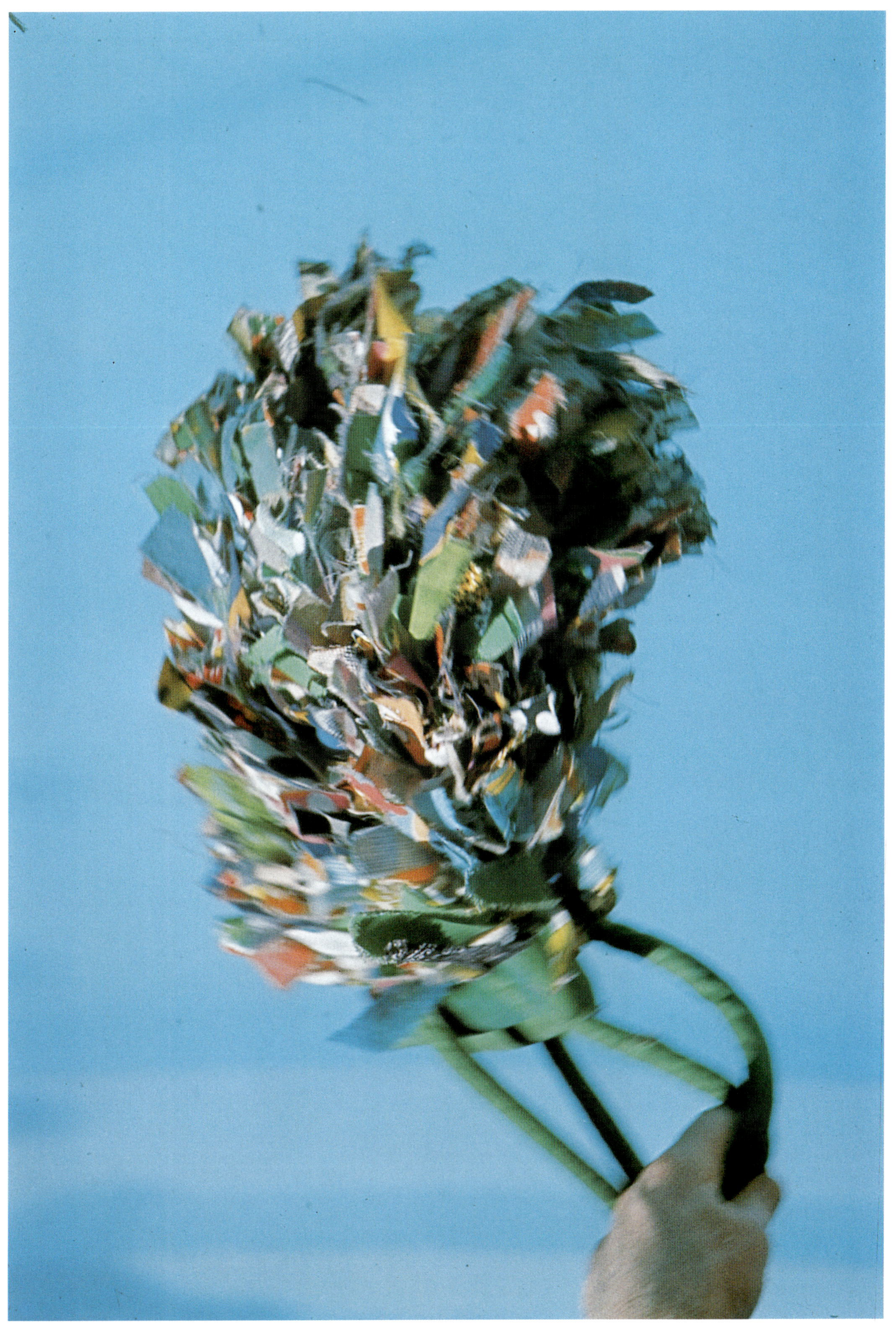

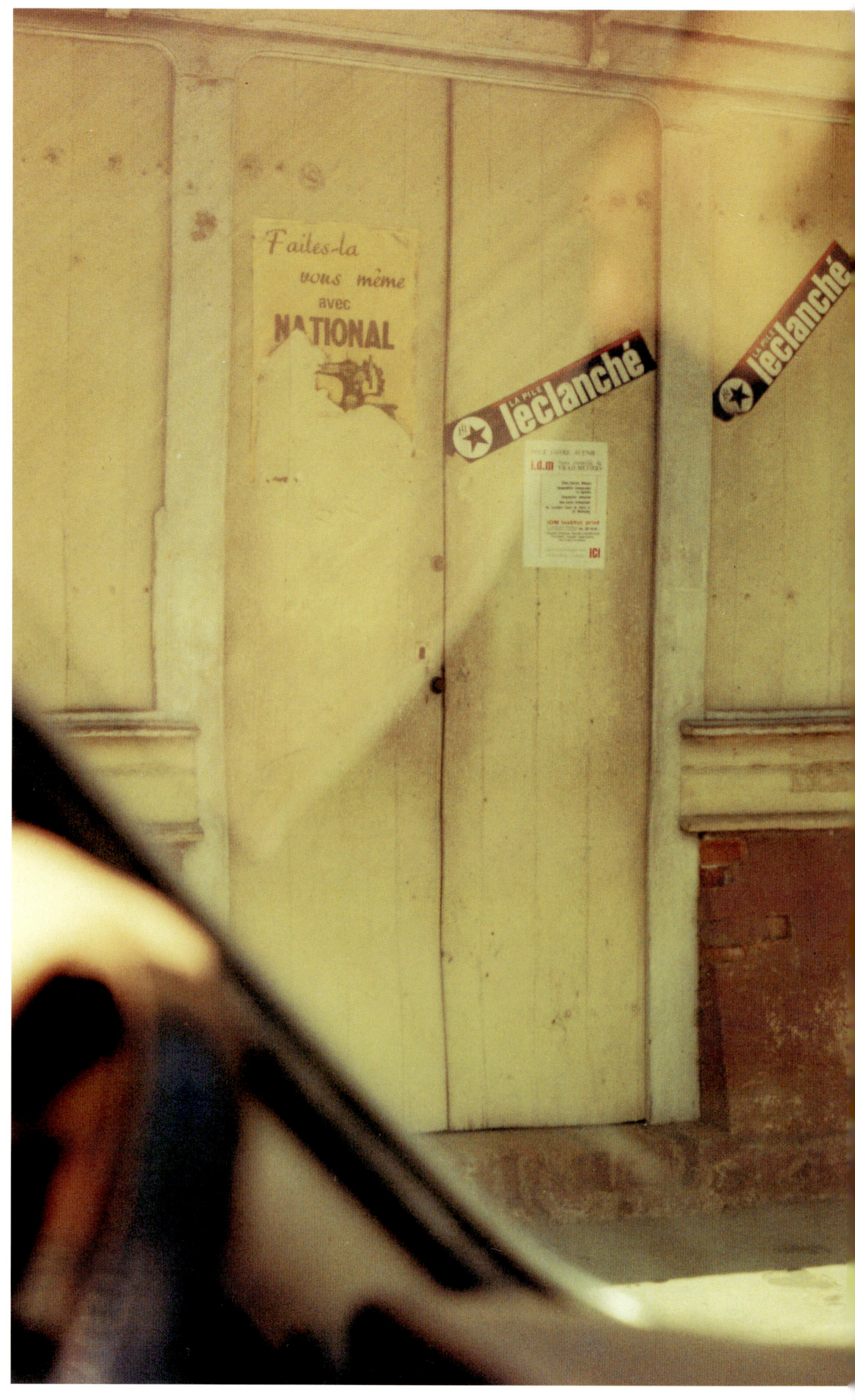
Faites-la
vous même
avec
NATIONAL
LA PILE
leclanché
LA PILE
leclanché

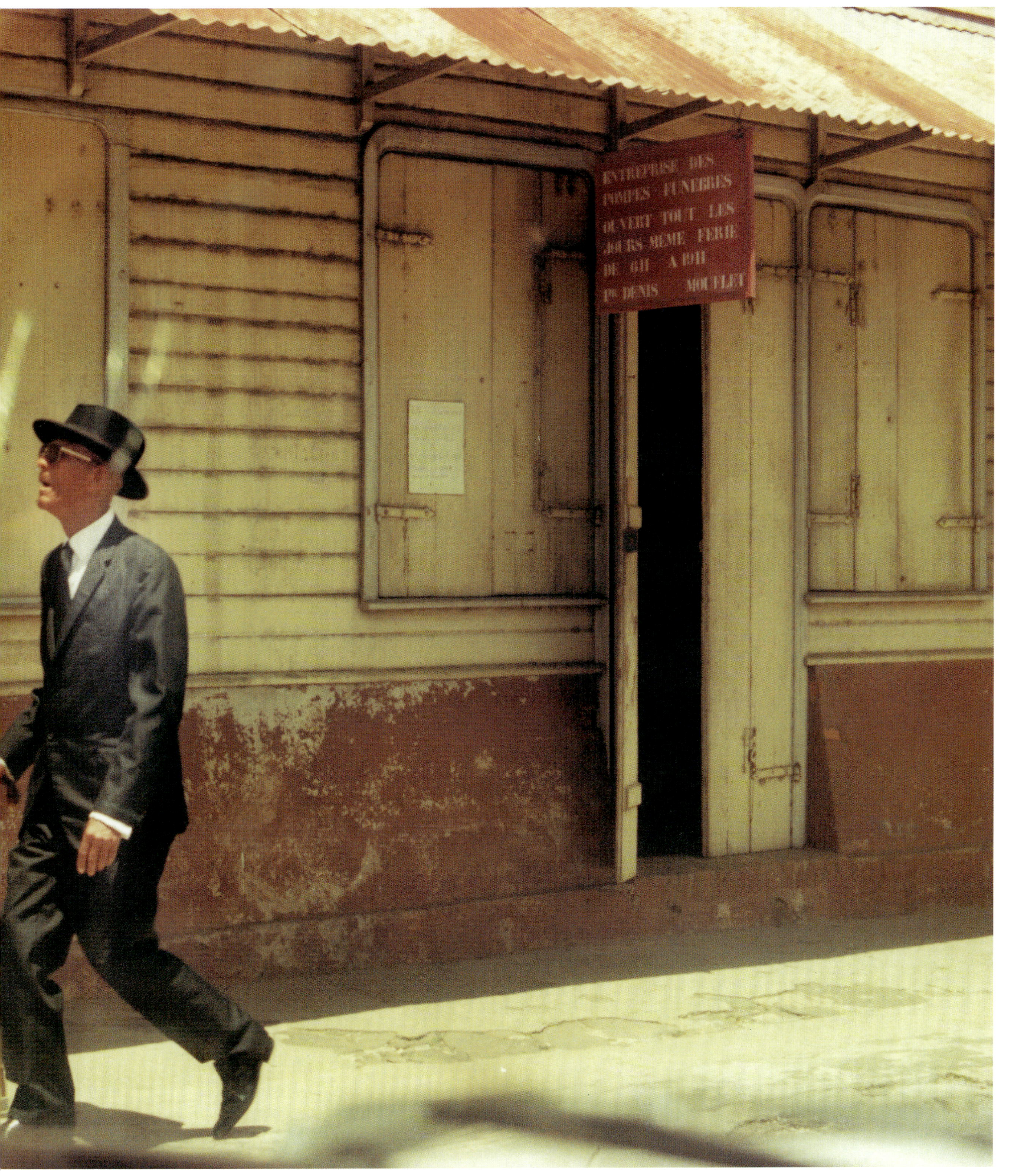
ENTREPRISE DES
POMPES FUNEBRES
OUVERT TOUT LES
JOURS MEME FERIE
DENIS MOUFLET

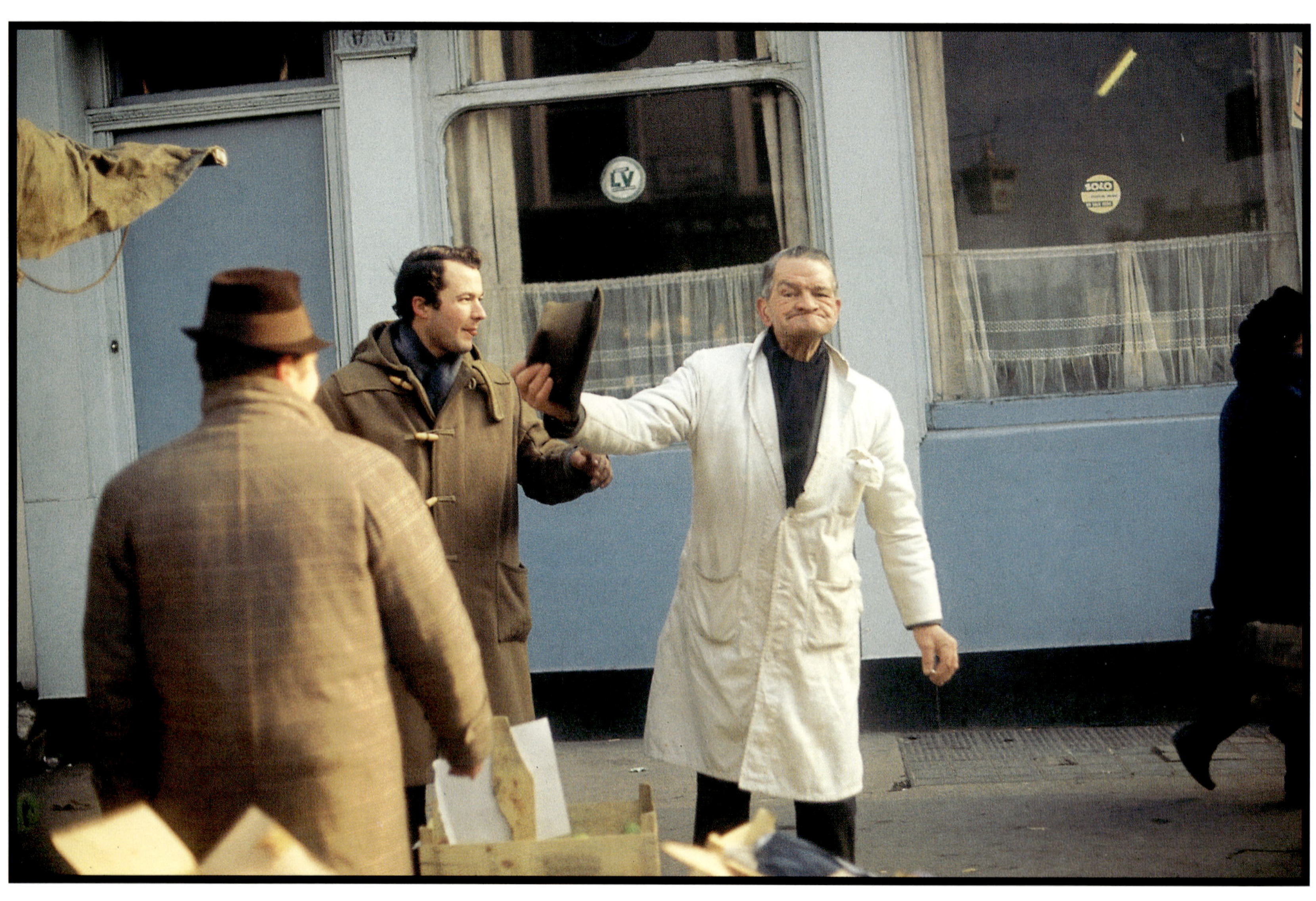
LV
SOLO

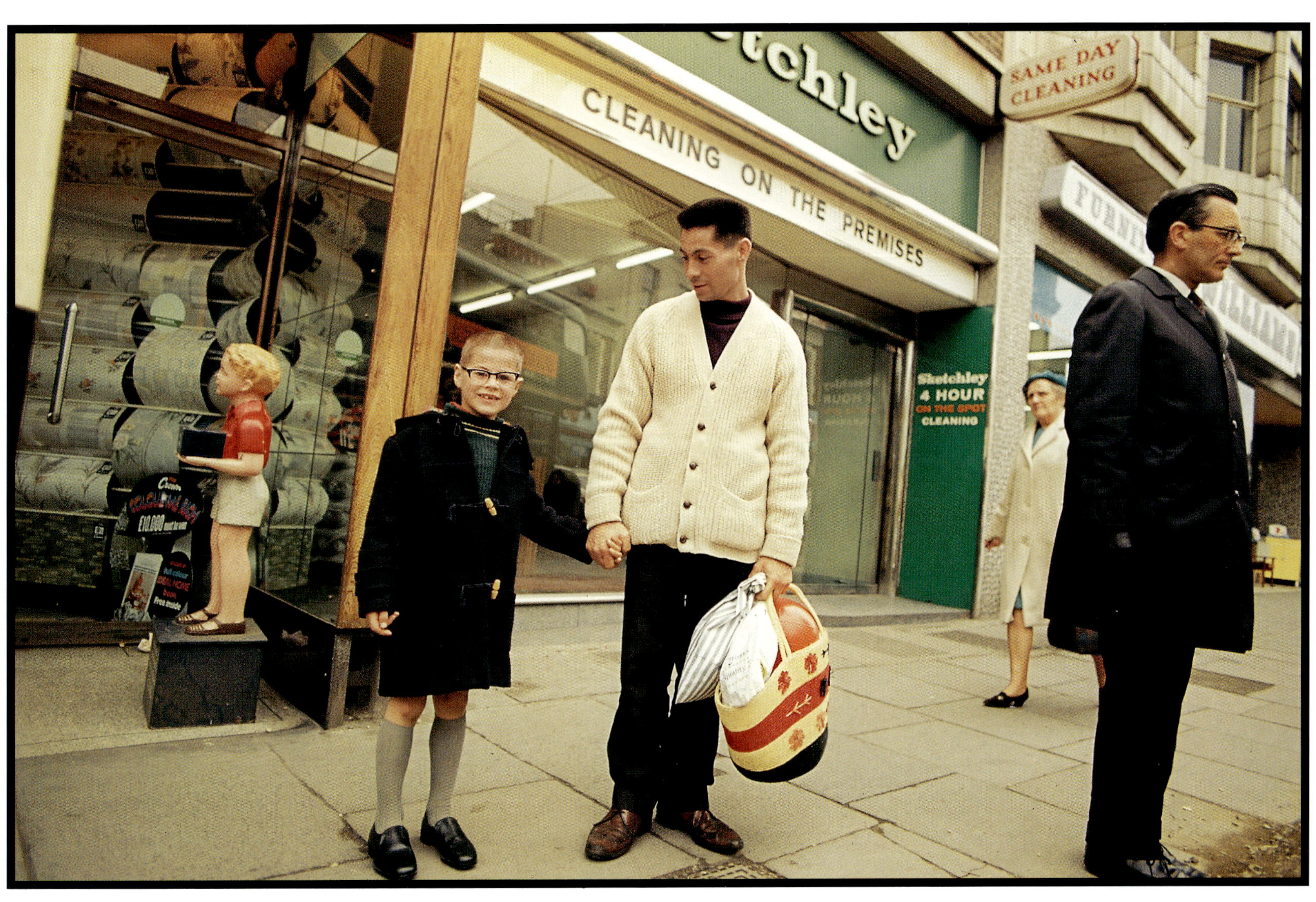
CLEANING ON THE PREMISES
SAME DAY CLEANING
Sketchley
4 HOUR
ON THE SPOT
CLEANING

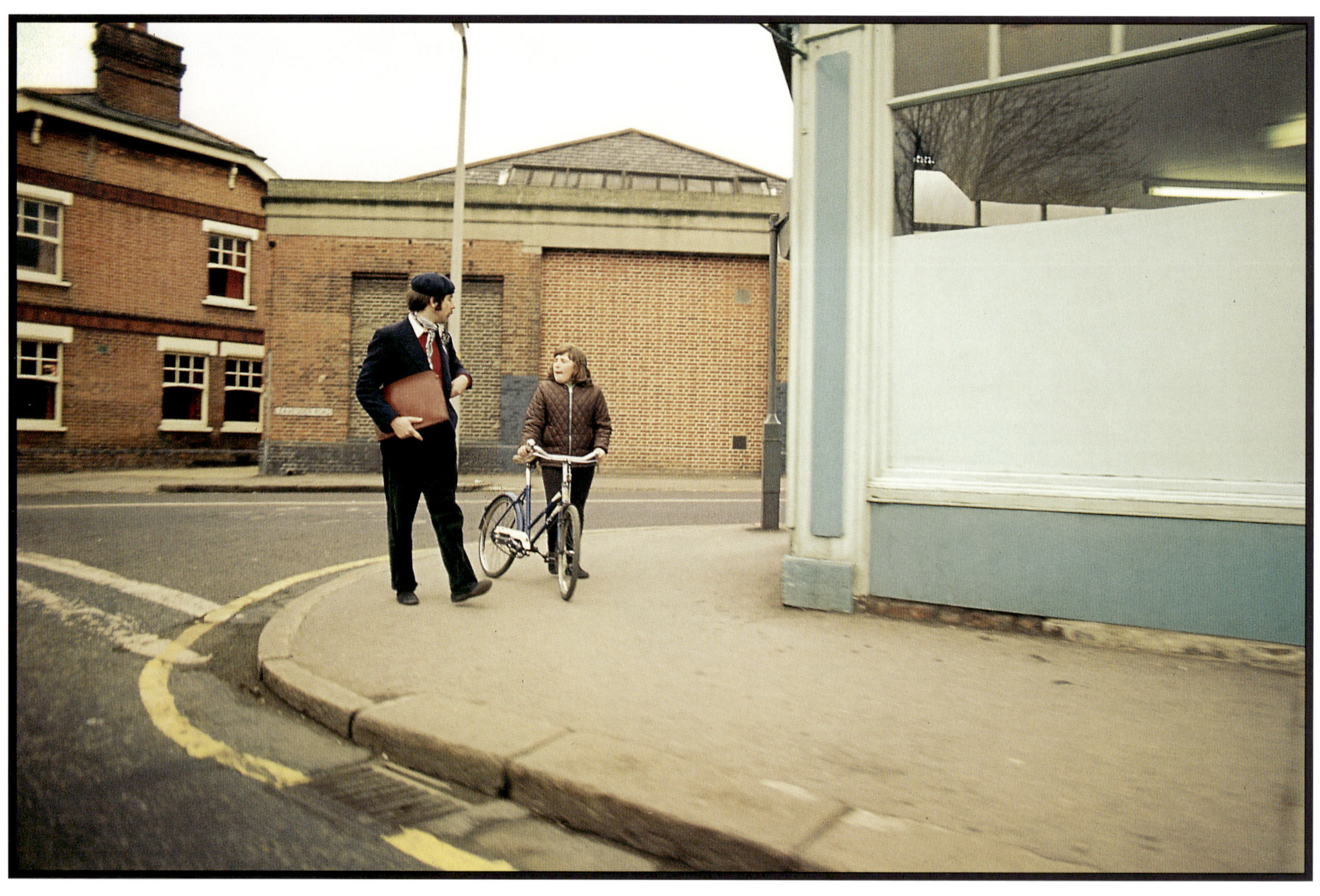

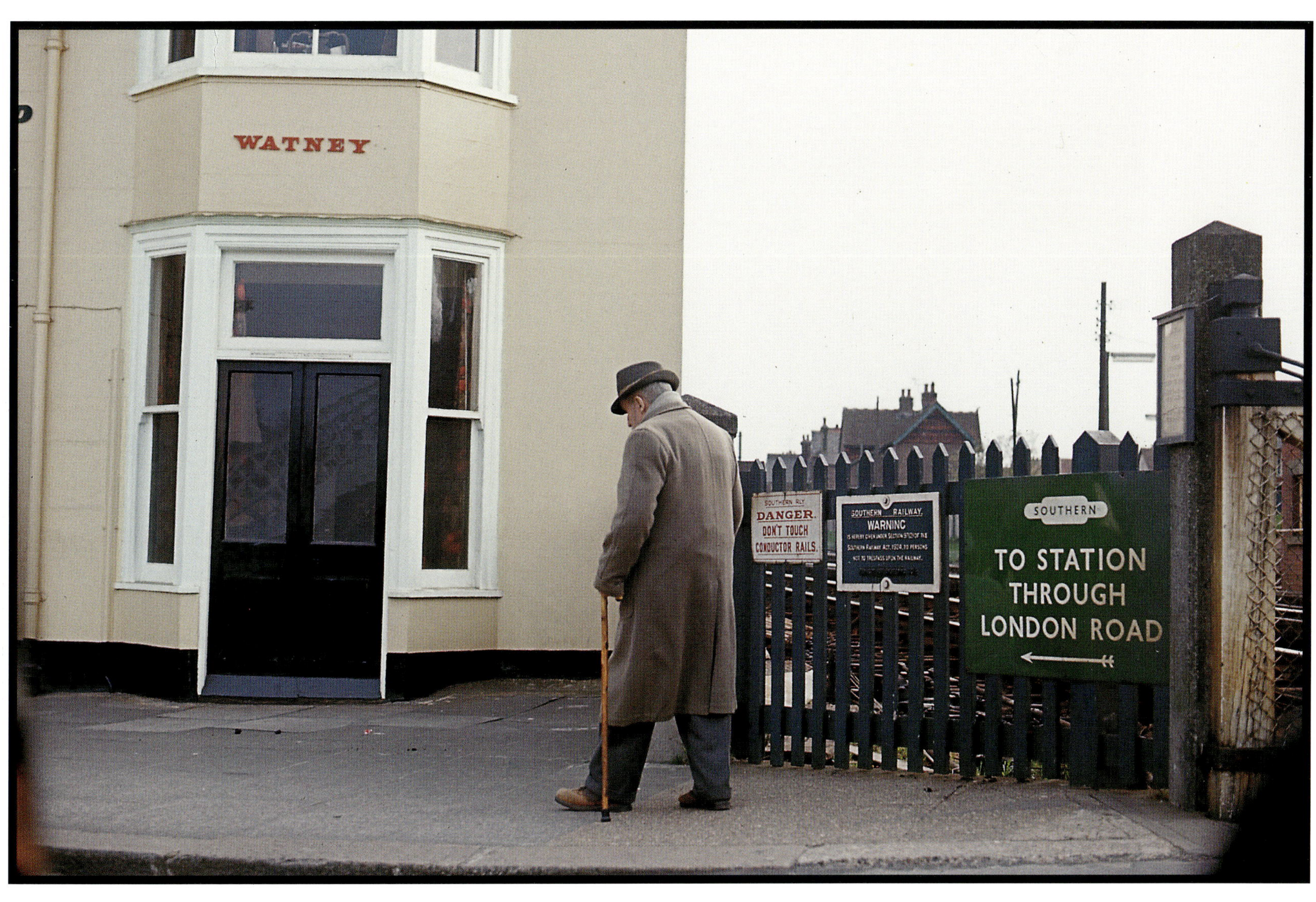
WATNEY
SOUTHERN RLY
DANGER.
DON'T TOUCH
CONDUCTOR RAILS.
SOUTHERN RAILWAY.
WARNING
SOUTHERN
TO STATION
THROUGH
LONDON ROAD

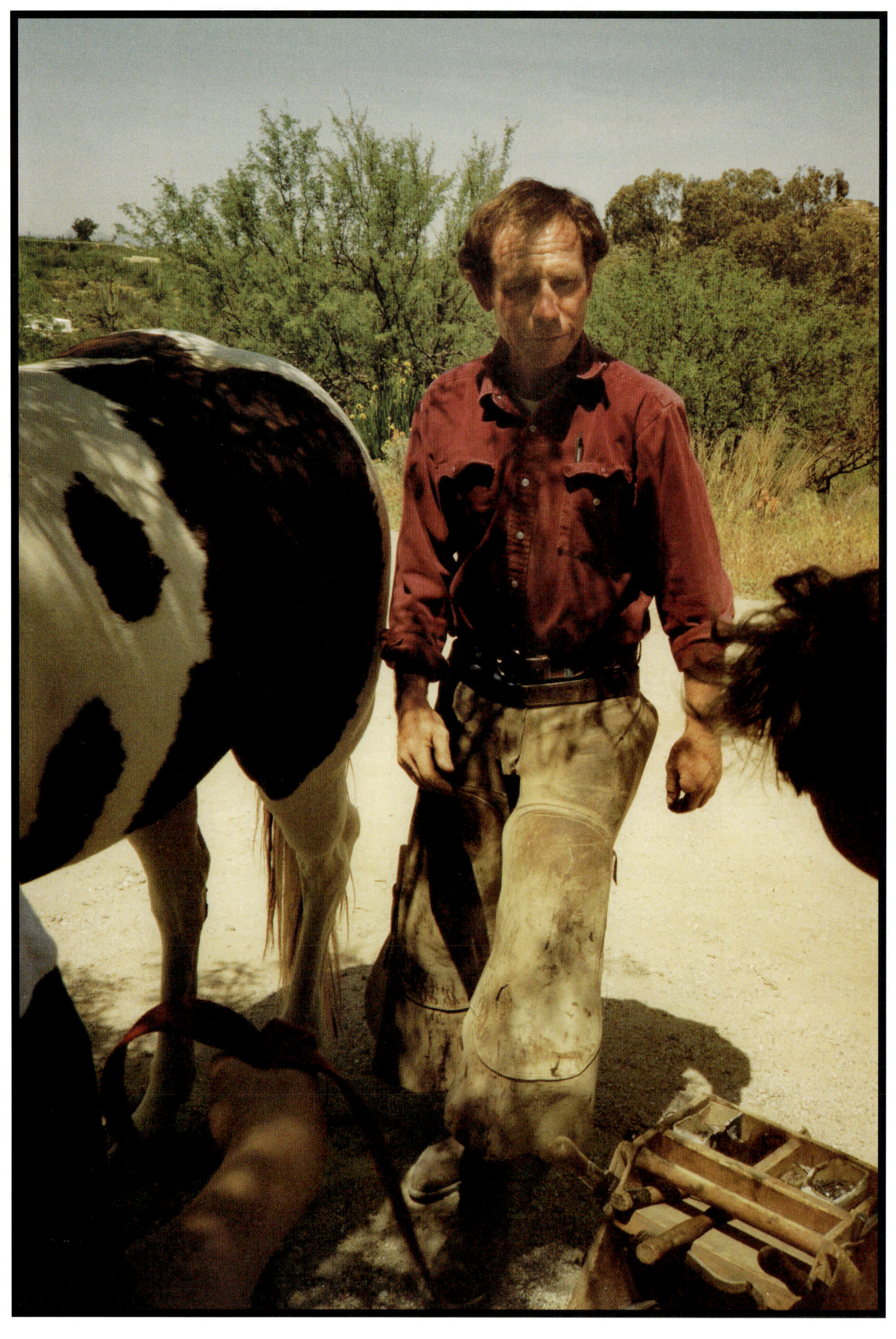

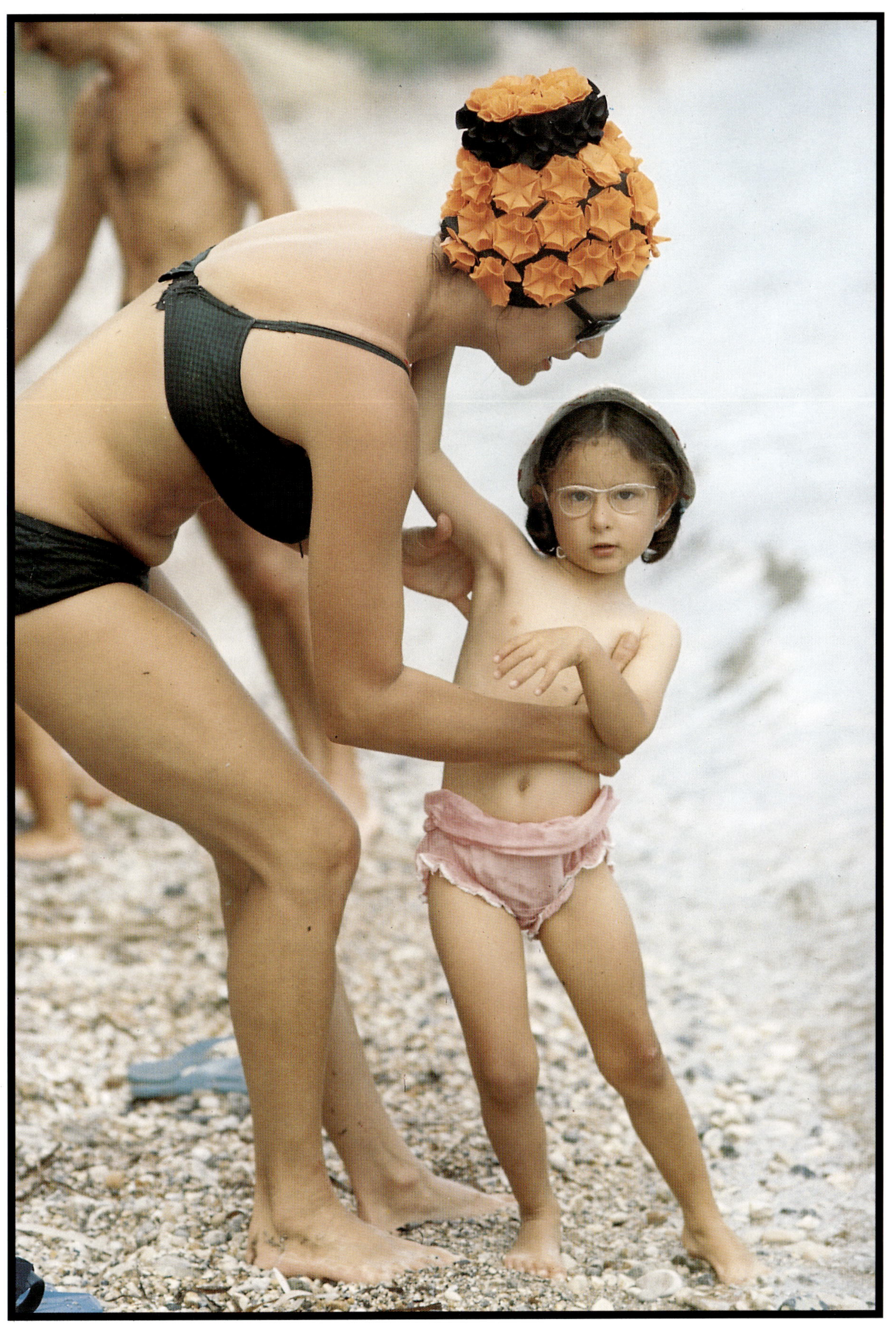

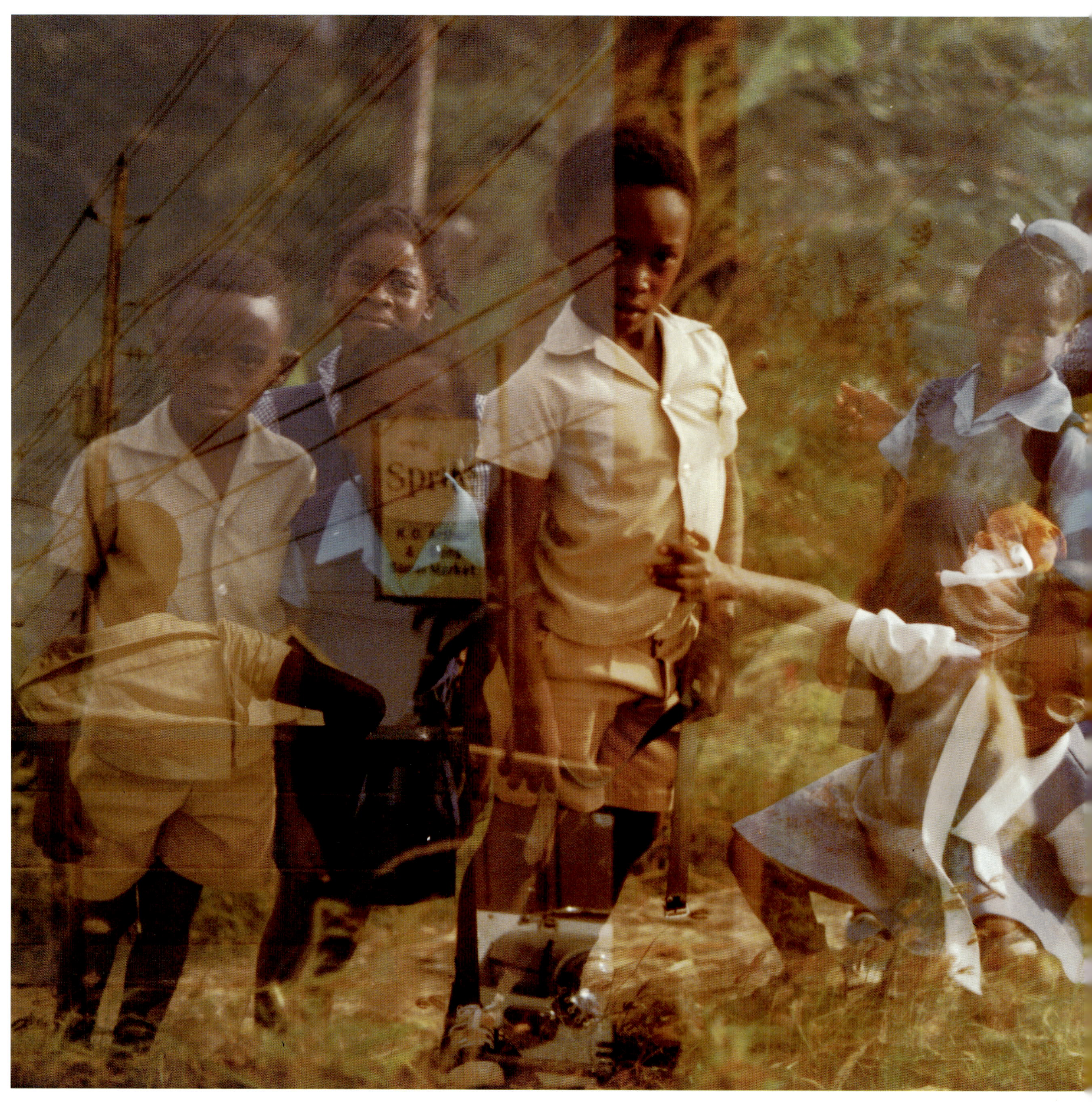

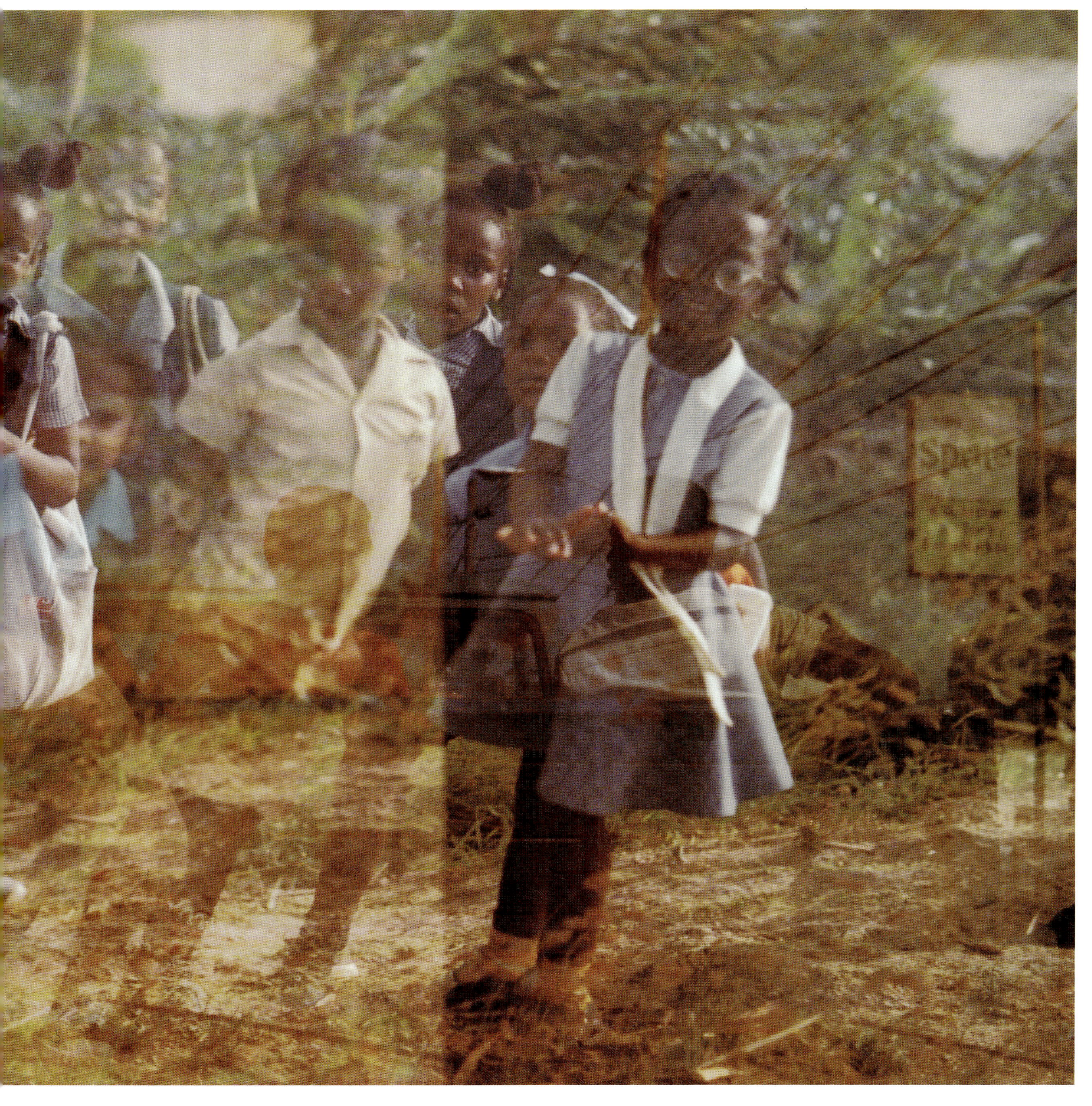

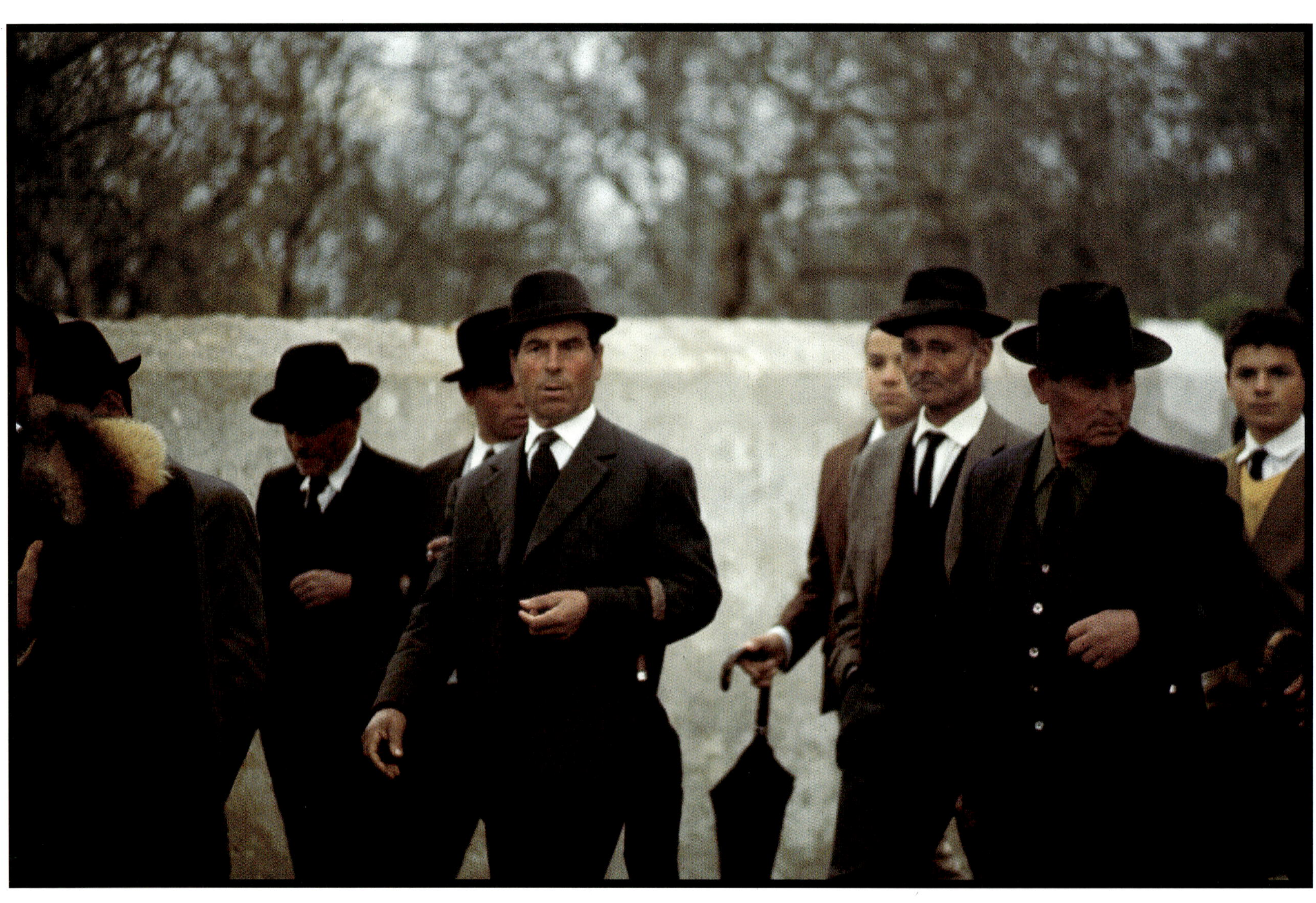

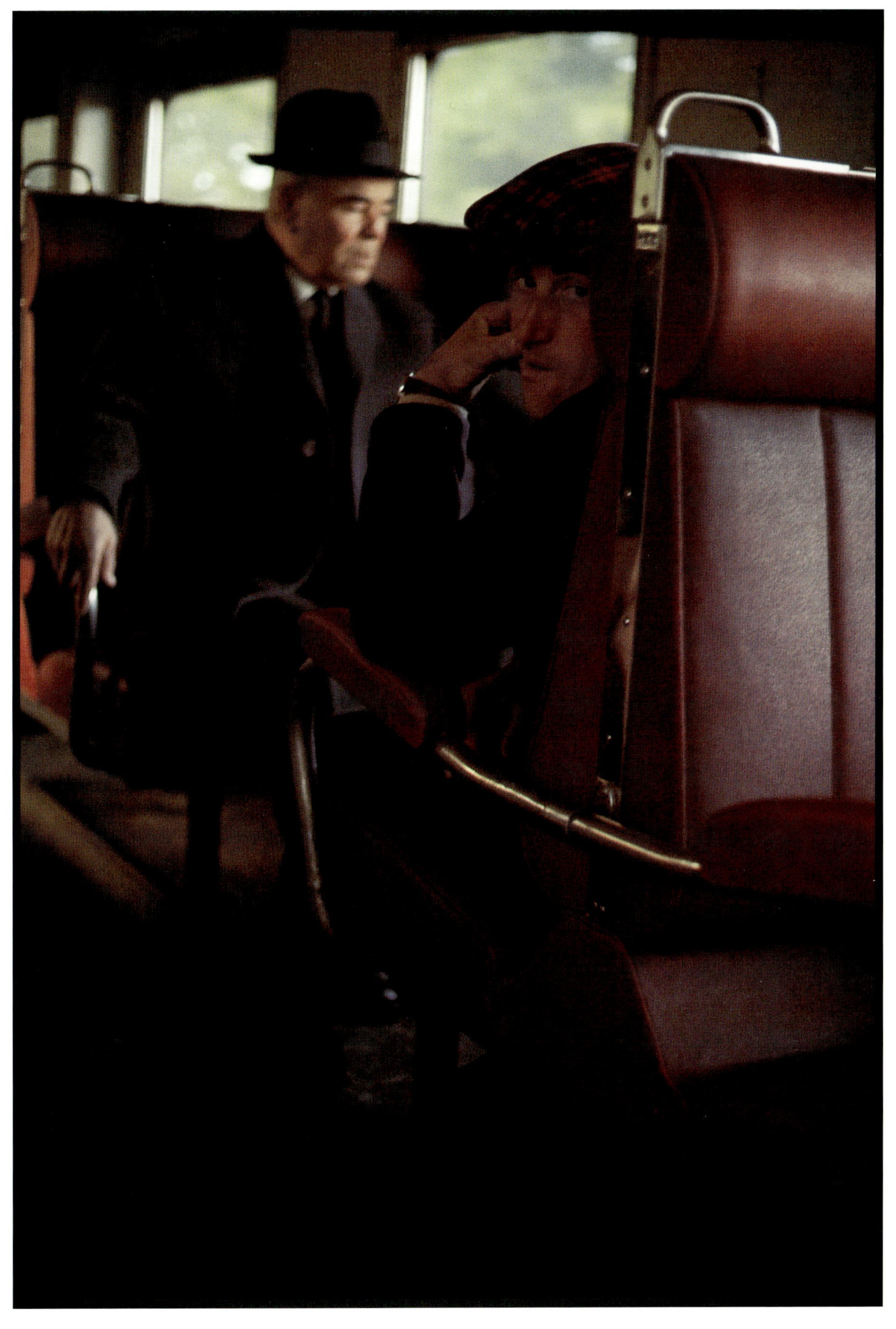

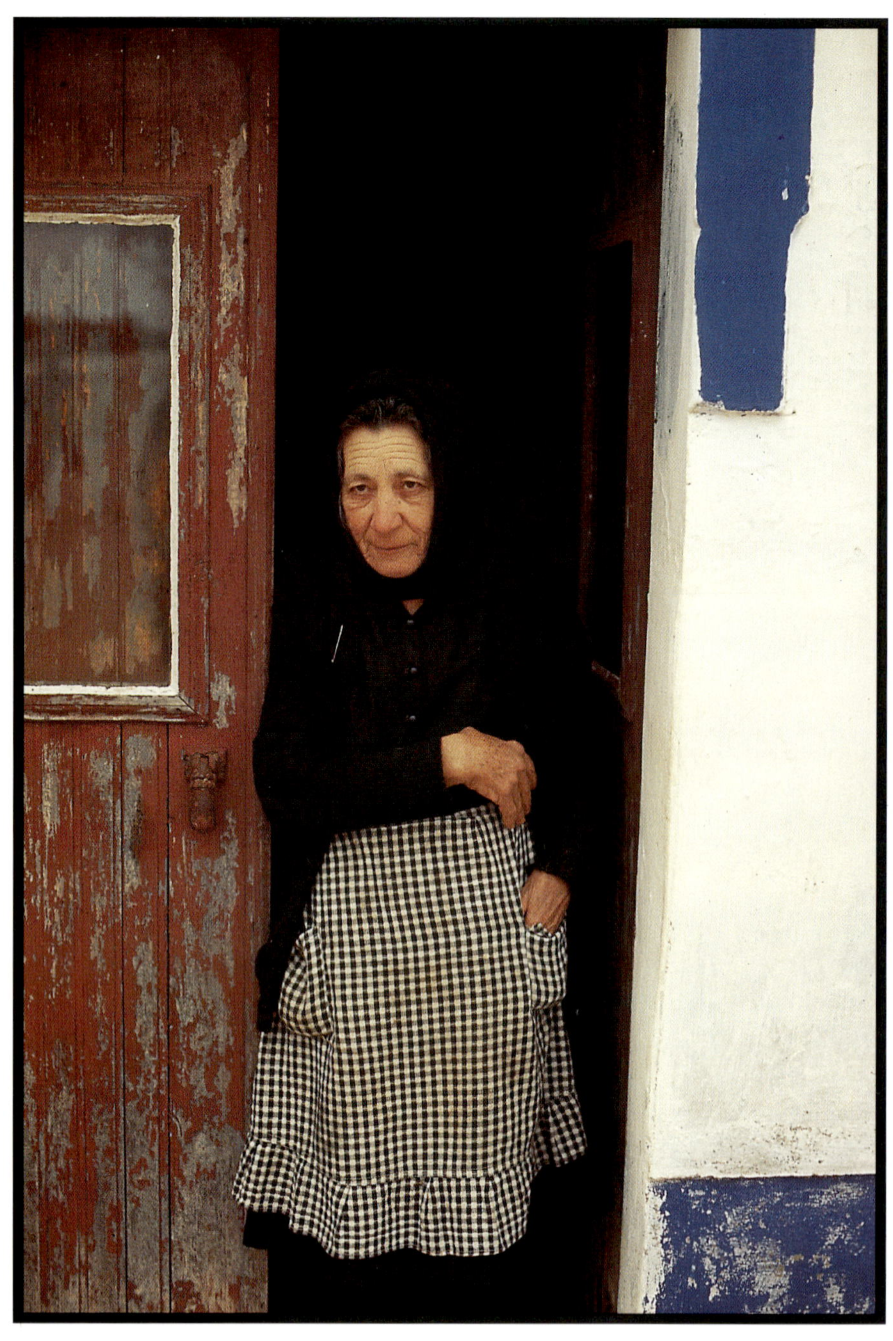

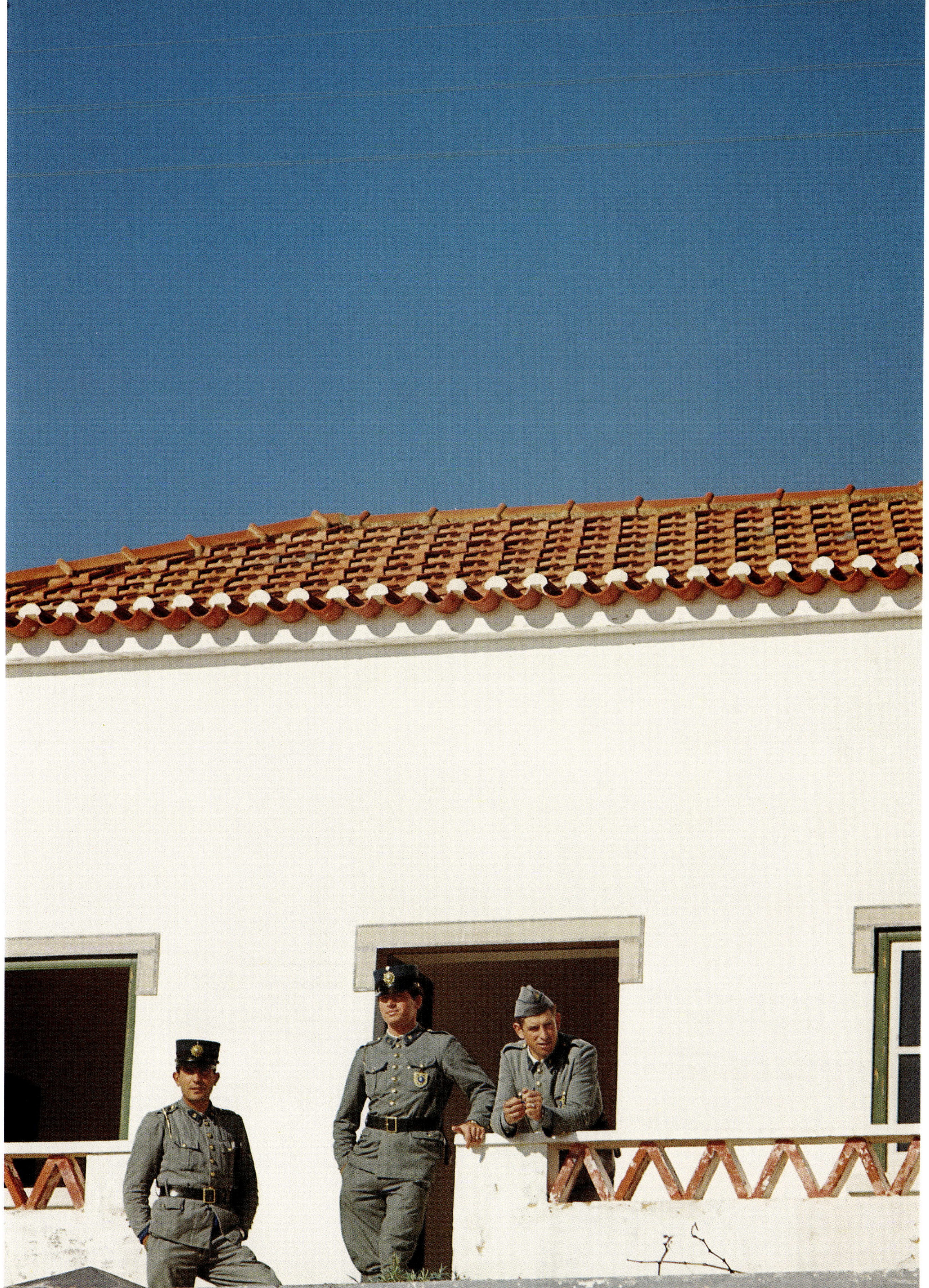

Woman tripping away from New Orleans
seeking a new direction

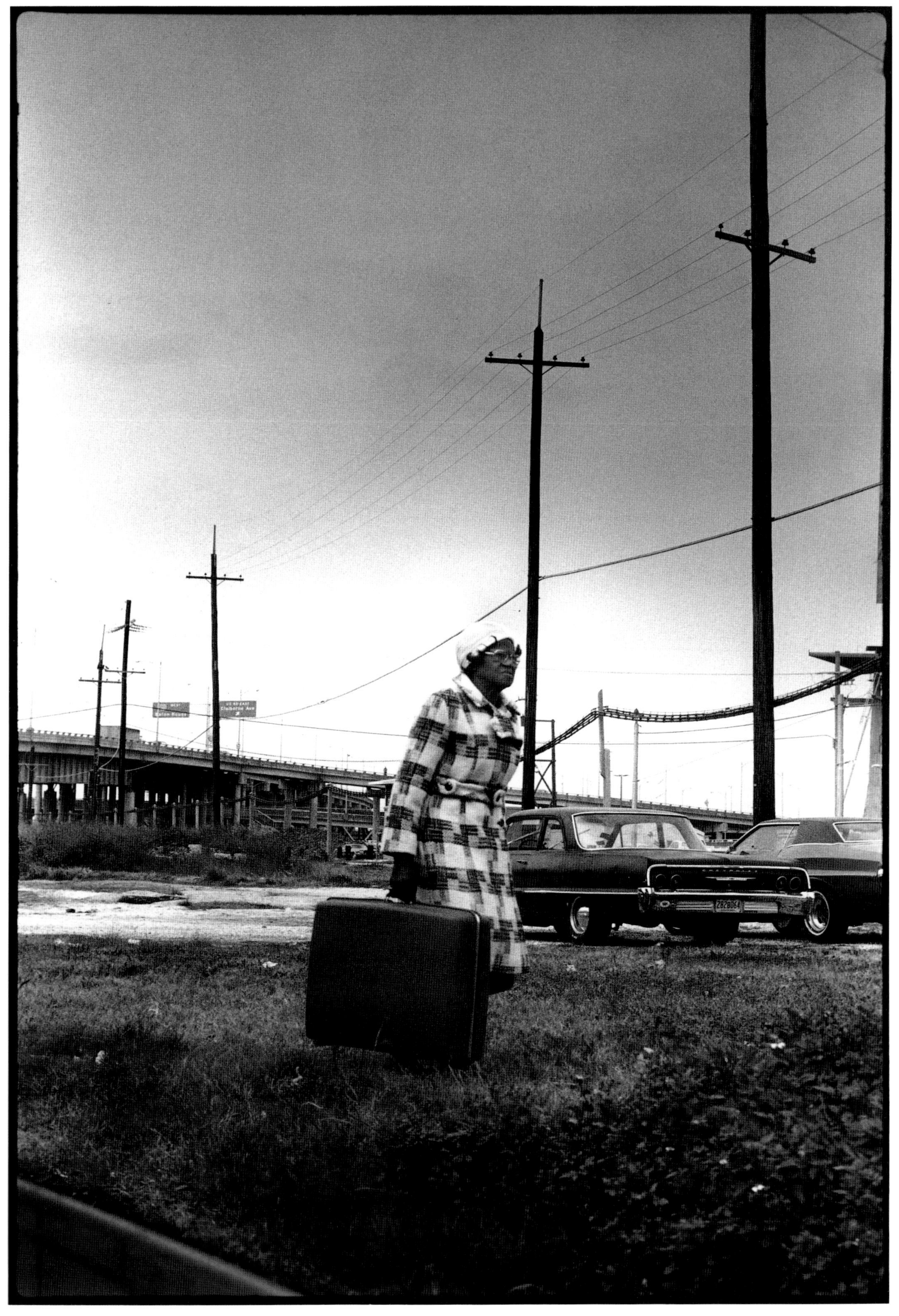
Claiborne Ave

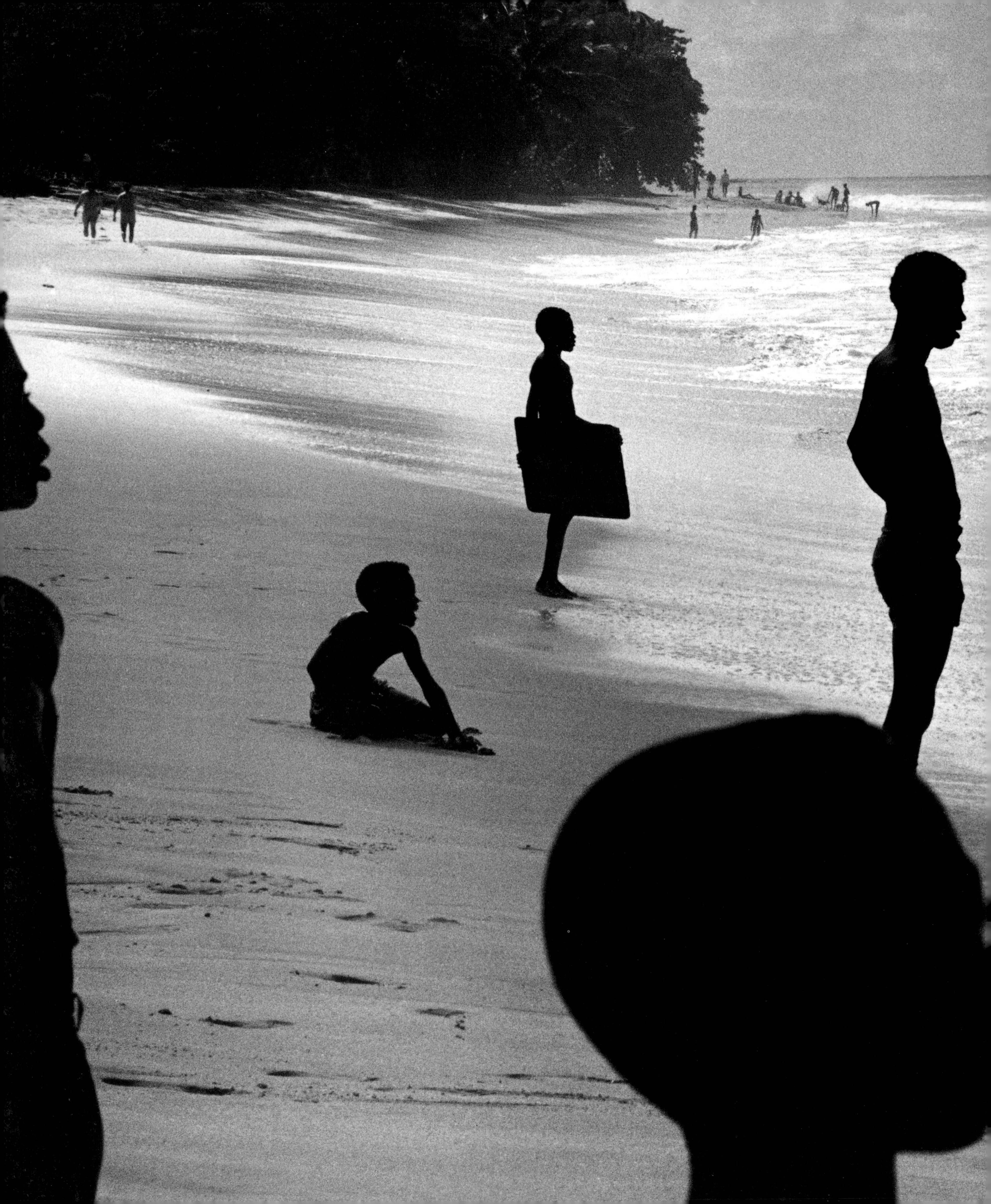

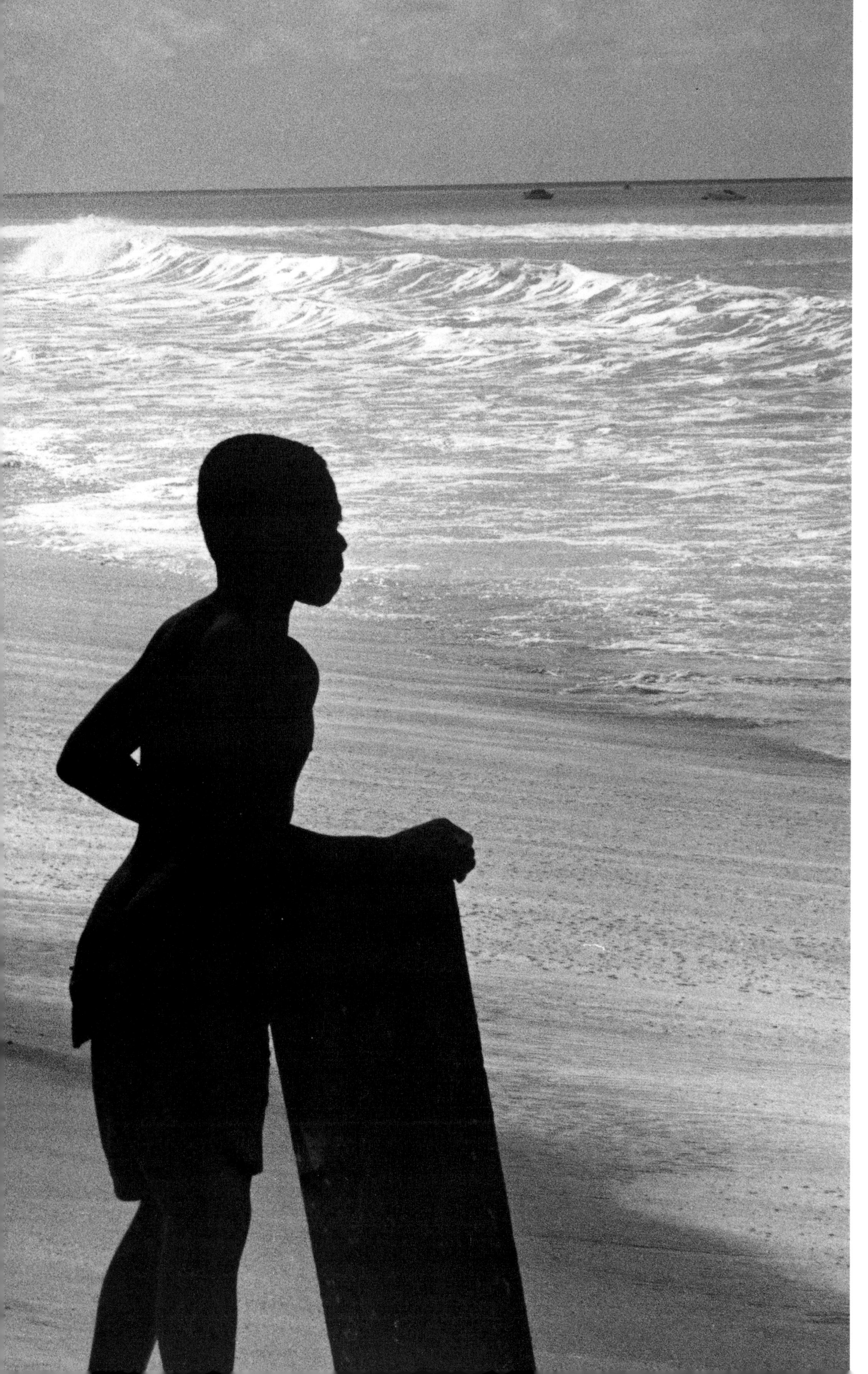

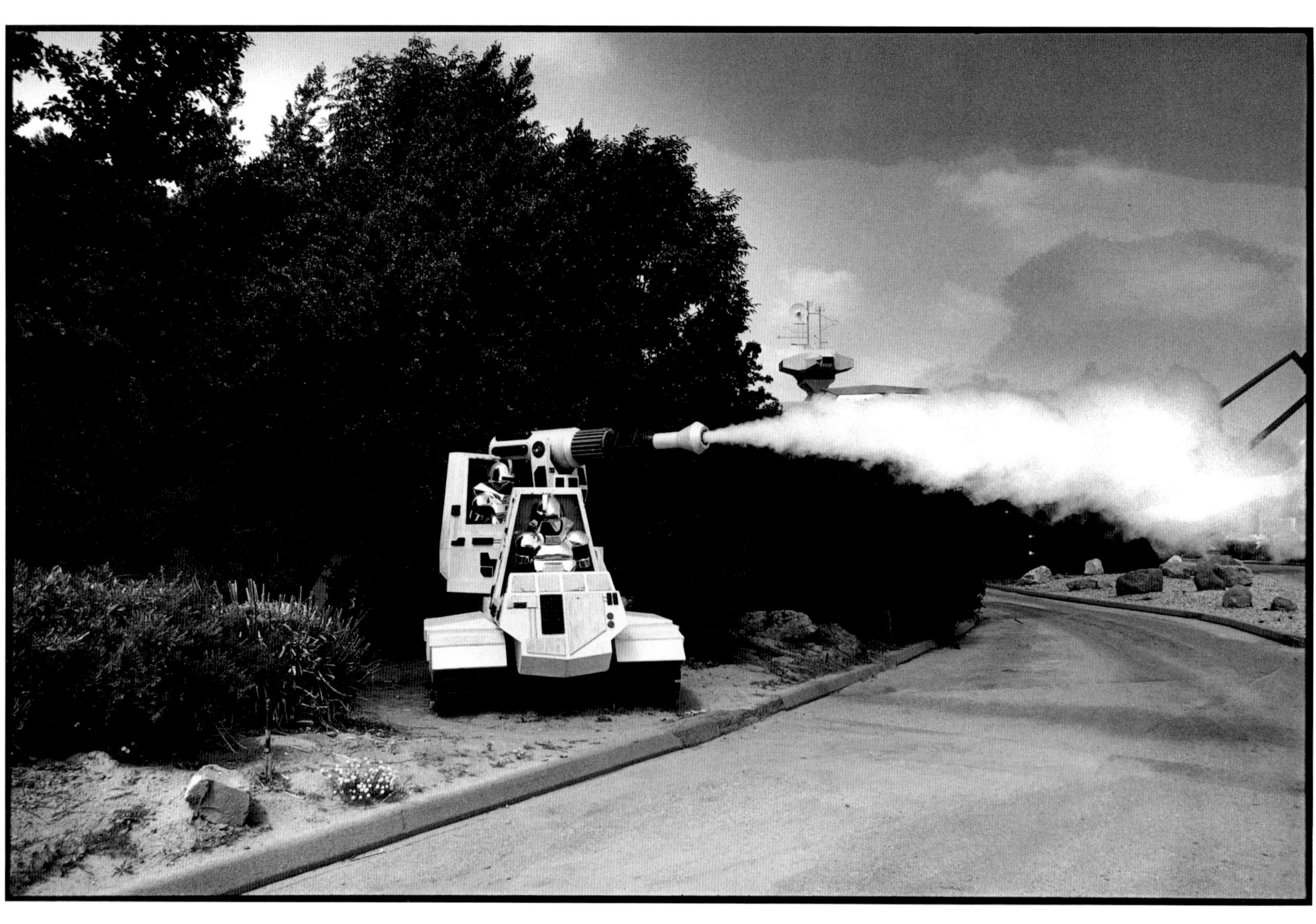

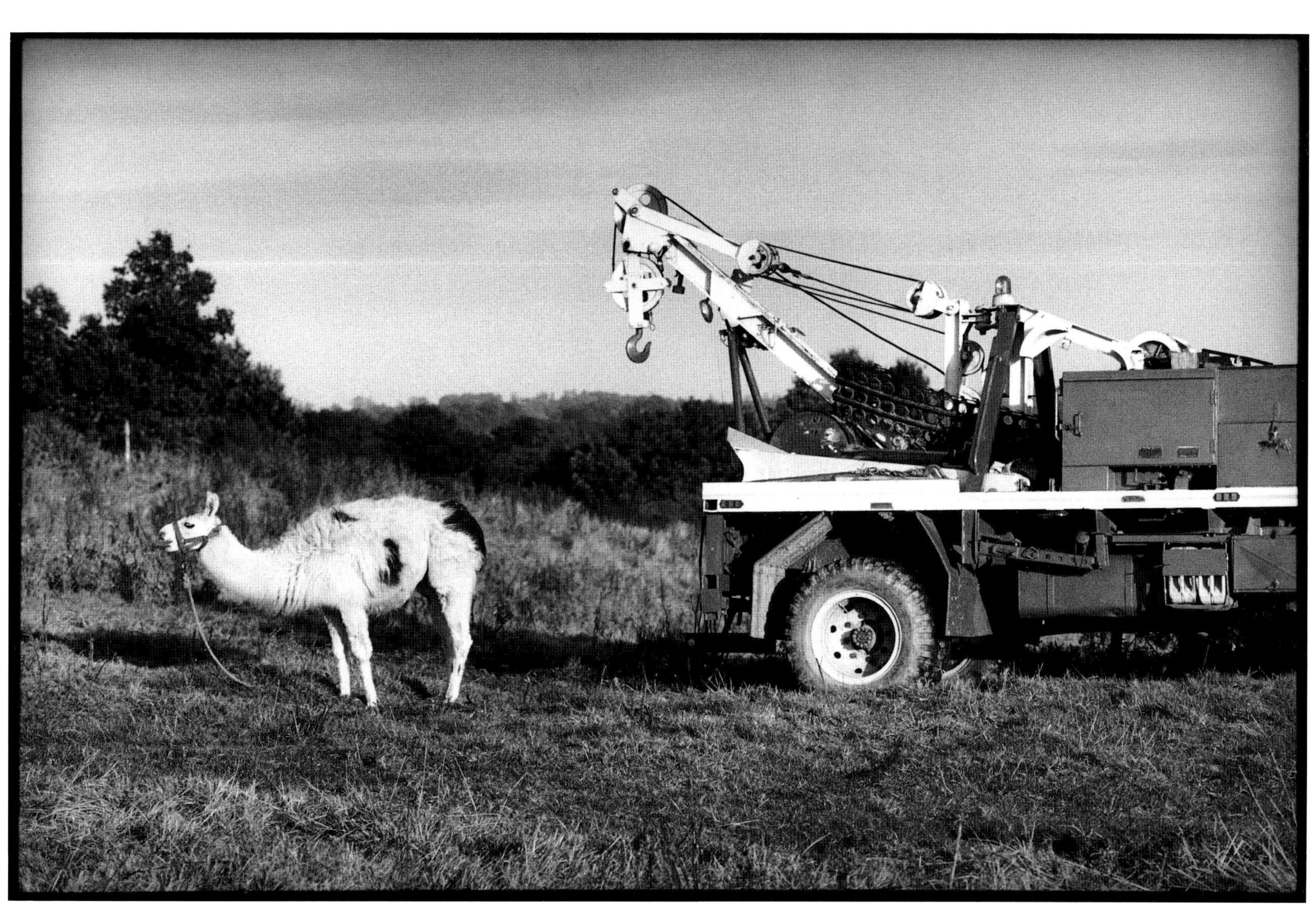

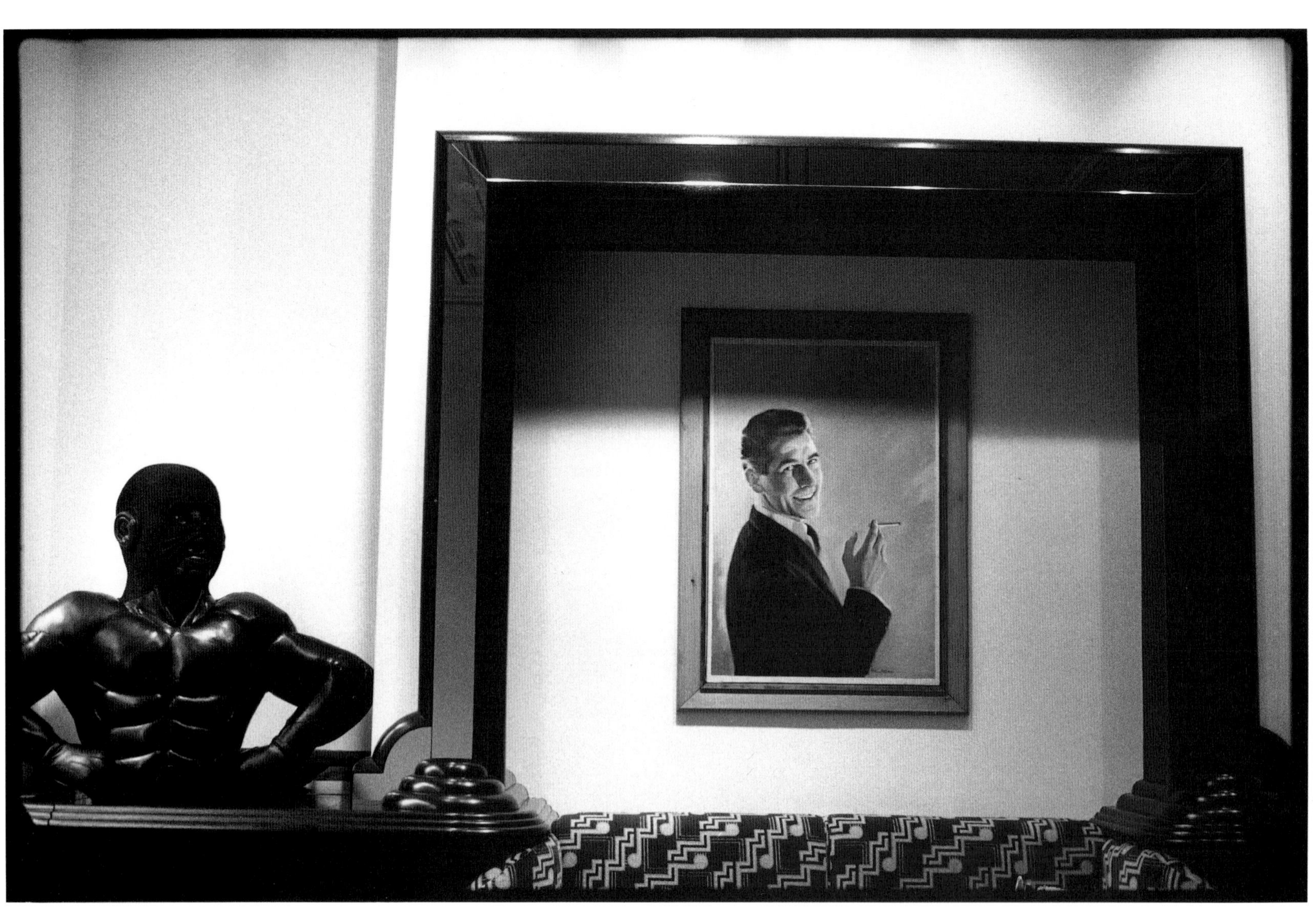

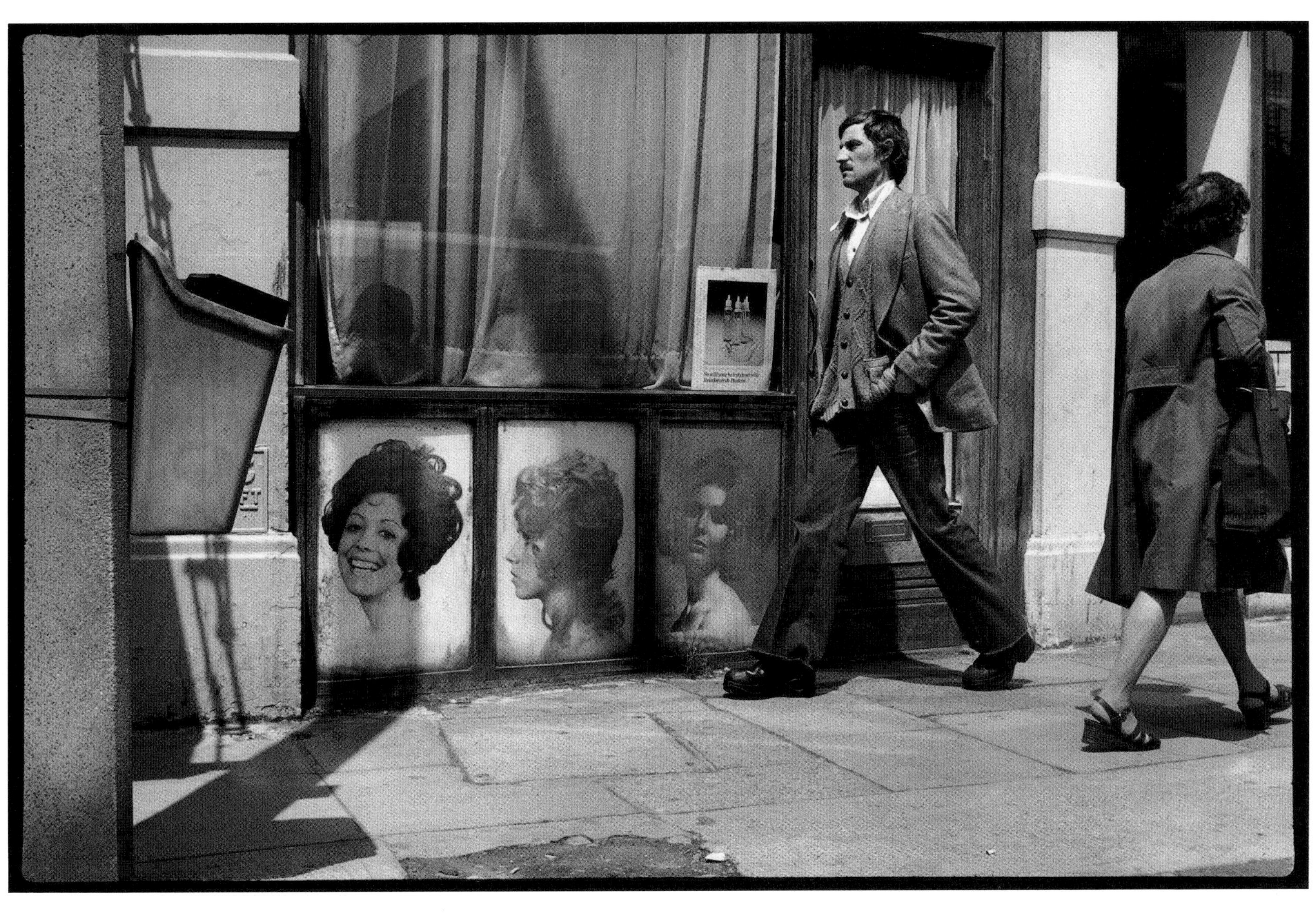

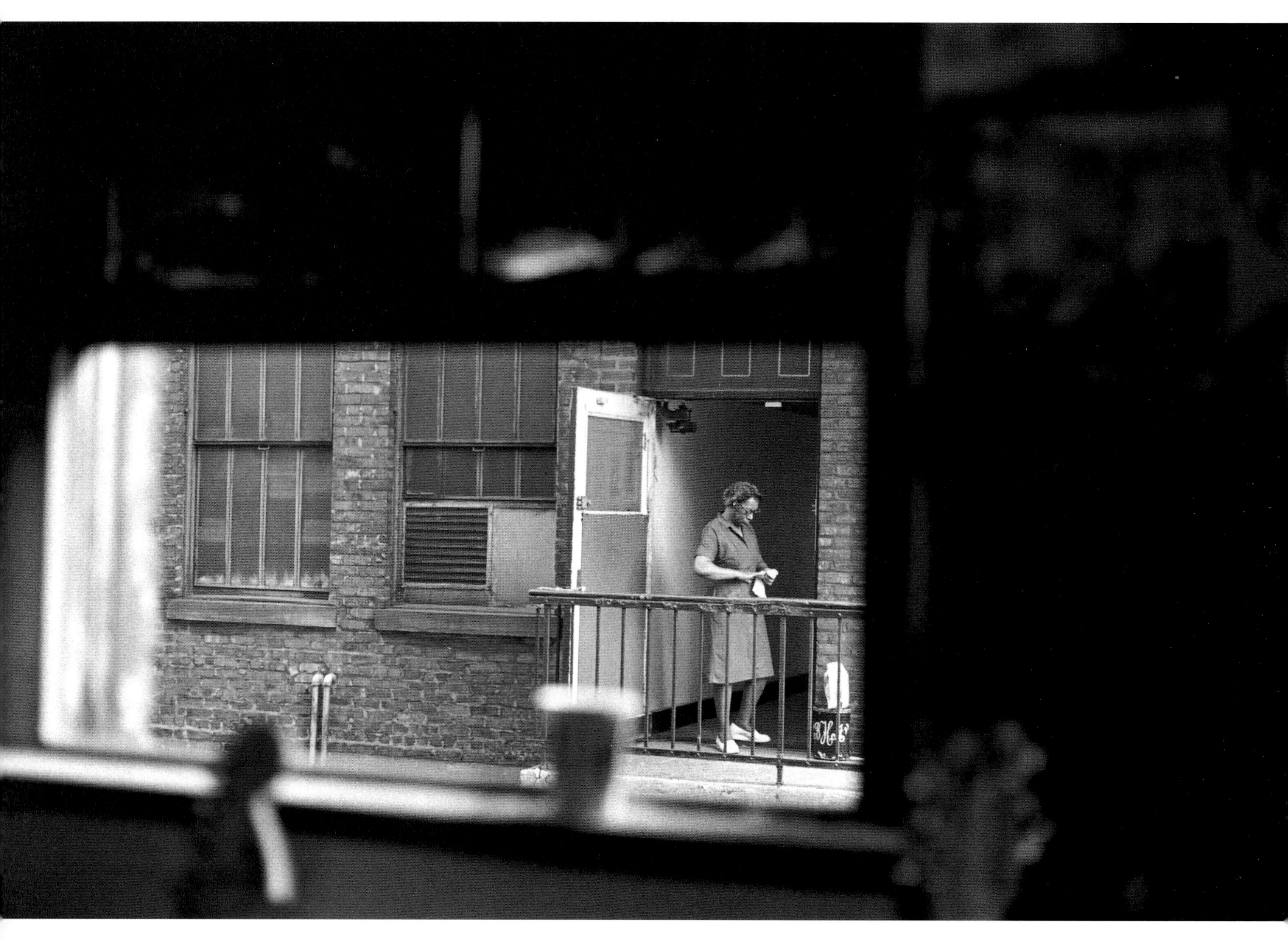

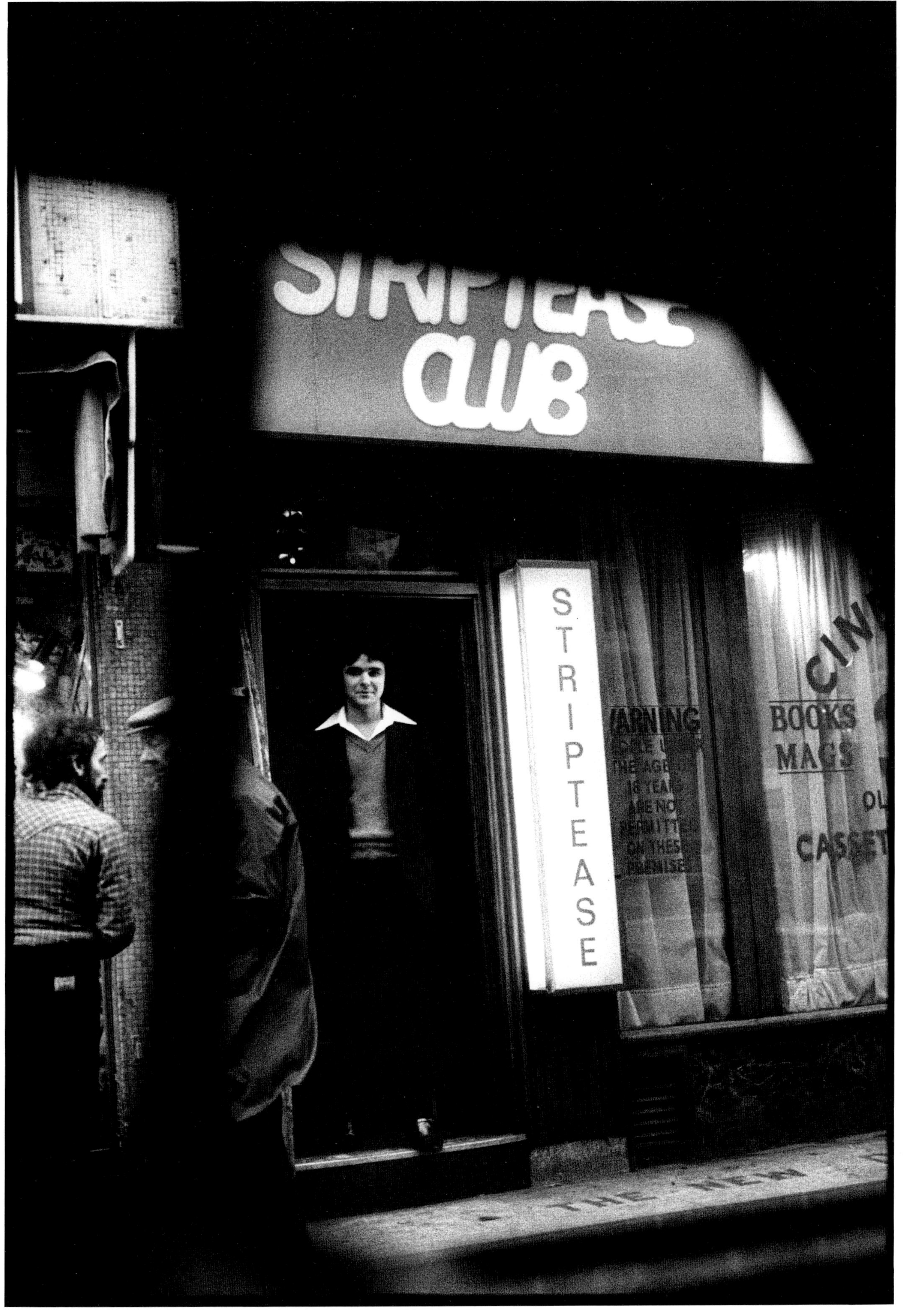
STRIPTEASE
CLUB
STRIPTEASE
BOOKS
MAGS

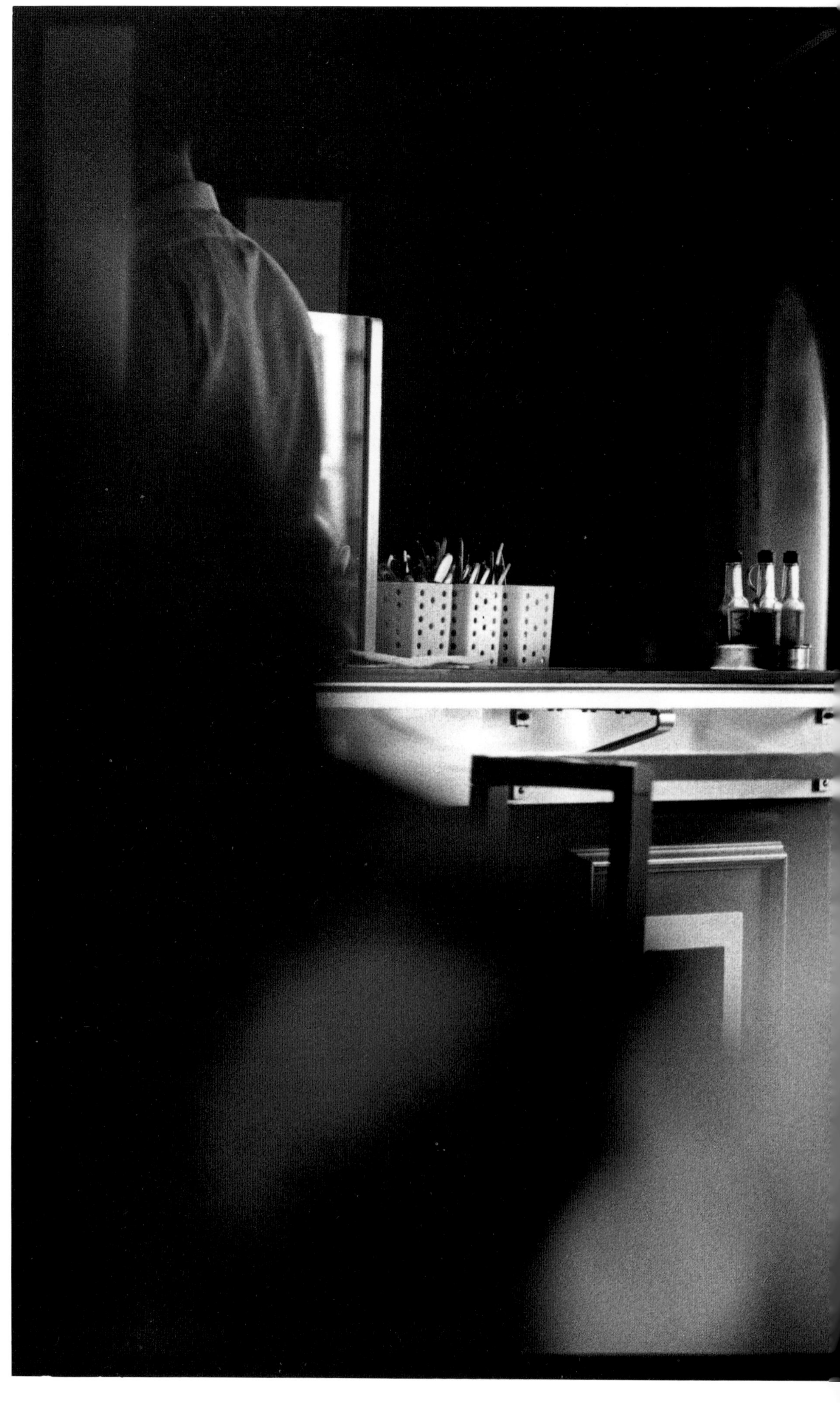

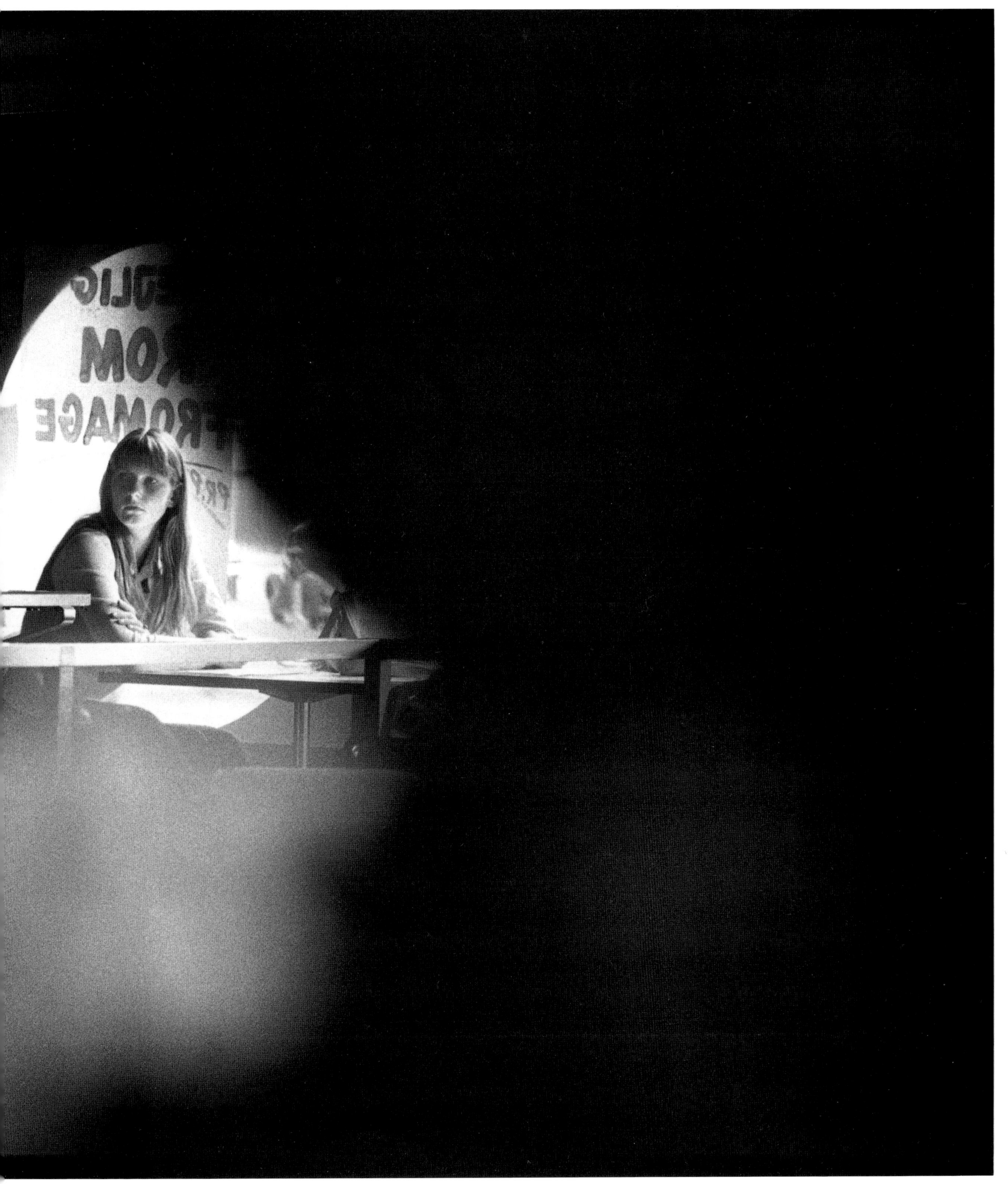

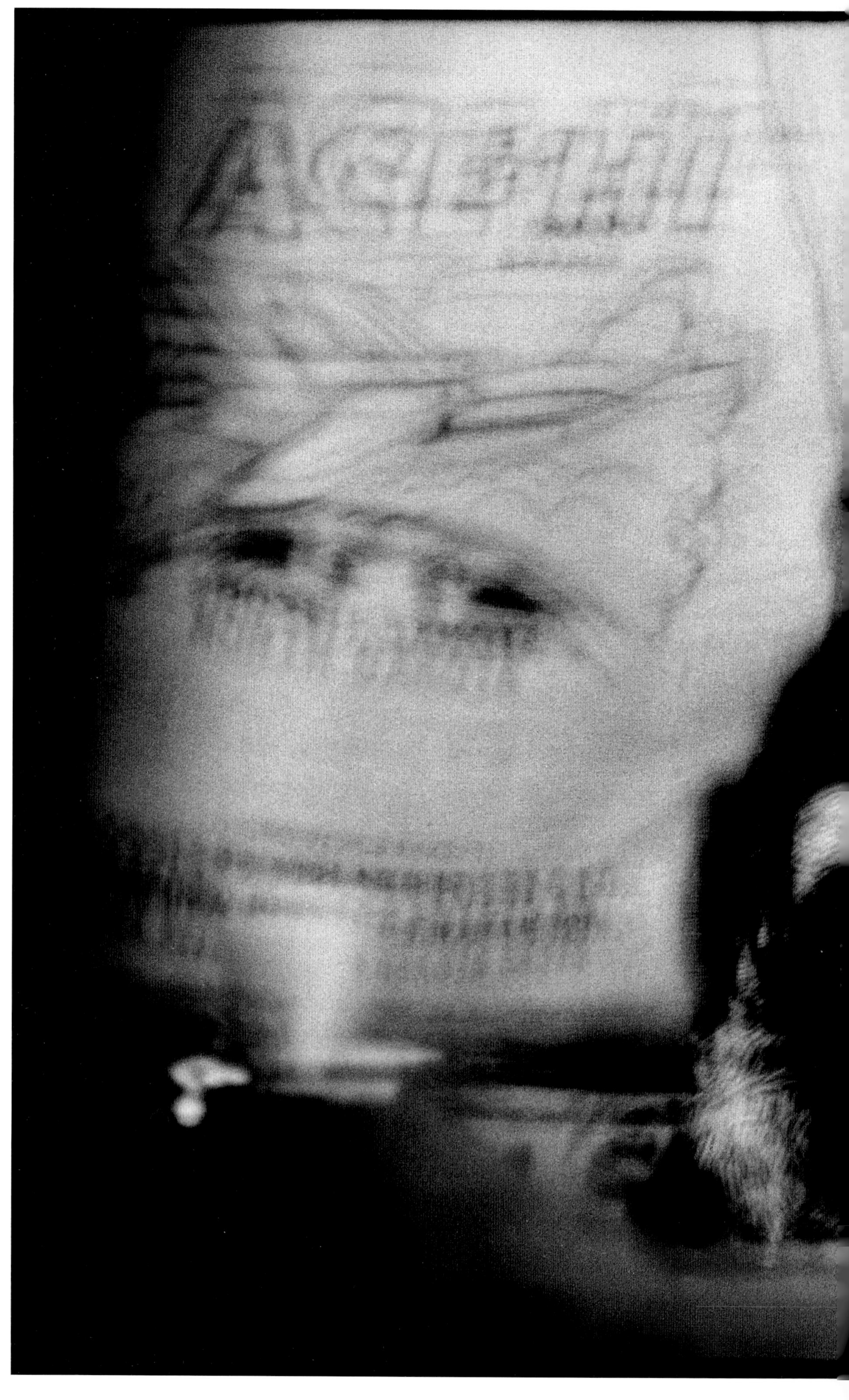

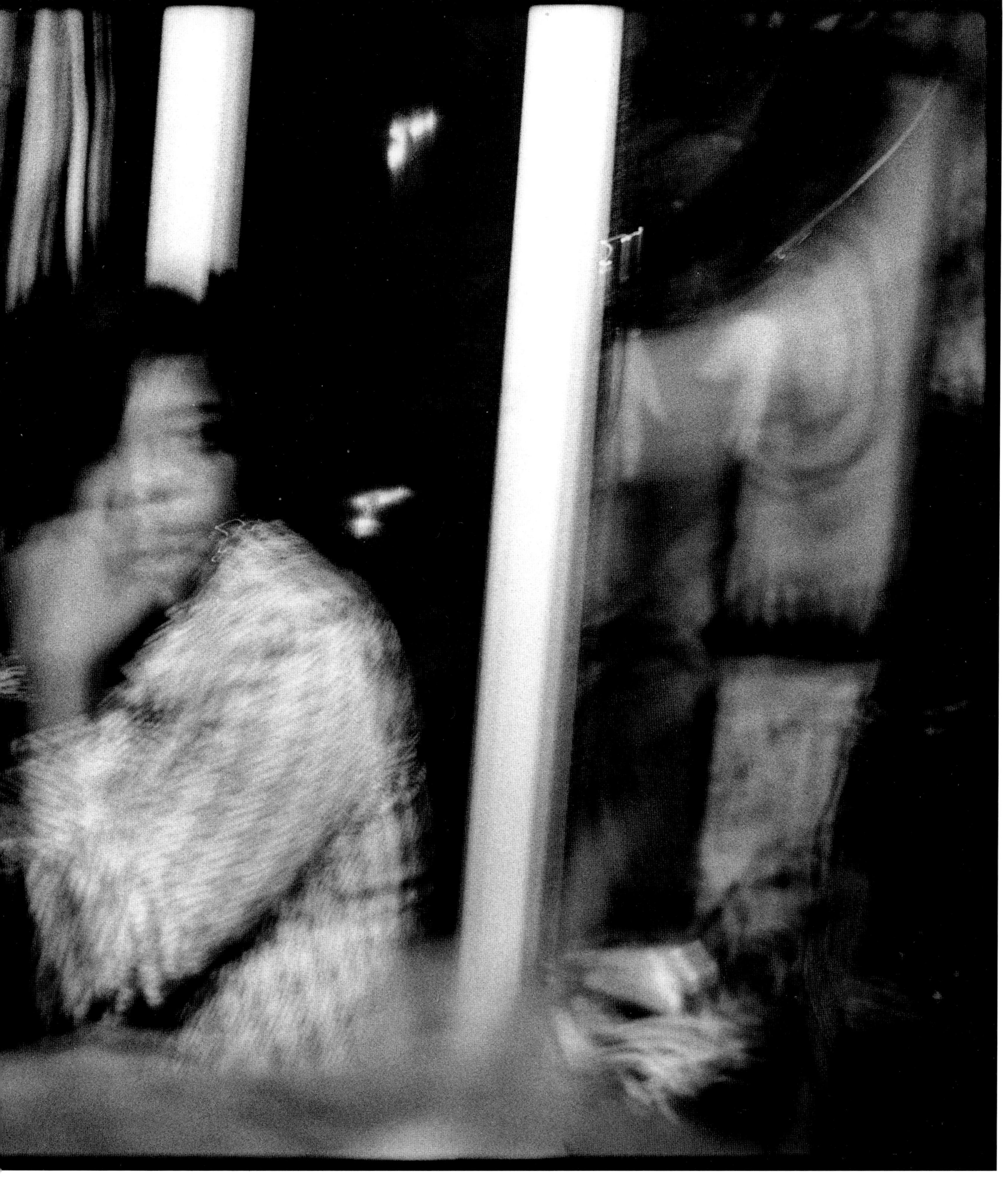

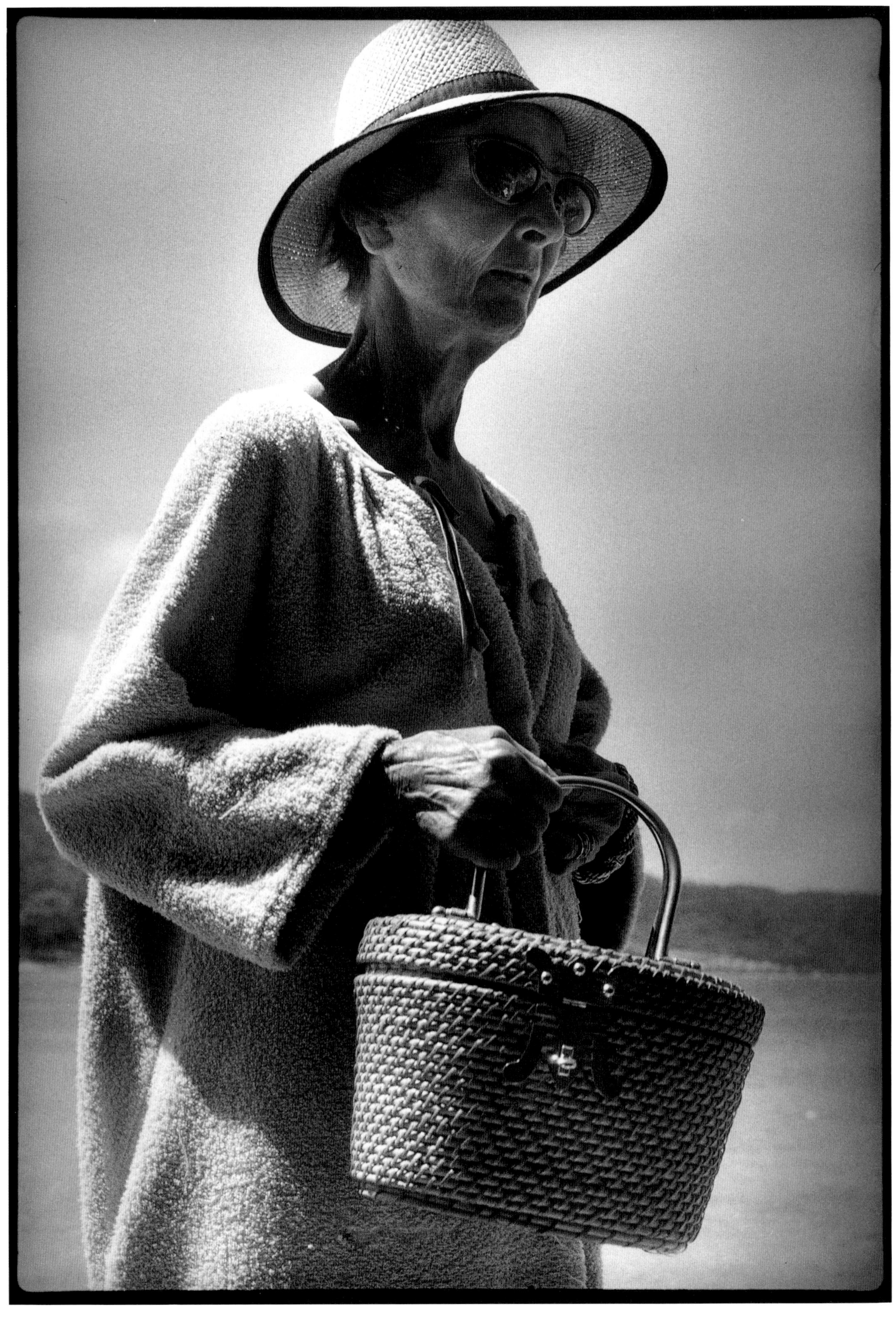

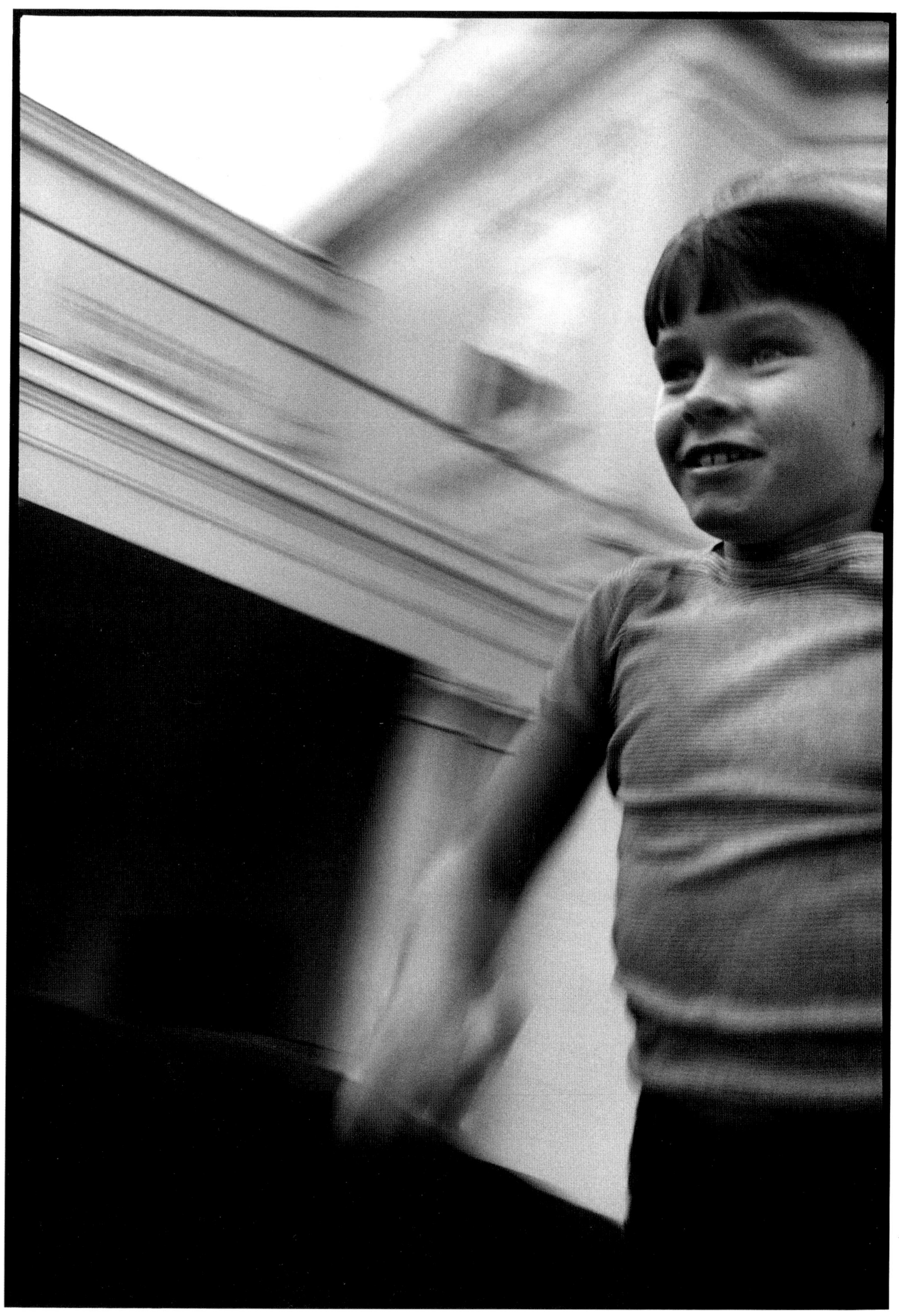

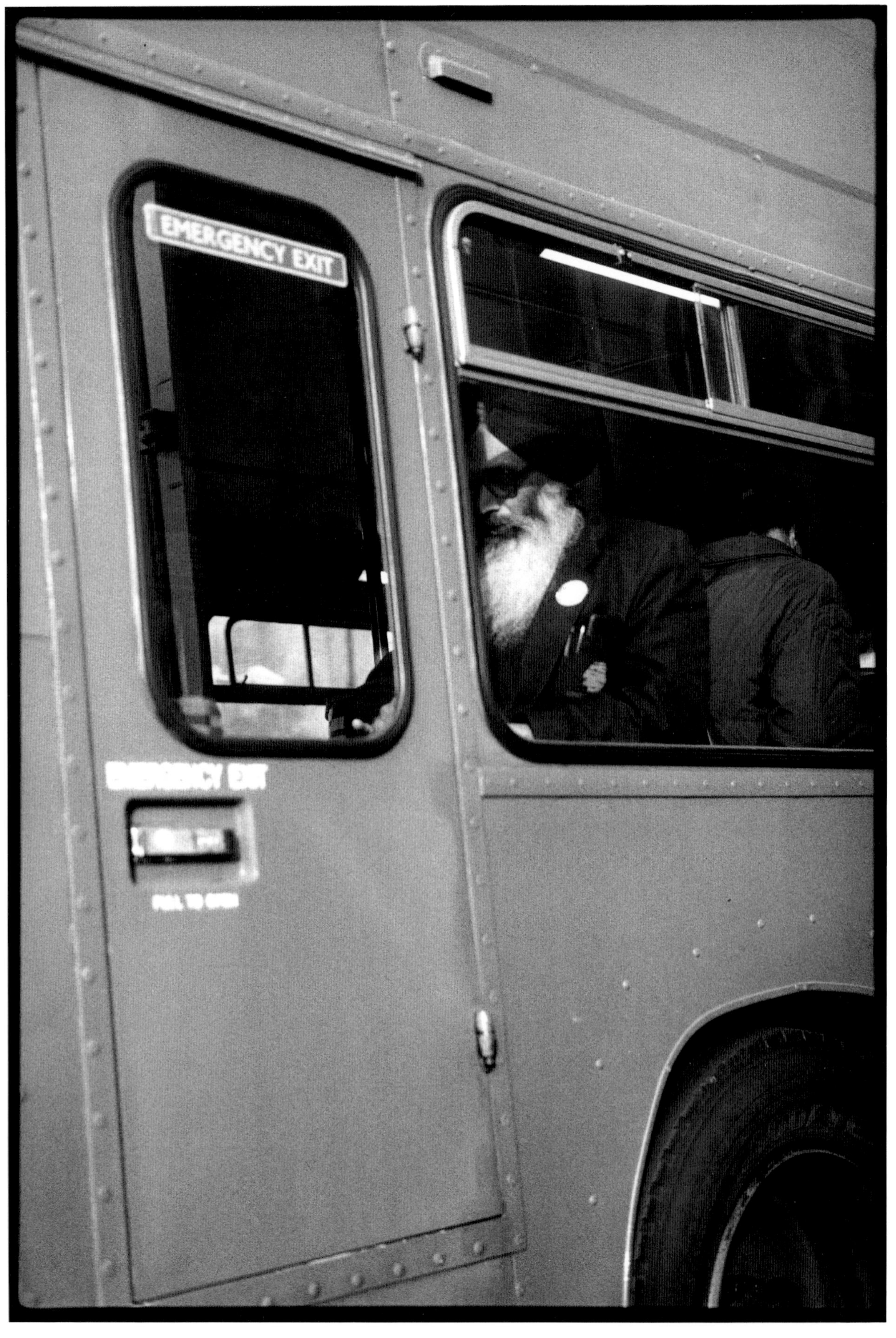
EMERGENCY EXIT
EMERGENCY EXIT

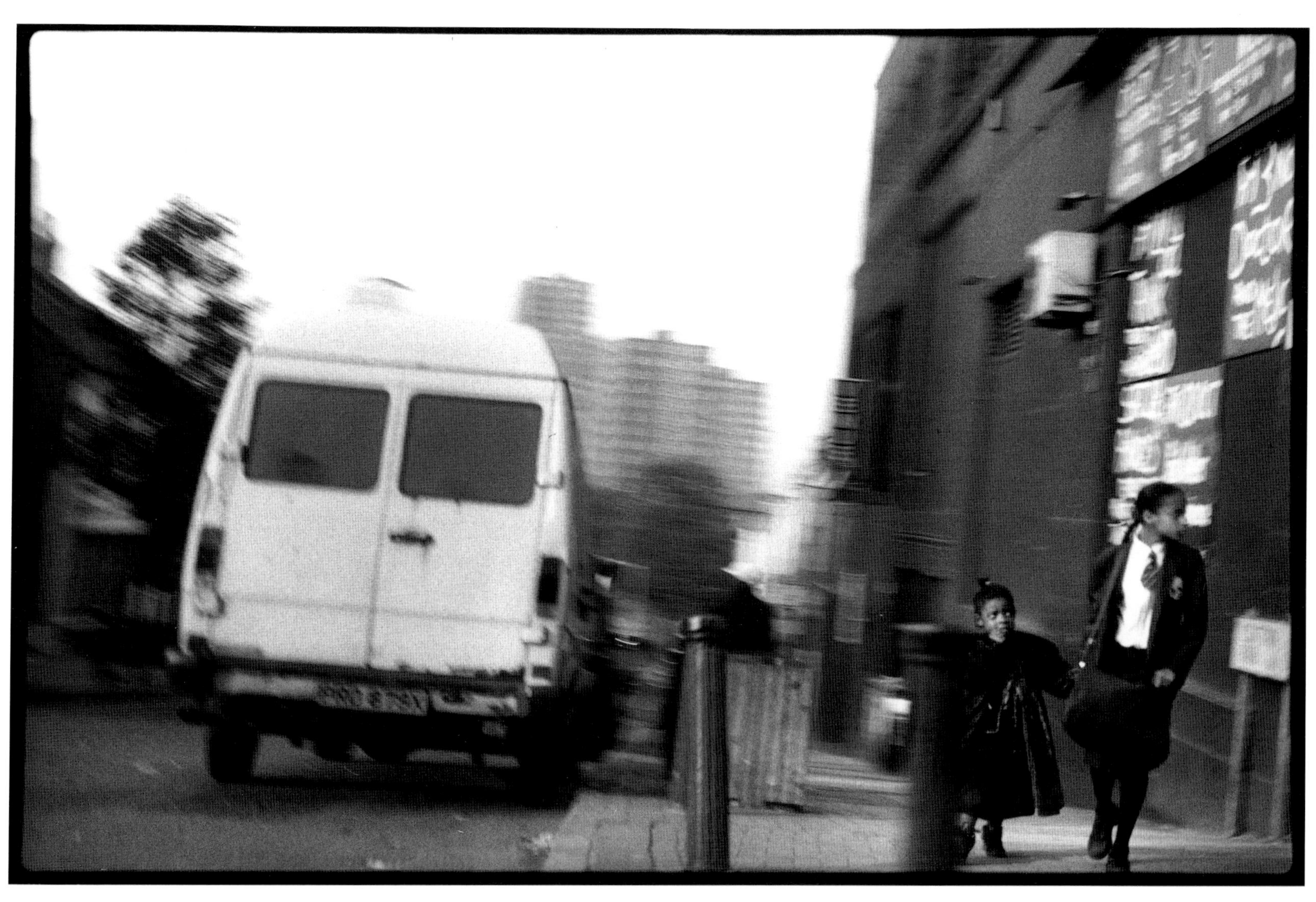

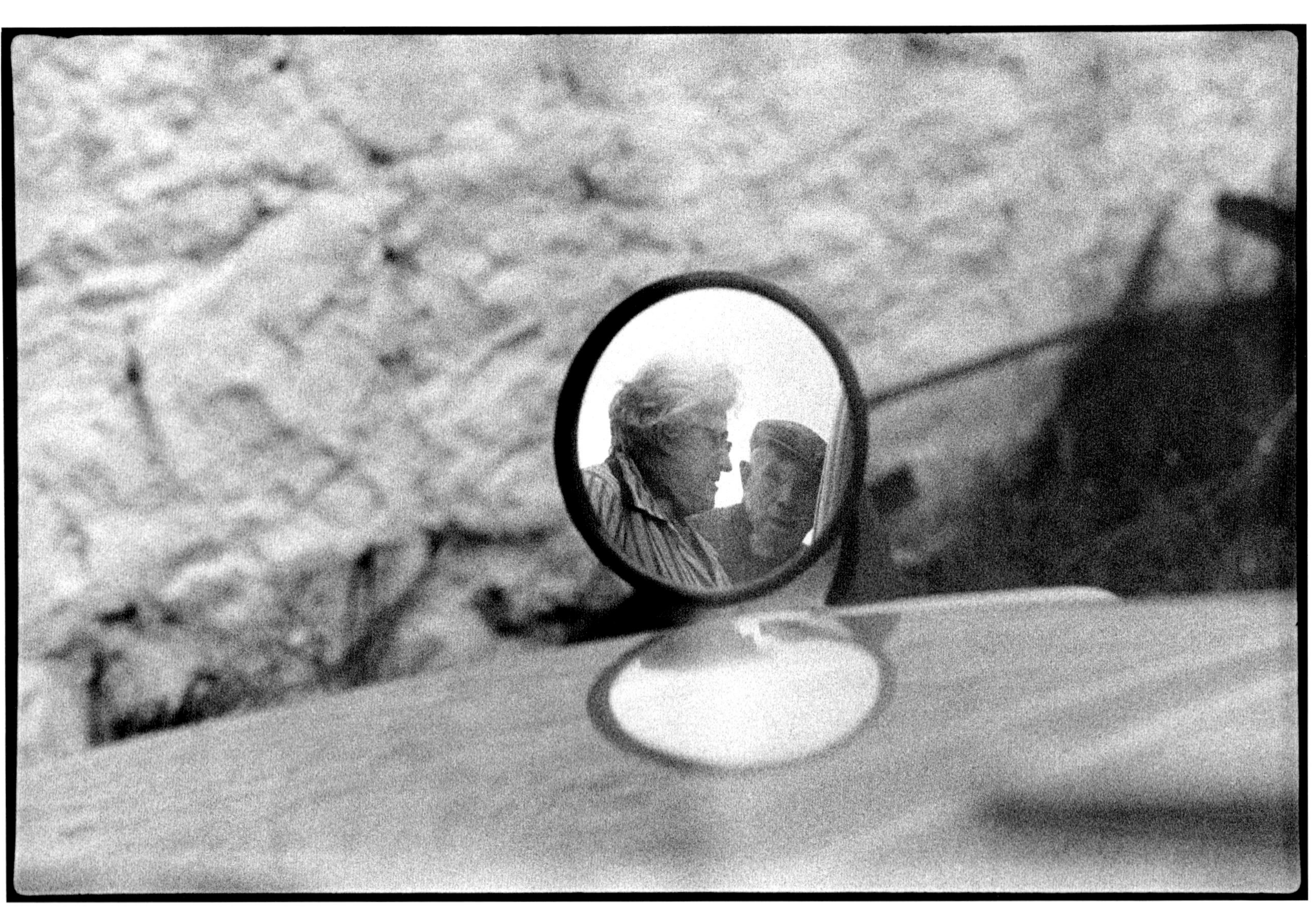

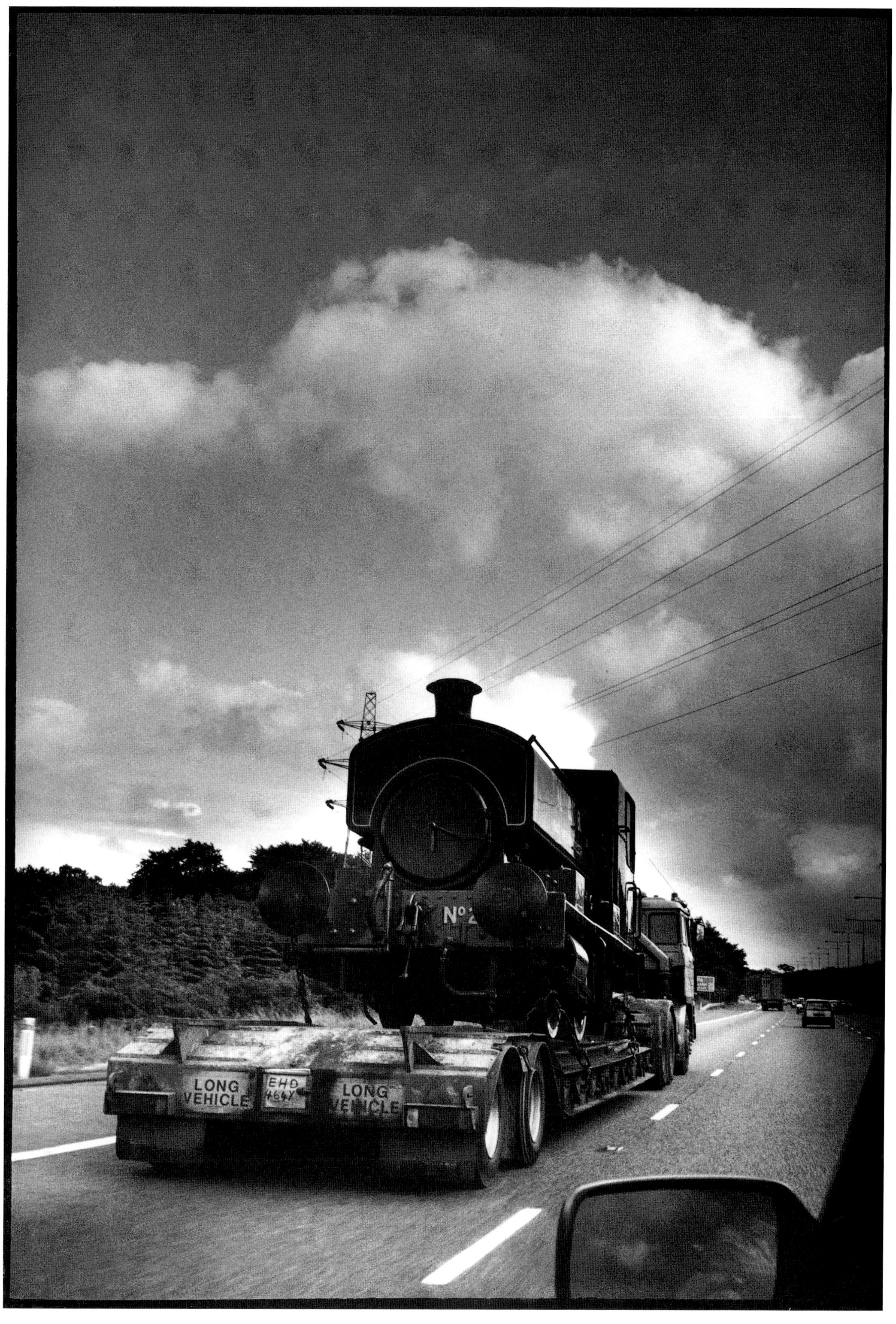
LONG VEHICLE
EHD 464Y
LONG VEHICLE

We kill with greed.

Natural world so fragile its future in our hands

Ends of The Earth

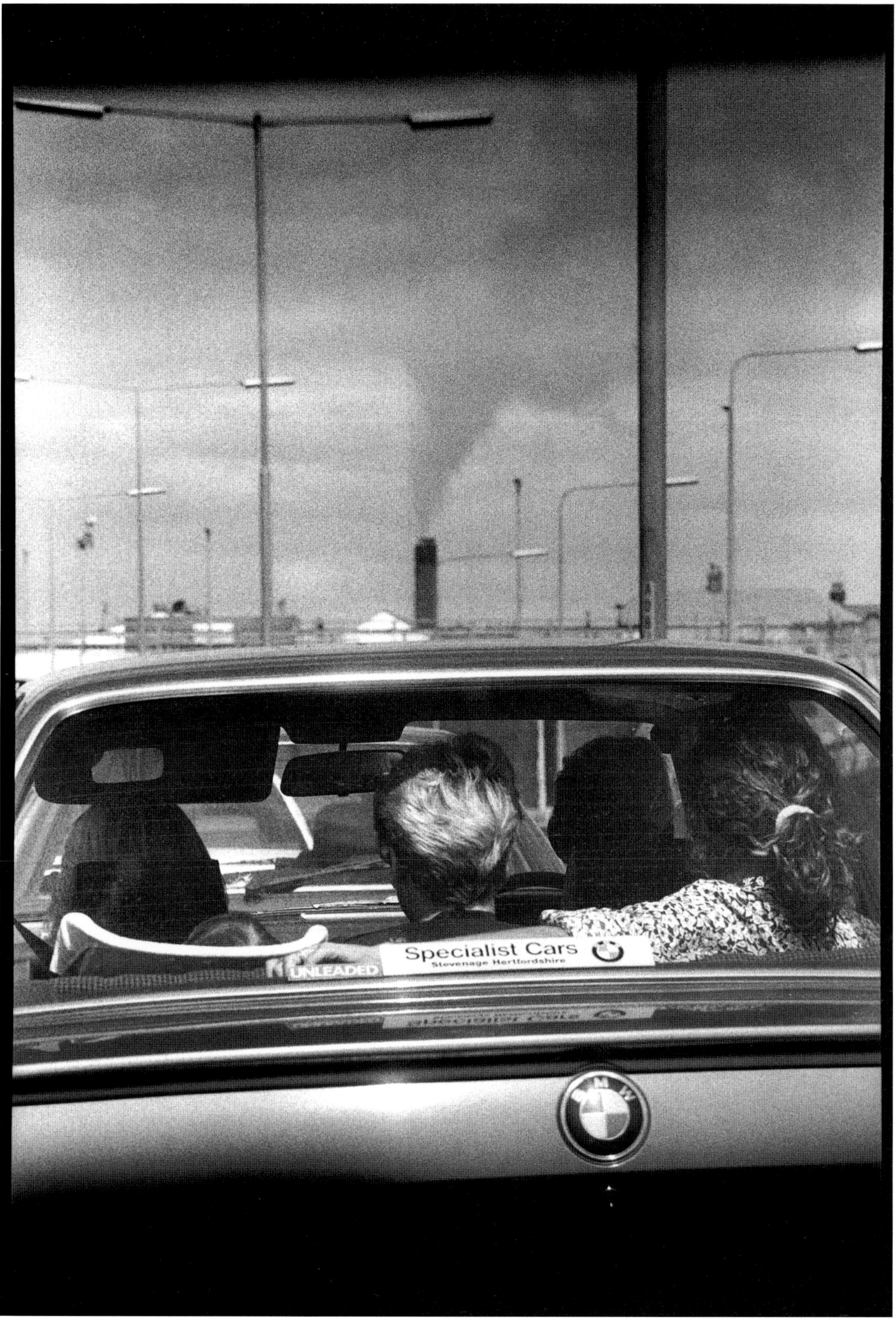

Specialist Cars
Stevenage Hertfordshire
UNLEADED

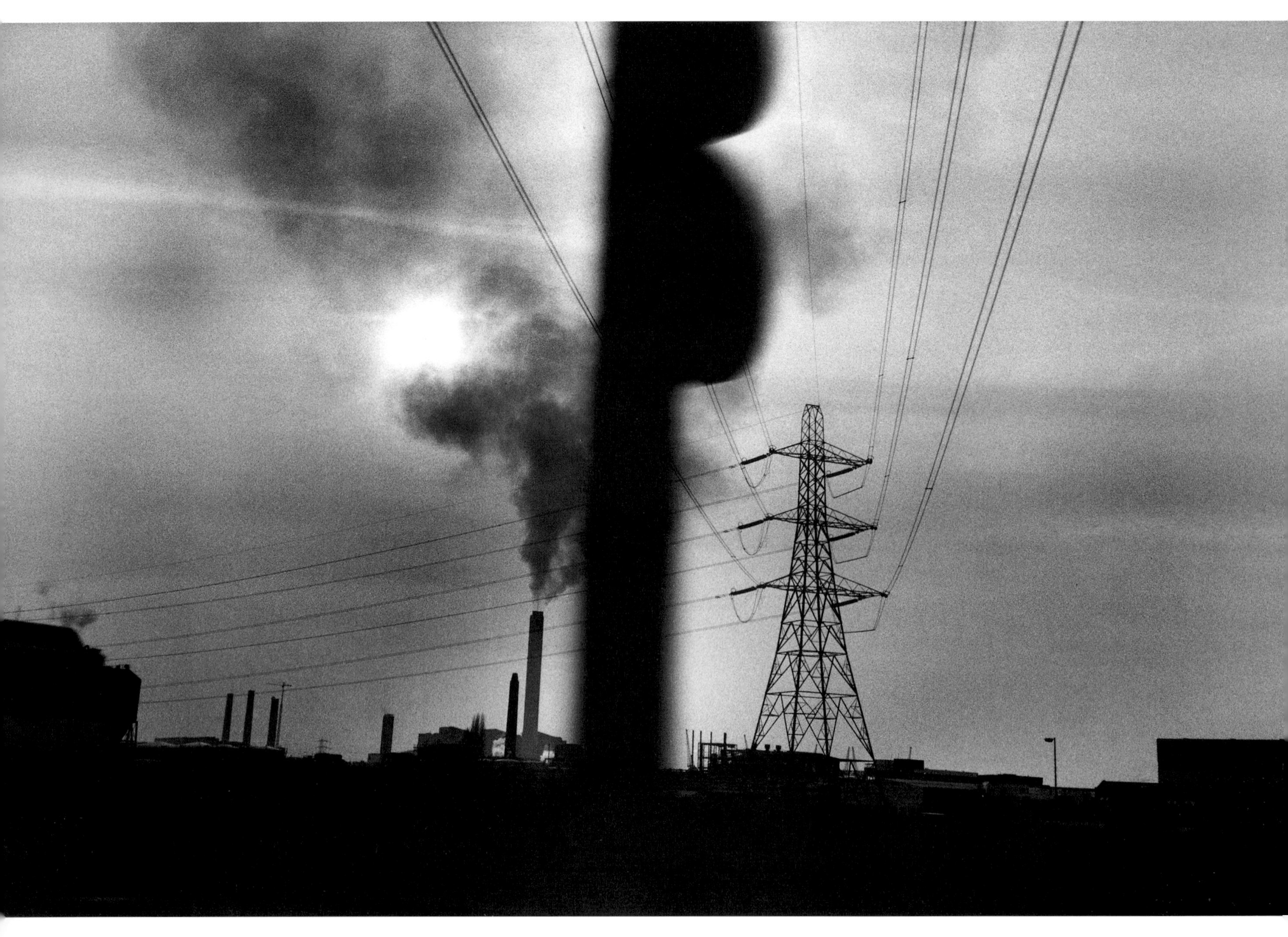

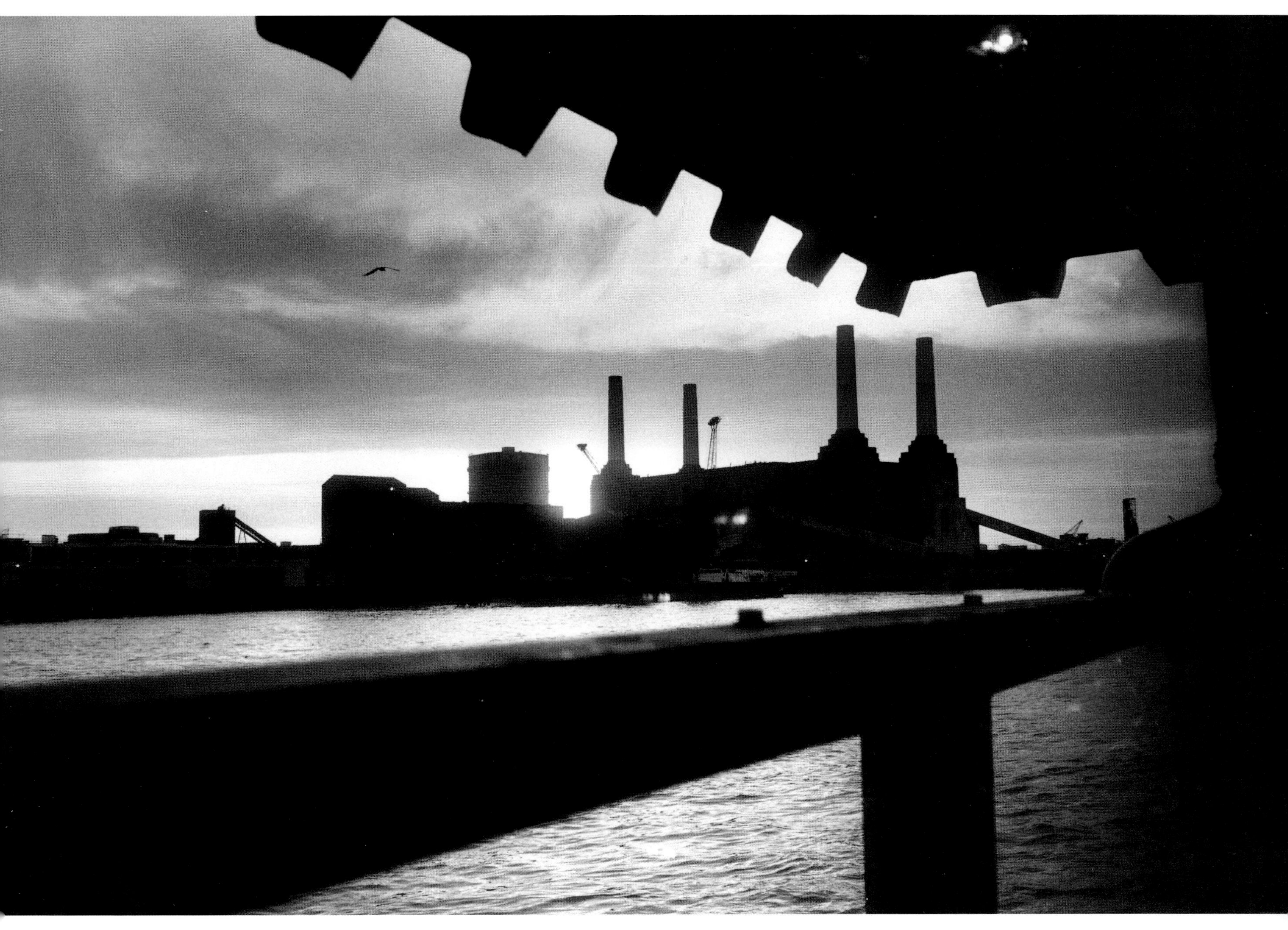

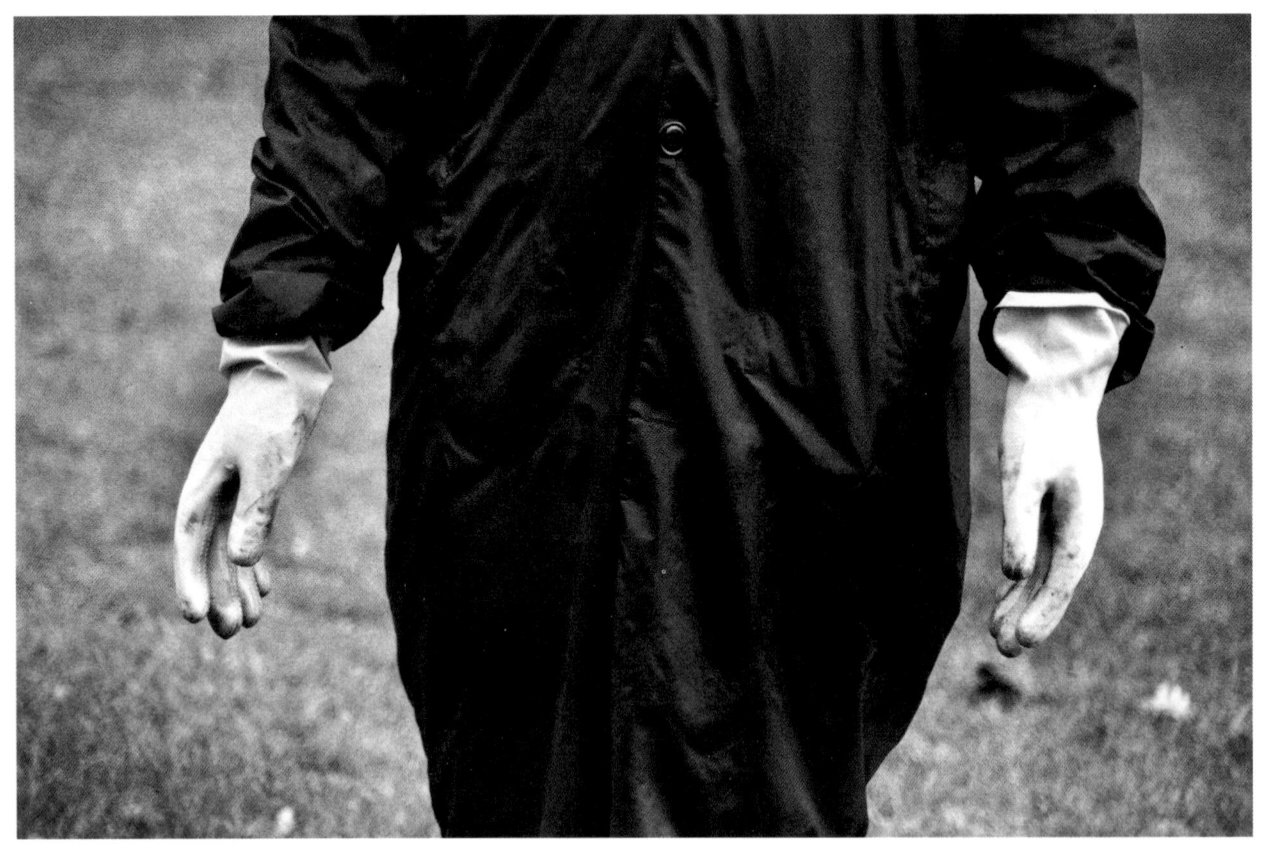

Destruction, poisoned wastelands —
only an ill bird destroys its own nest.

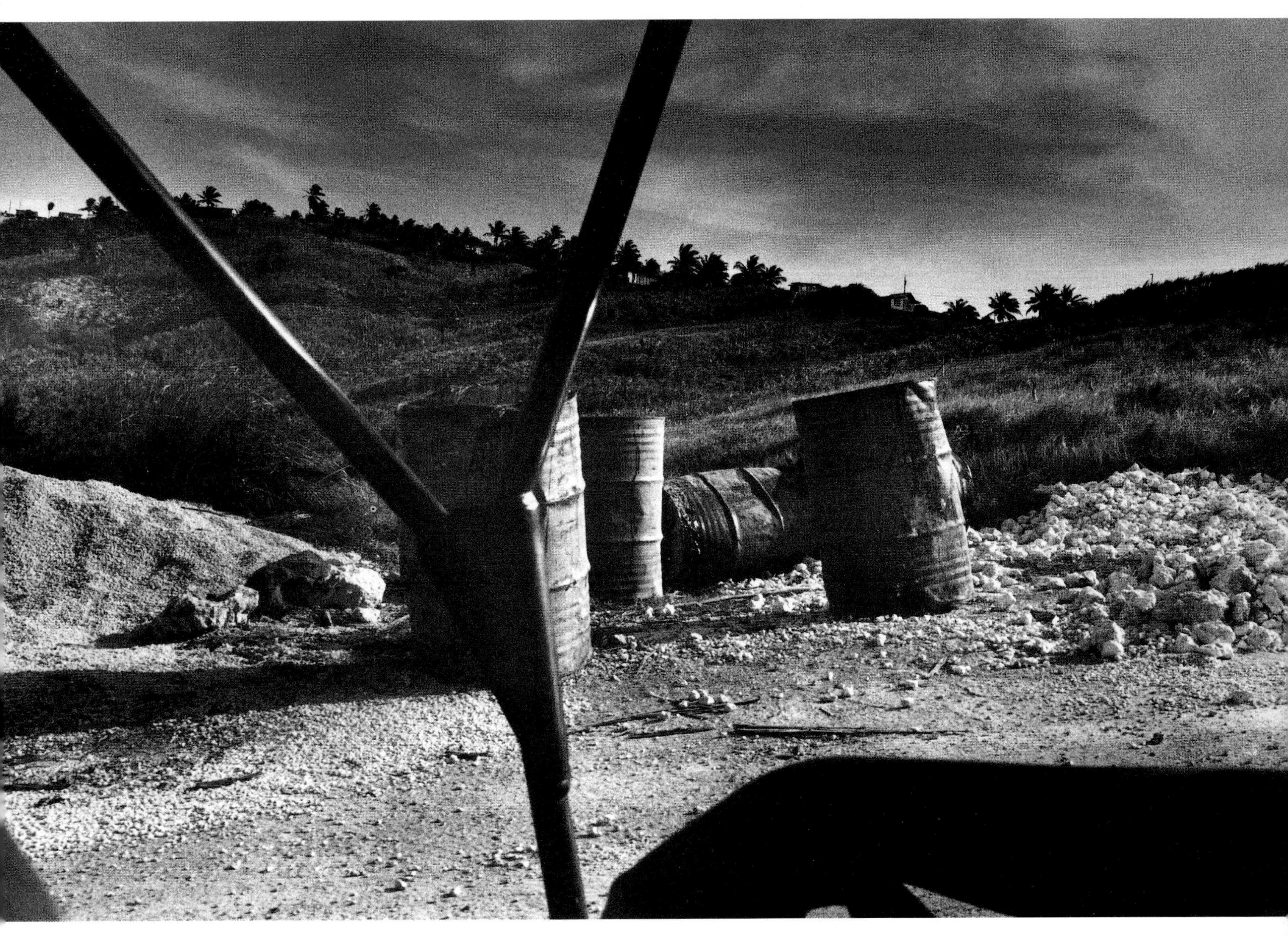

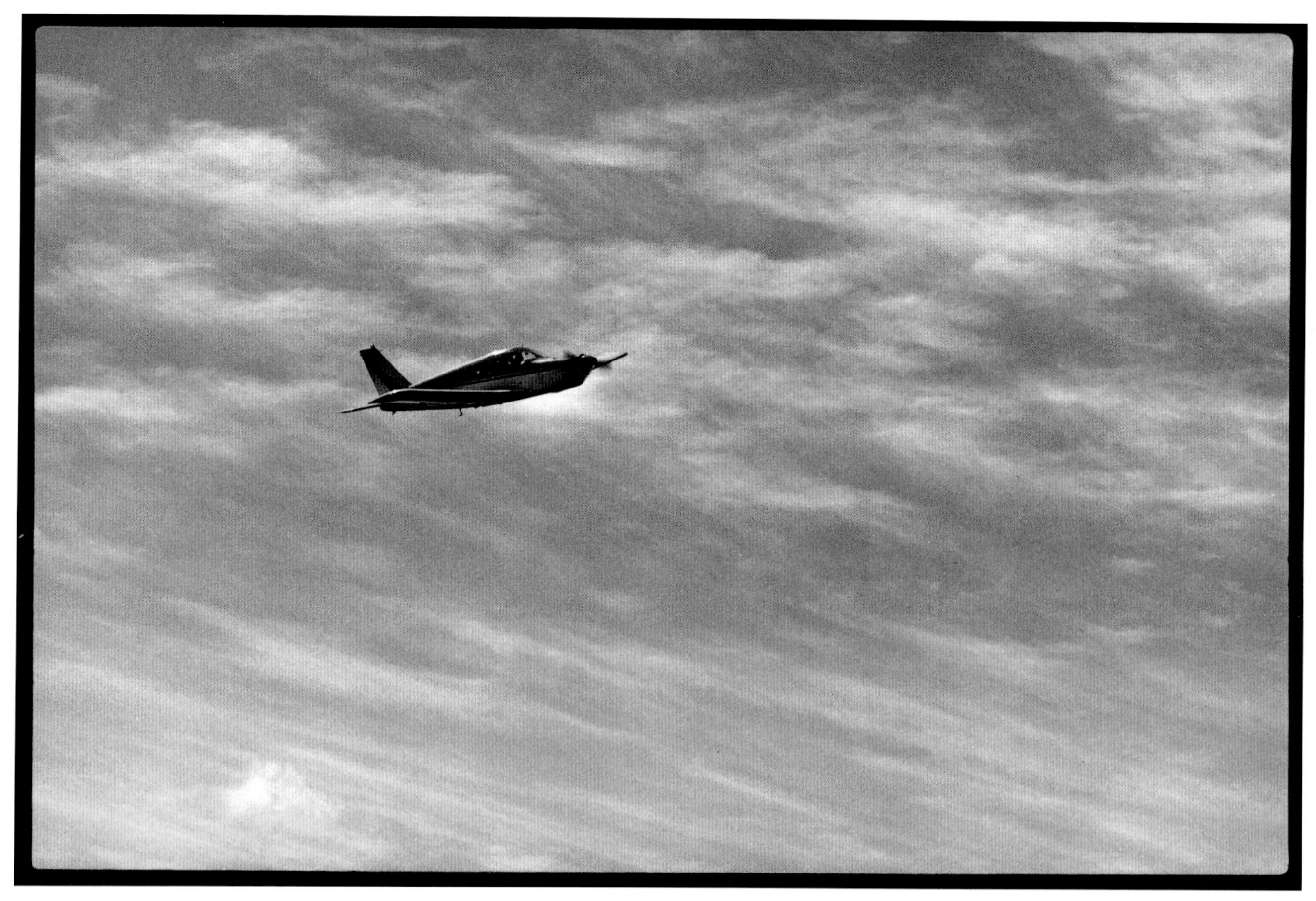

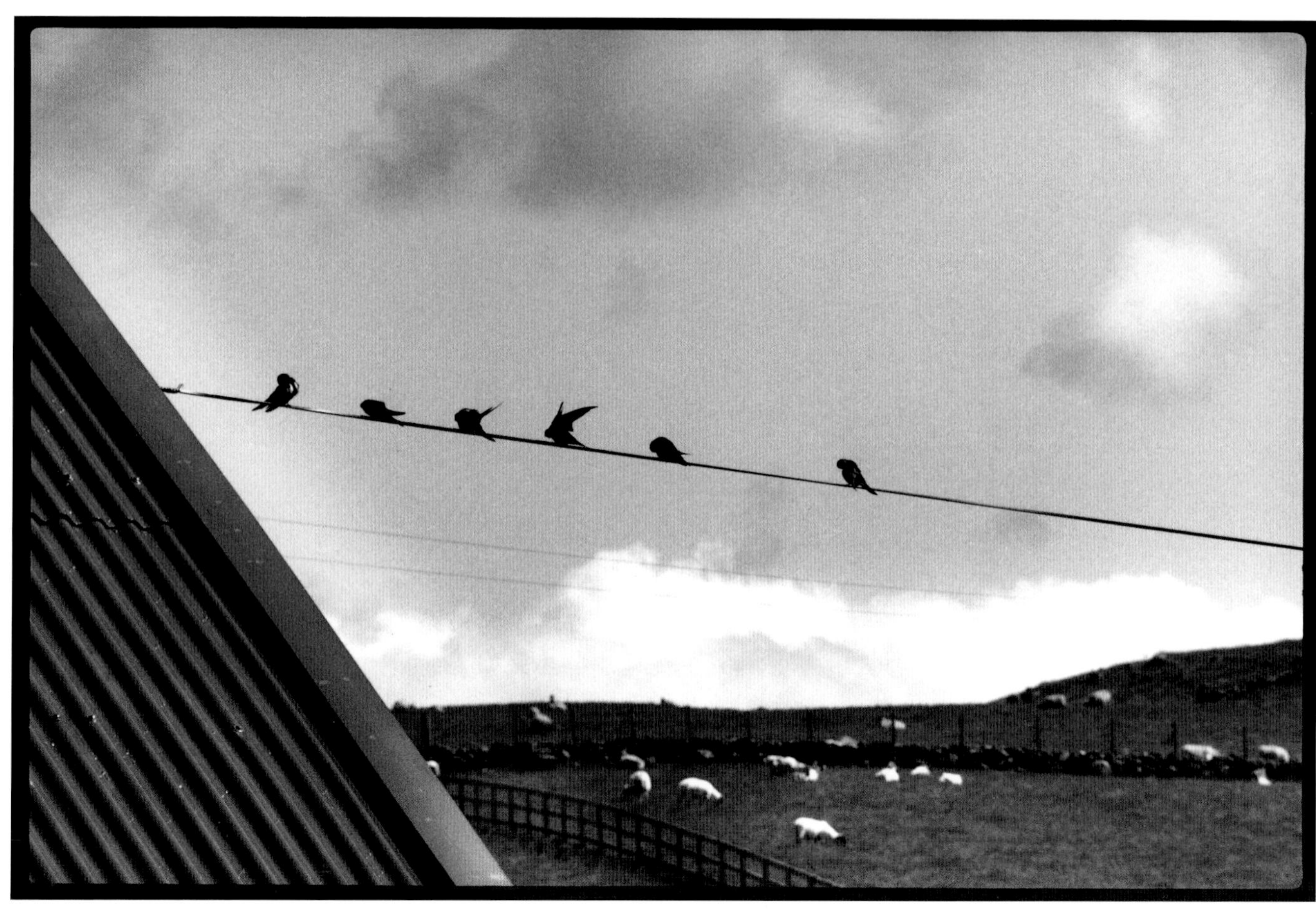

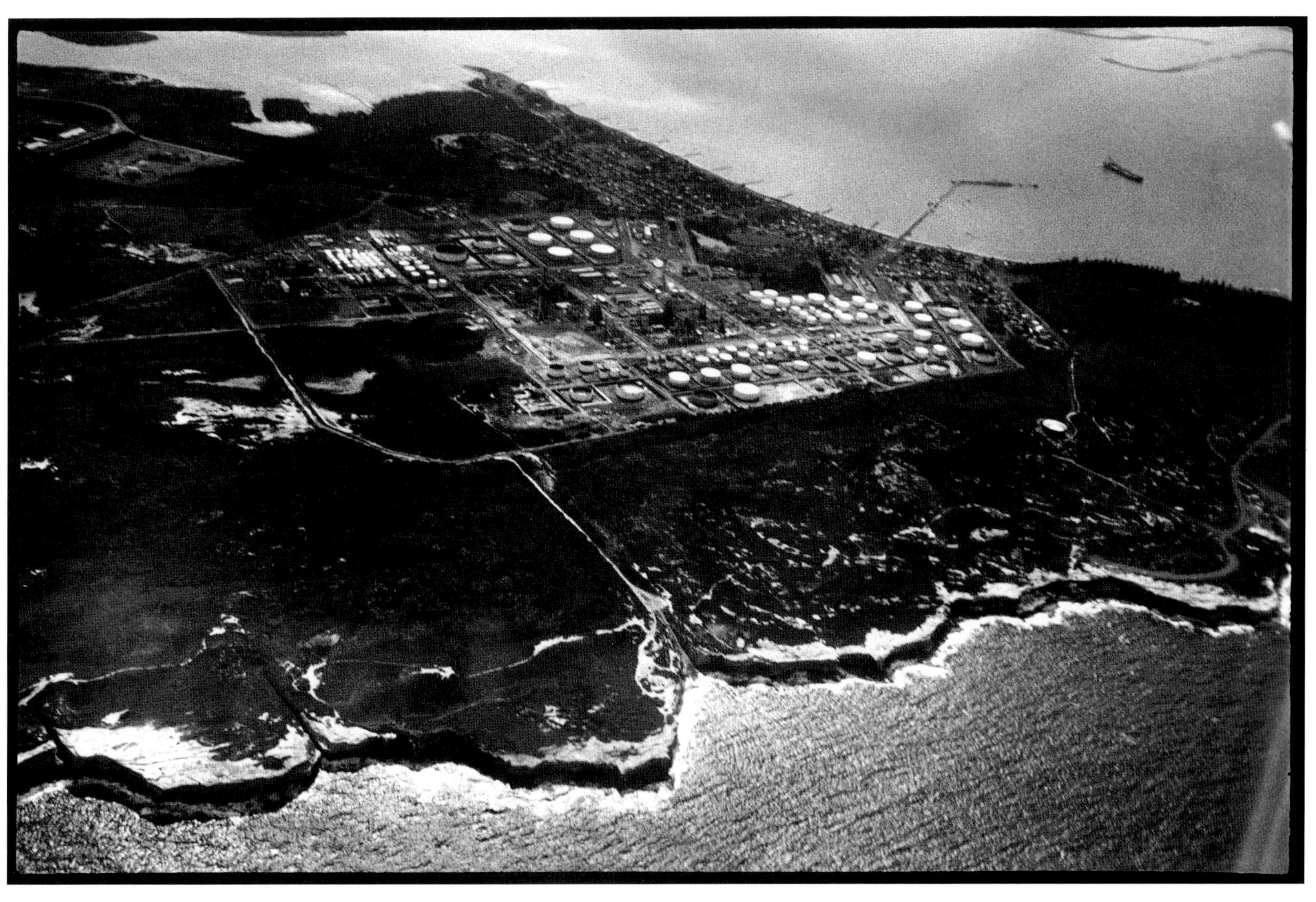

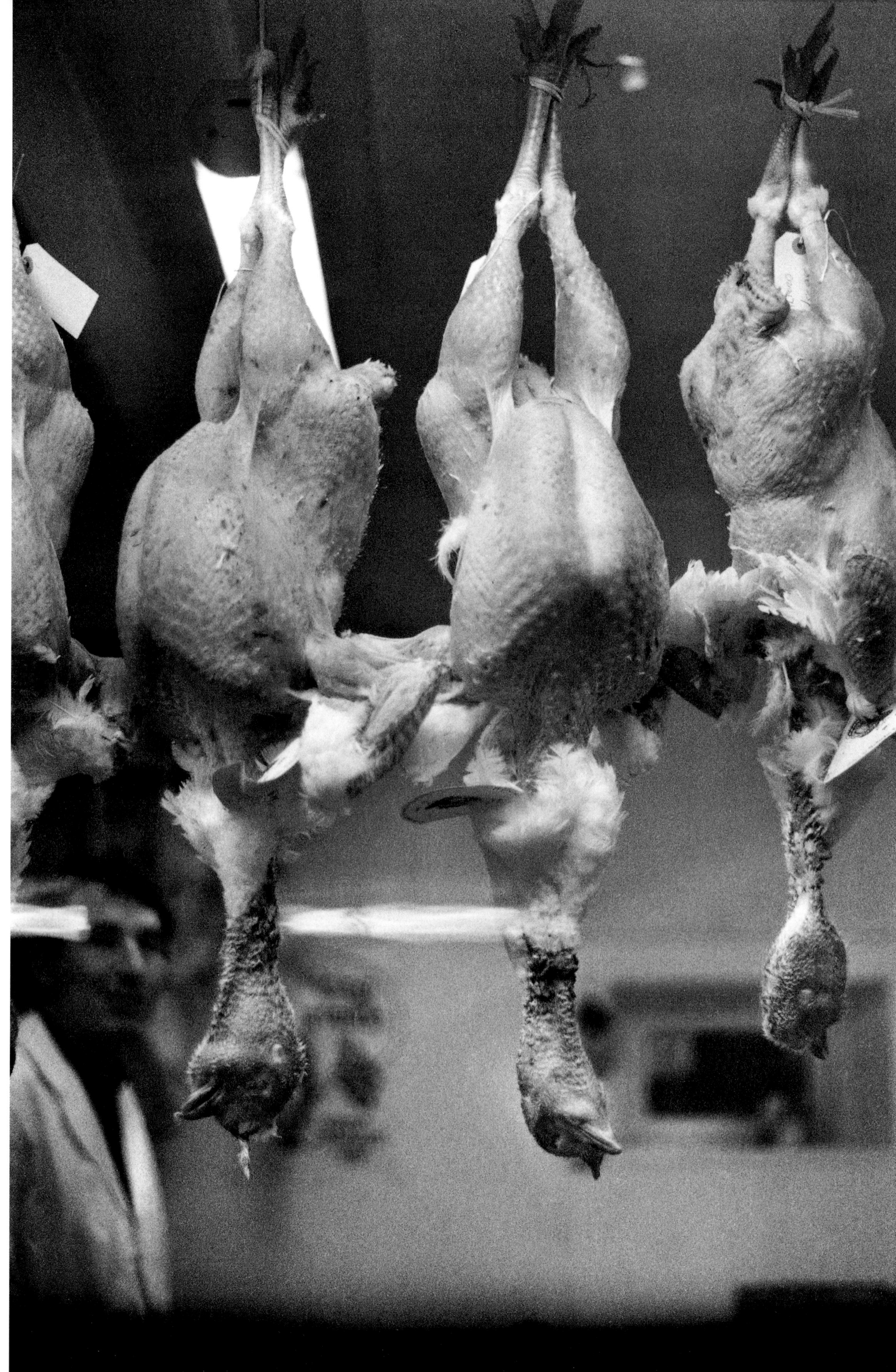

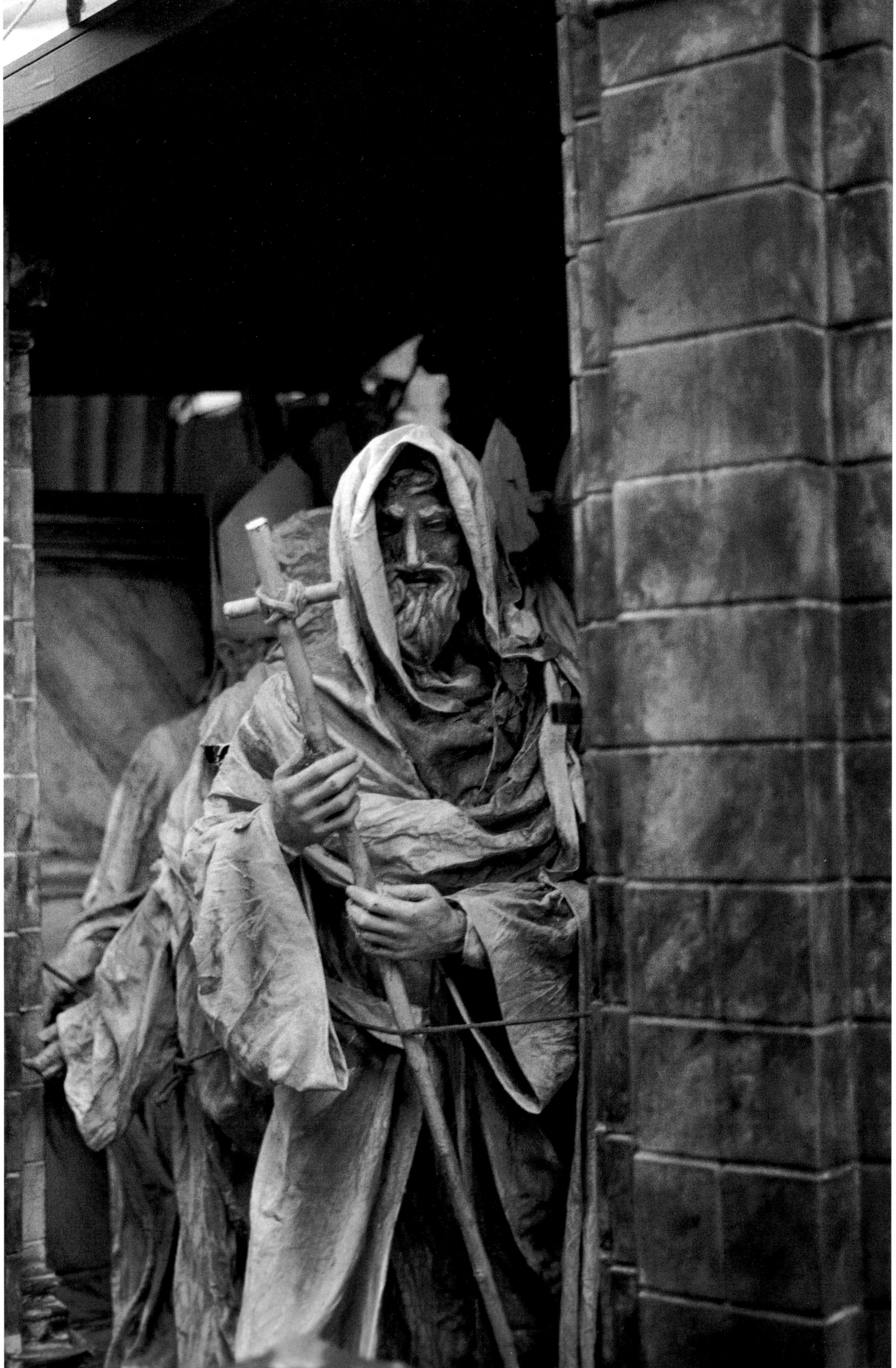

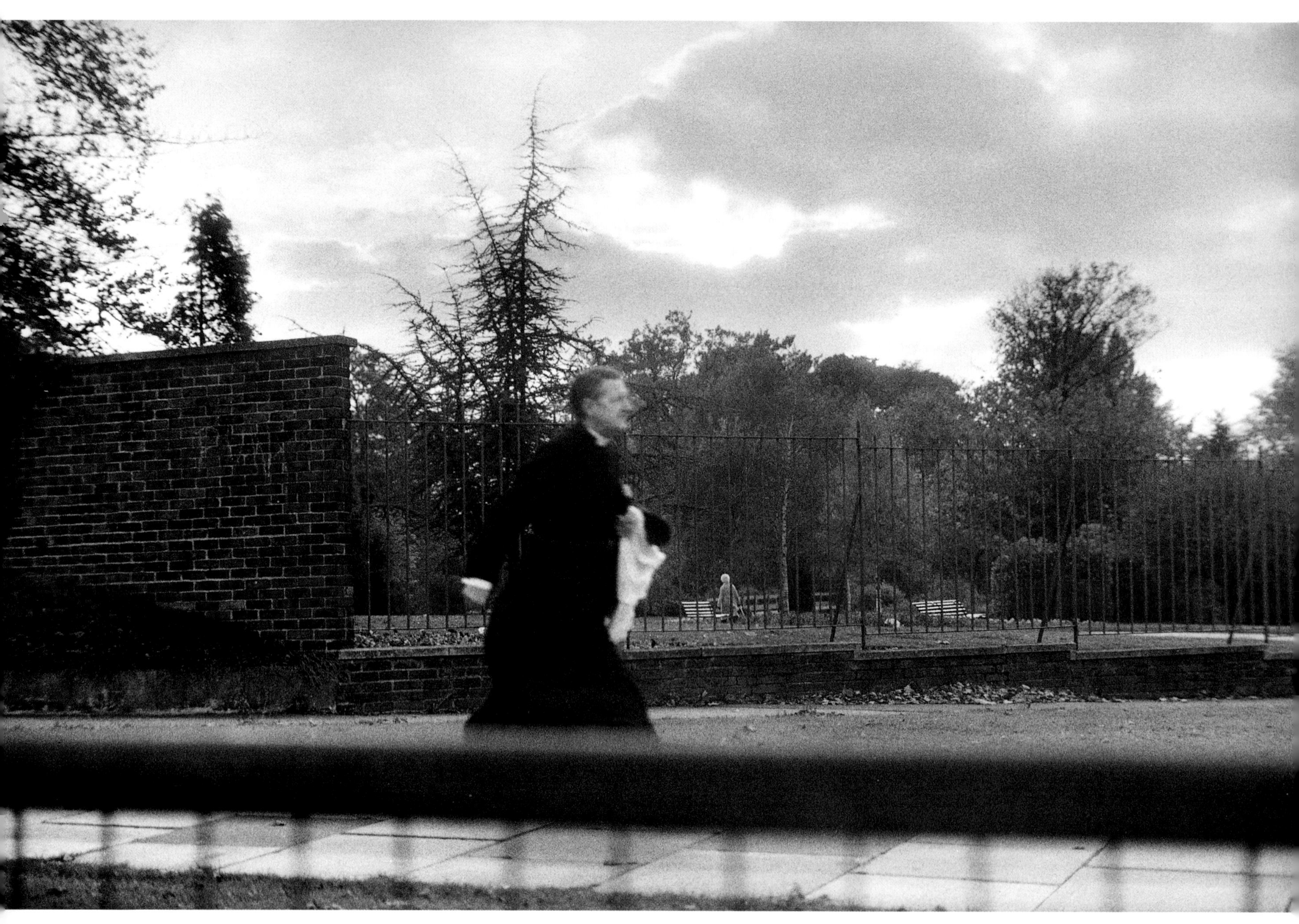

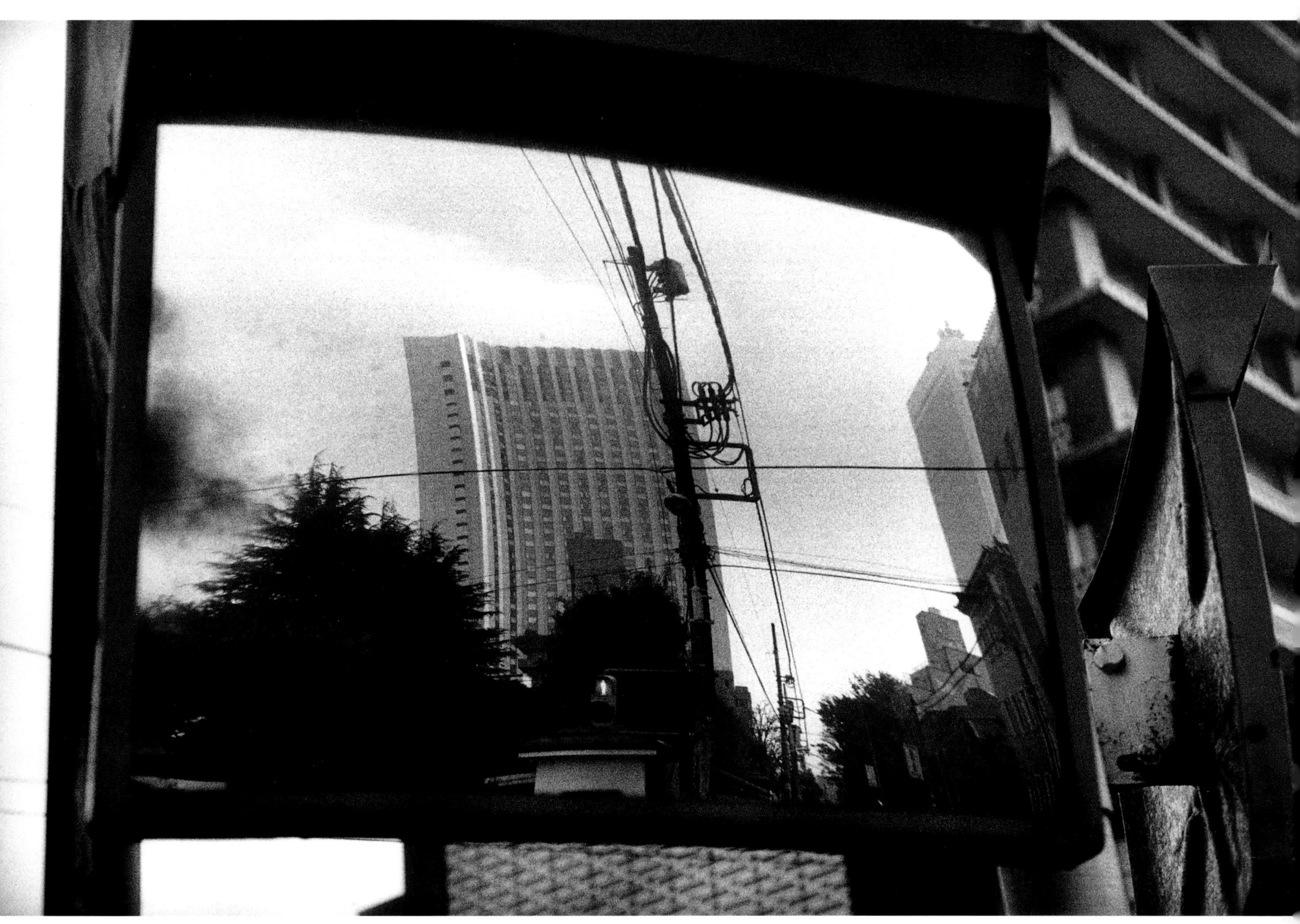

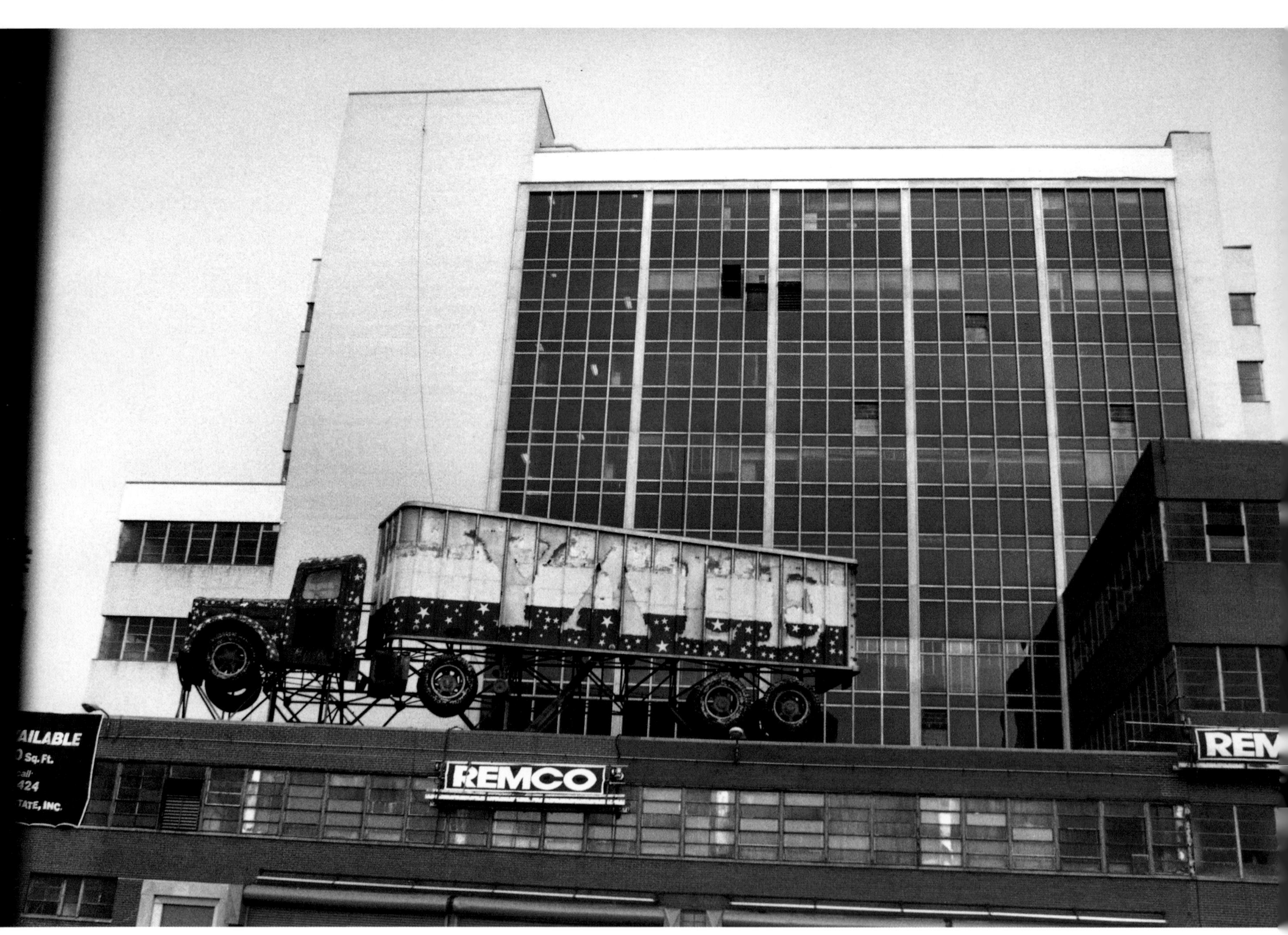
AILABLE
Sq. Ft.
424
TATE, INC.
REMCO
REM

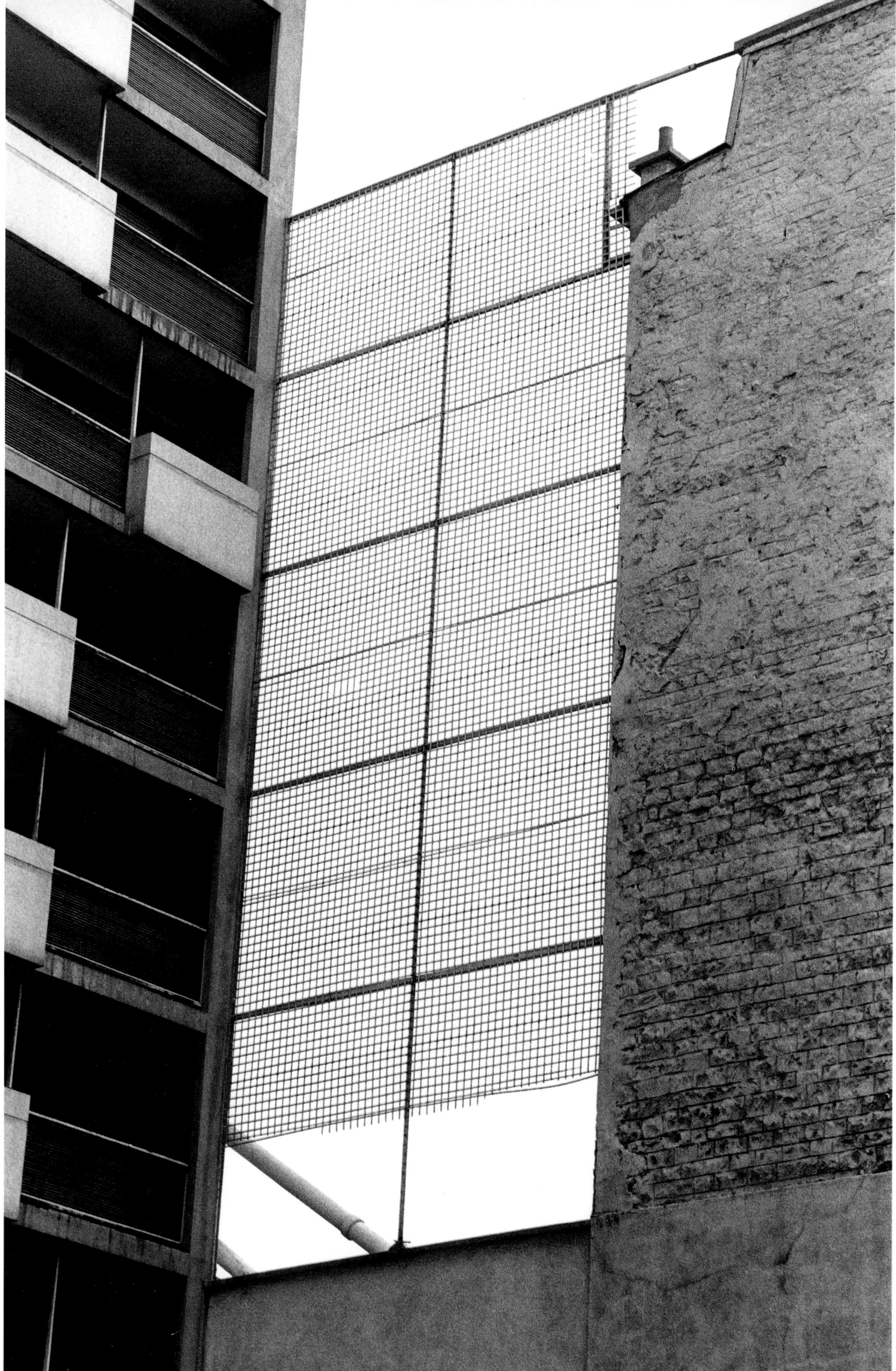

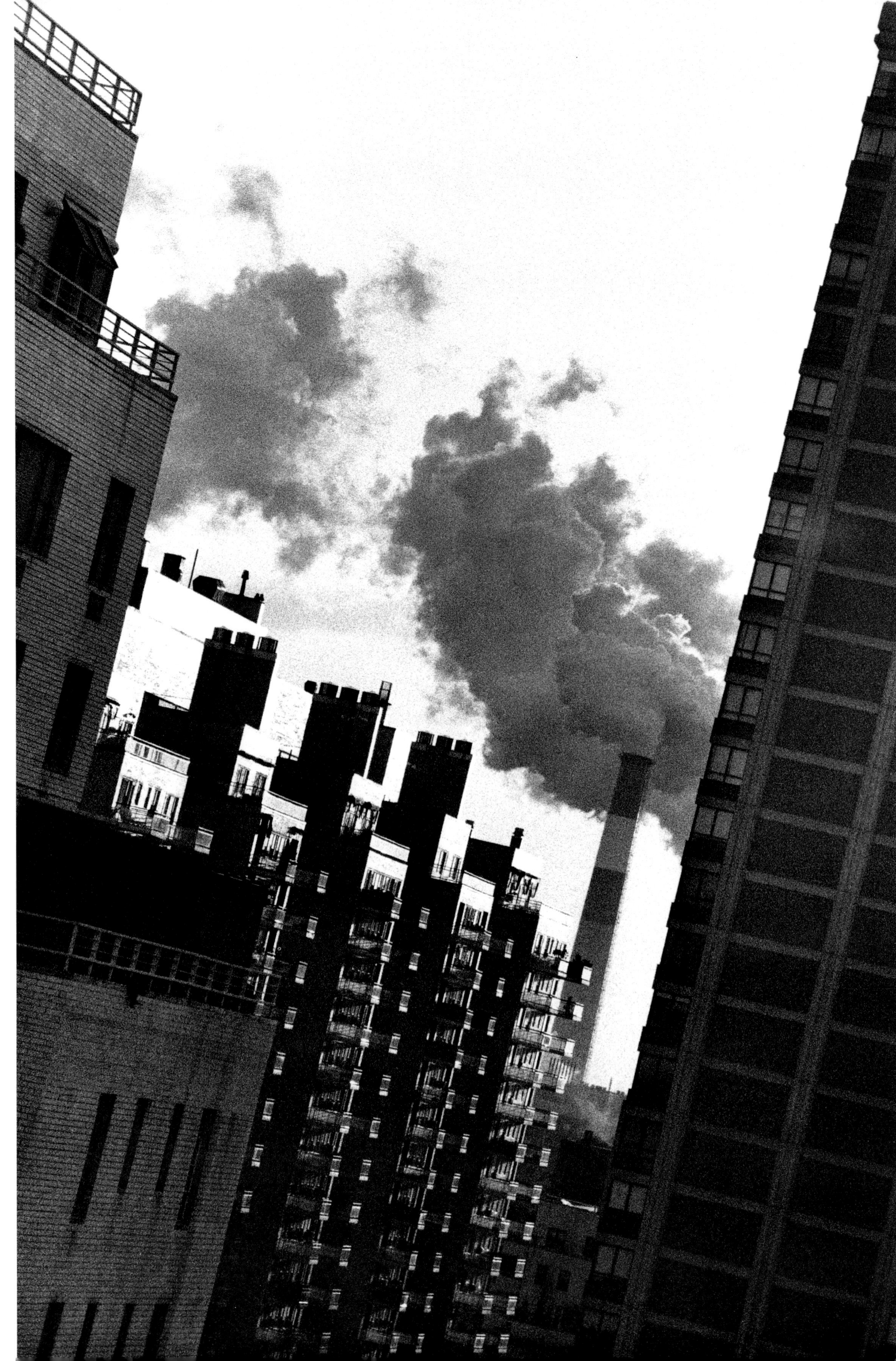

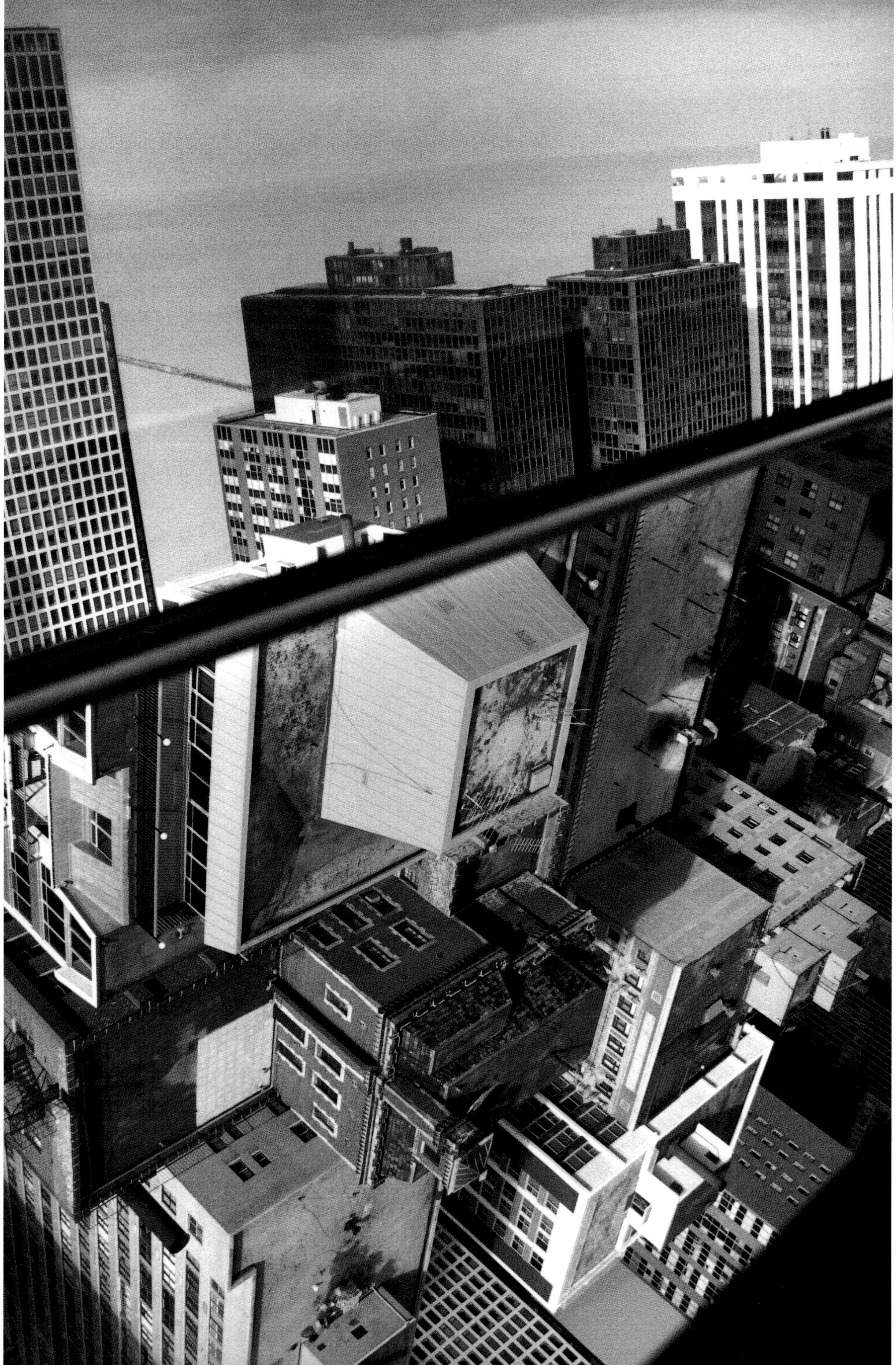

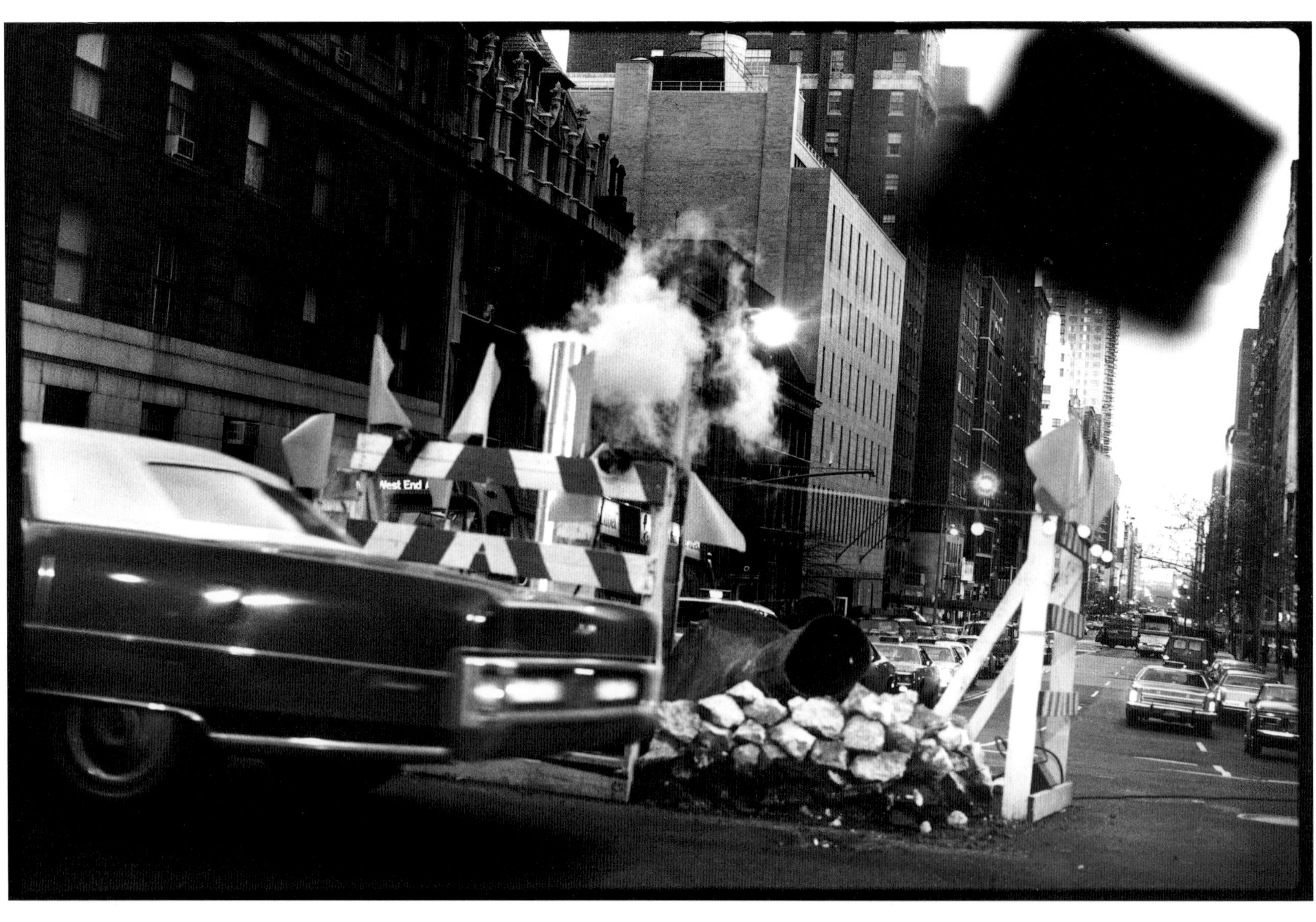
West End

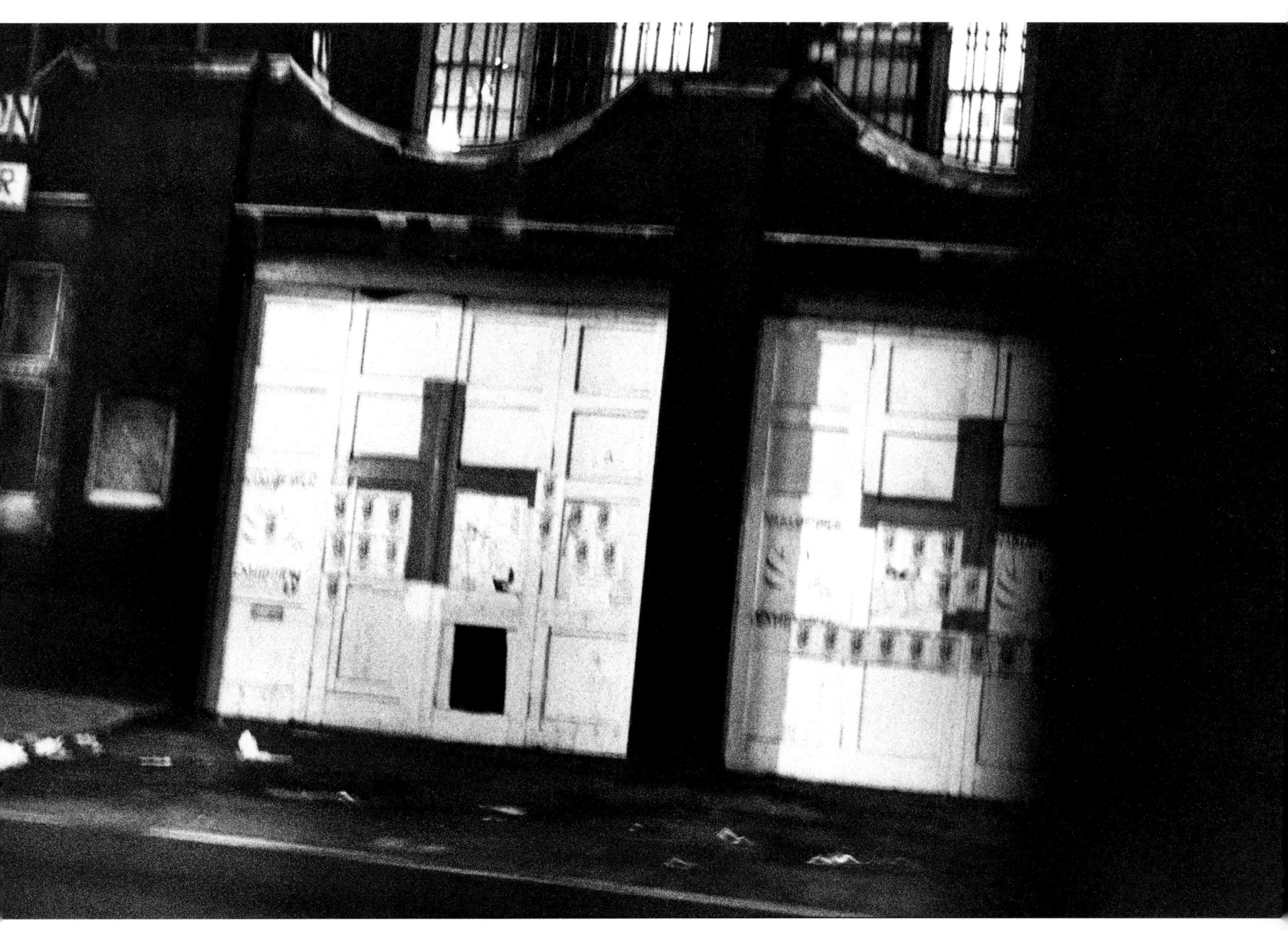

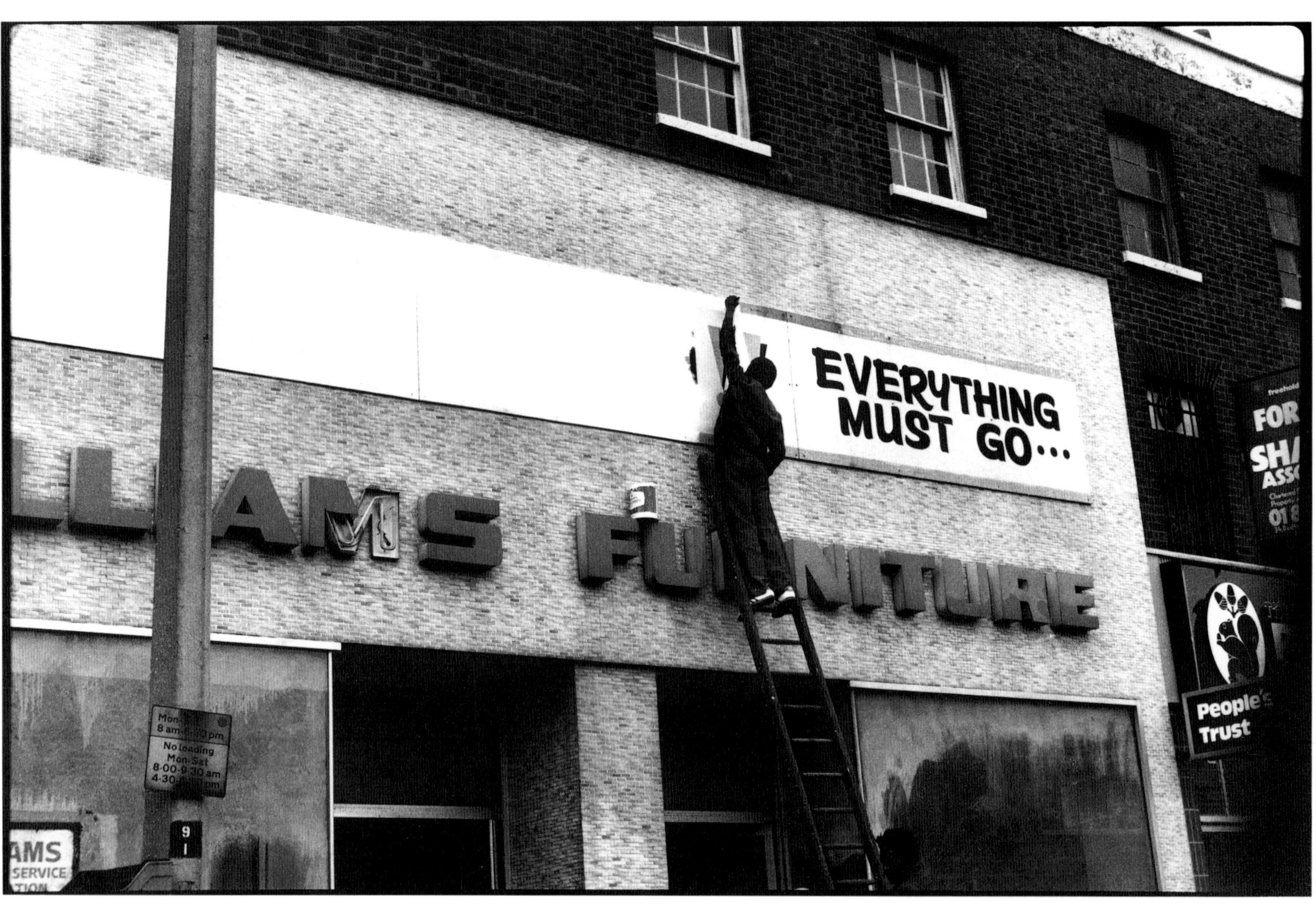
EVERYTHING
MUST GO…
No Loading
Mon-Sat
People's
Trust

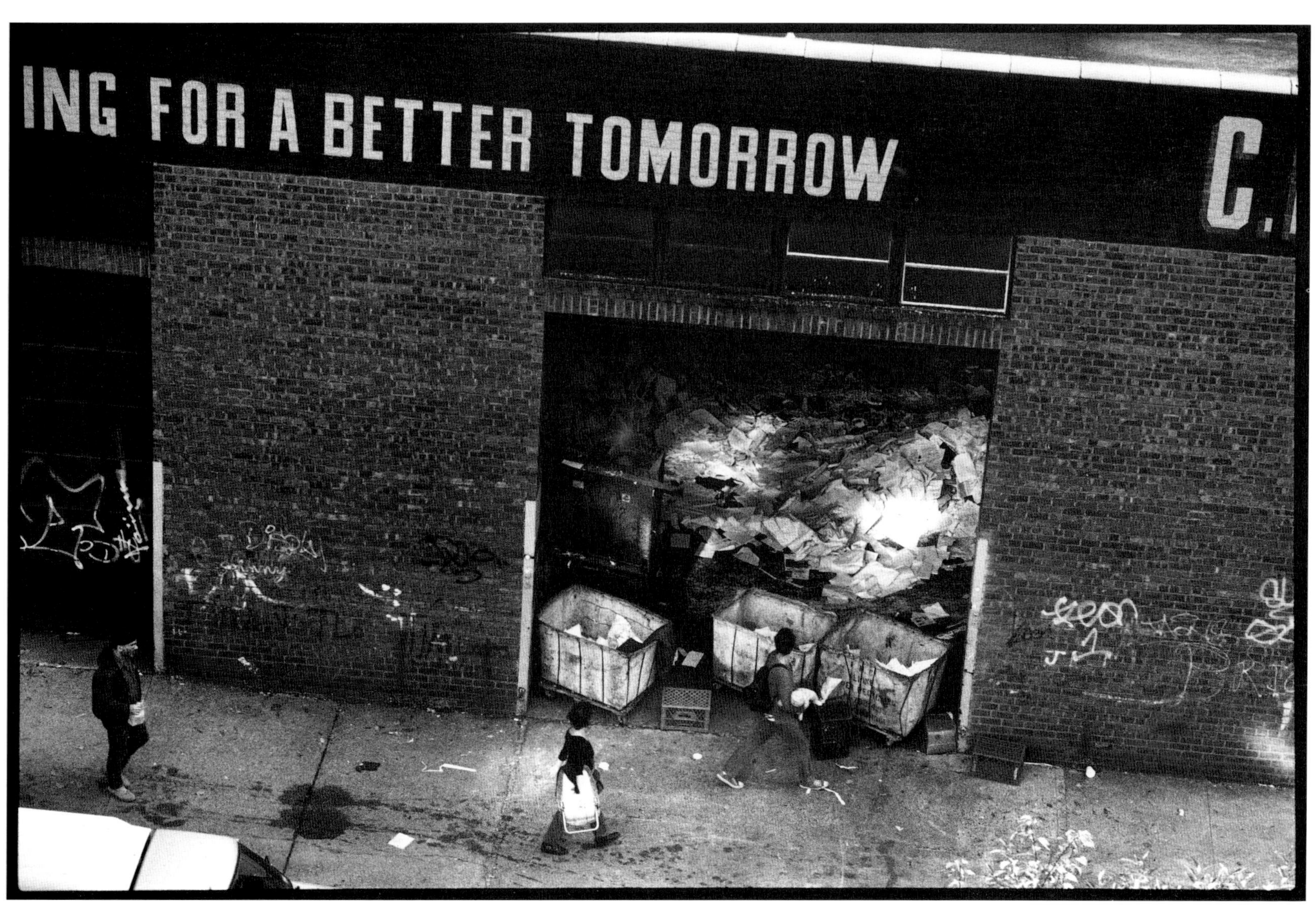
ING FOR A BETTER TOMORROW
C.

We would head off to anywhere
and drive until we were getting lost.

getting lost

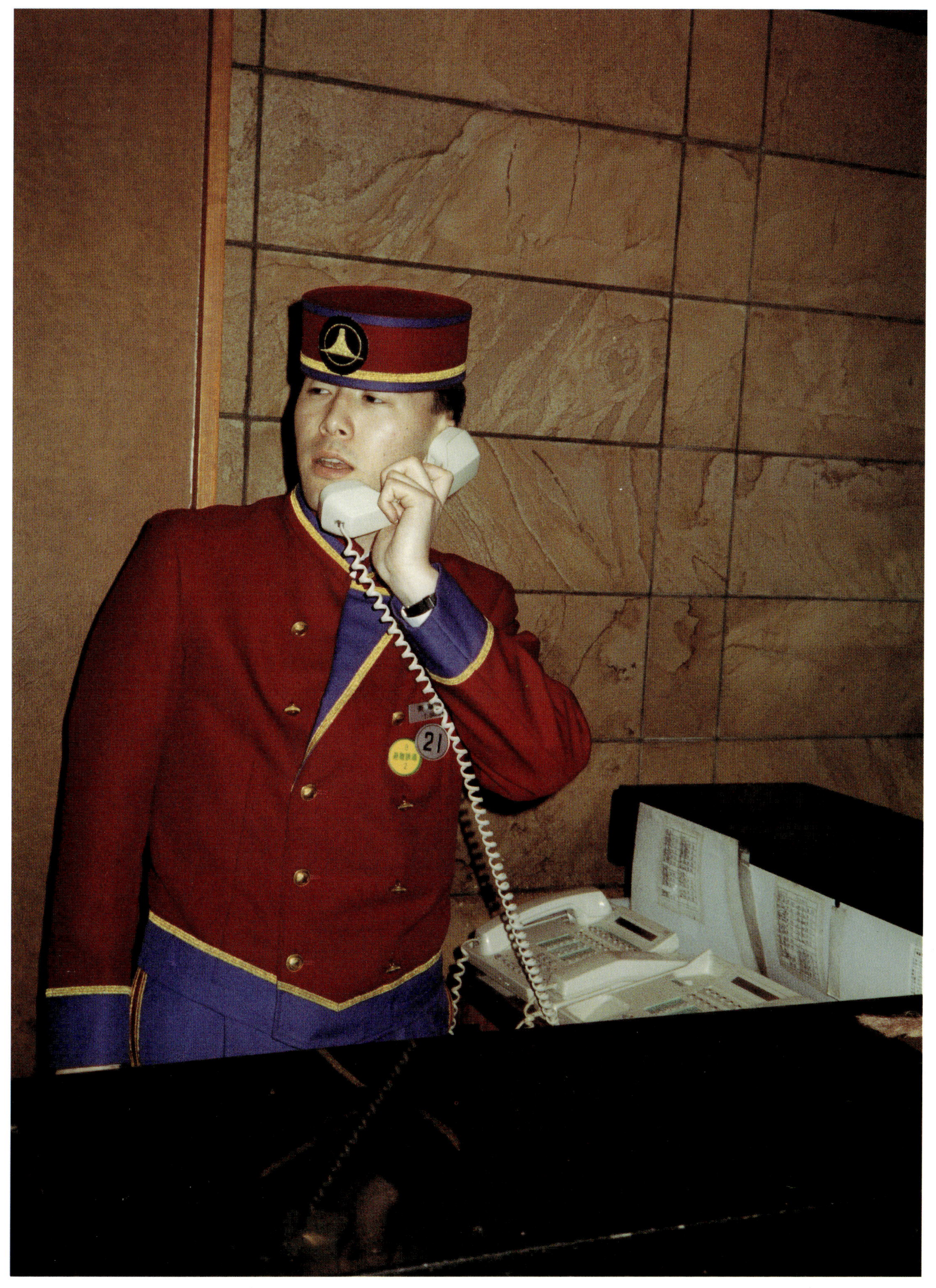
21

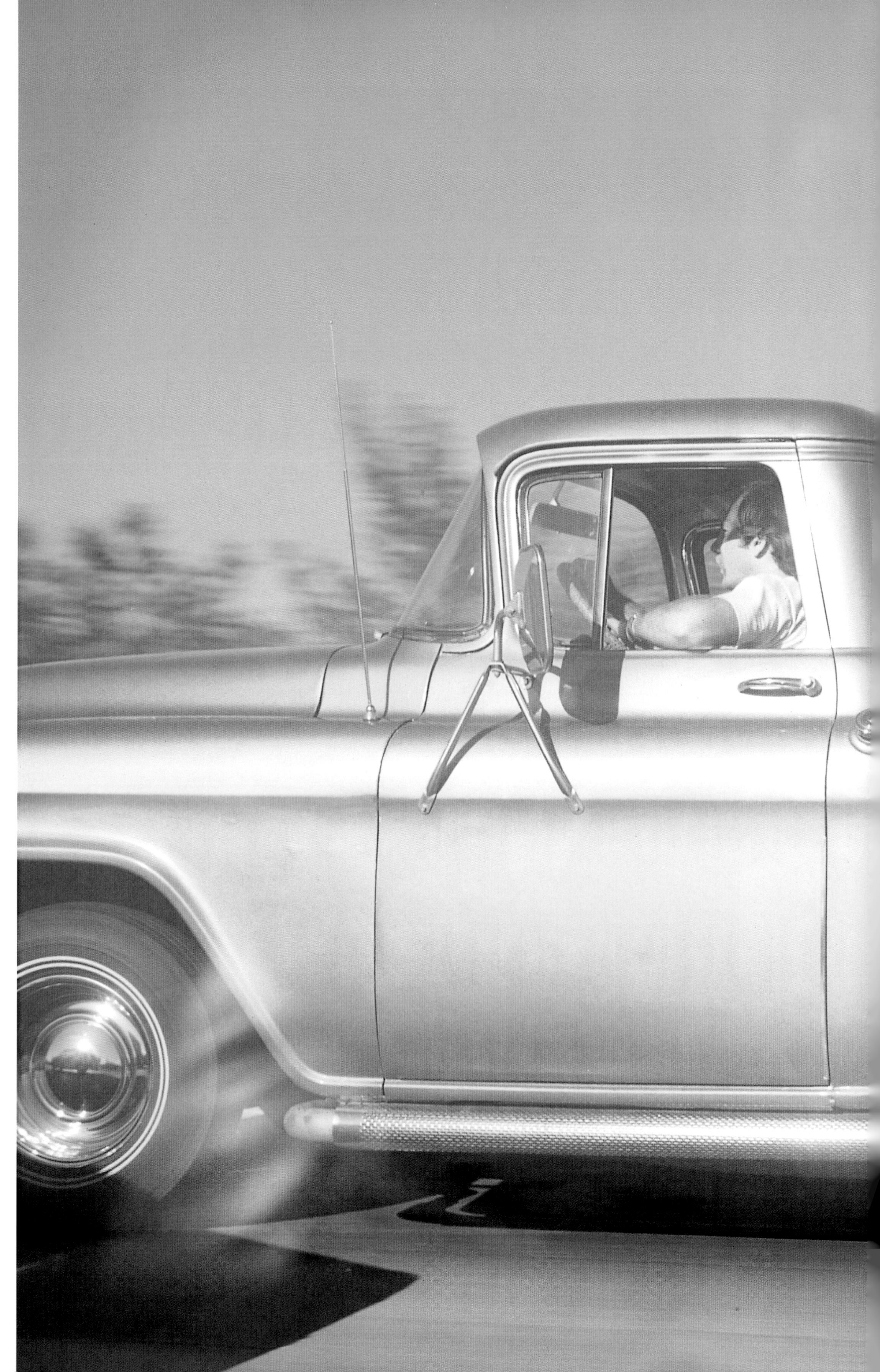

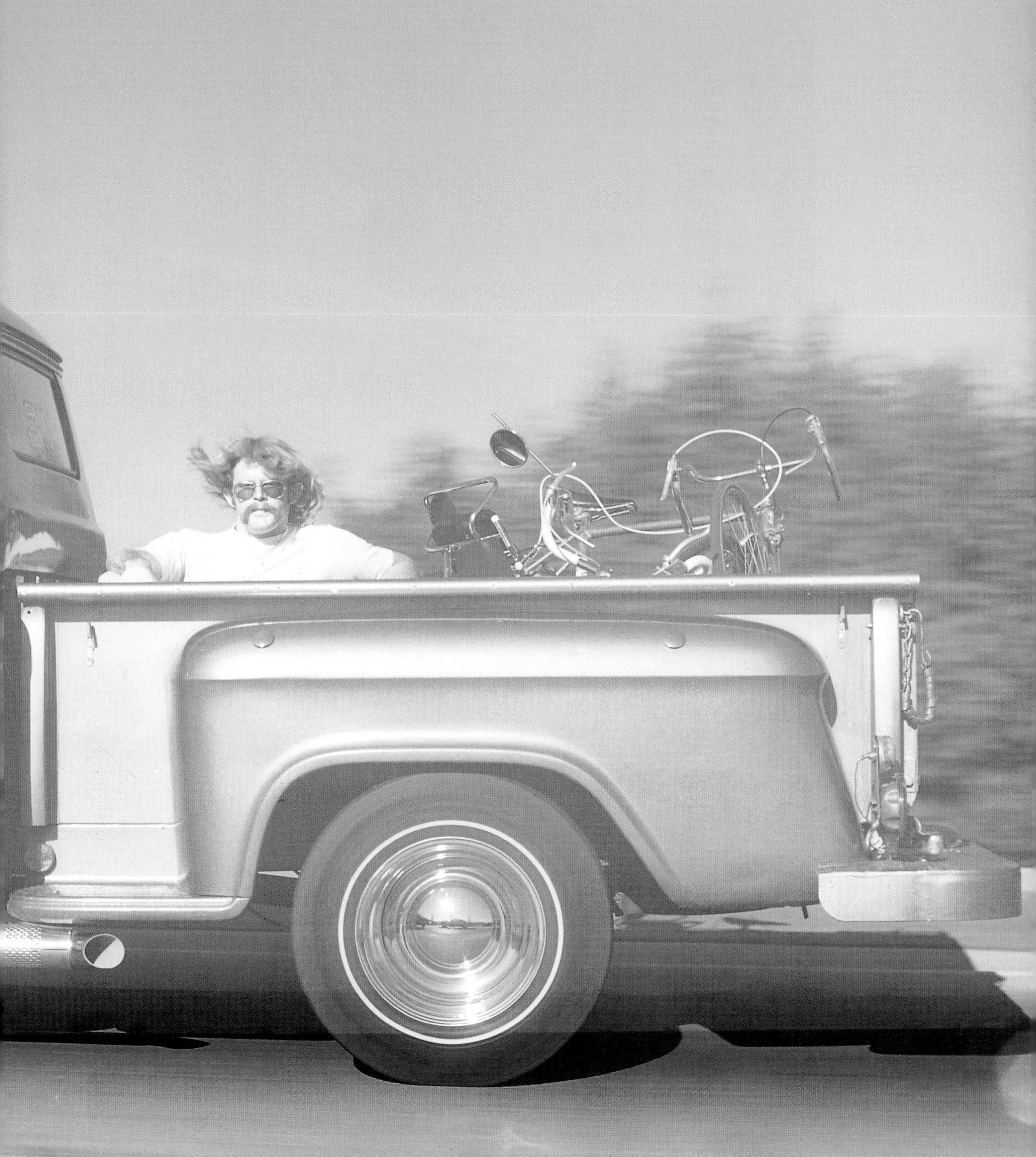

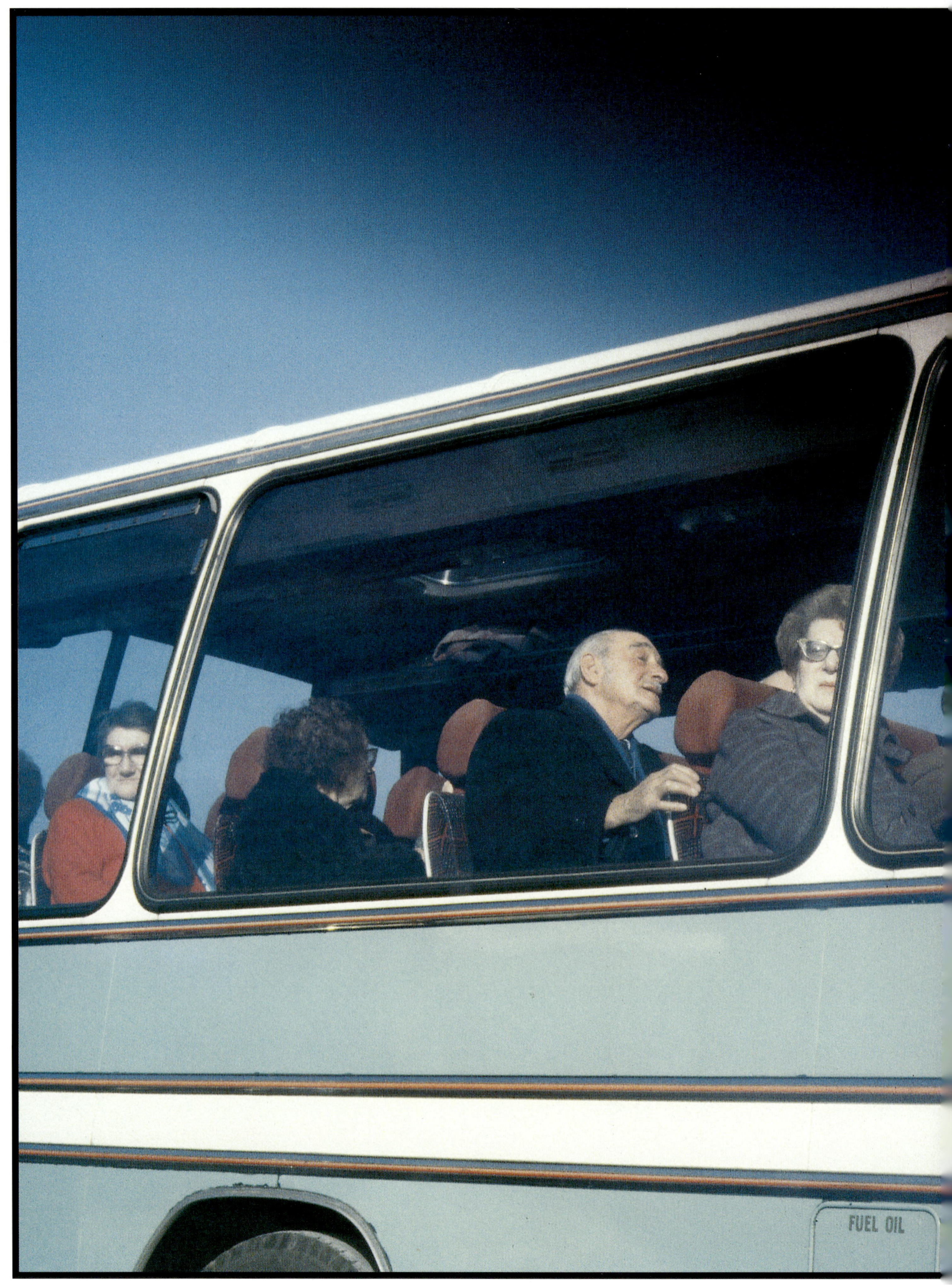
FUEL OIL

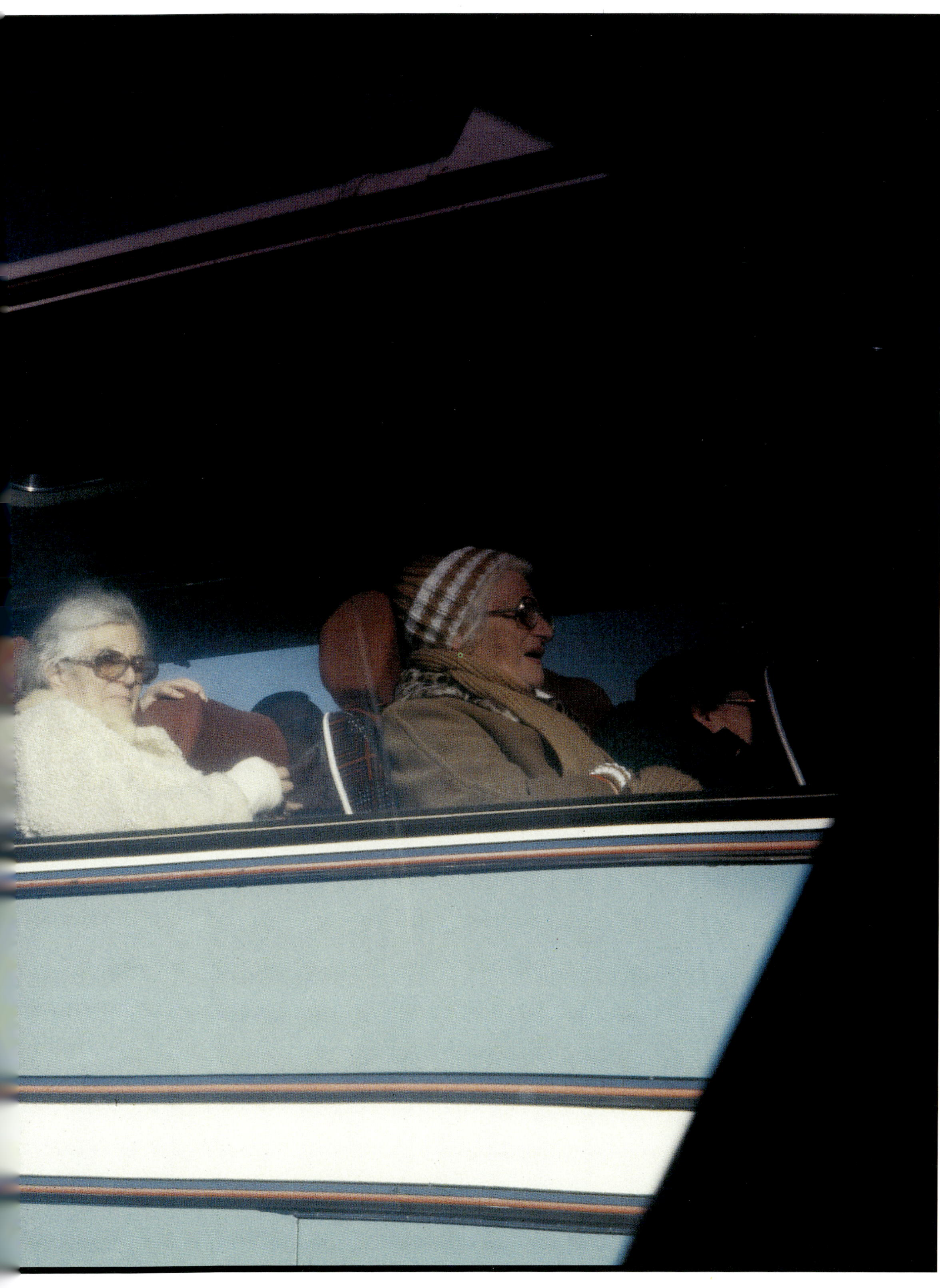

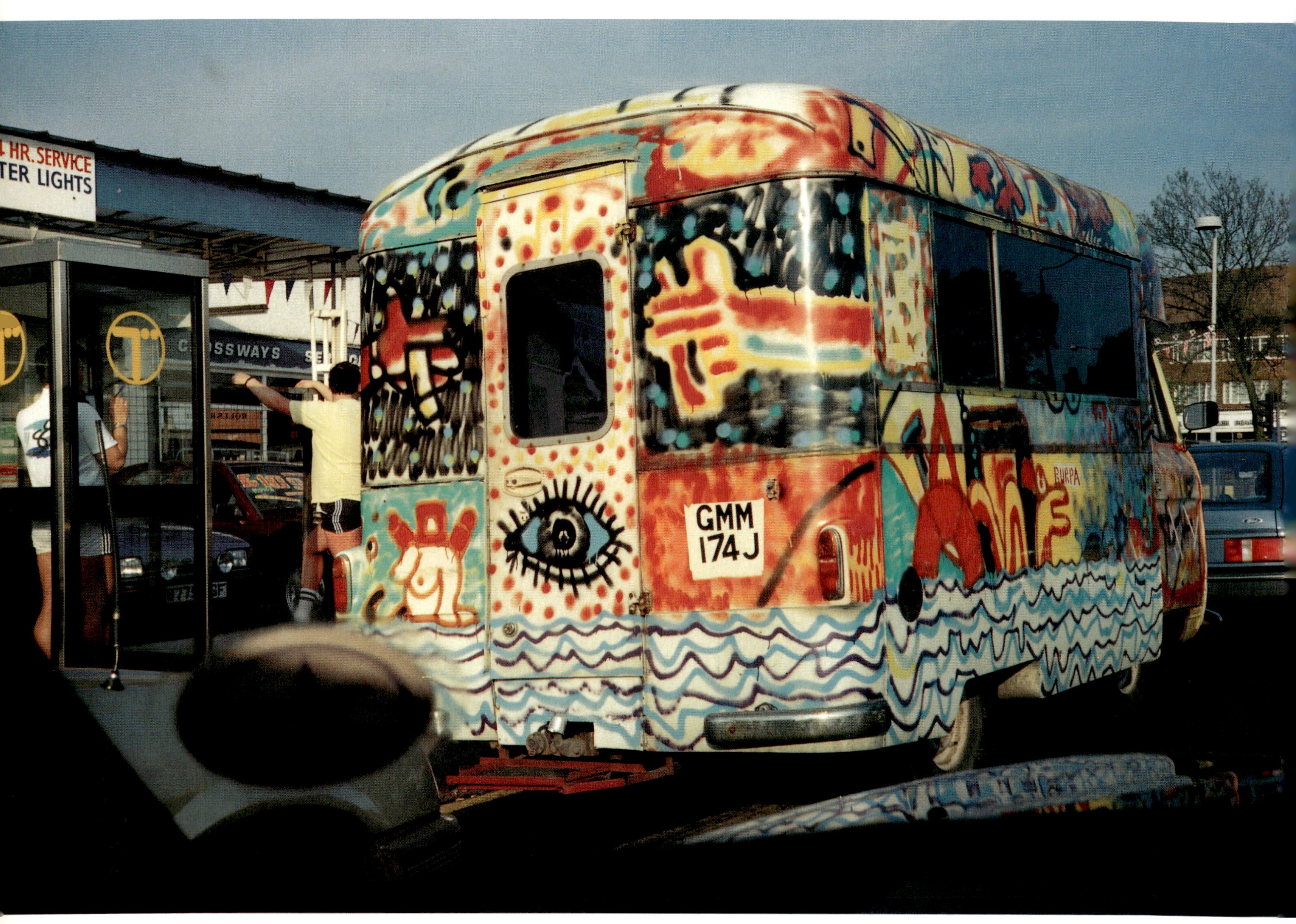
HR. SERVICE
TER LIGHTS
GMM
174 J

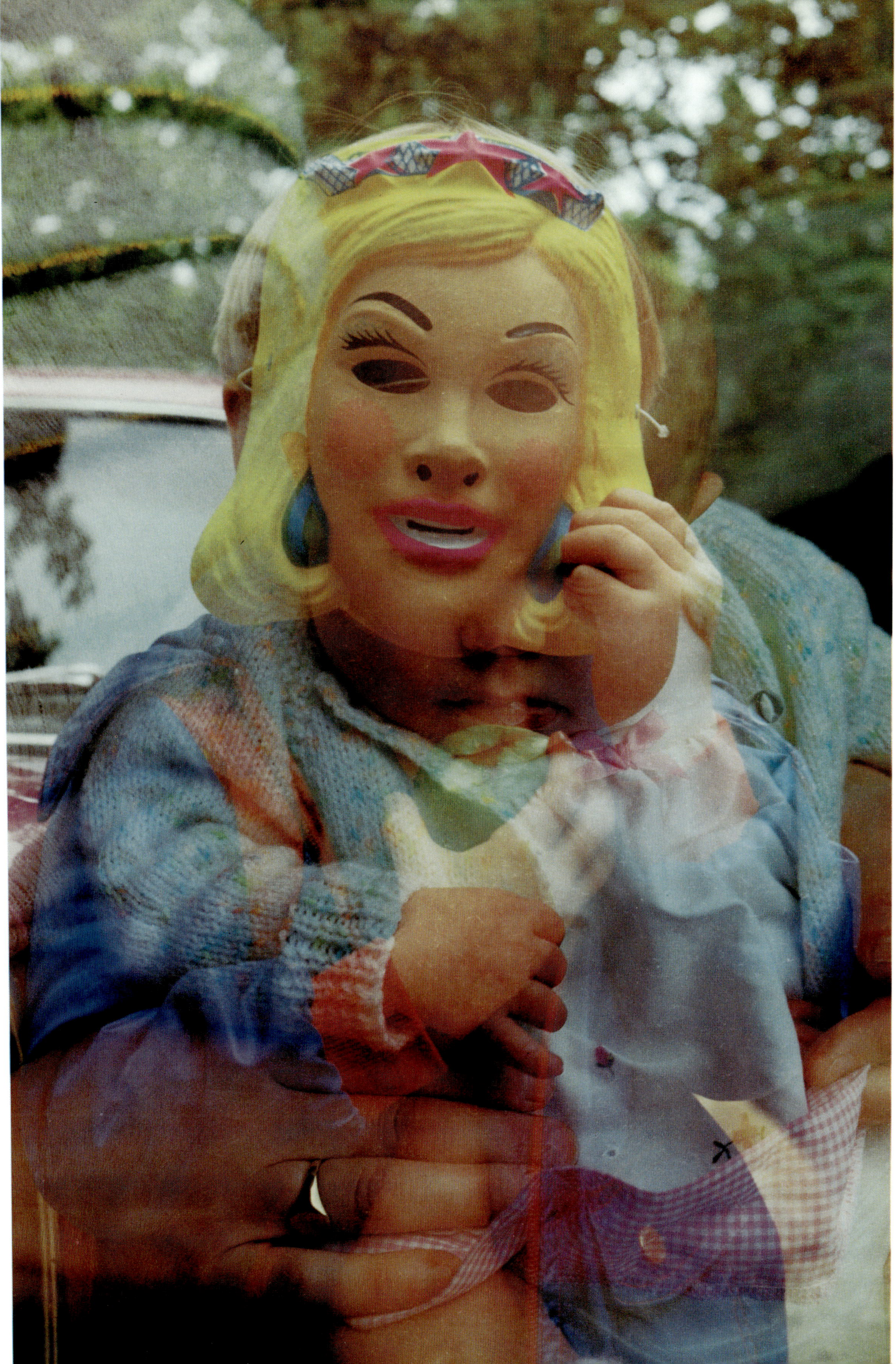

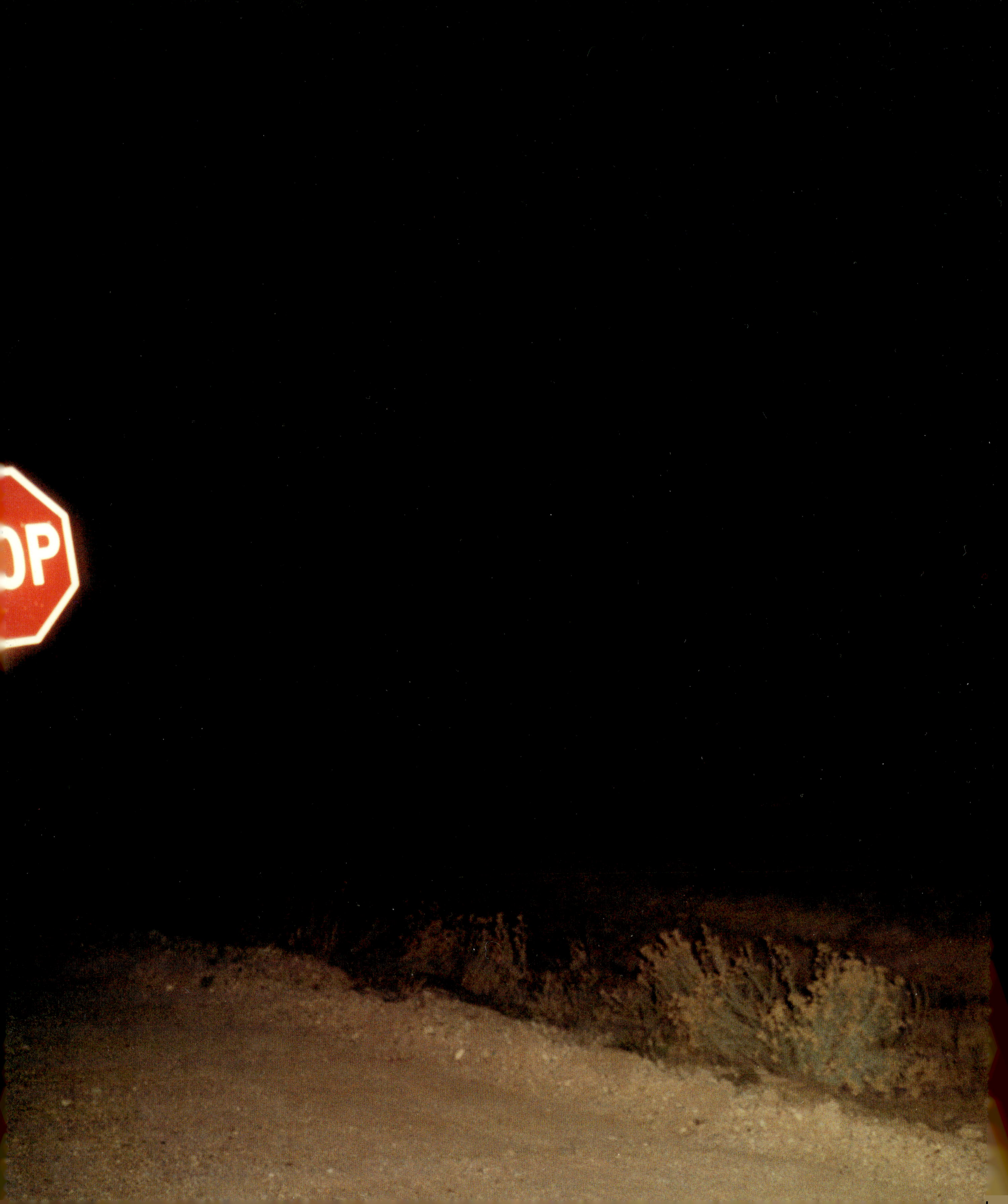

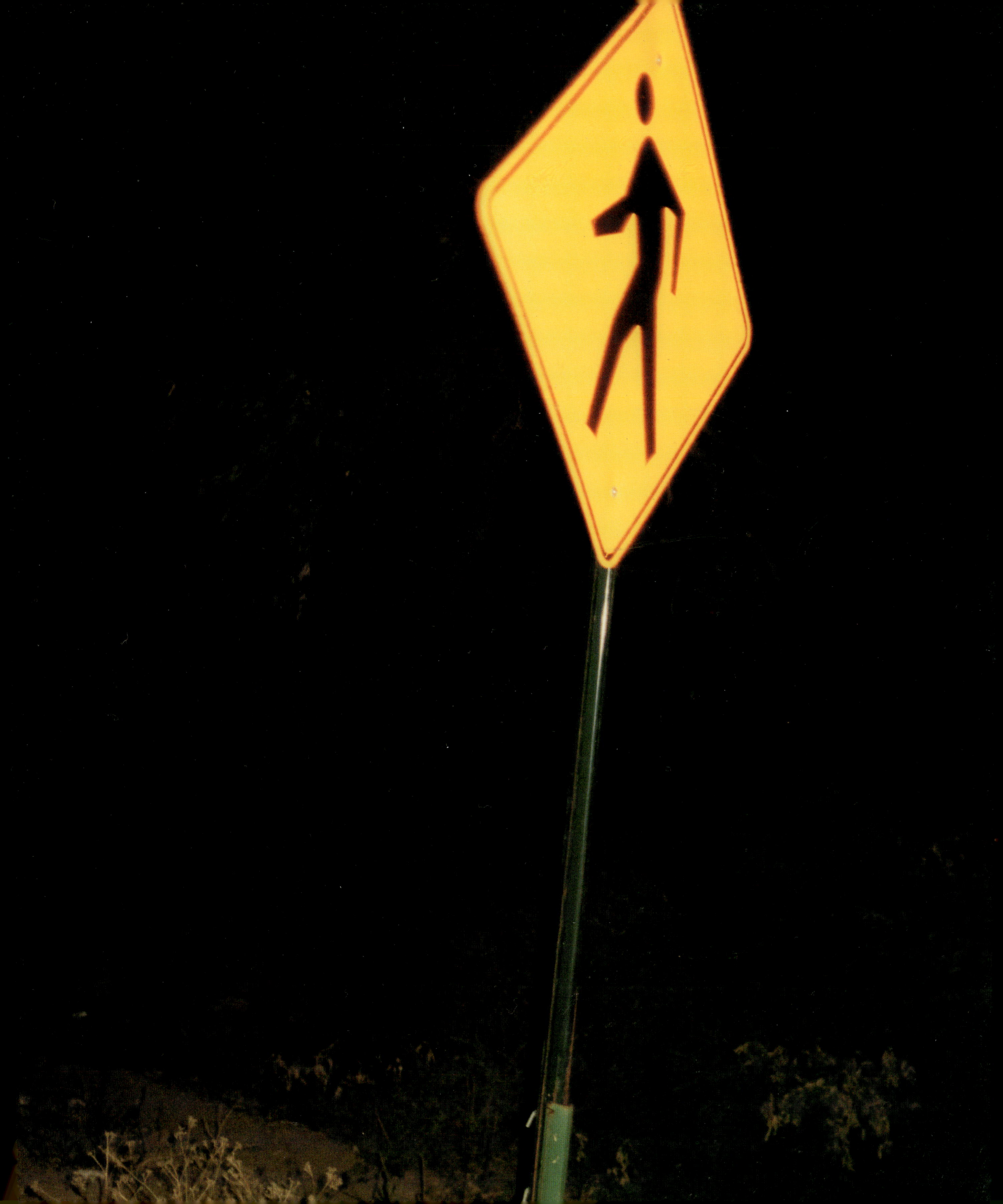

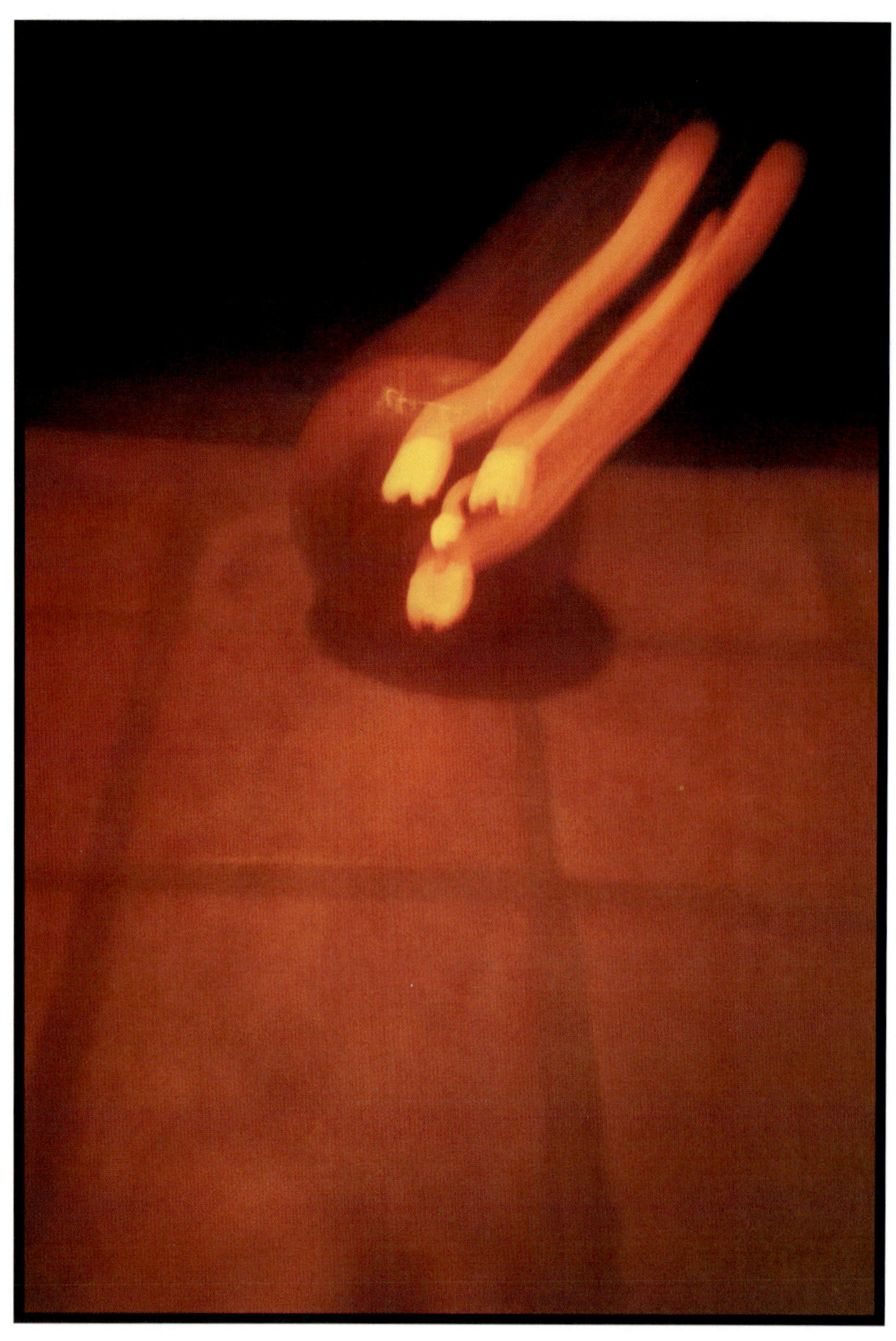

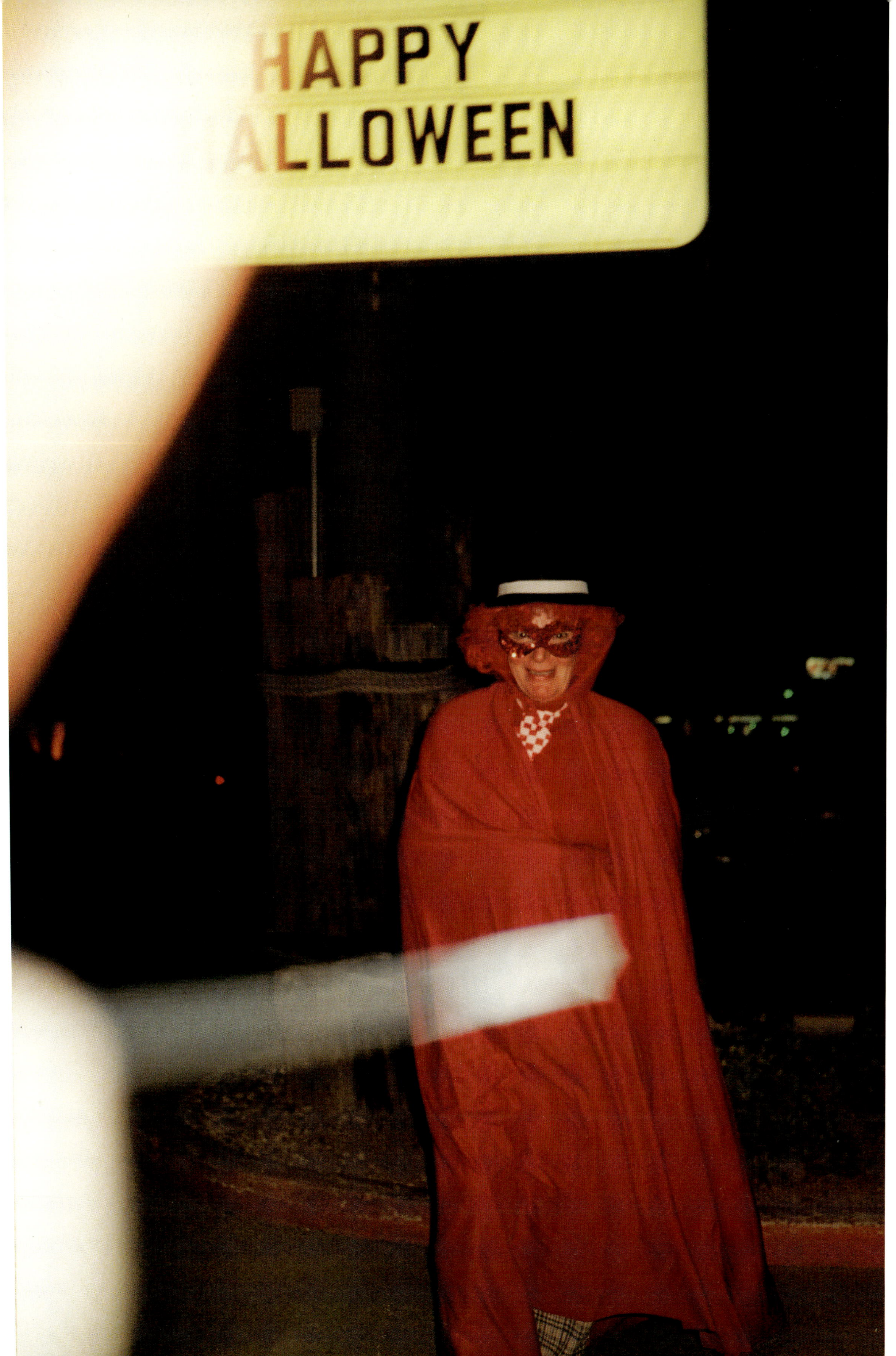
HAPPY
ALLOWEEN

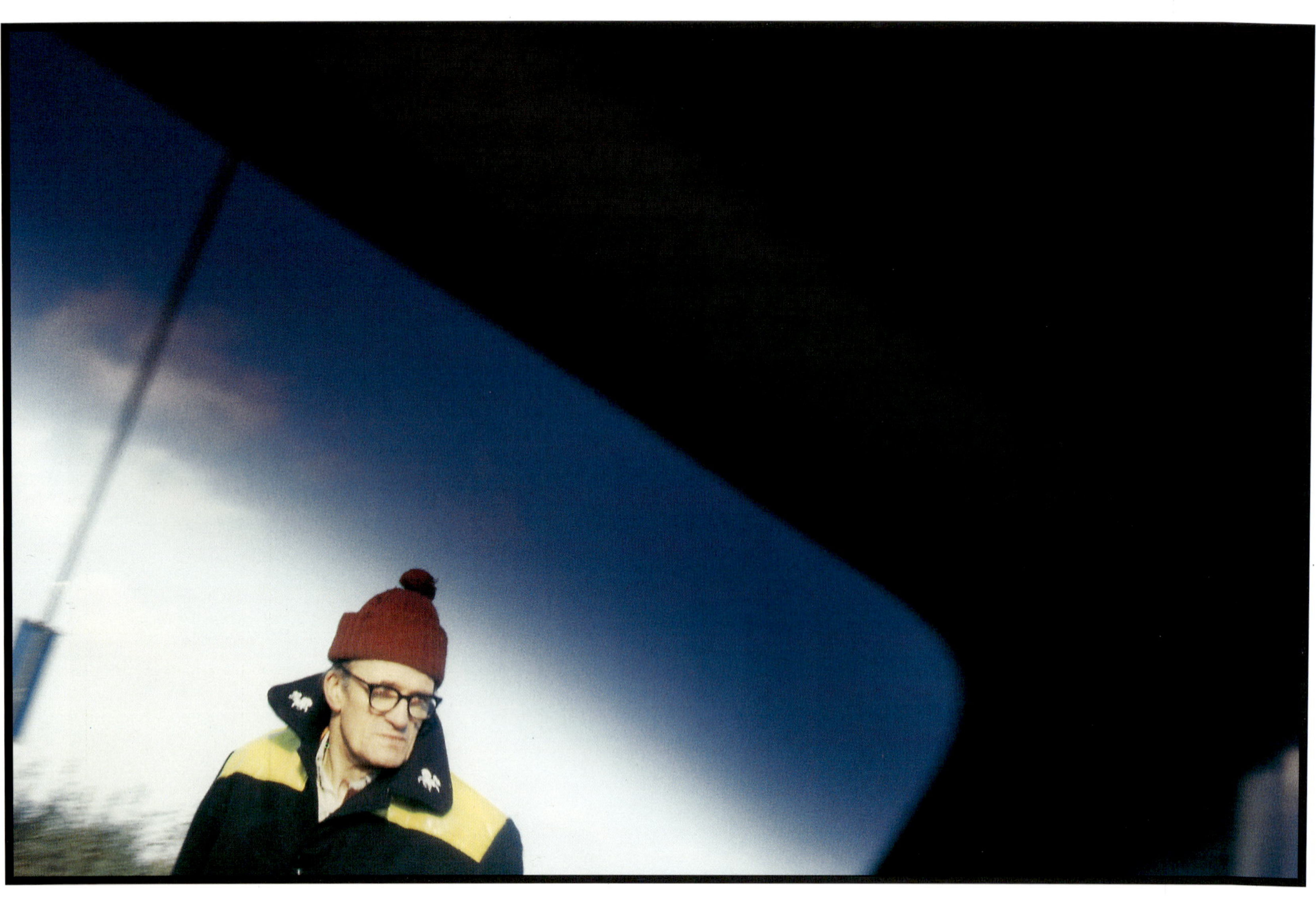

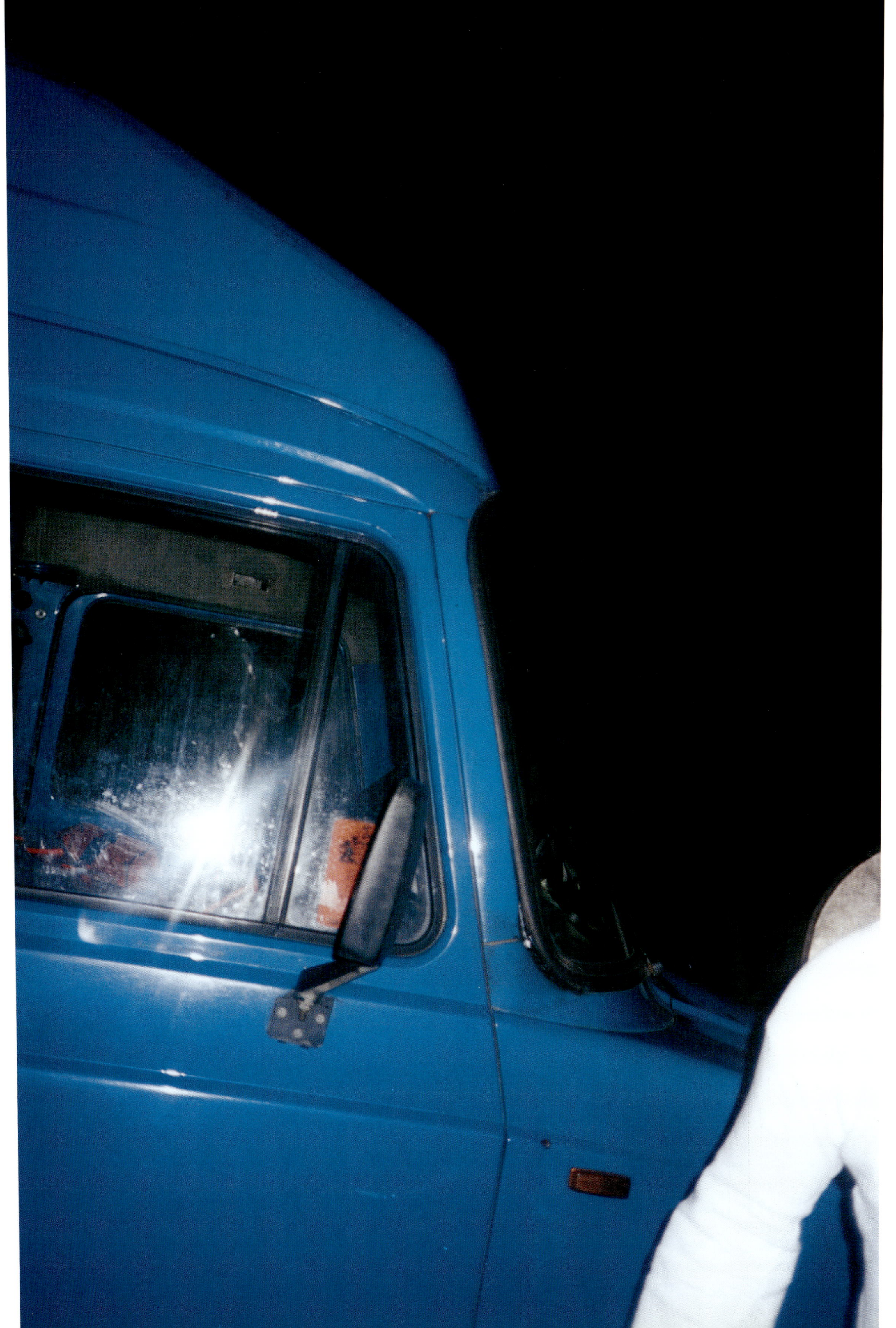

Spiritual horse floating in my heart,
free my mind from teachings: no guilt.

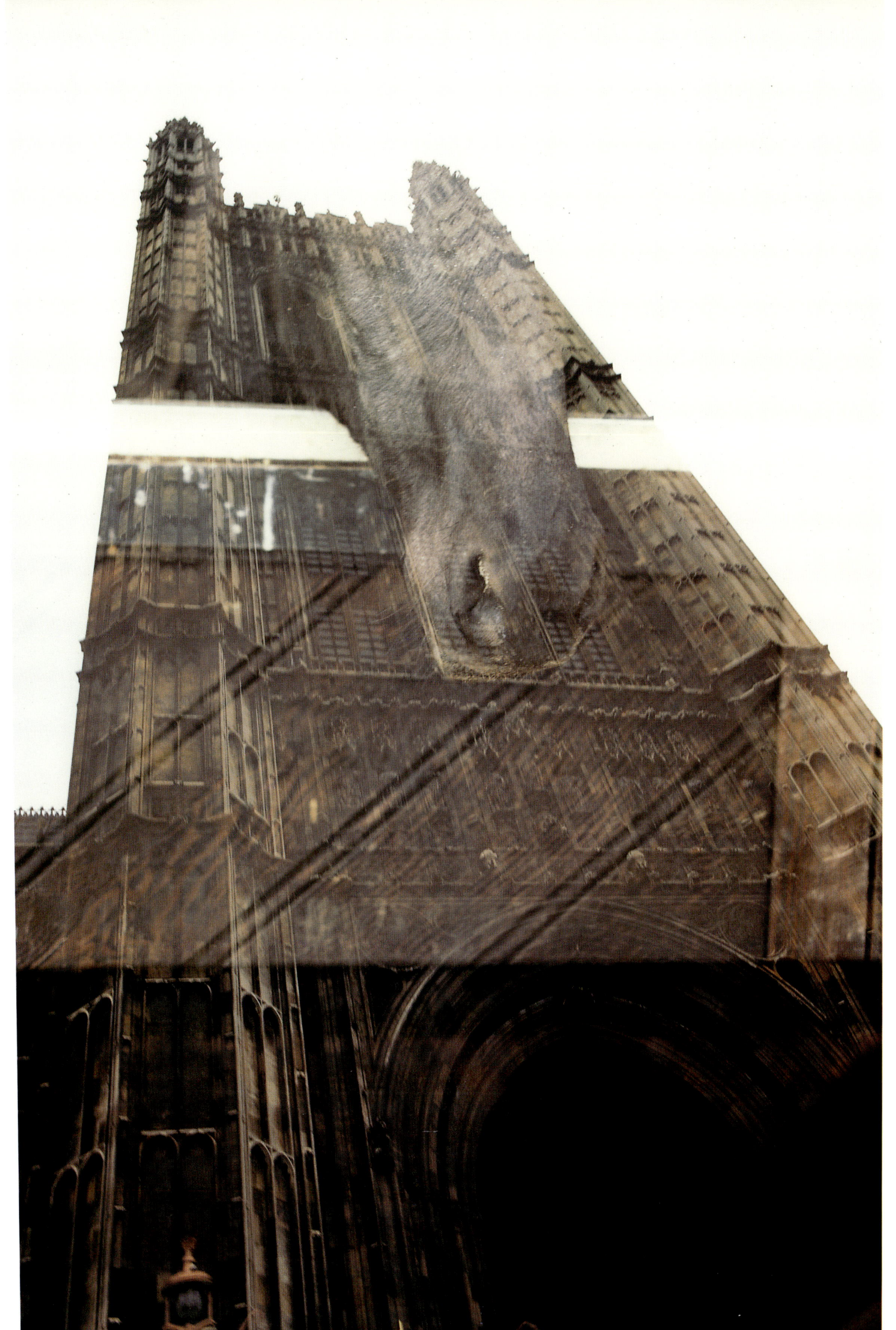

Random elements unrelated
combine — accentuate weirdness.

Detour

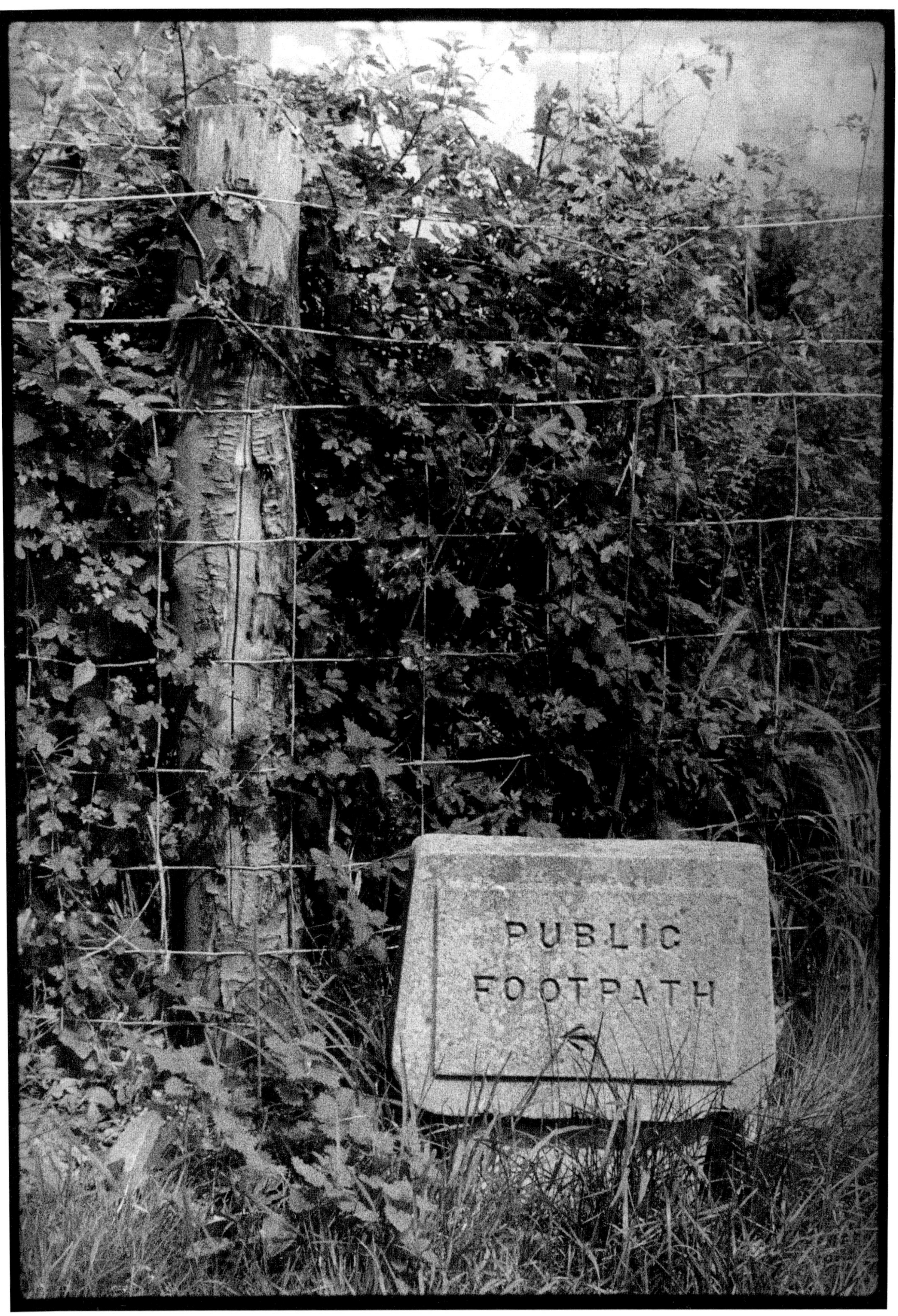
PUBLIC
FOOTPATH

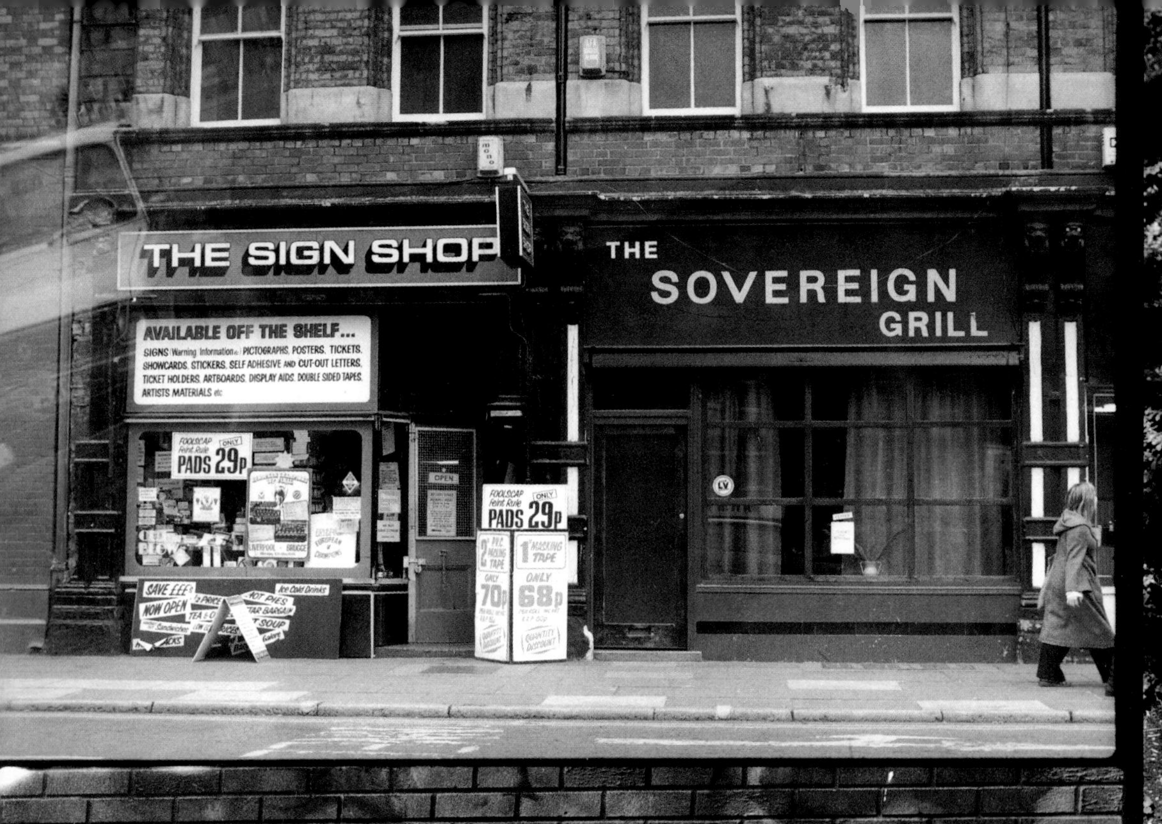
THE SIGN SHOP
THE SOVEREIGN GRILL
AVAILABLE OFF THE SHELF...
PADS 29p

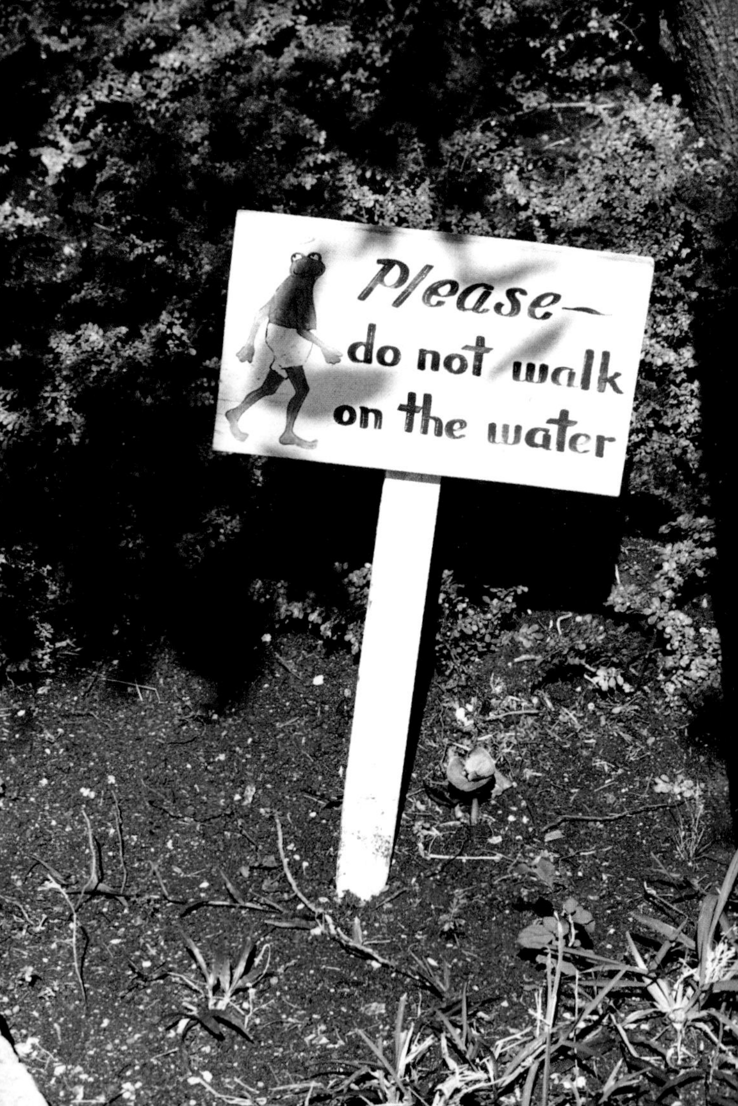
Please—
do not walk
on the water

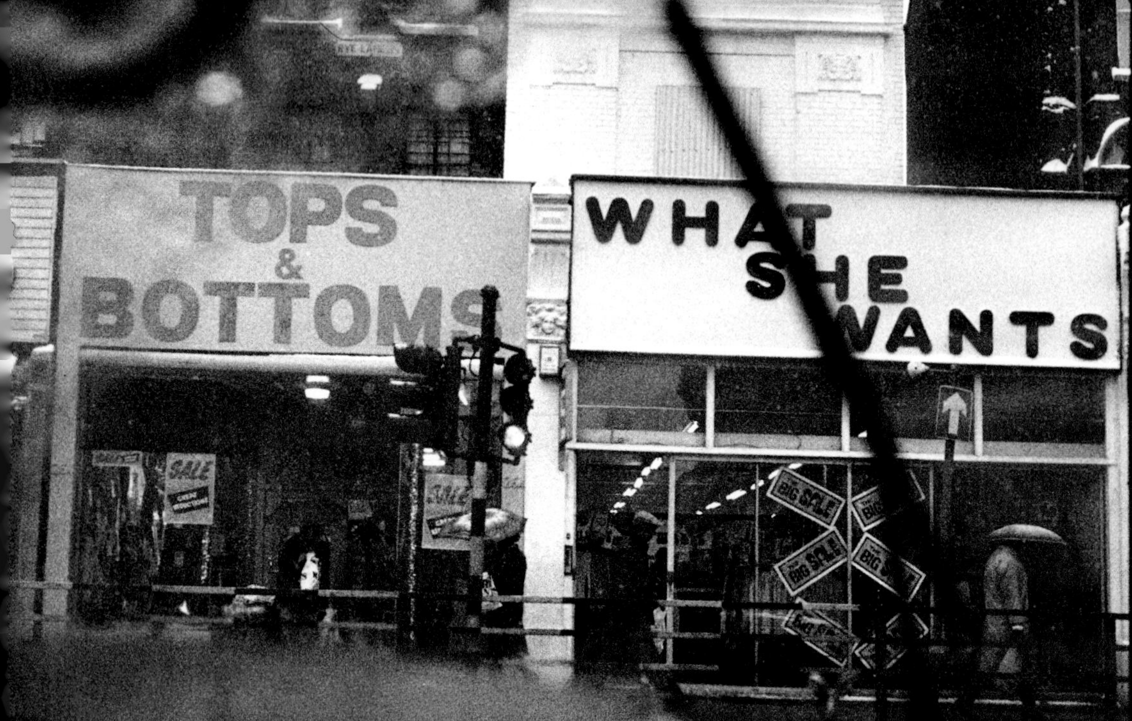
TOPS & BOTTOMS
WHAT SHE WANTS

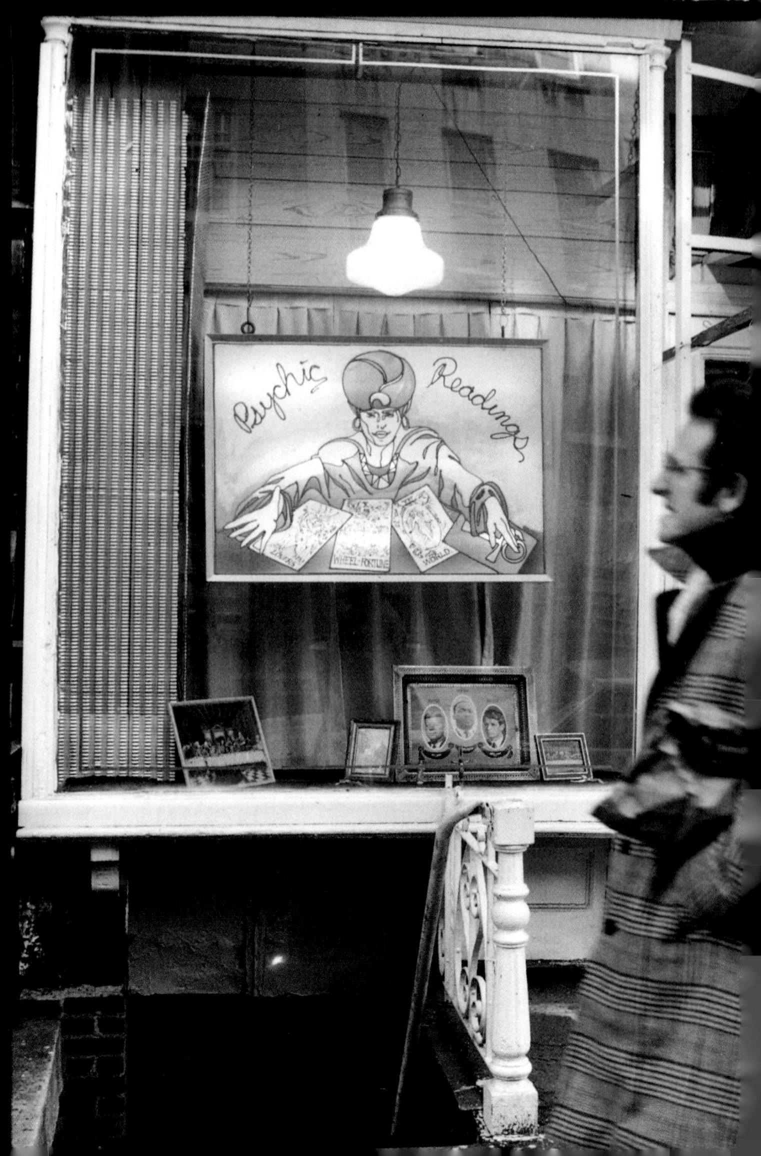
Psychic Readings

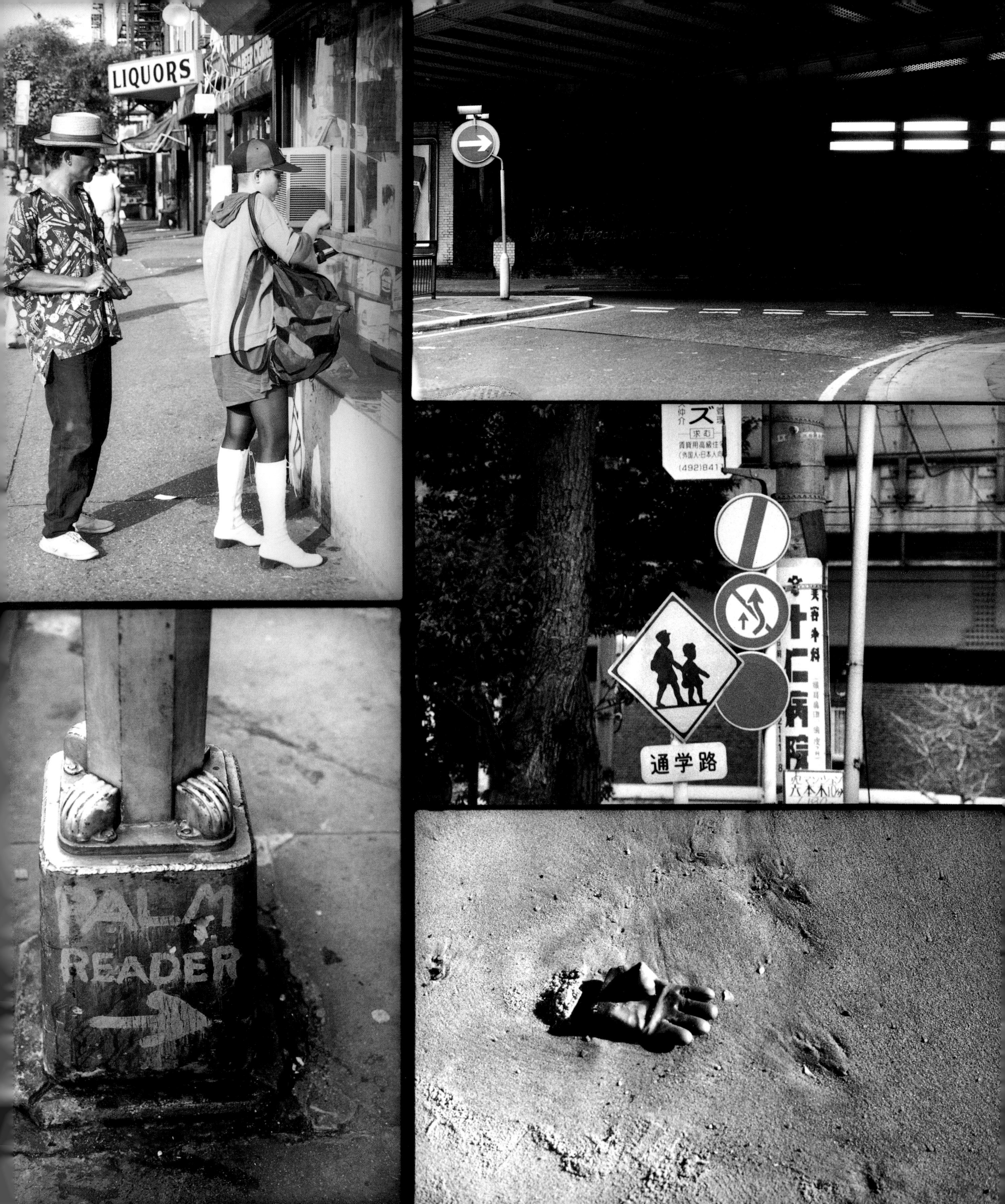
LIQUORS
通学路
PALM
READER

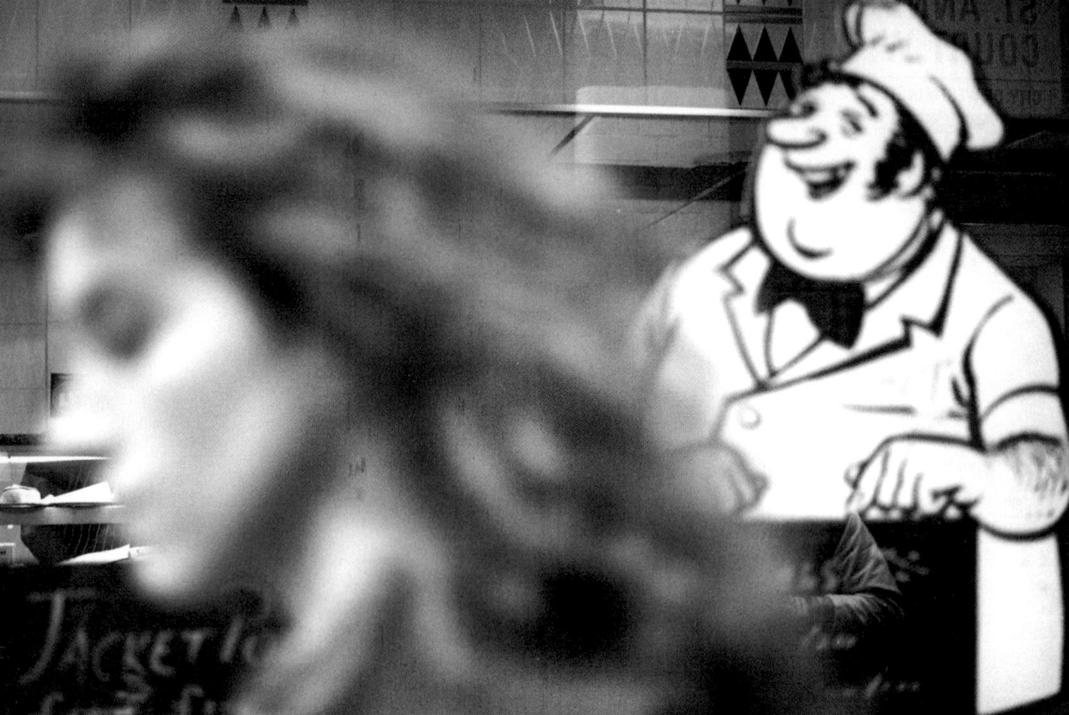
FIZZ
BOMB

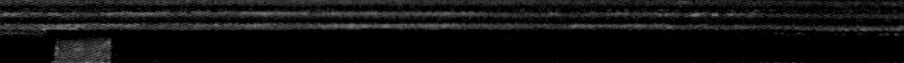
GET IT AT PAGE'S

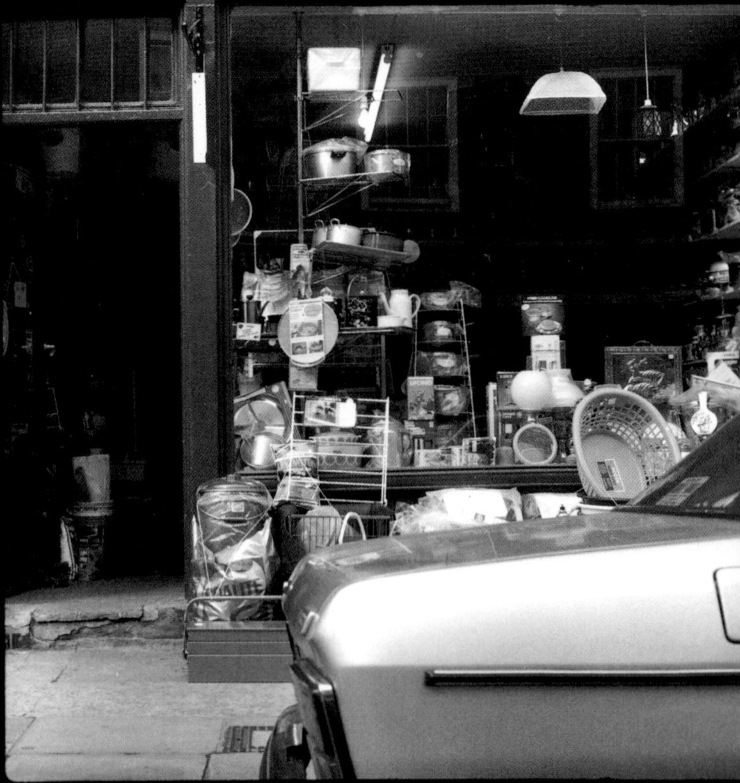

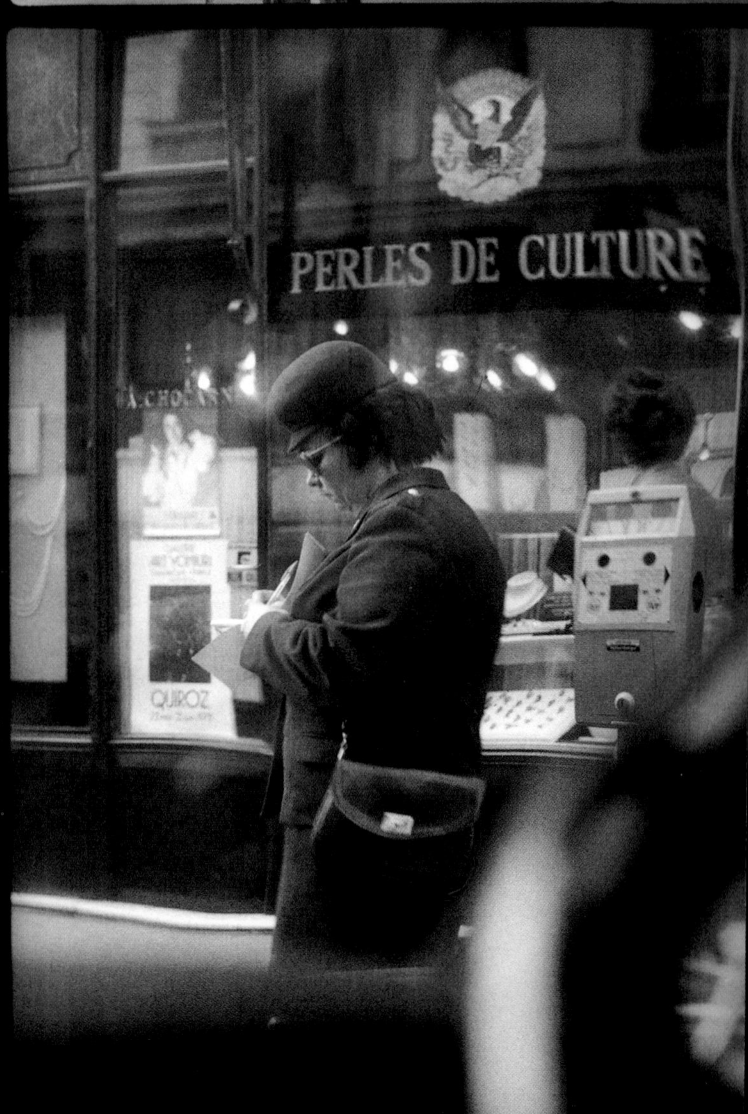
PERLES DE CULTURE
QUIROZ

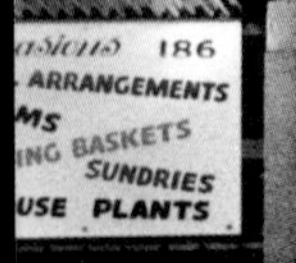
186
ARRANGEMENTS
SUNDRIES
PLANTS
AZALEA

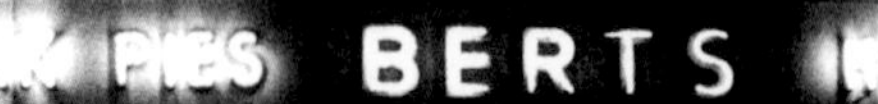
BERTS

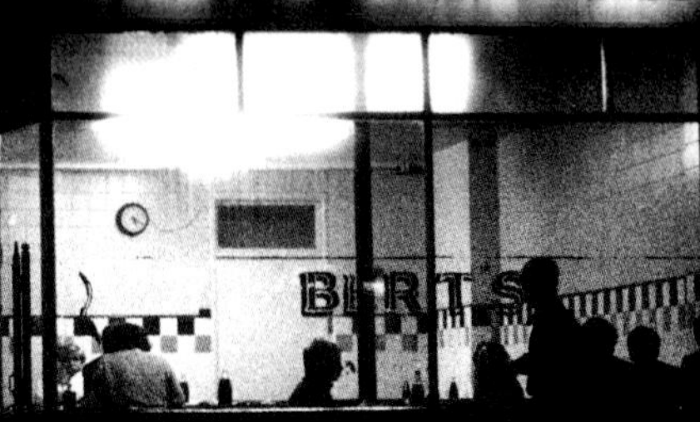
BERTS

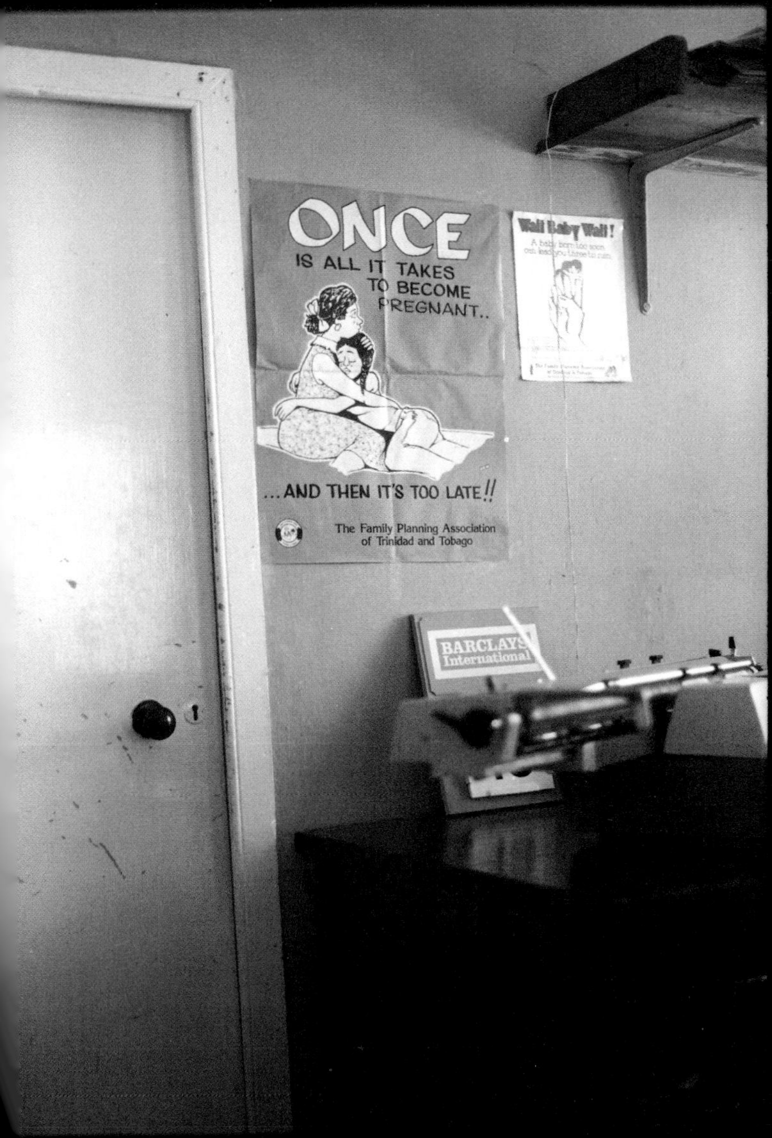

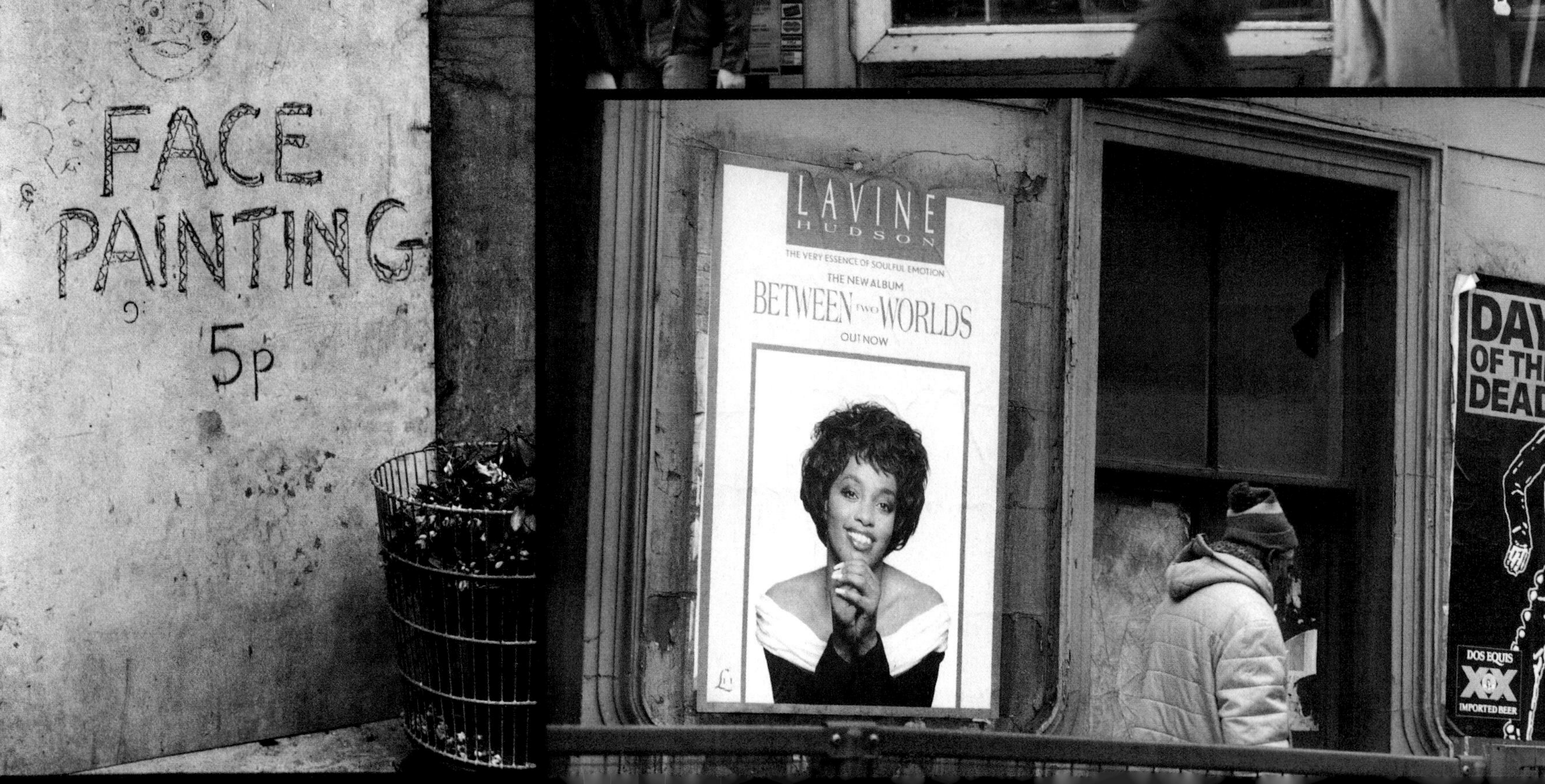
ONCE
IS ALL IT TAKES
TO BECOME
PREGNANT..
...AND THEN IT'S TOO LATE!!
The Family Planning Association
of Trinidad and Tobago
BARCLAYS
International
Van Gils 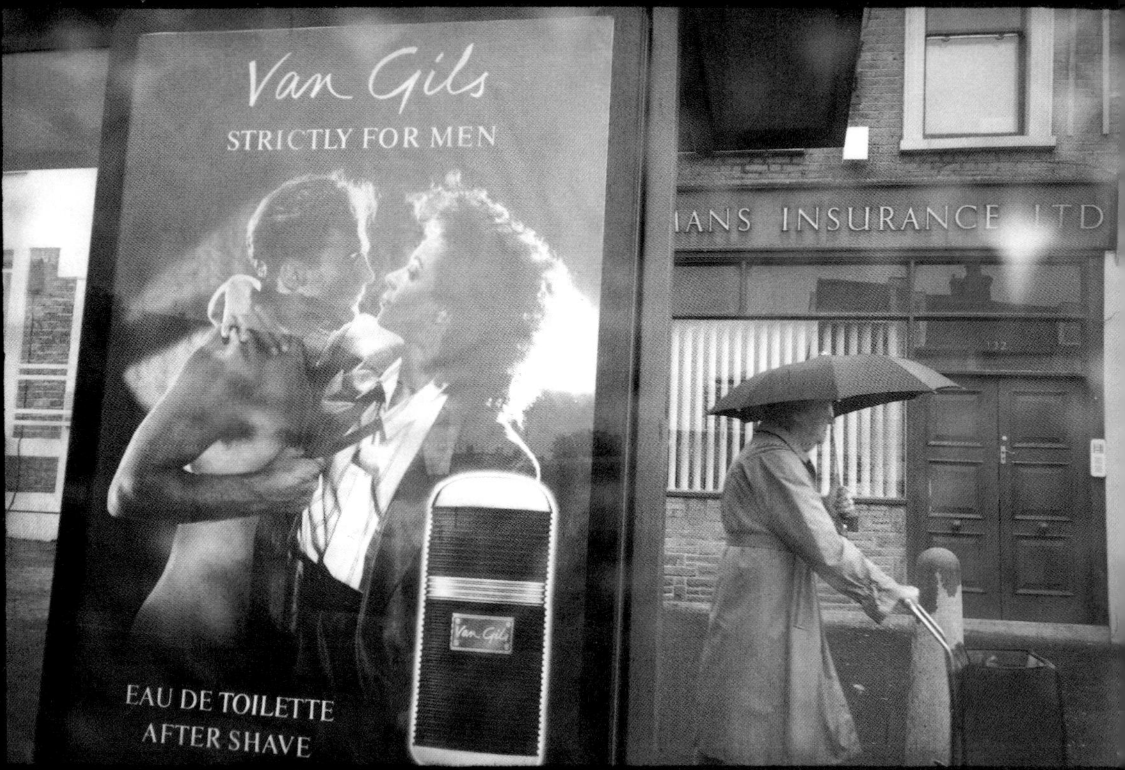
STRICTLY FOR MEN
EAU DE TOILETTE
AFTER SHAVE
Van Gils
IANS INSURANCE LTD
"LEATHER MAN" 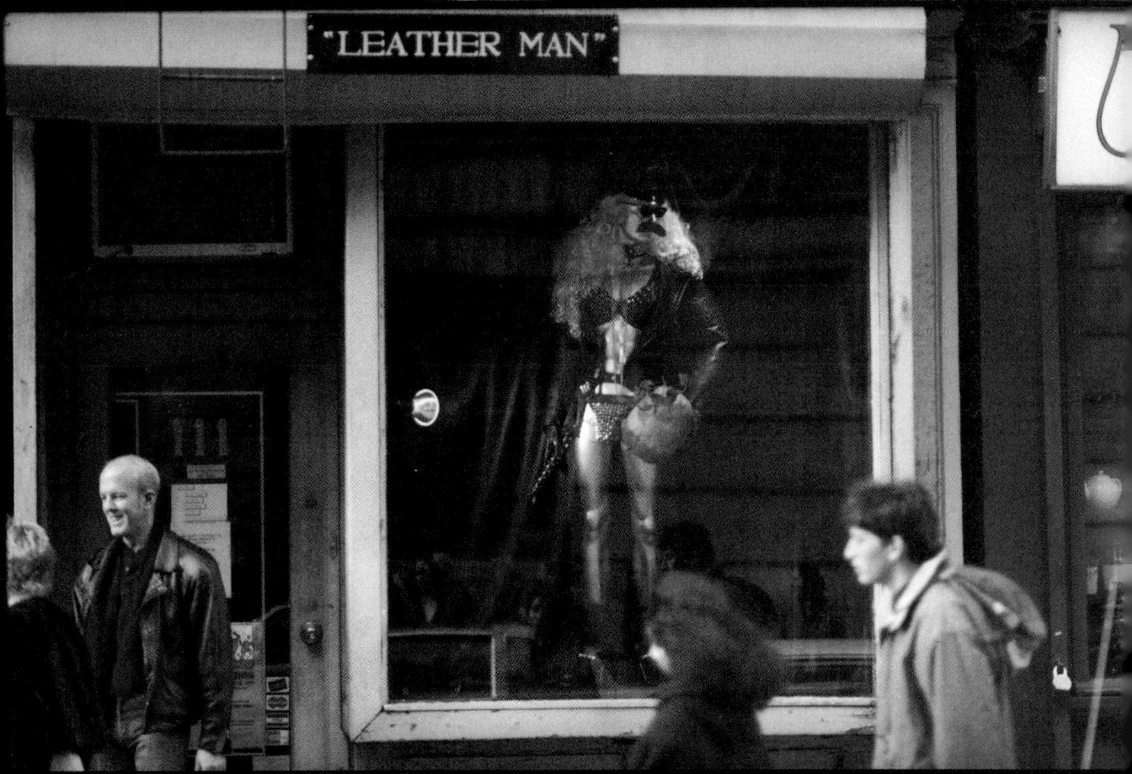
FACE 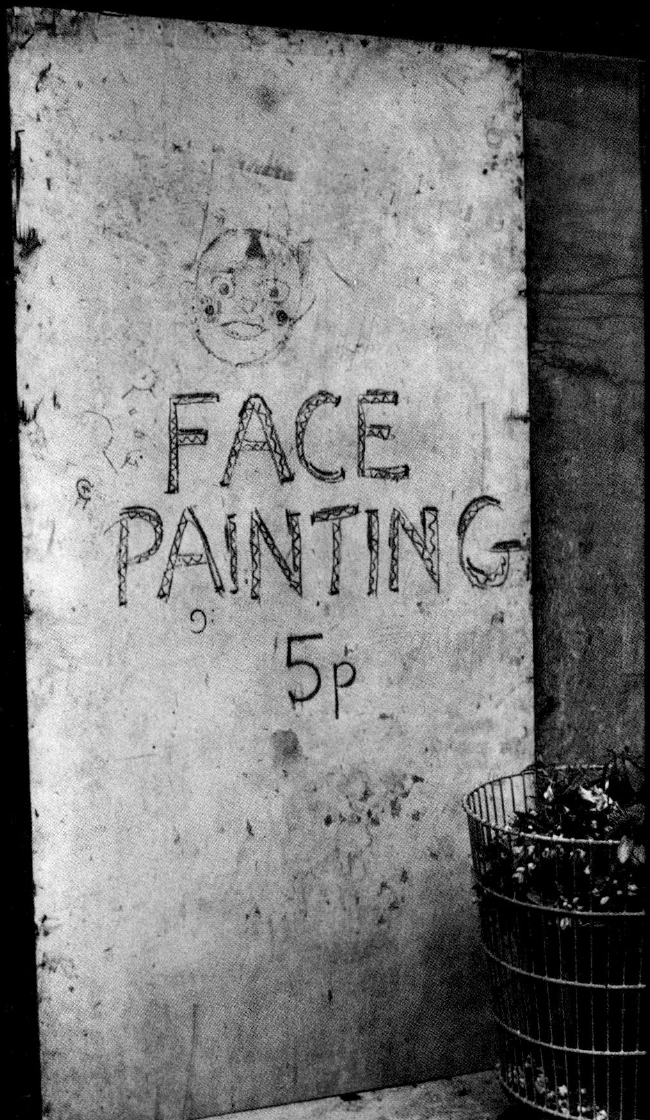
PAINTING
5p
LAVINE
HUDSON
THE VERY ESSENCE OF SOULFUL EMOTION
THE NEW ALBUM
BETWEEN TWO WORLDS
OUT NOW
DAY
OF THE
DEAD
DOS EQUIS
XX
IMPORTED BEER

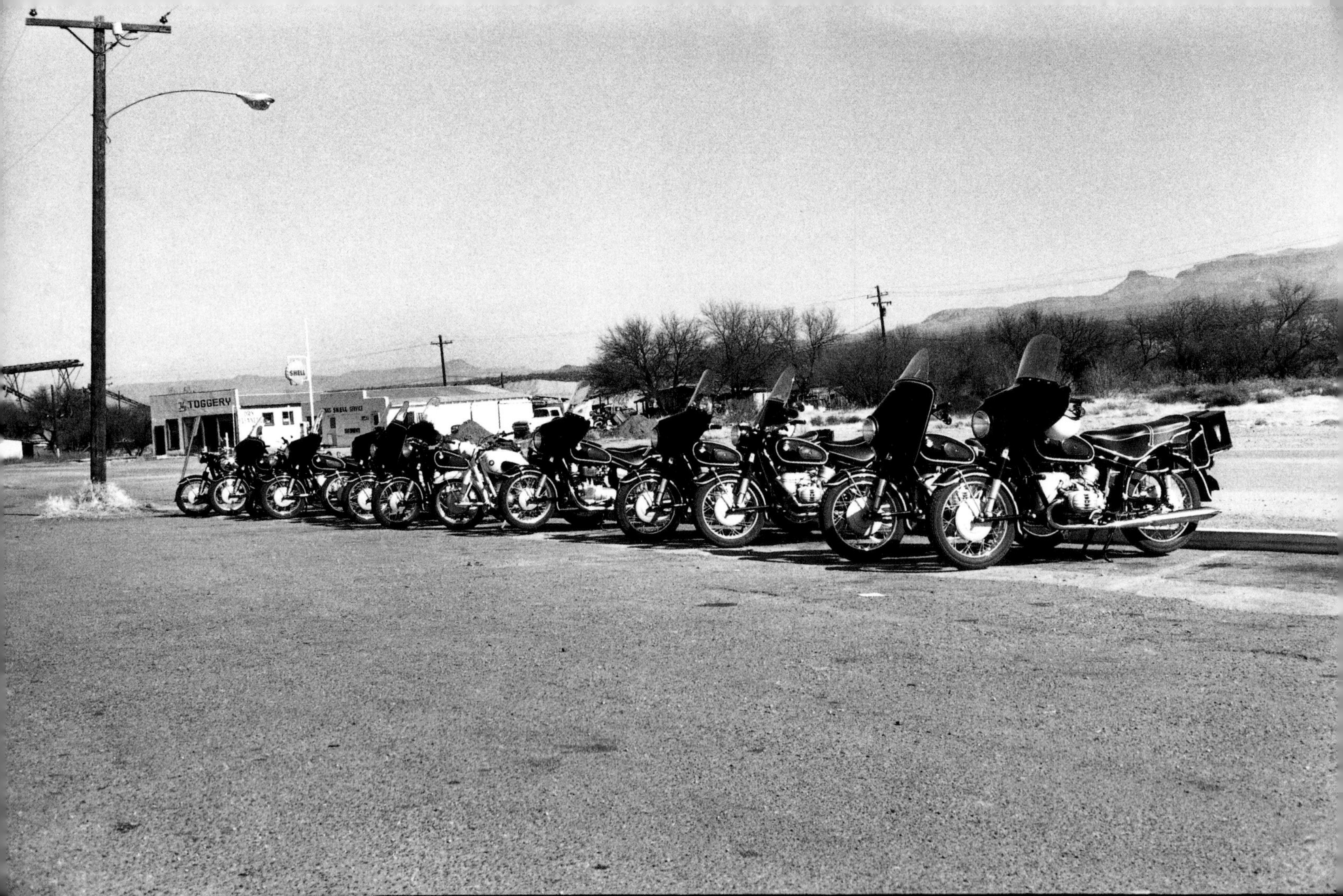

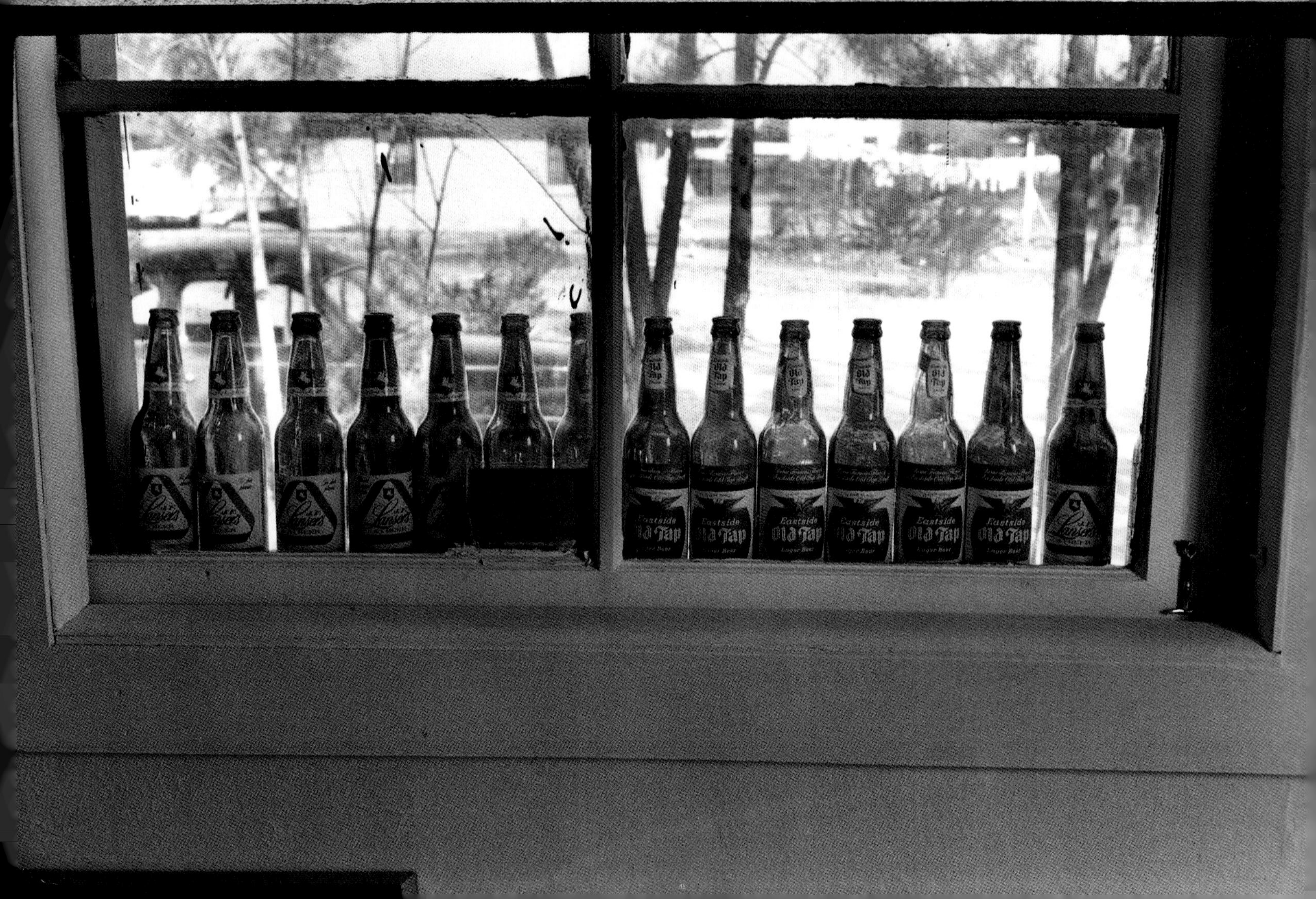

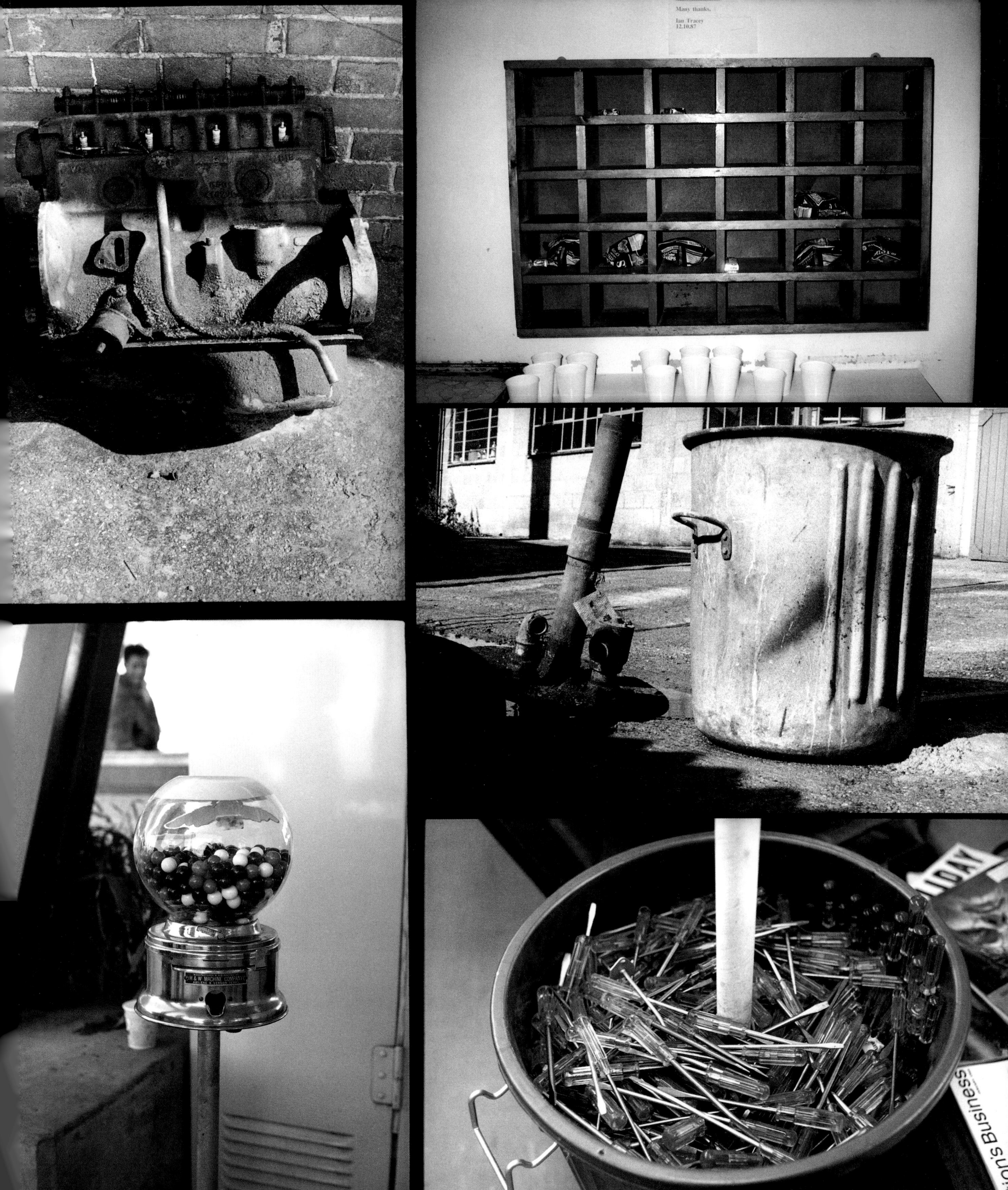
Many thanks.
Ian Tracey
12.10.87
H & W MACHINE COMPANY
ion's Business

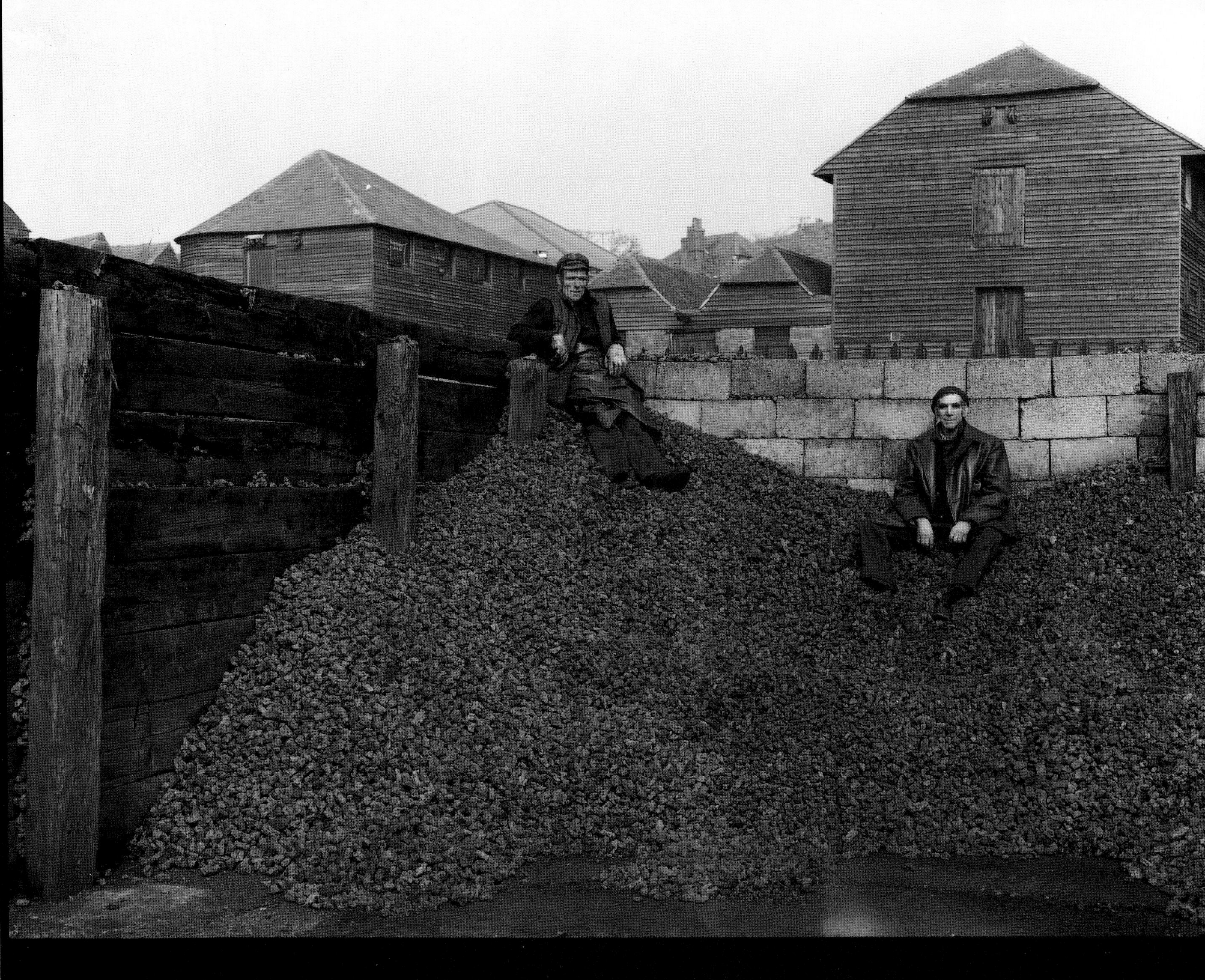

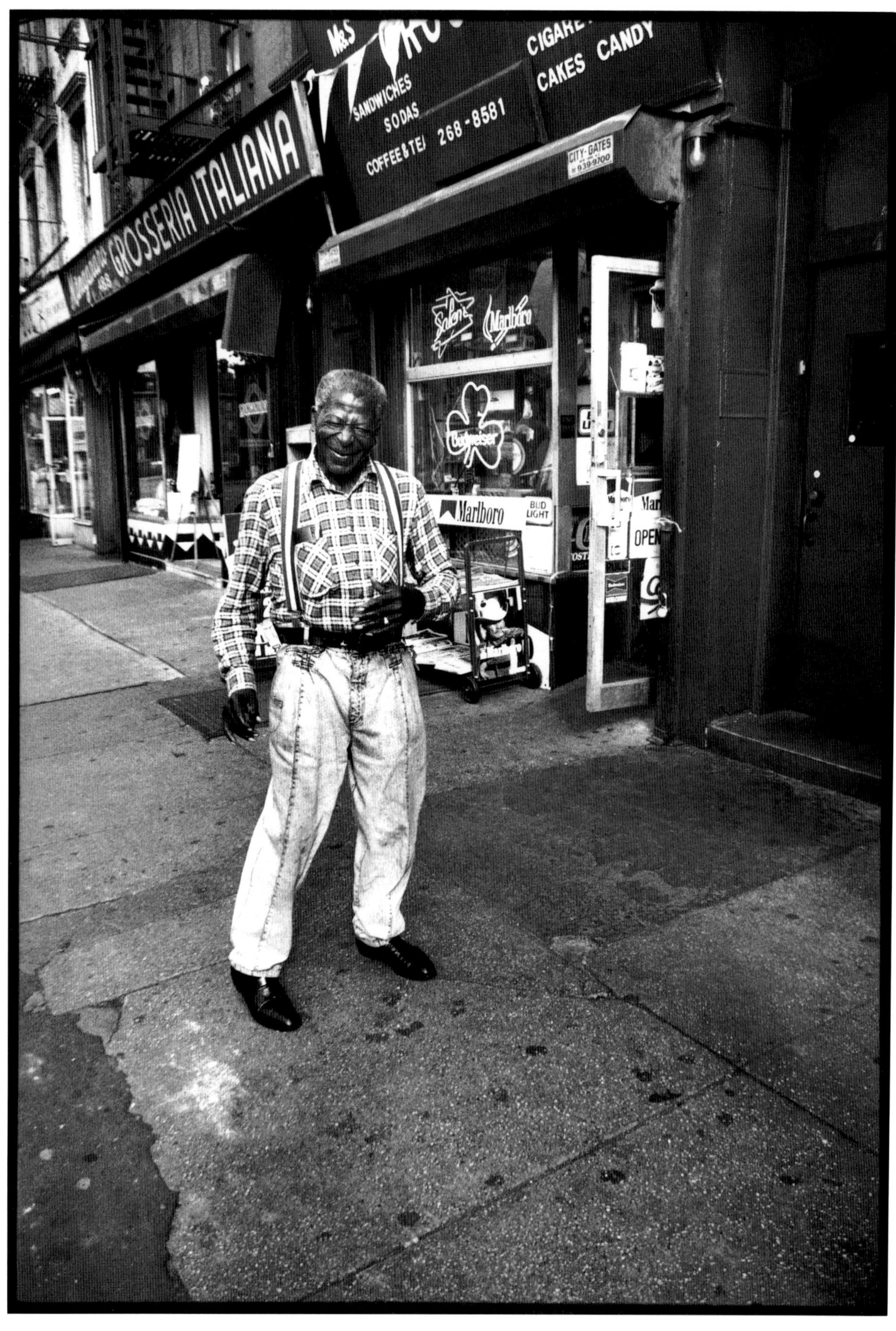
GROSSERIA ITALIANA
SANDWICHES
SODAS
COFFEE & TEA
268-8581
CIGARE
CAKES CANDY
CITY-GATES
Marlboro
BUD LIGHT
OPEN

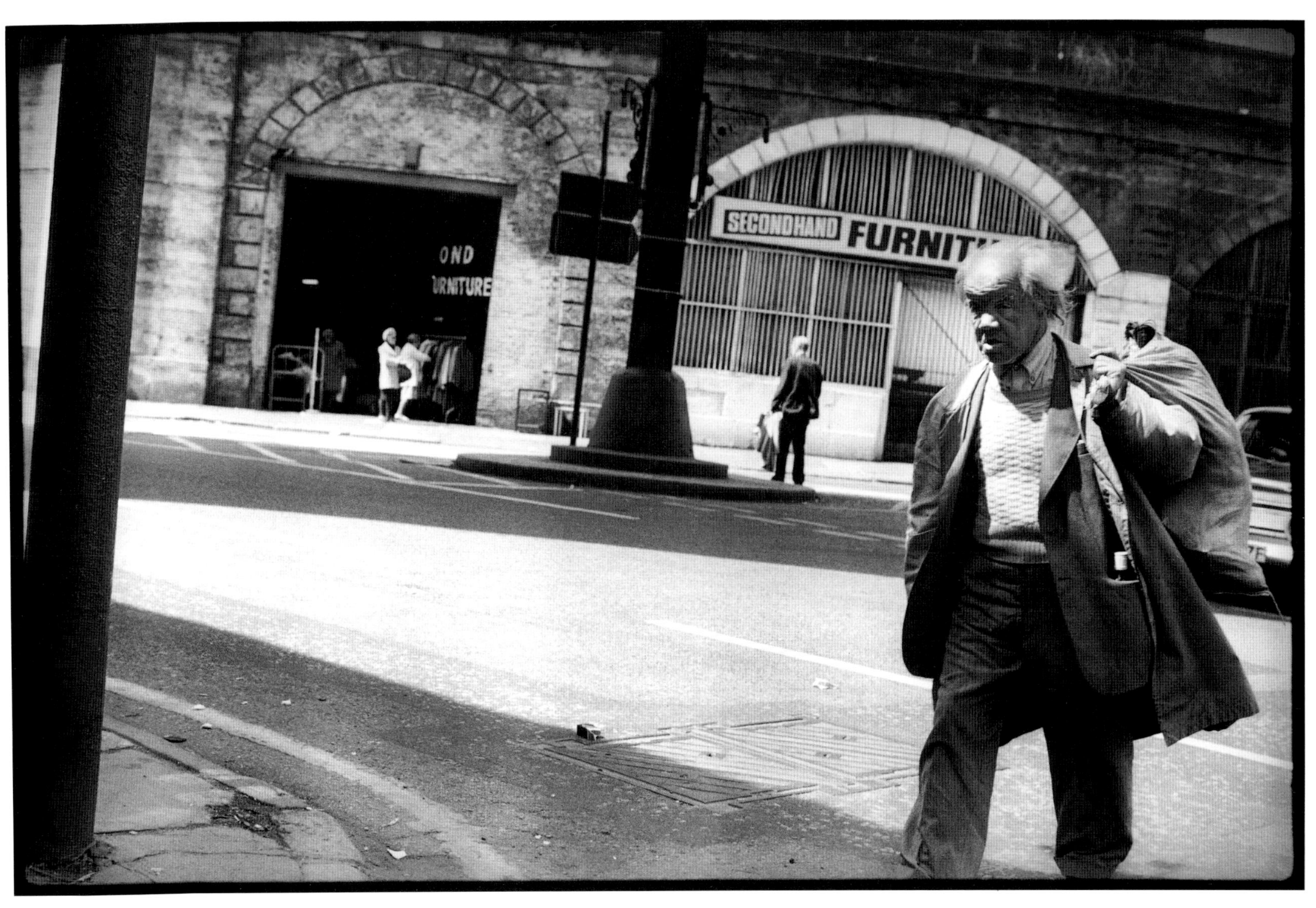
OND
URNITURE
SECONDHAND
FURNIT

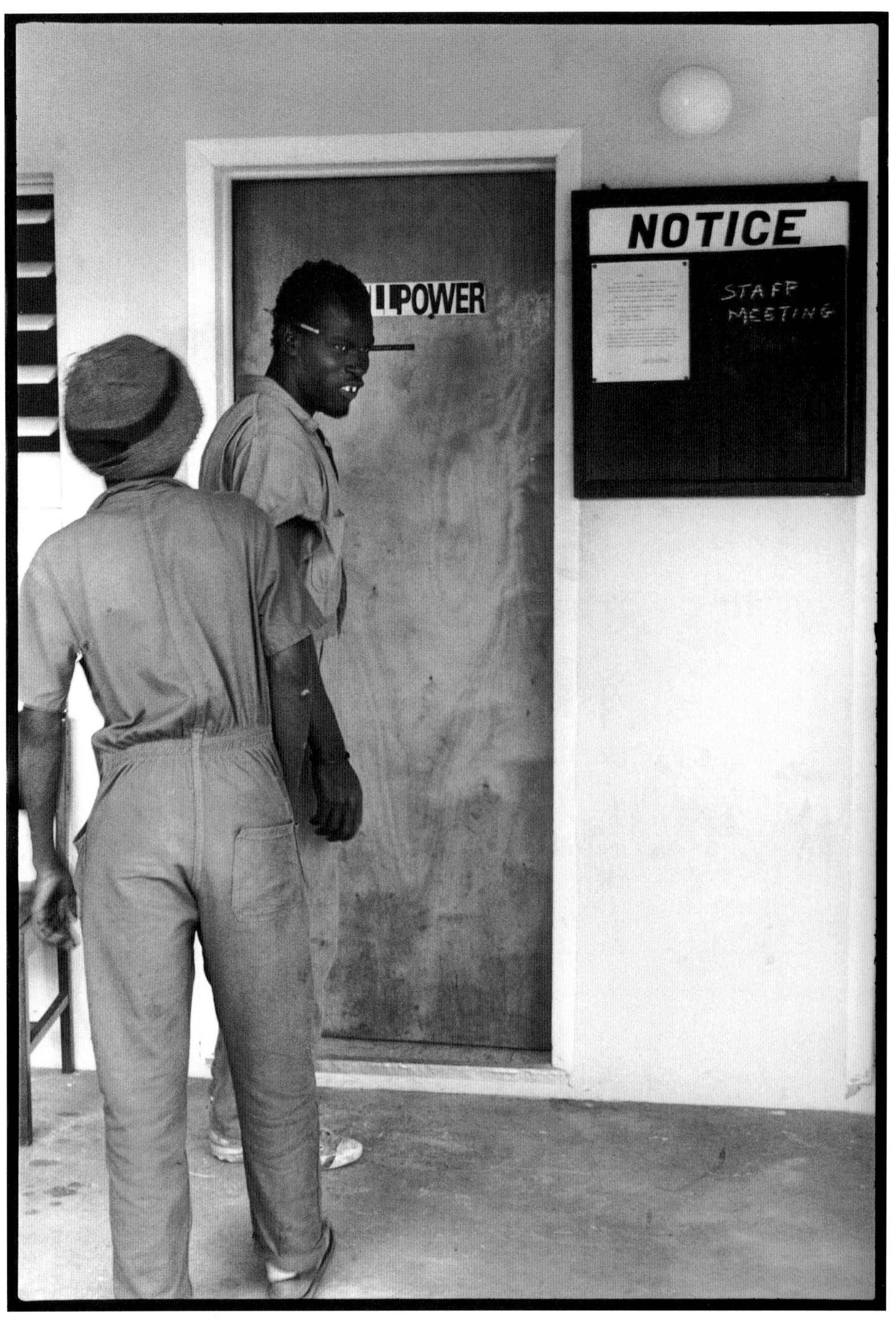
LLPOWER
NOTICE
STAFF
MEETING

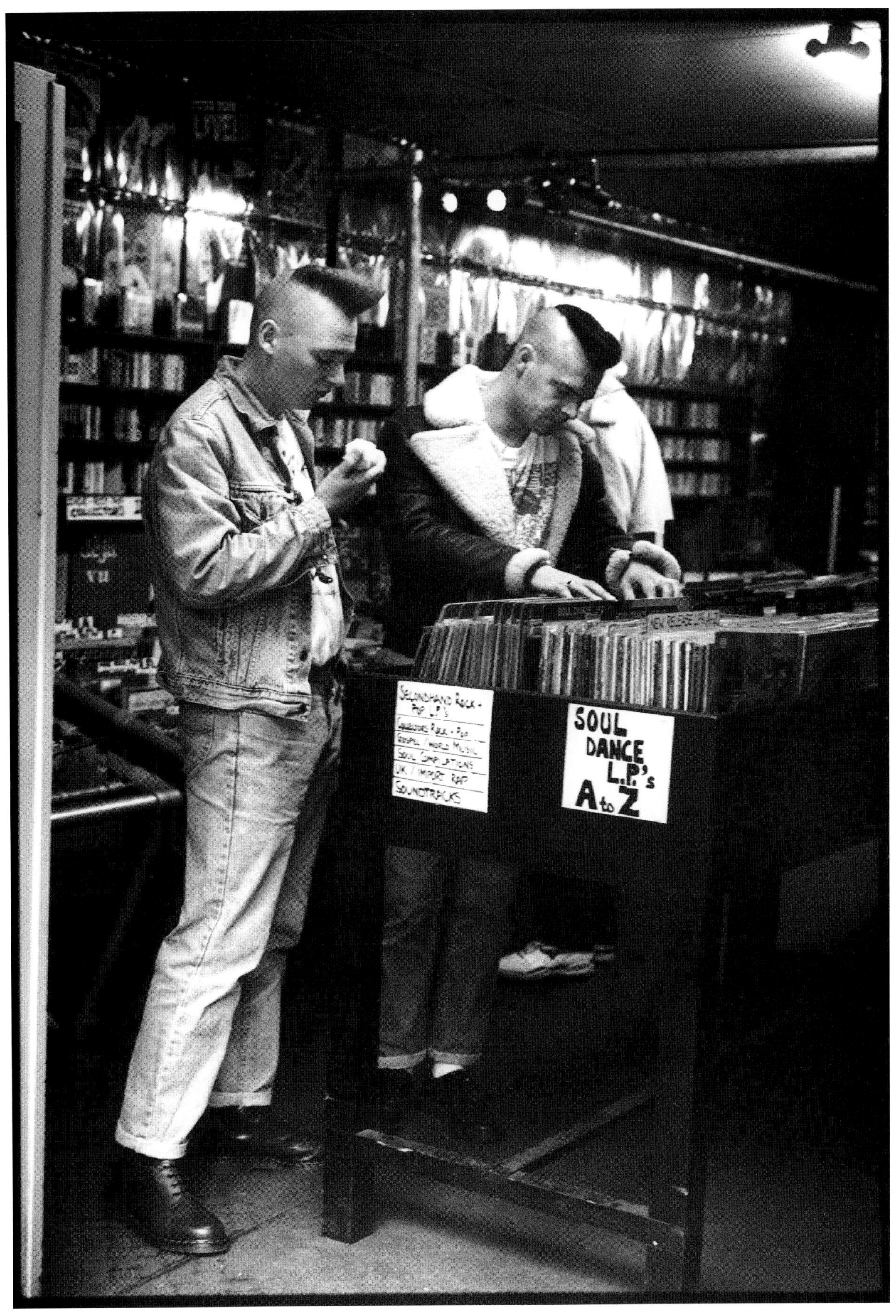
SECONDHAND ROCK + POP L.P.'s
ROCK + POP
GOSPEL / WORLD MUSIC
SOUL COMPILATIONS
UK / IMPORT RAP
SOUNDTRACKS
SOUL DANCE L.P.'s A to Z
NEW RELEASE

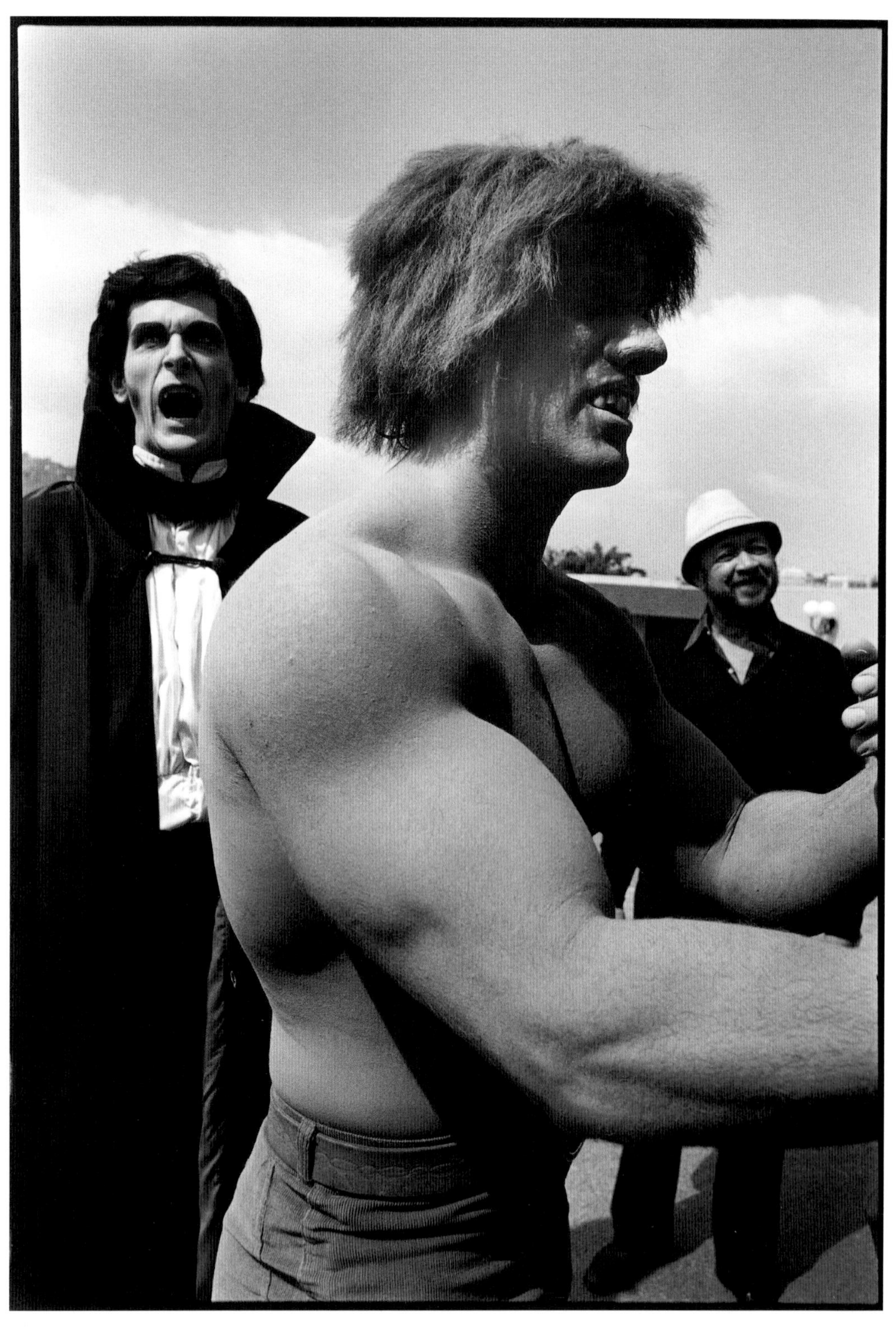

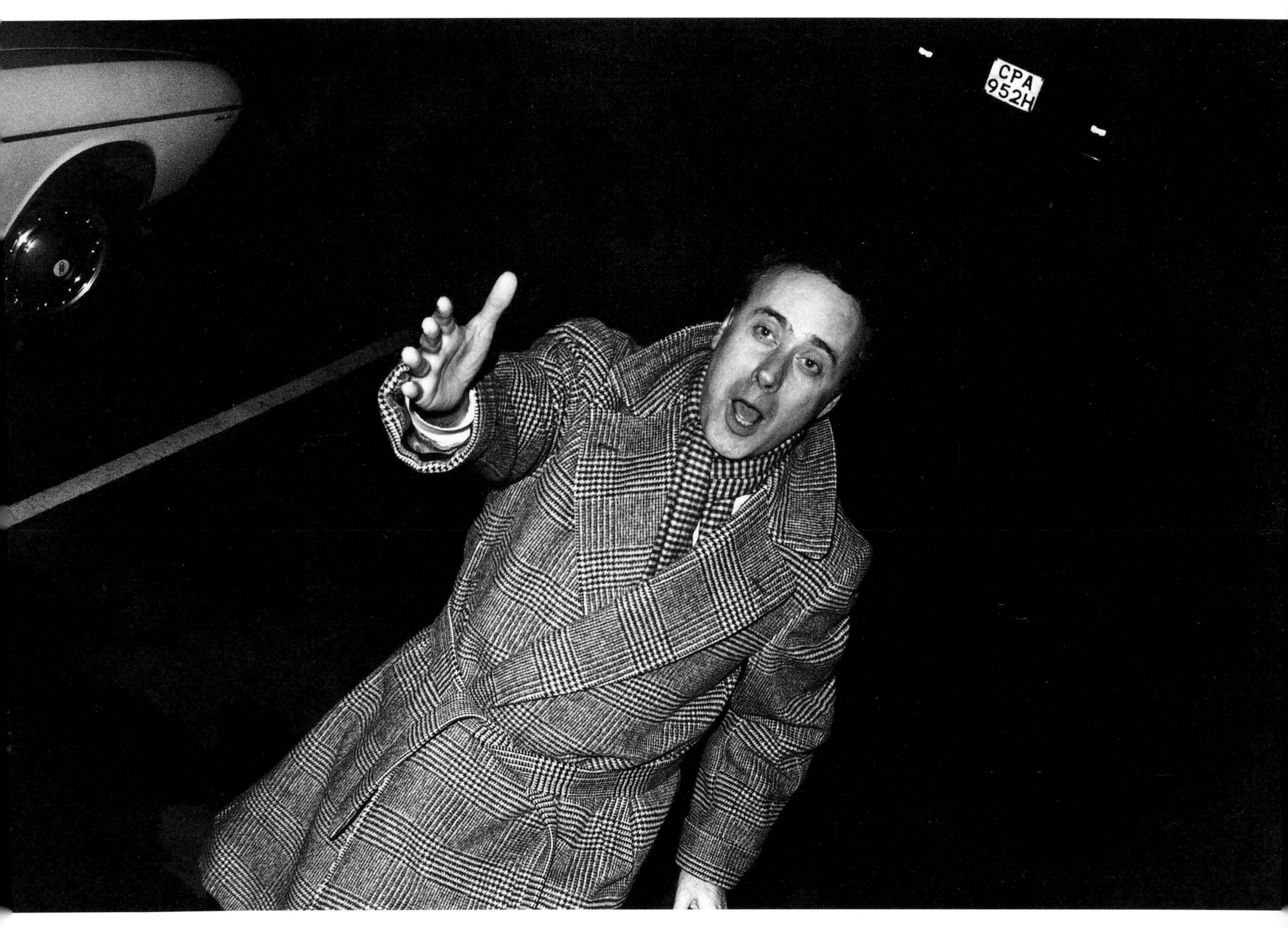
CPA
952H

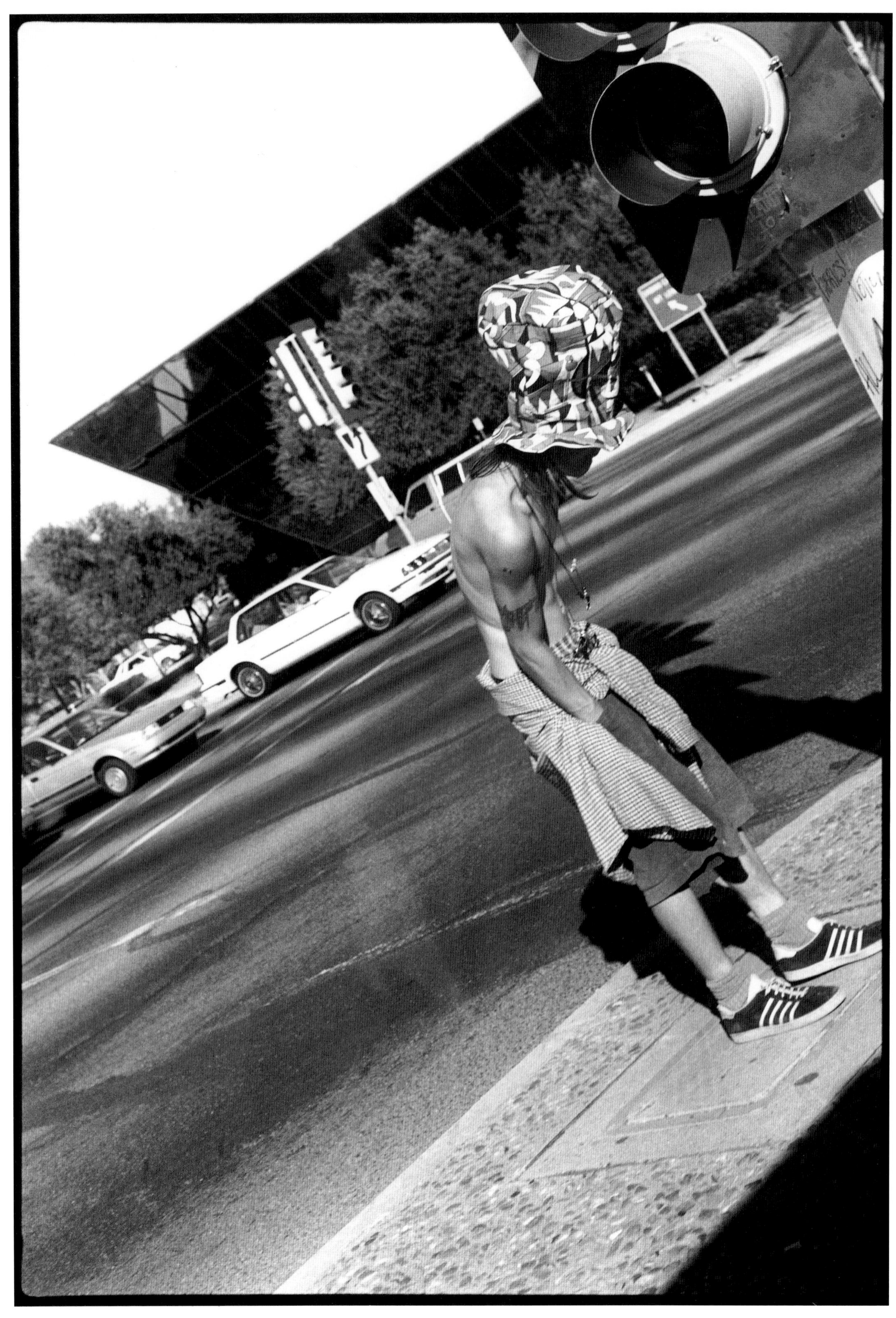

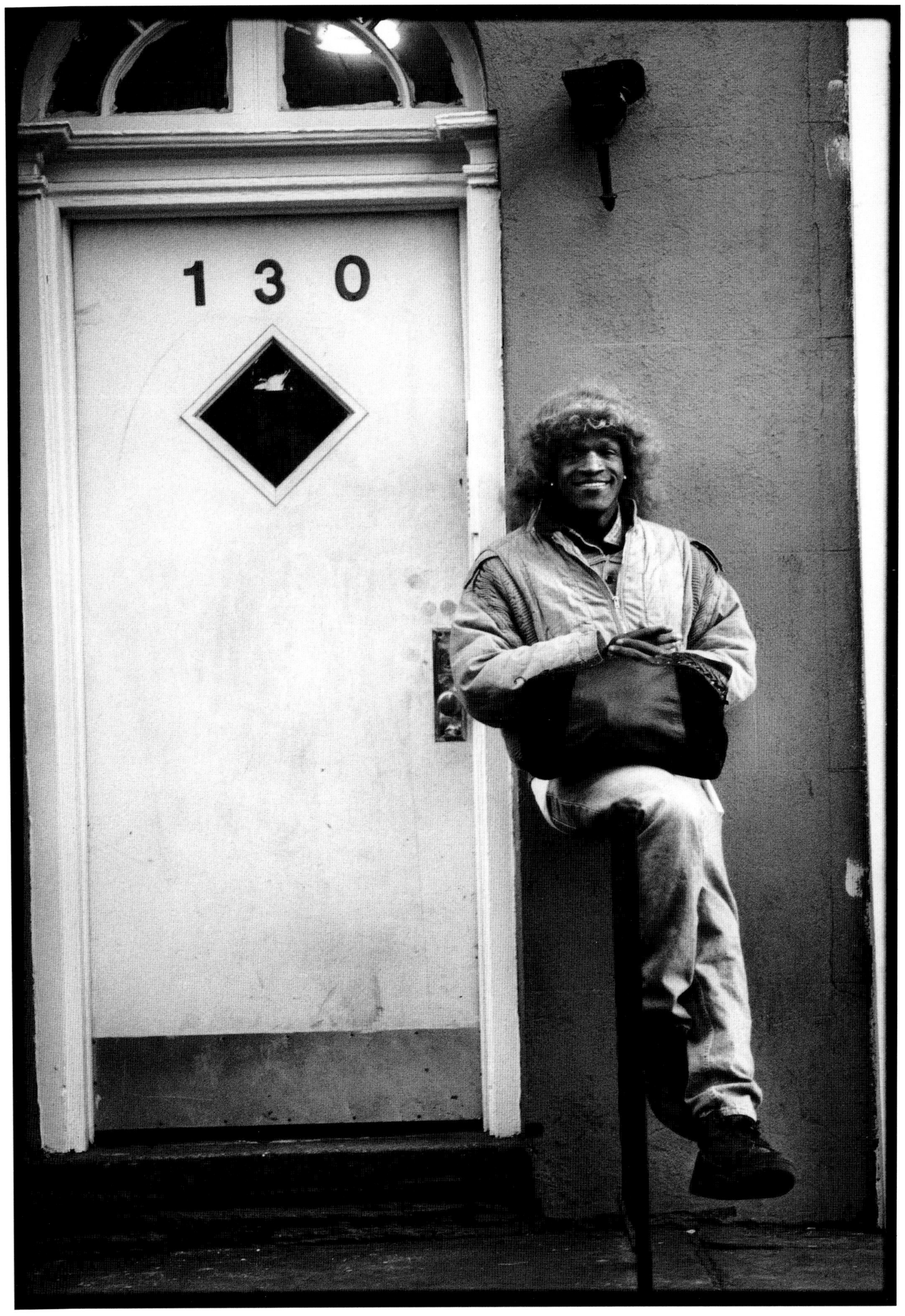
130

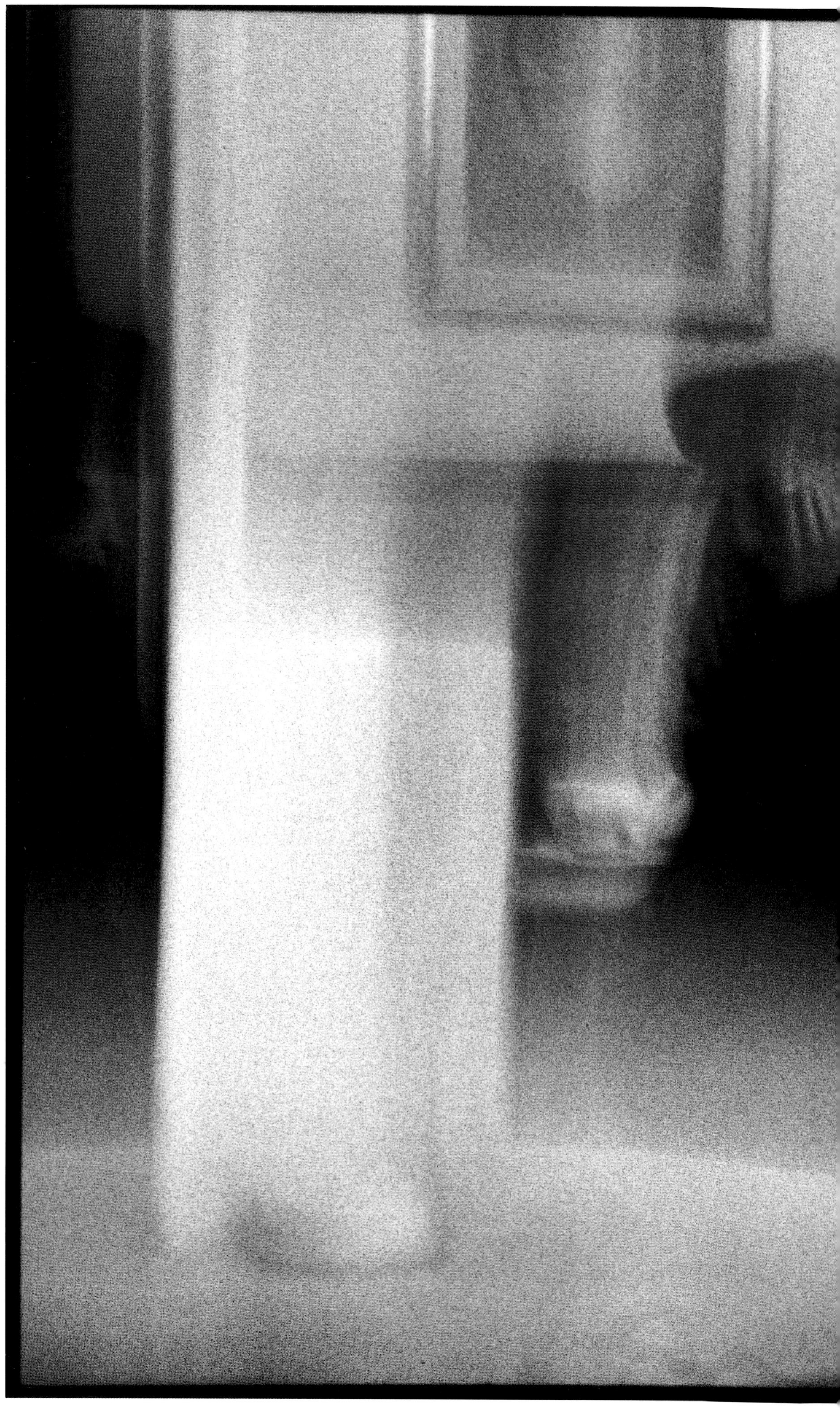

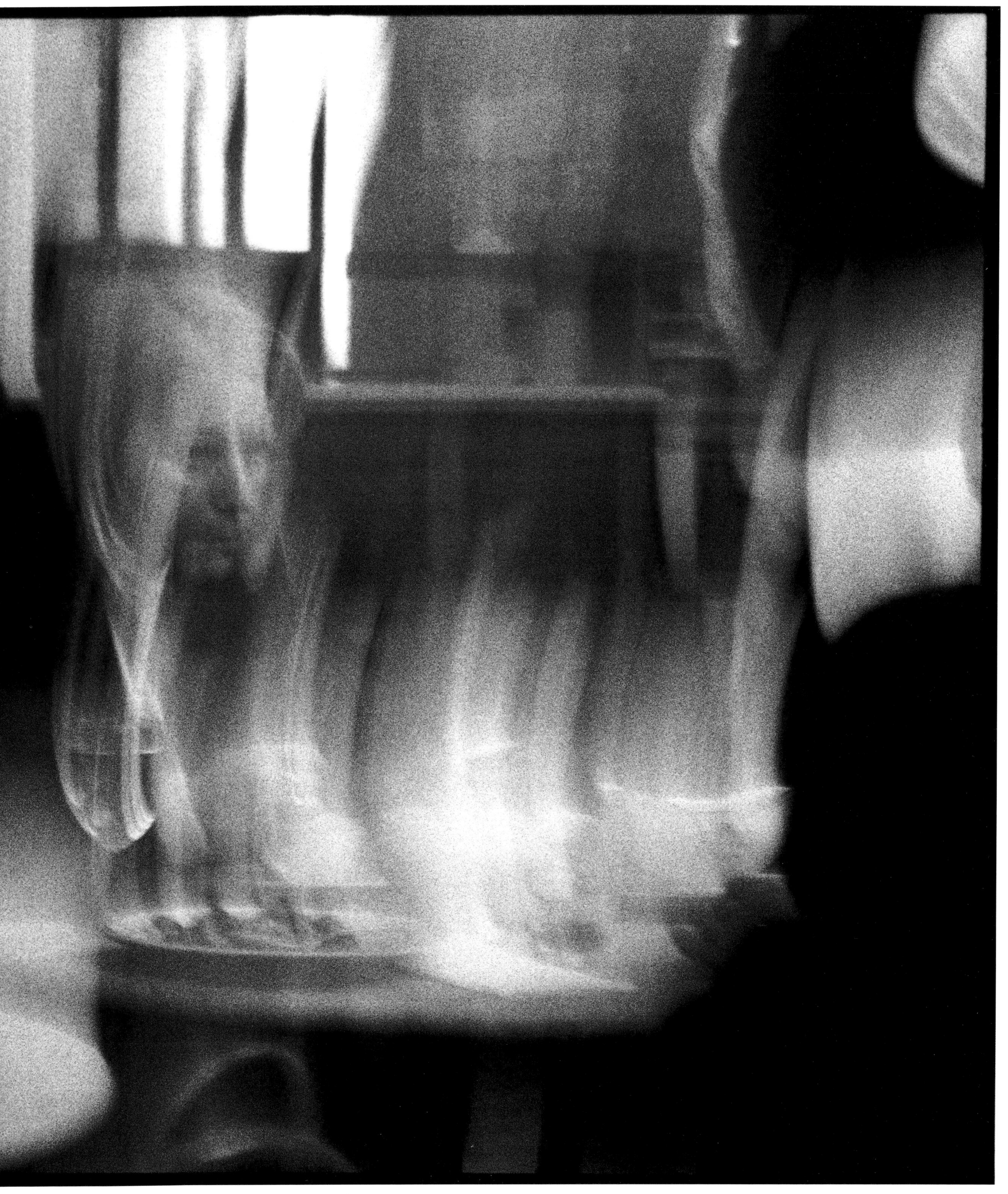

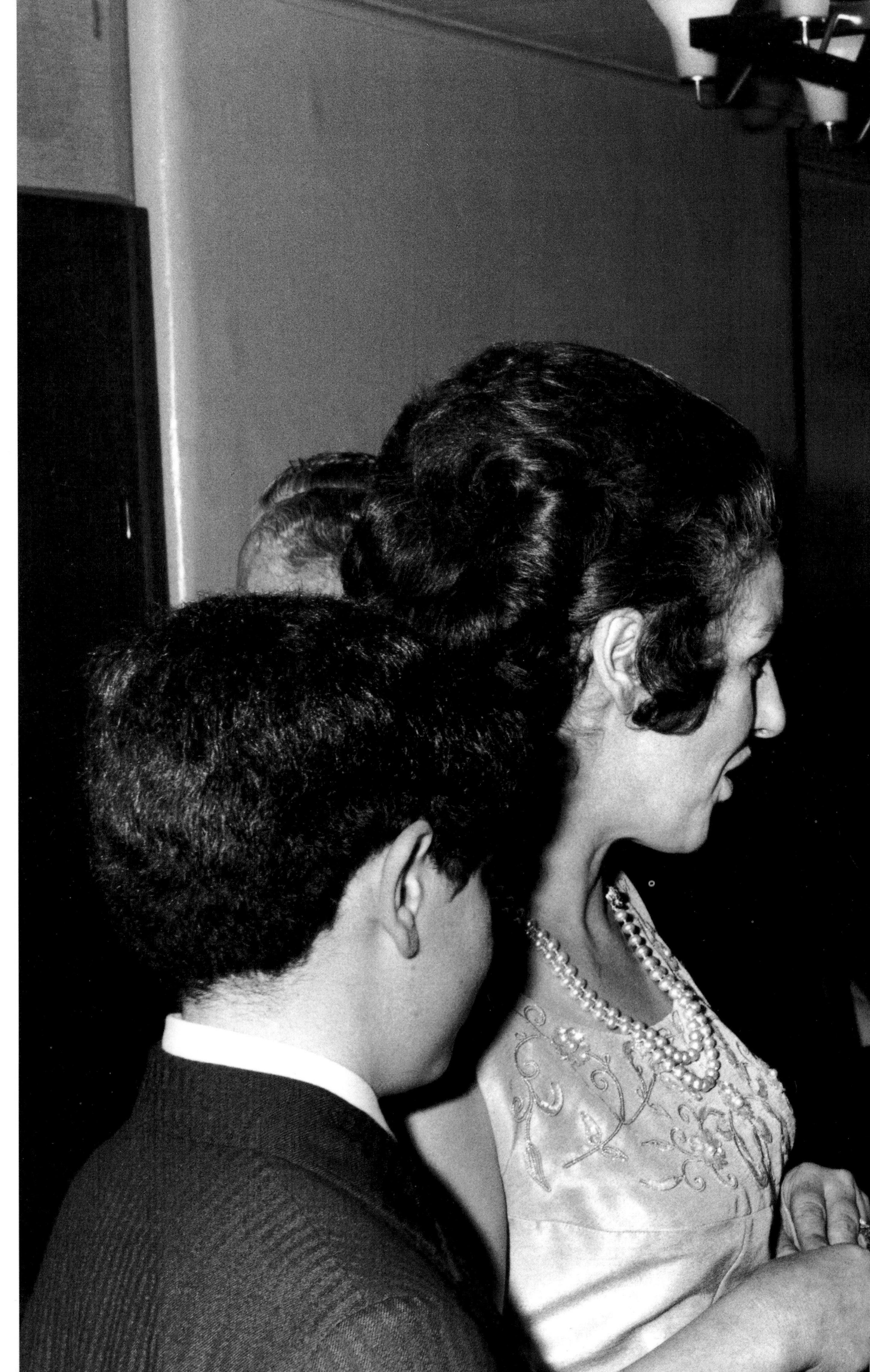

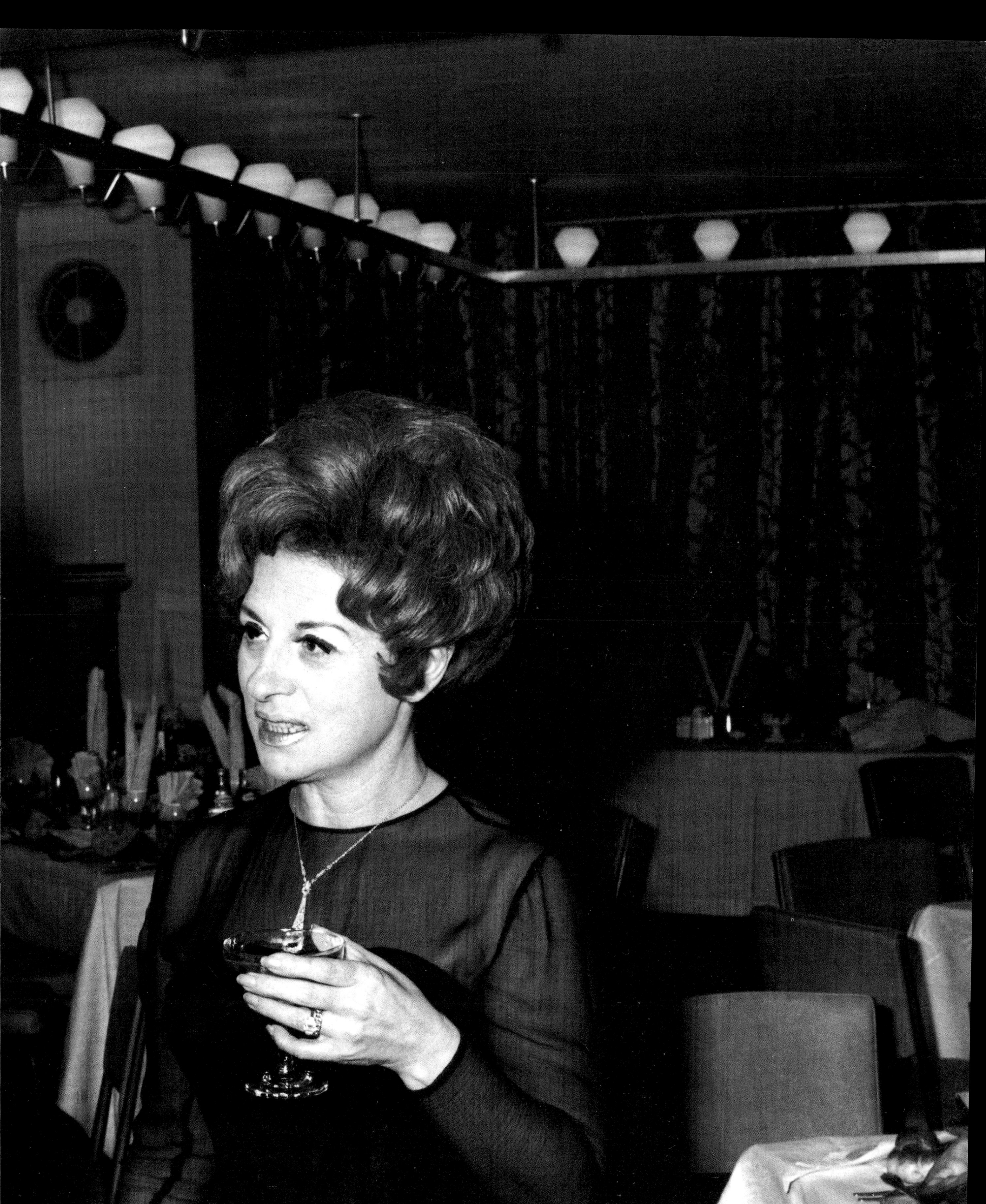

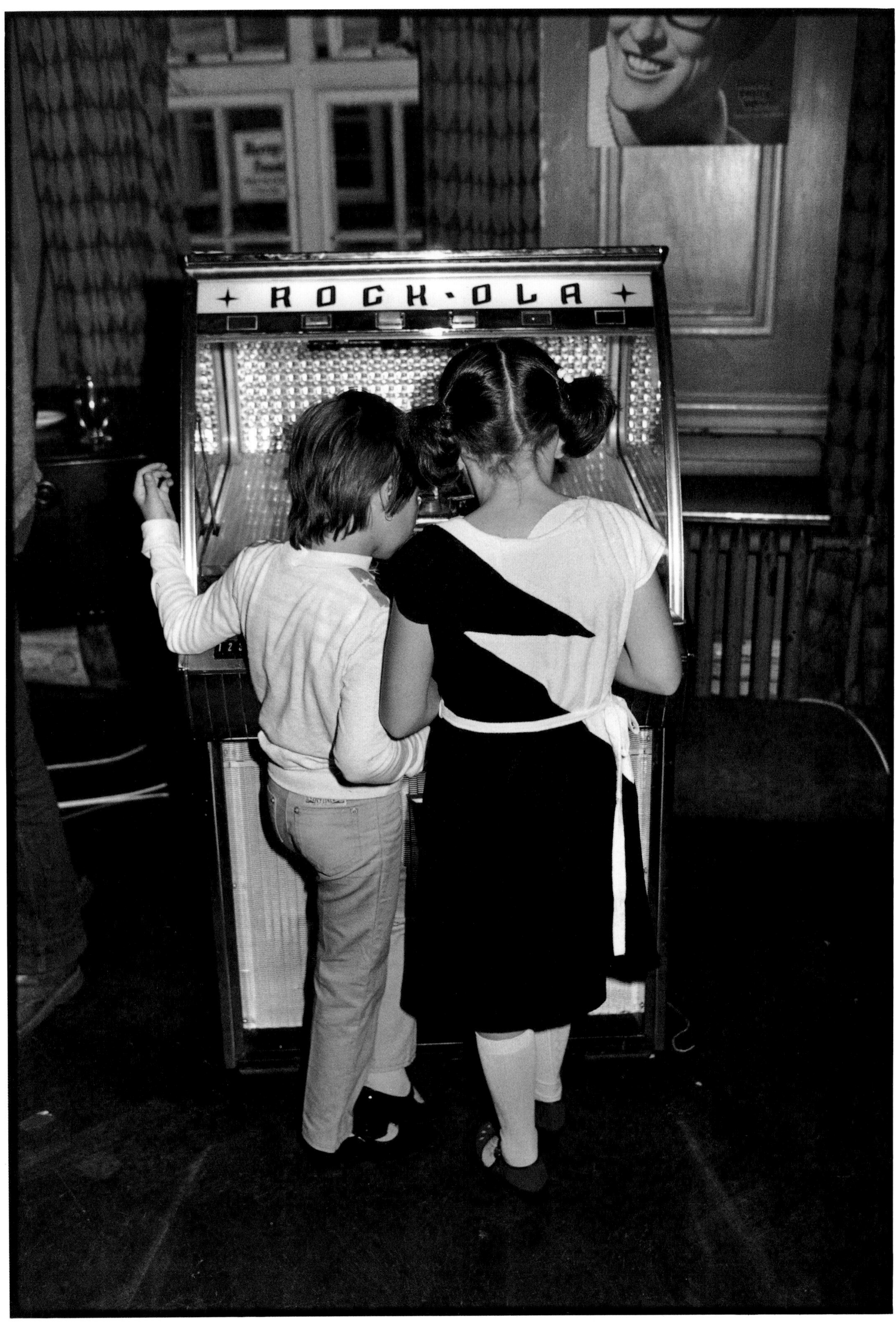
ROCK·OLA

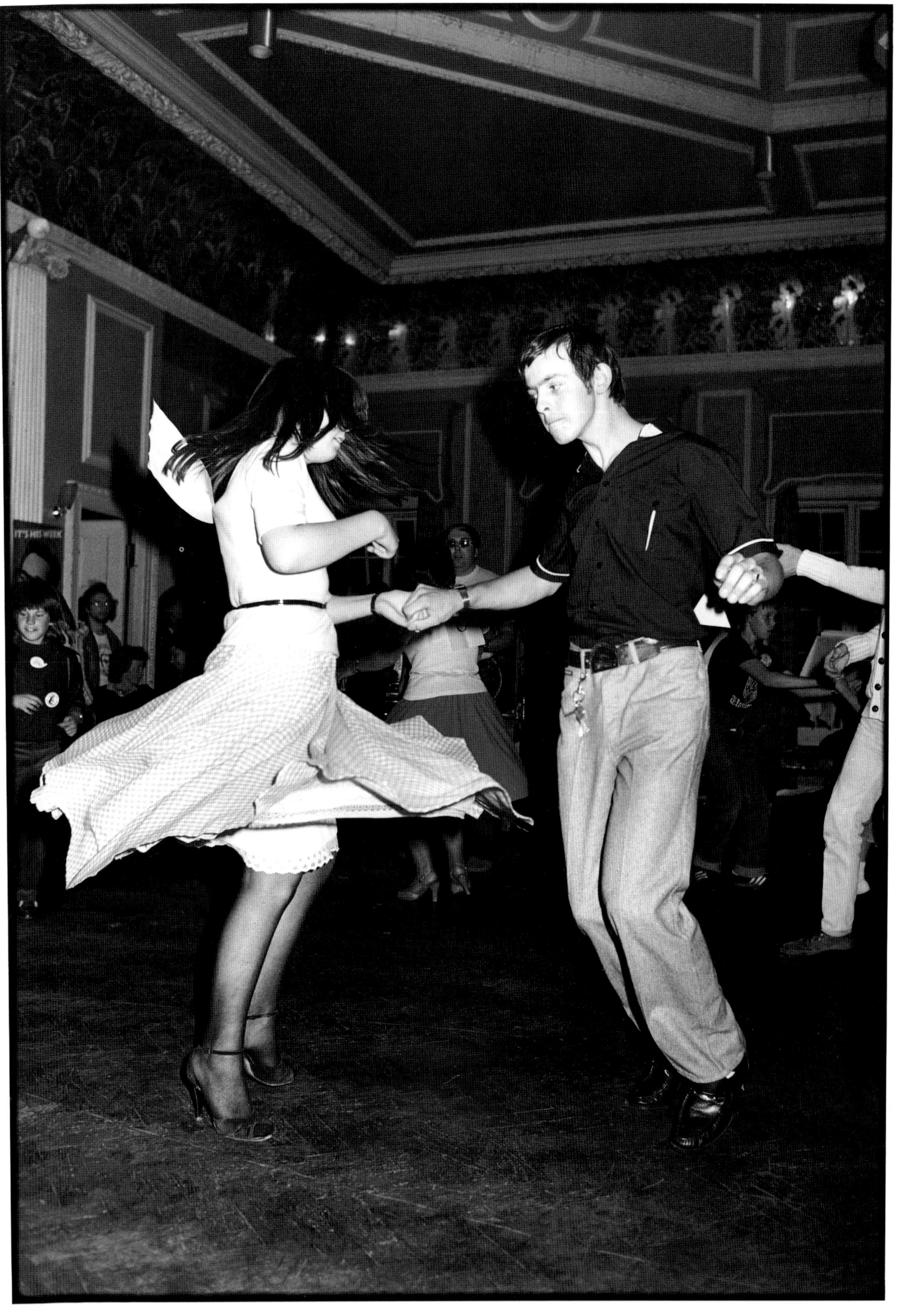

Constant traveling, rehearsals, preparation —
hurry up and wait

On The road again

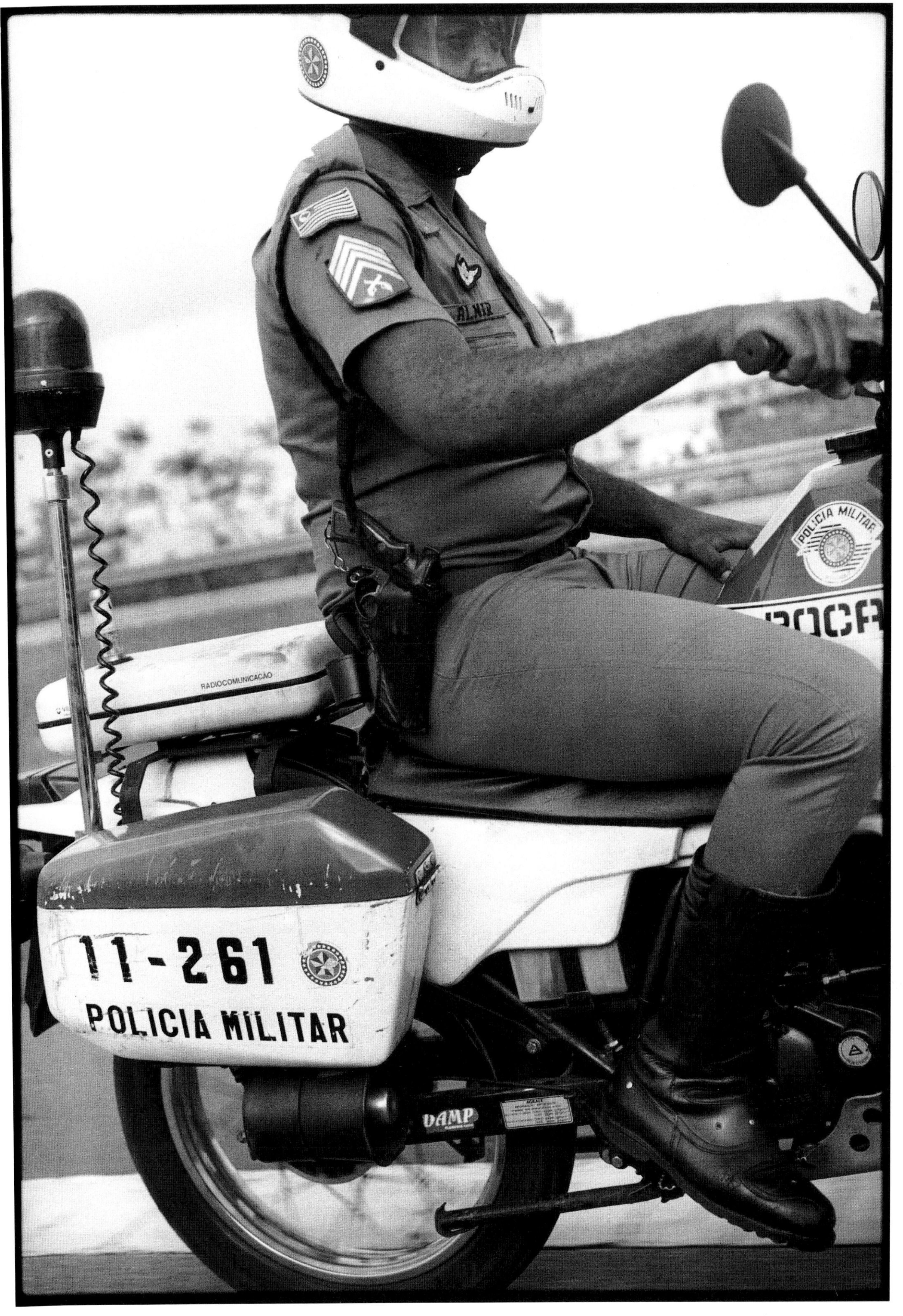
11-261
POLICIA MILITAR
POLICIA MILITAR
RADIOCOMUNICAÇÃO

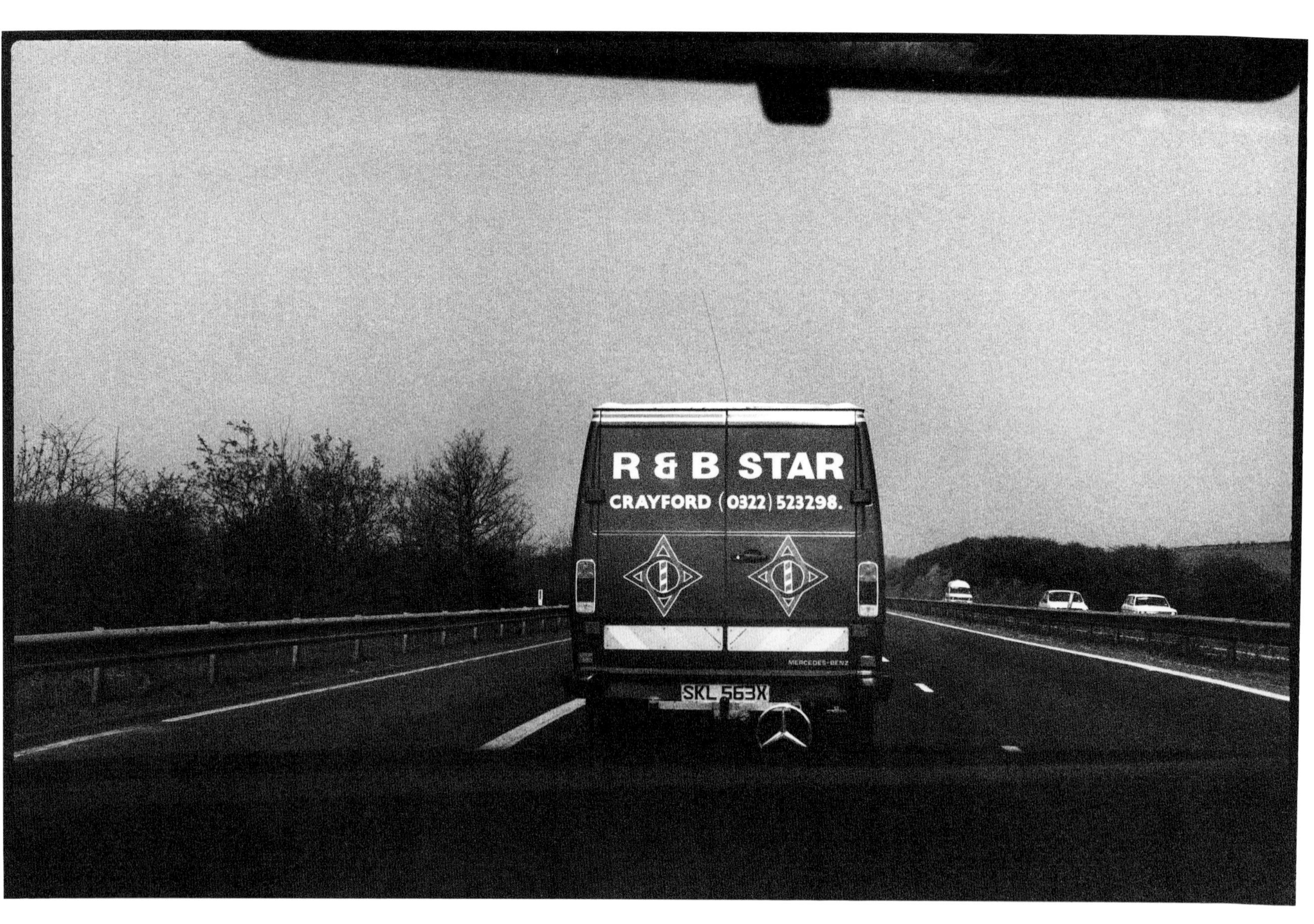
R & B STAR
CRAYFORD (0322) 523298.
SKL 563X

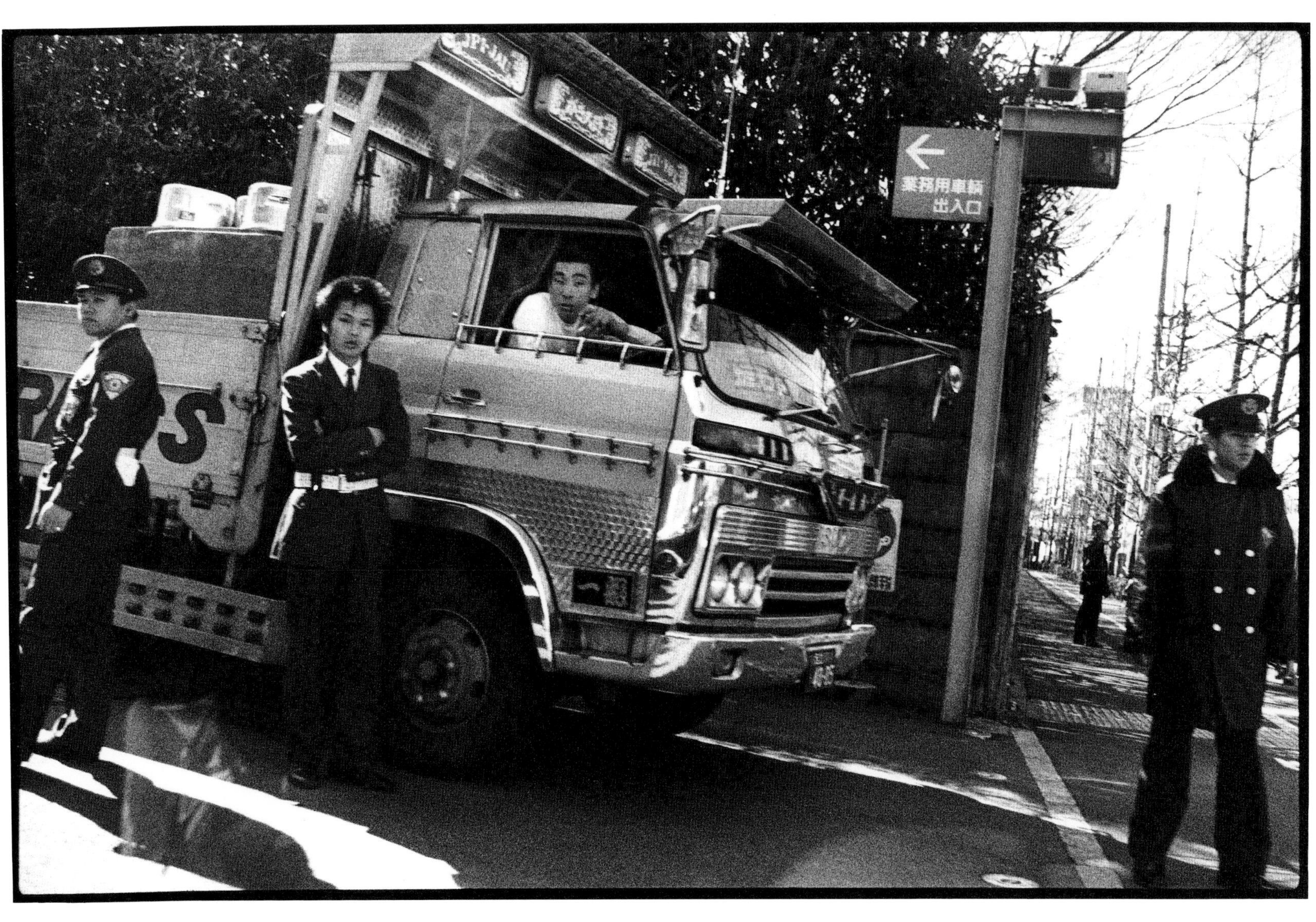
業務用車輌
出入口

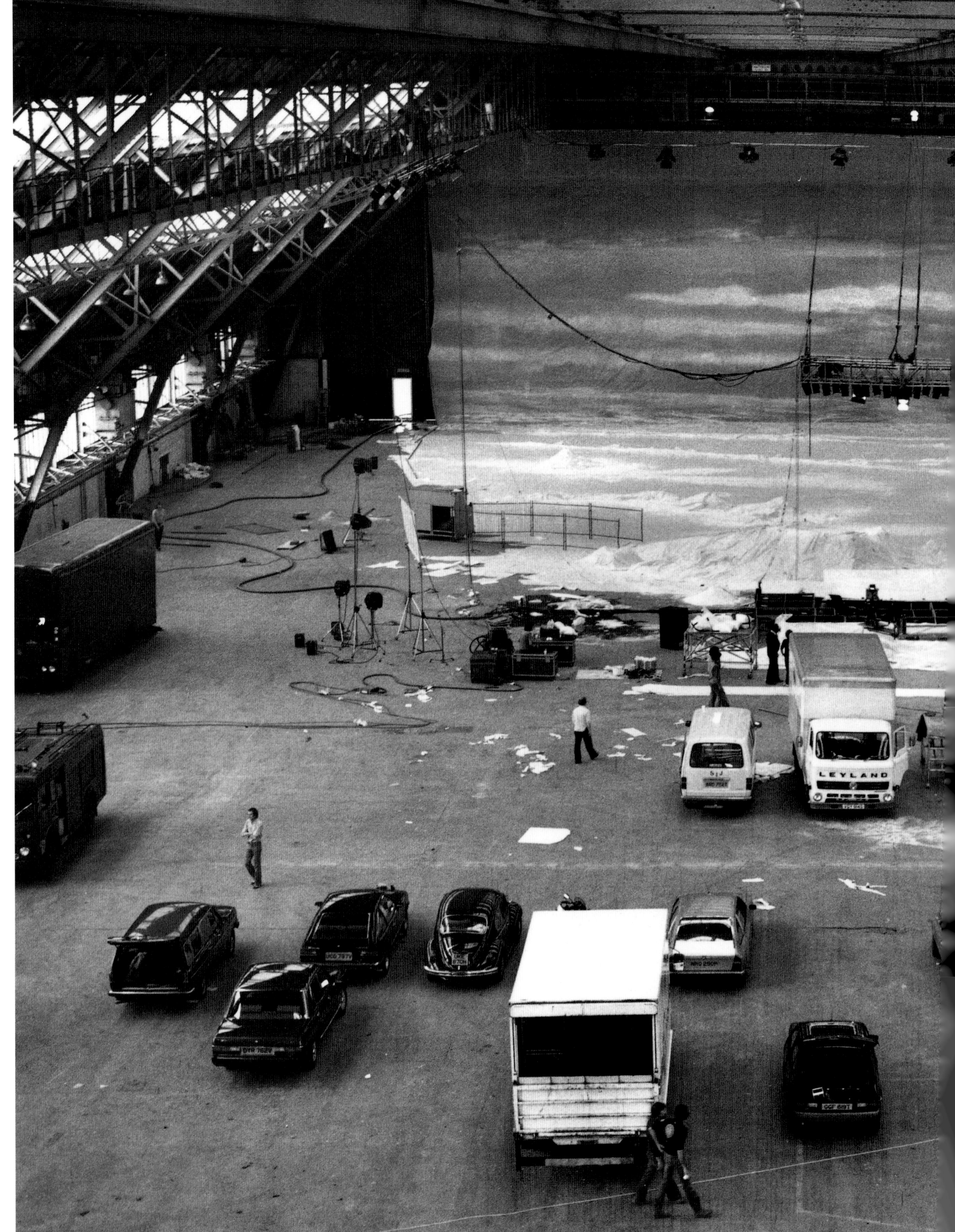
LEYLAND

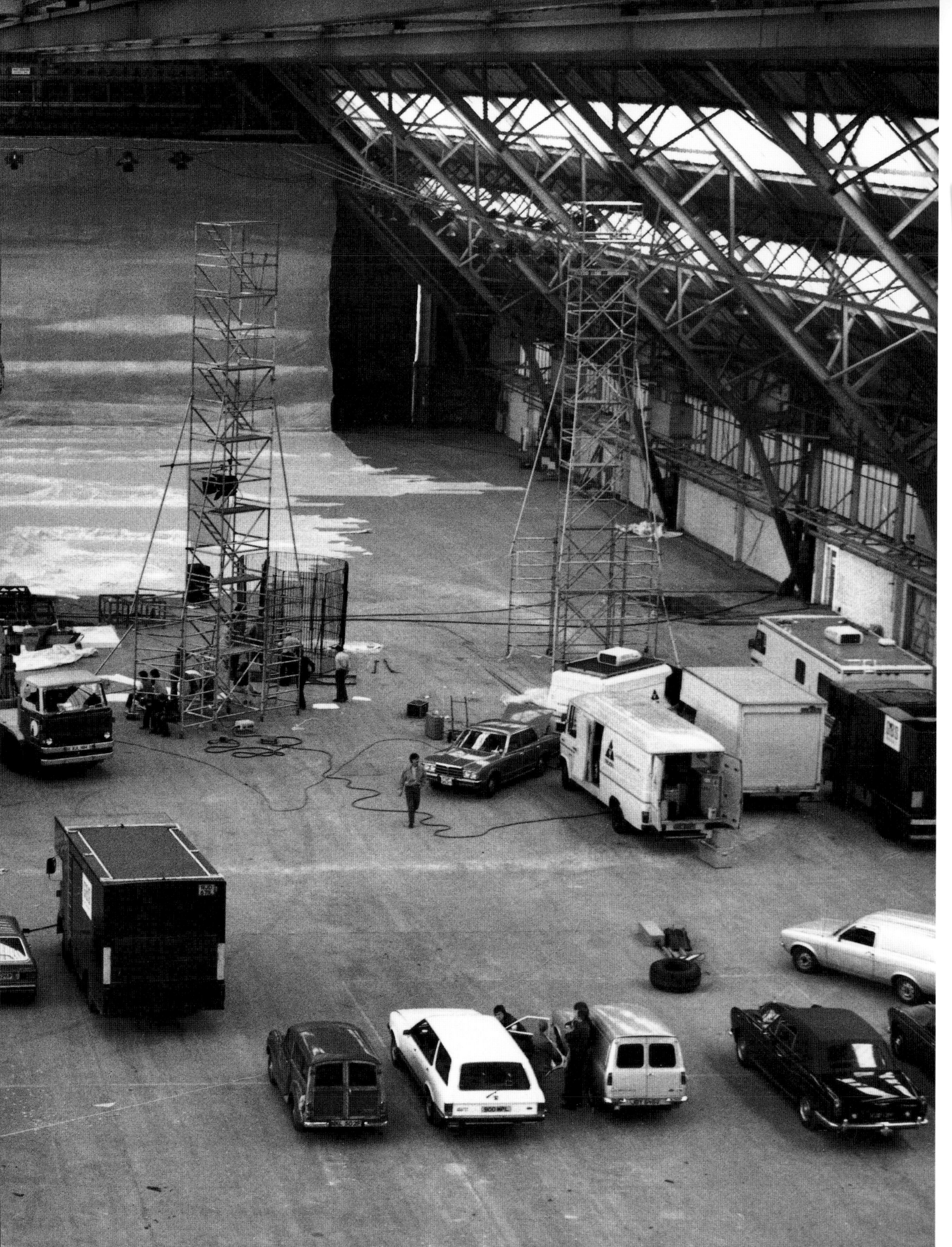

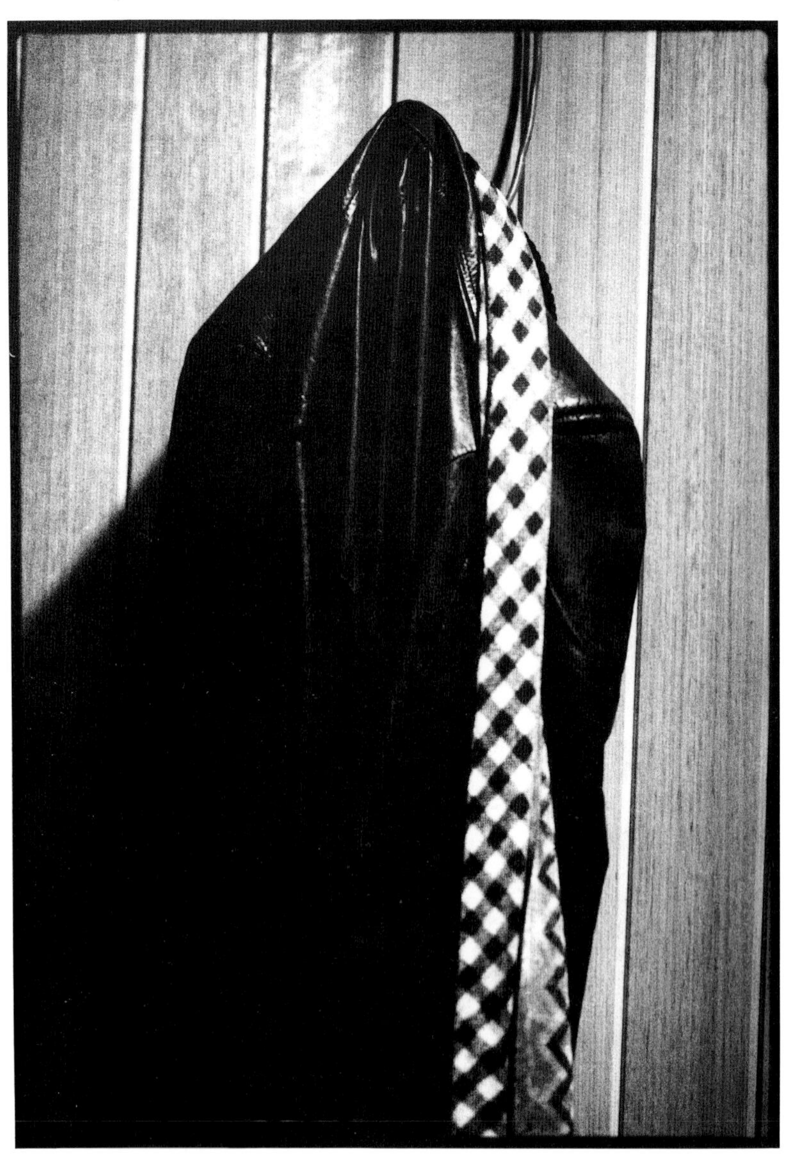

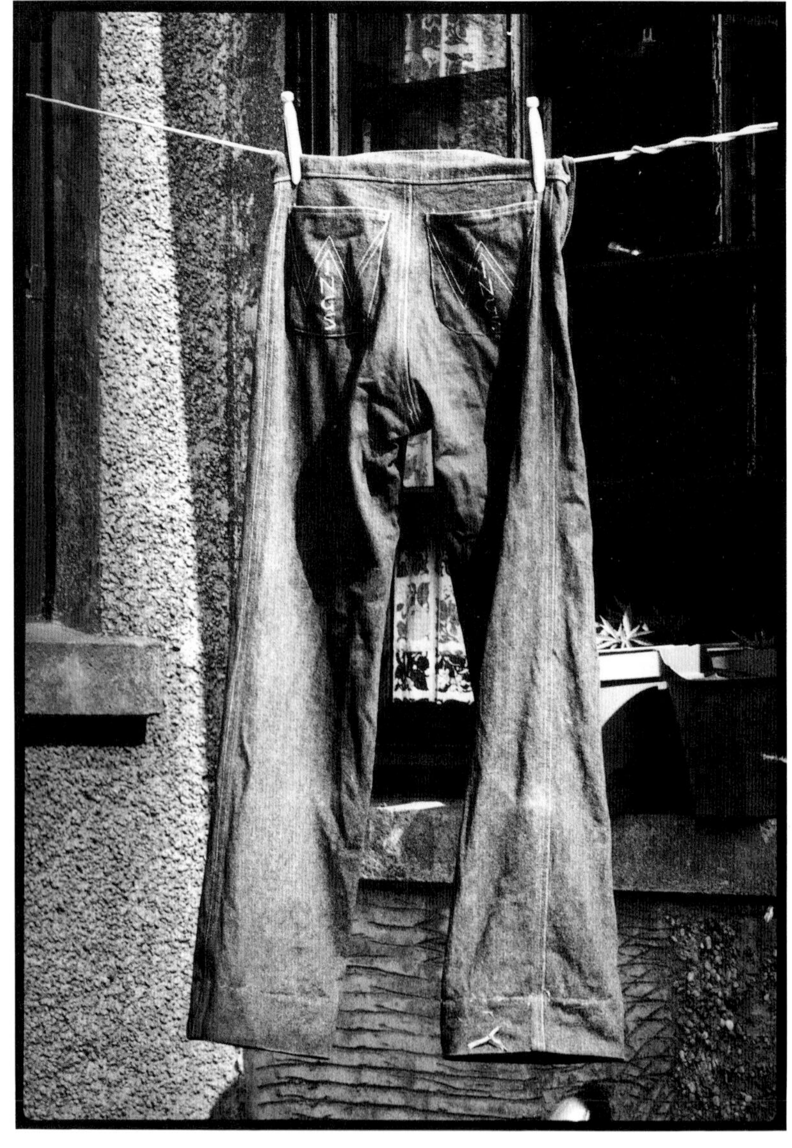

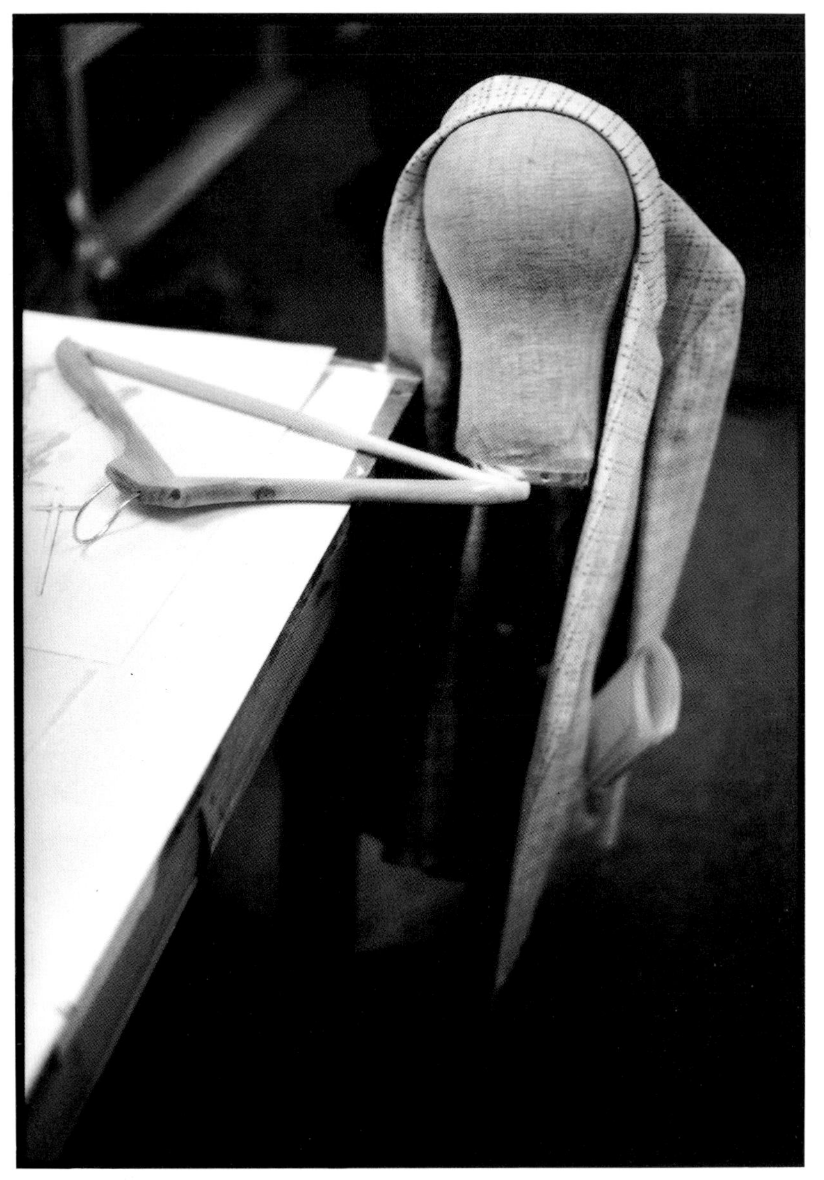

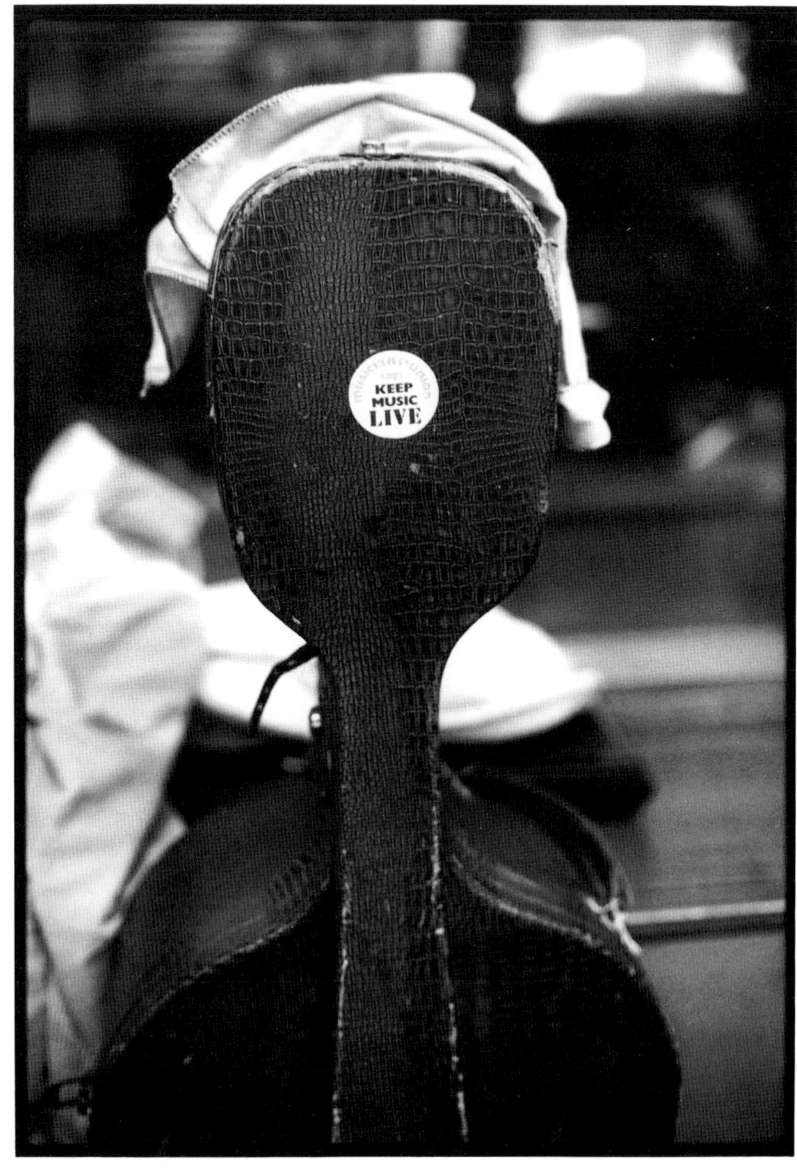
KEEP
MUSIC
LIVE

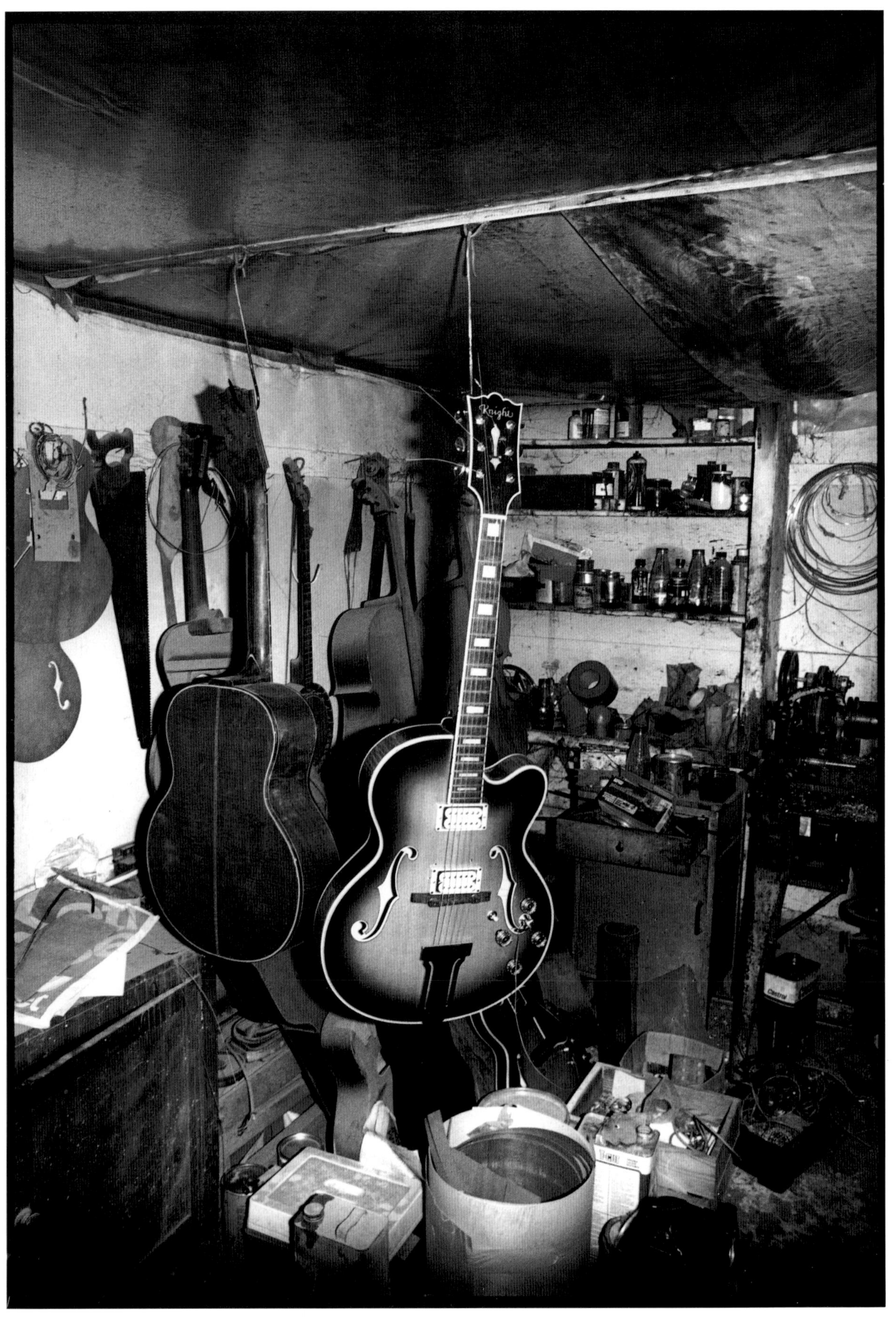
Knight

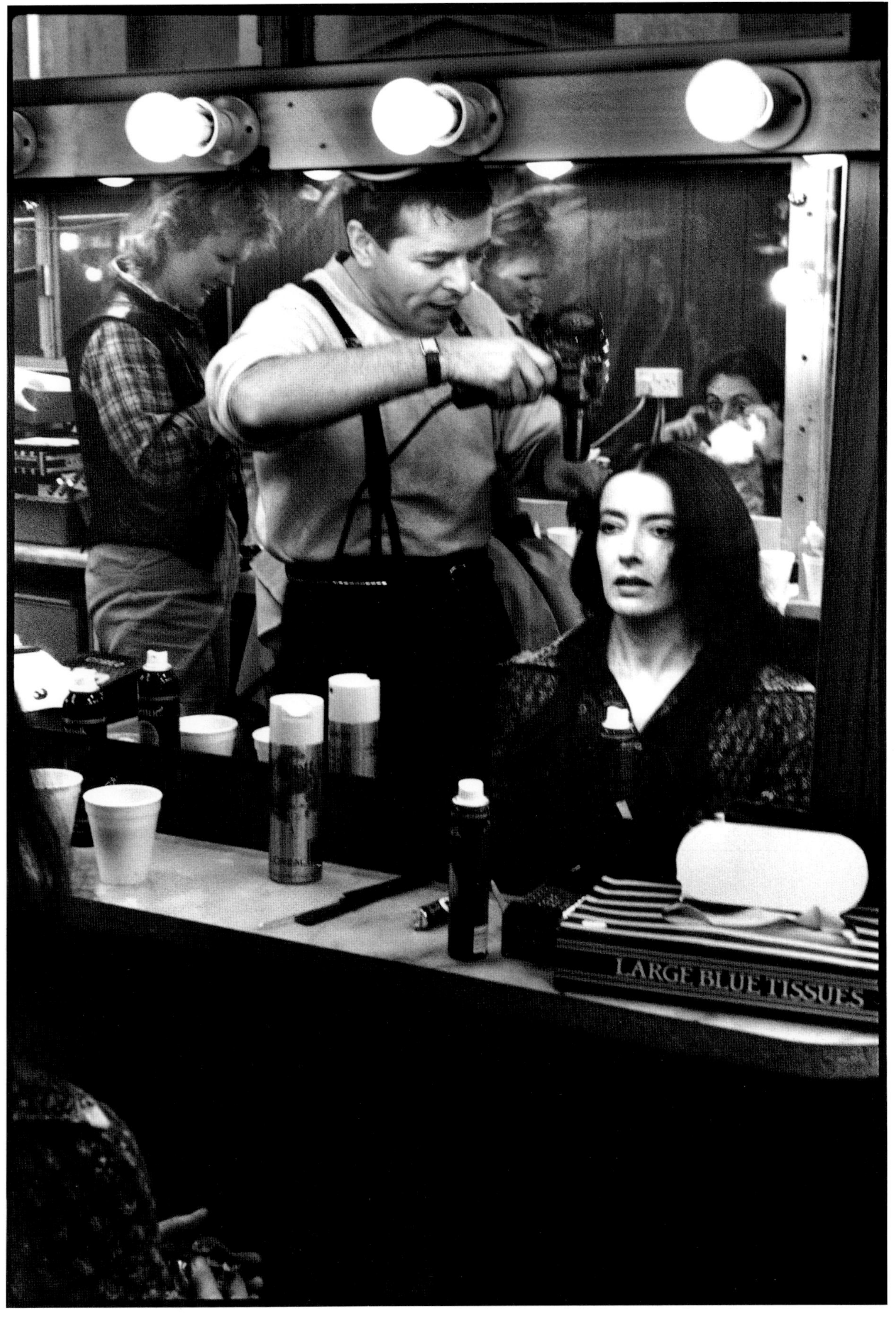
LARGE BLUE TISSUES

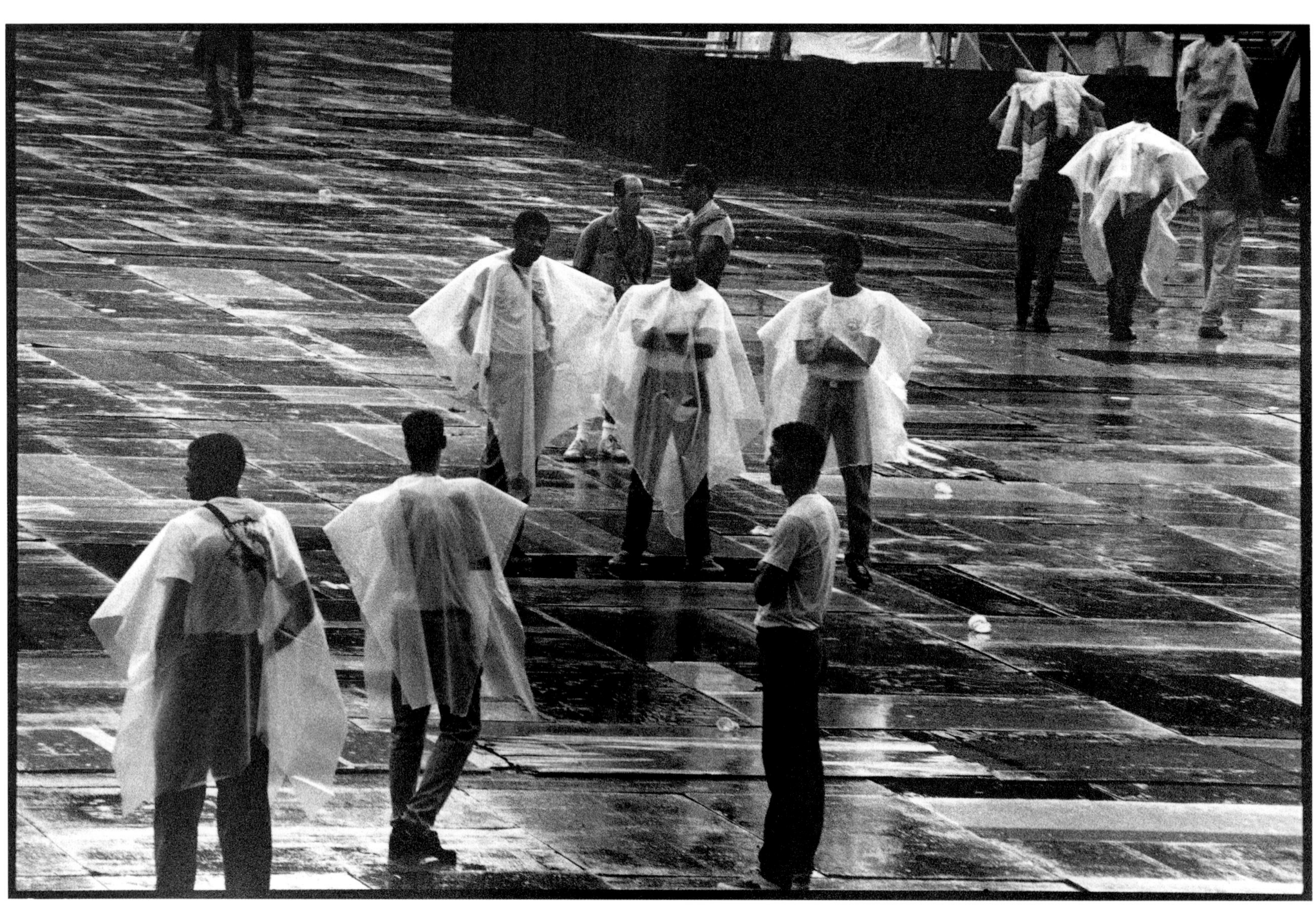

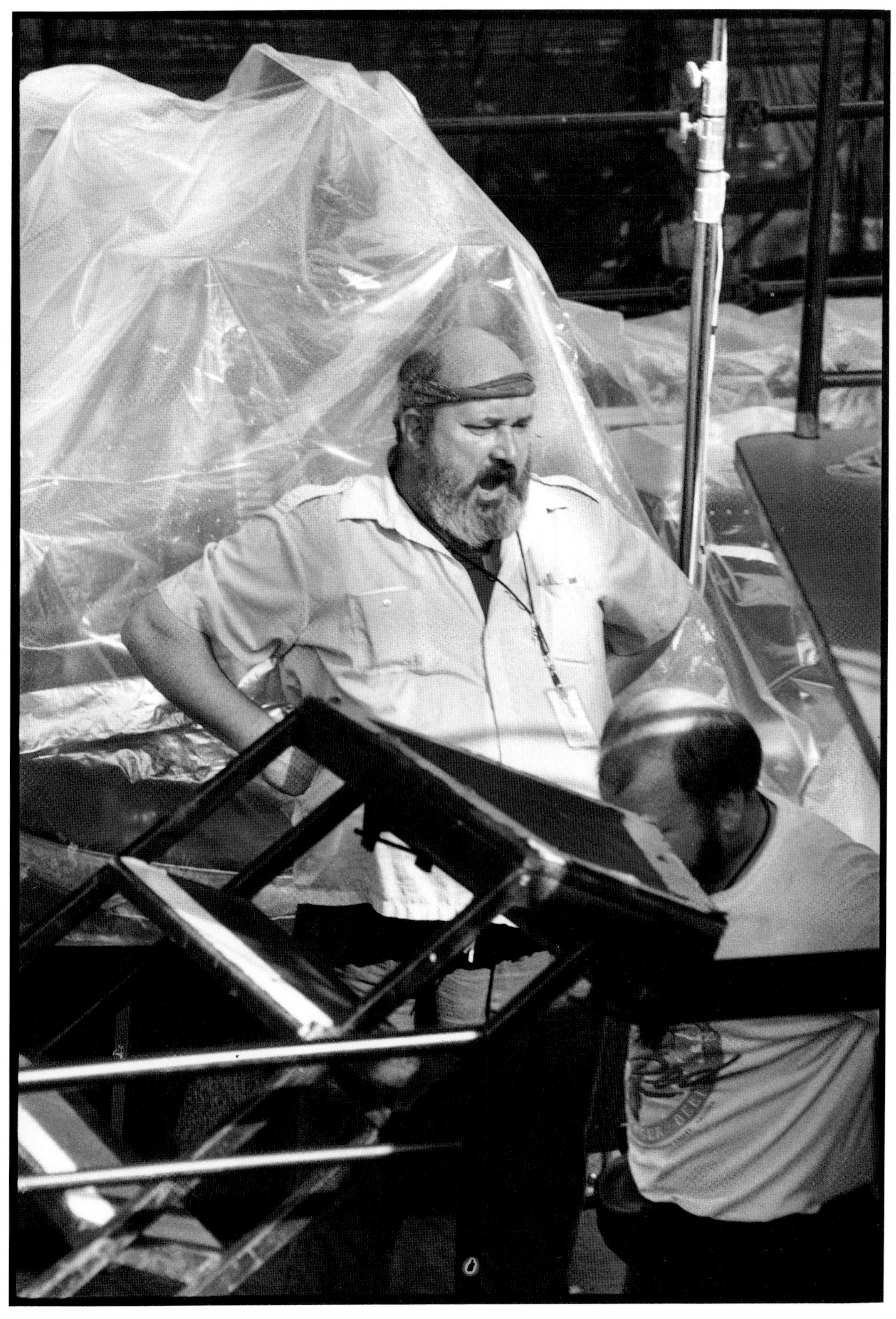

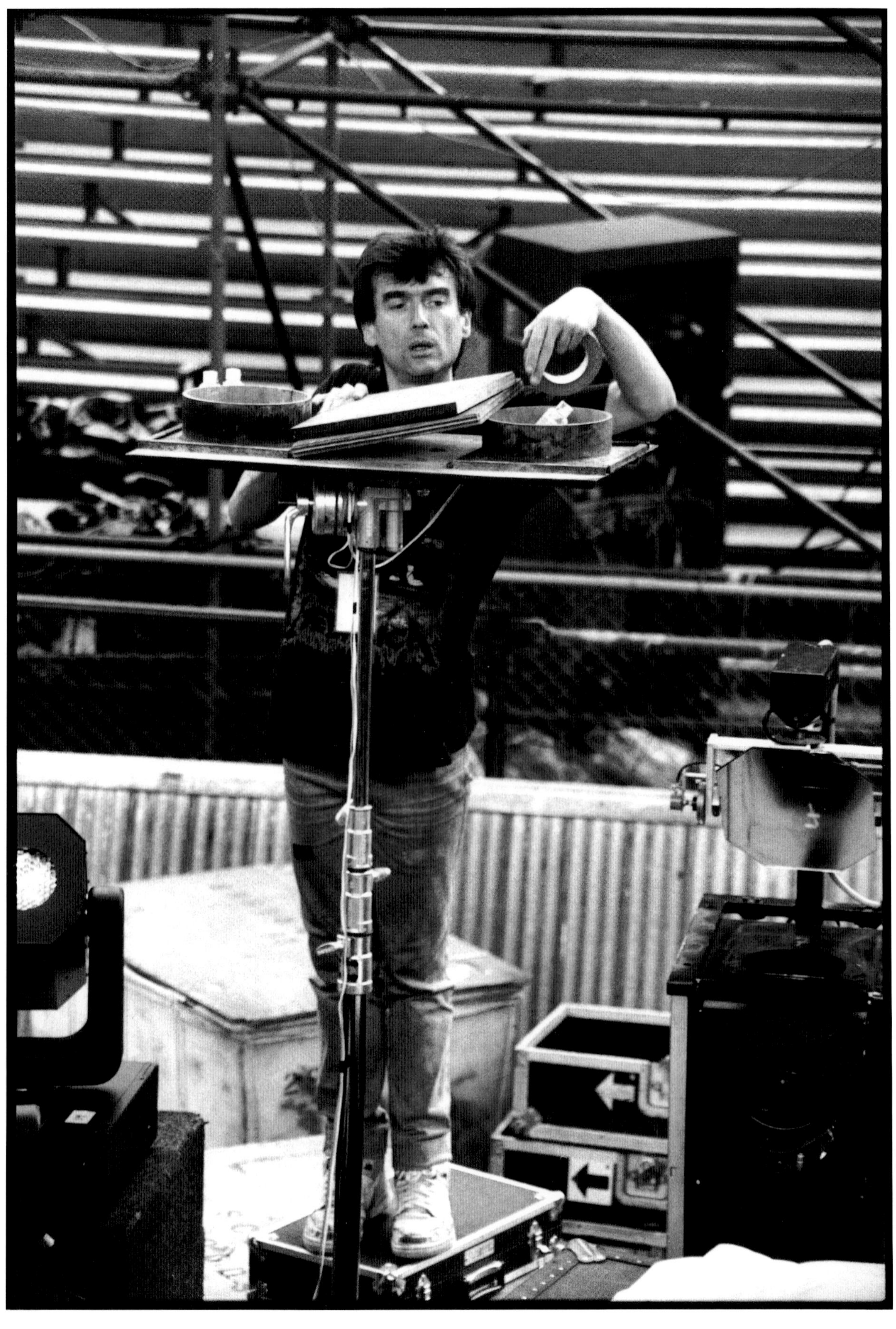

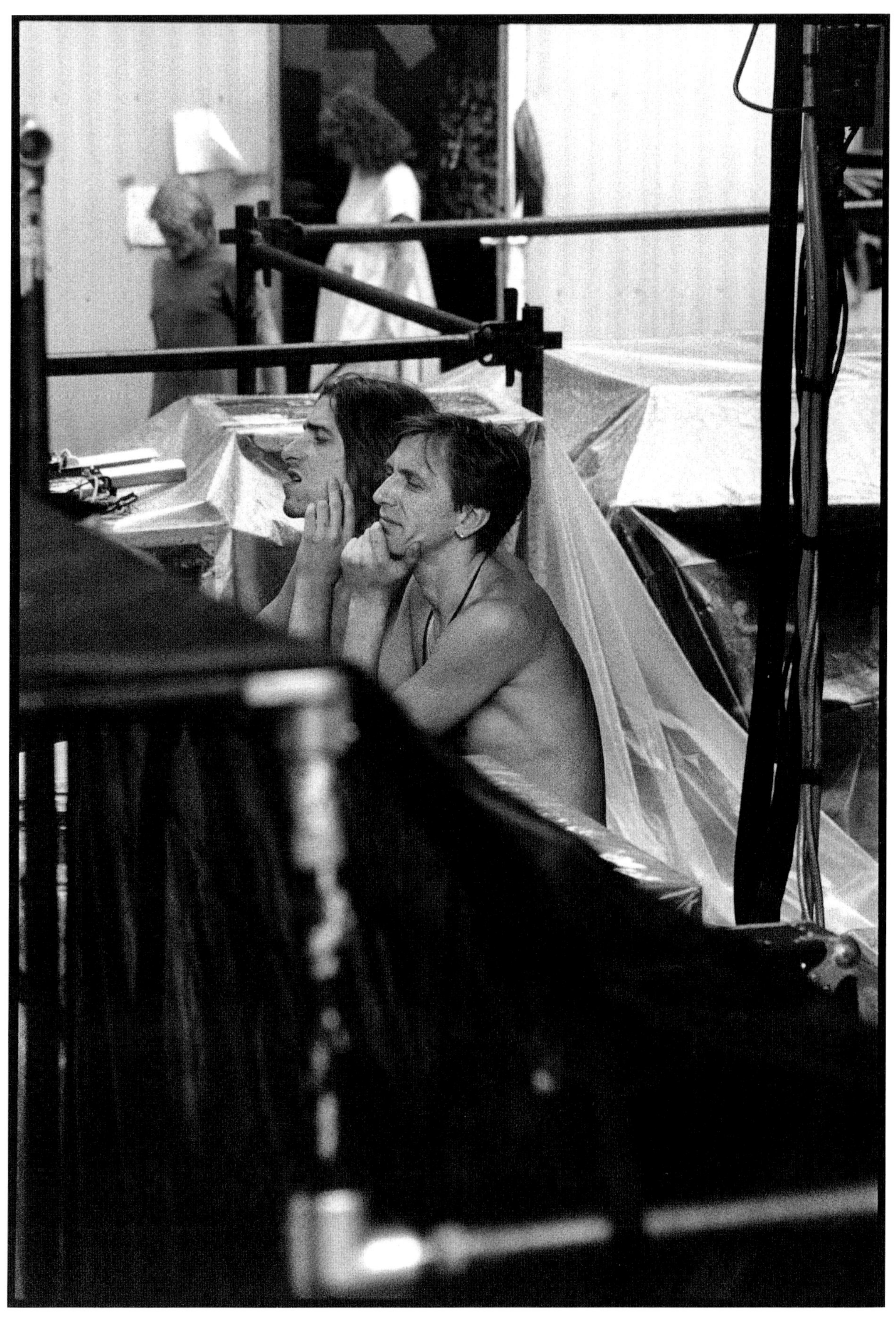

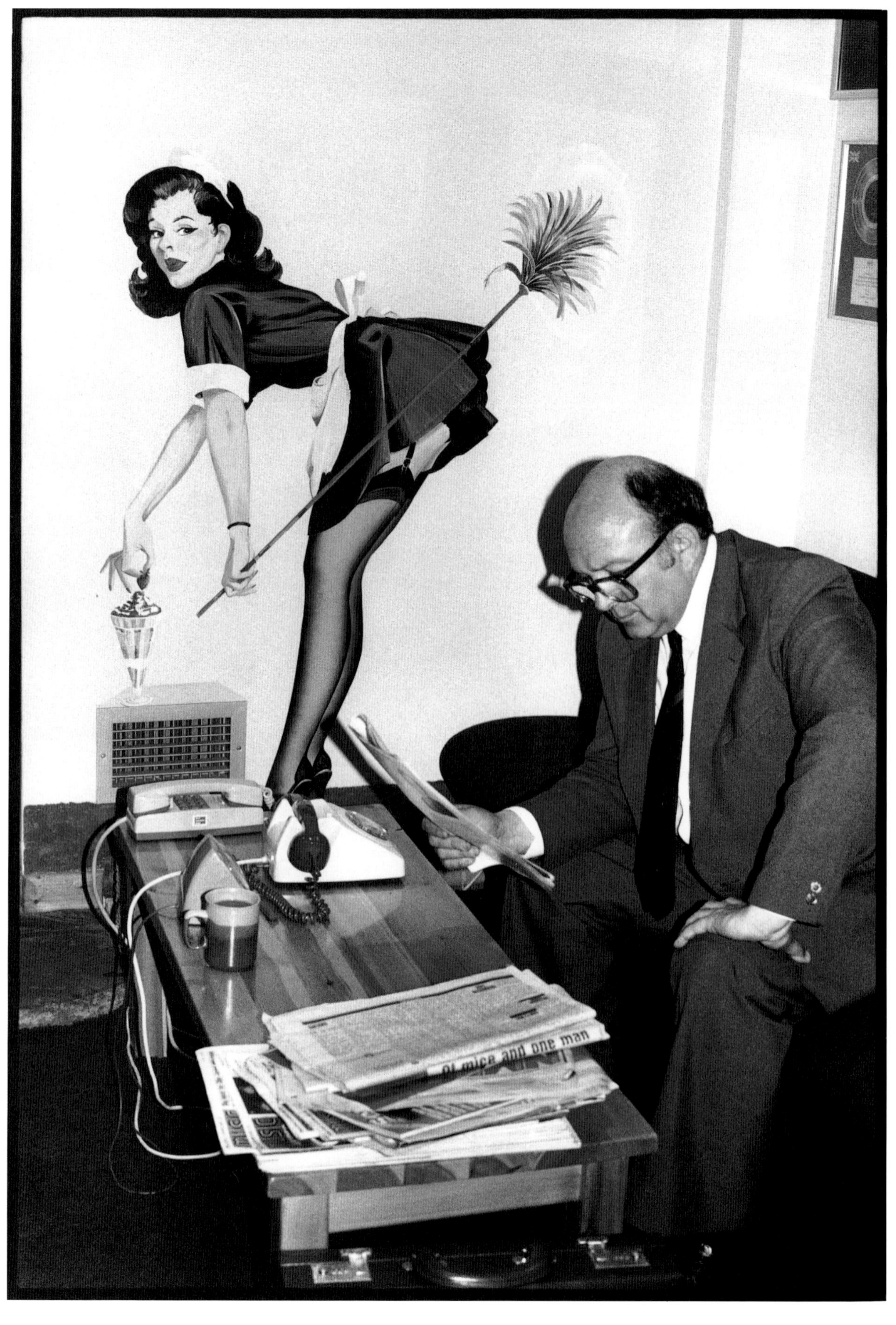
of mice and one man

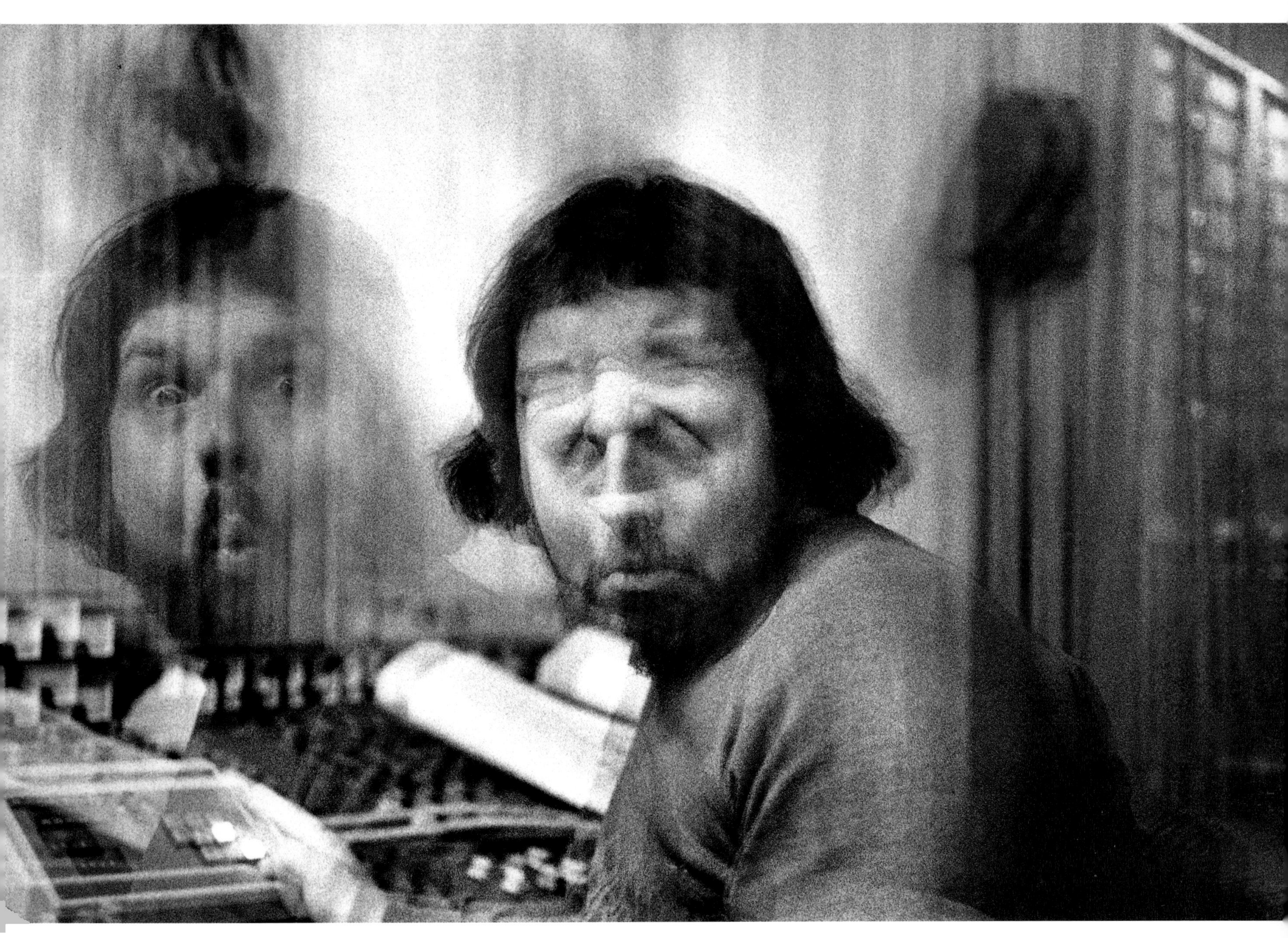

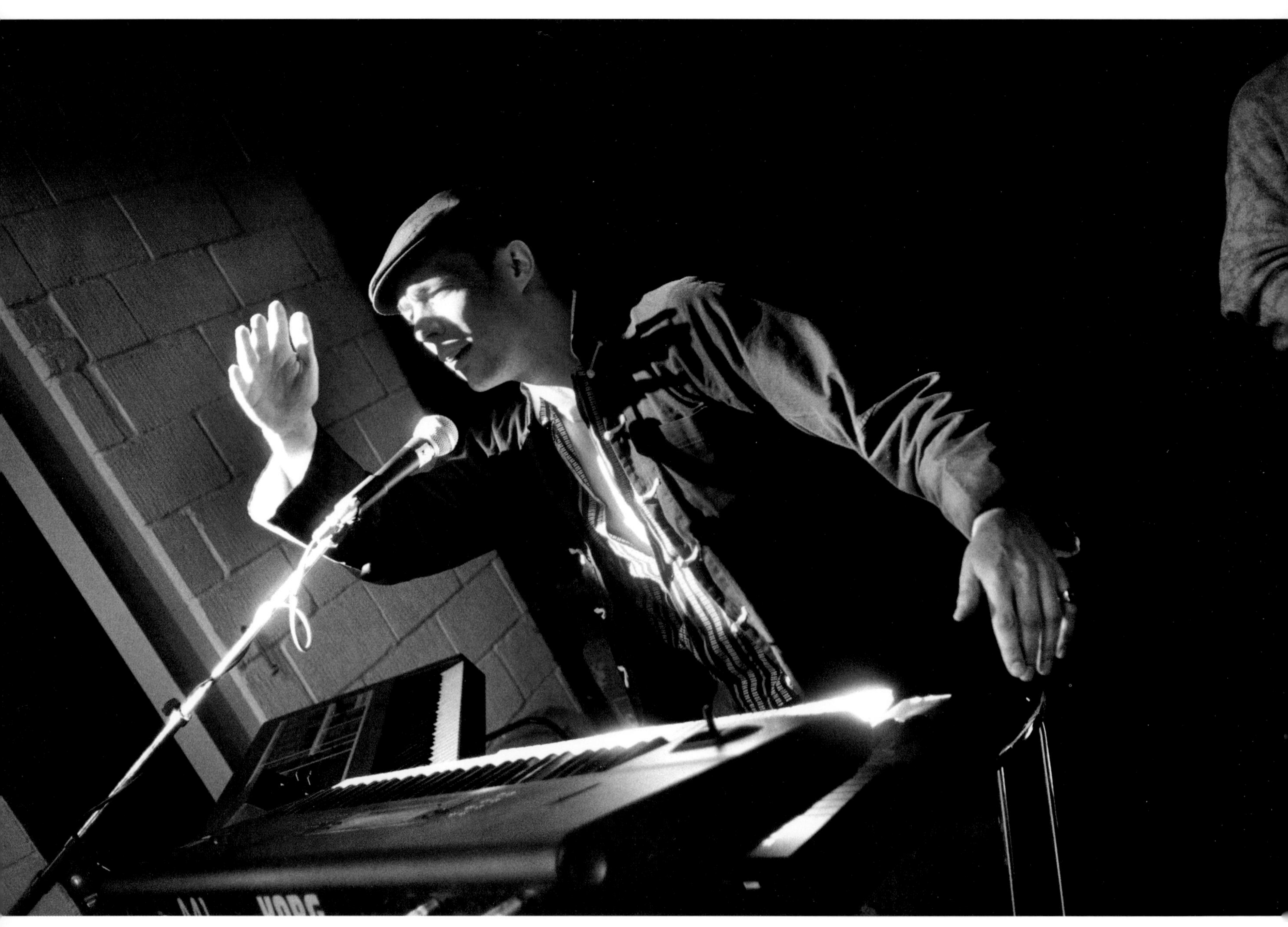

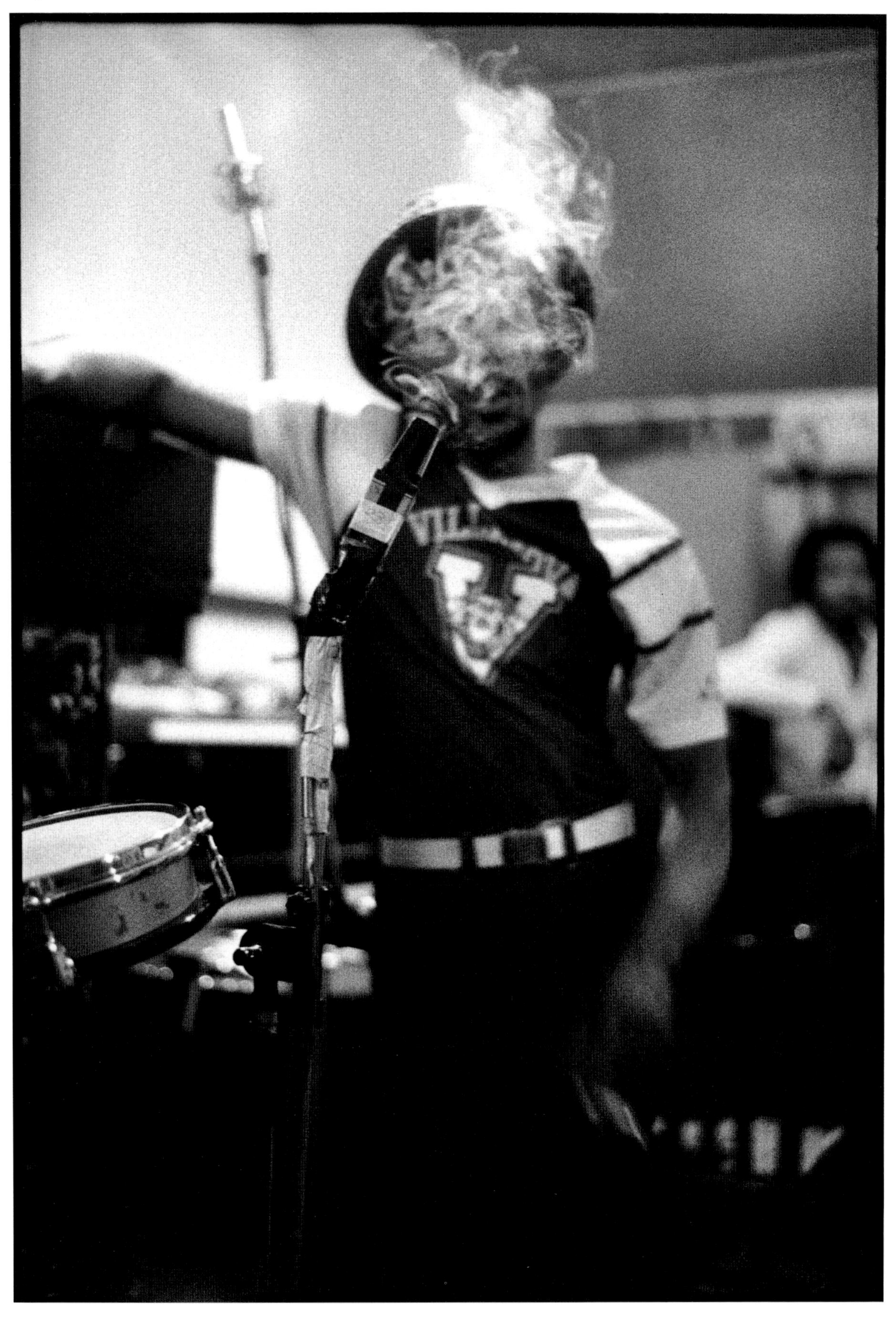

Margaret Cameron, Fox-Talbot, old techniques,
printing with the sun

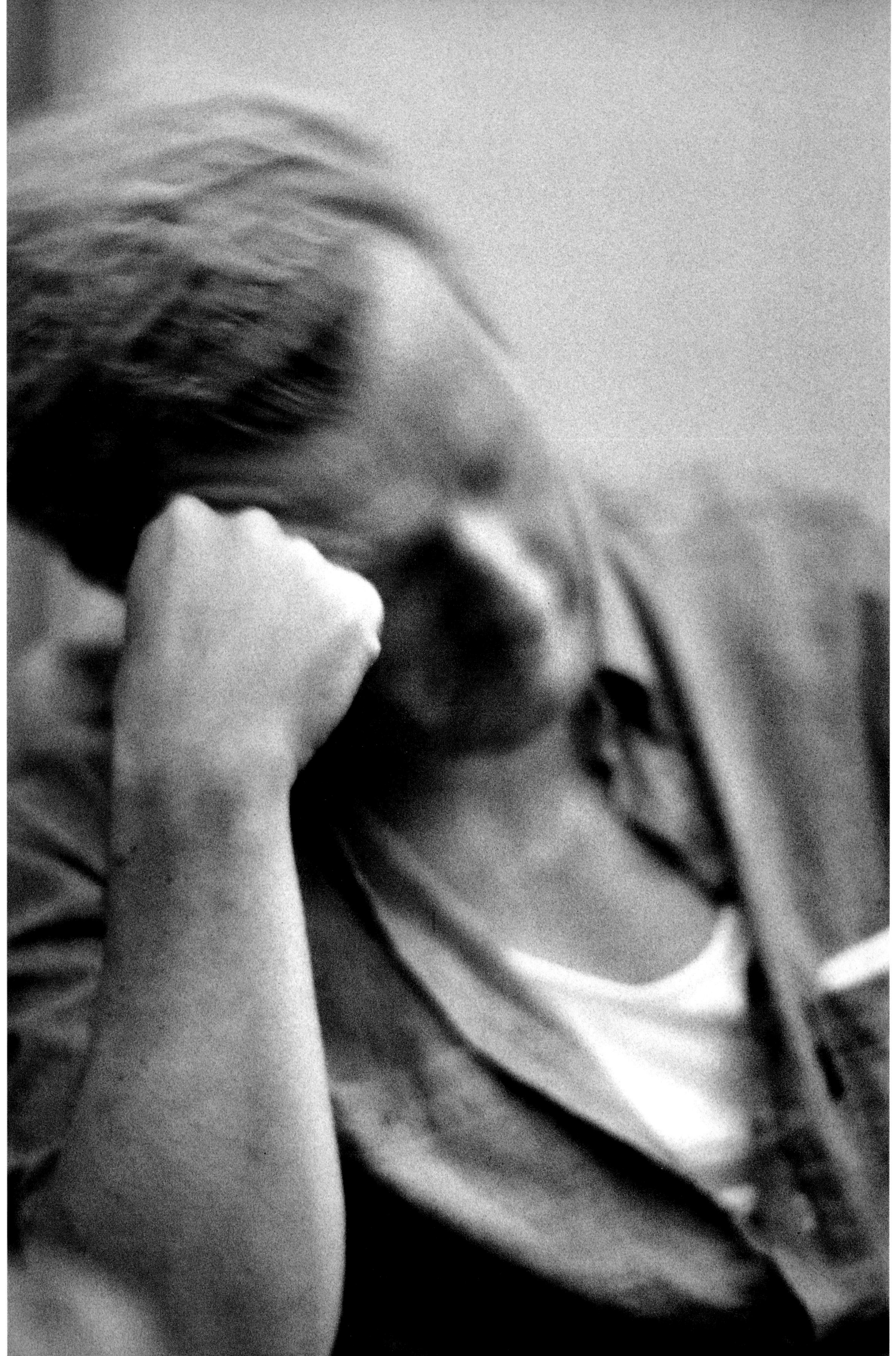

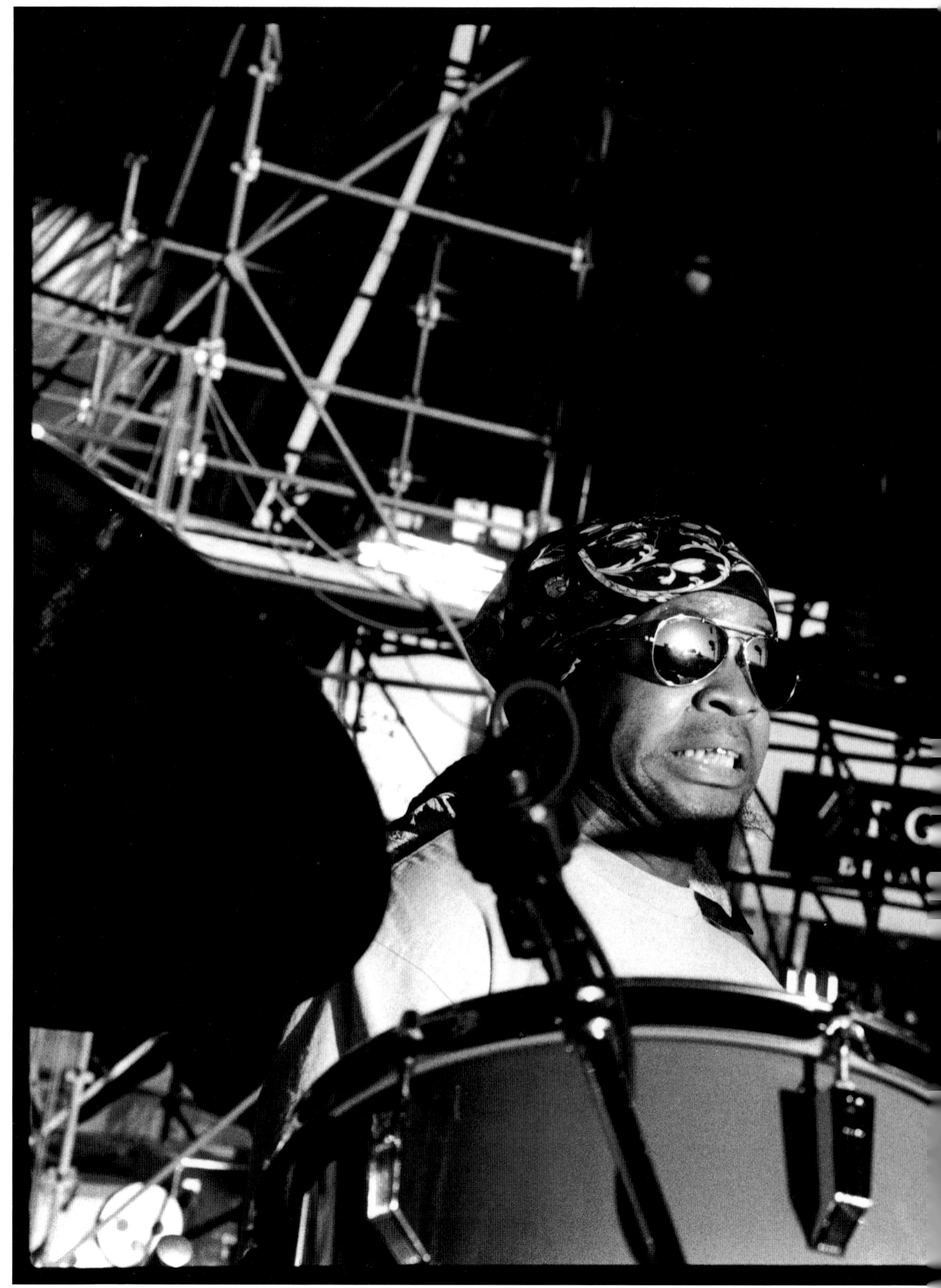

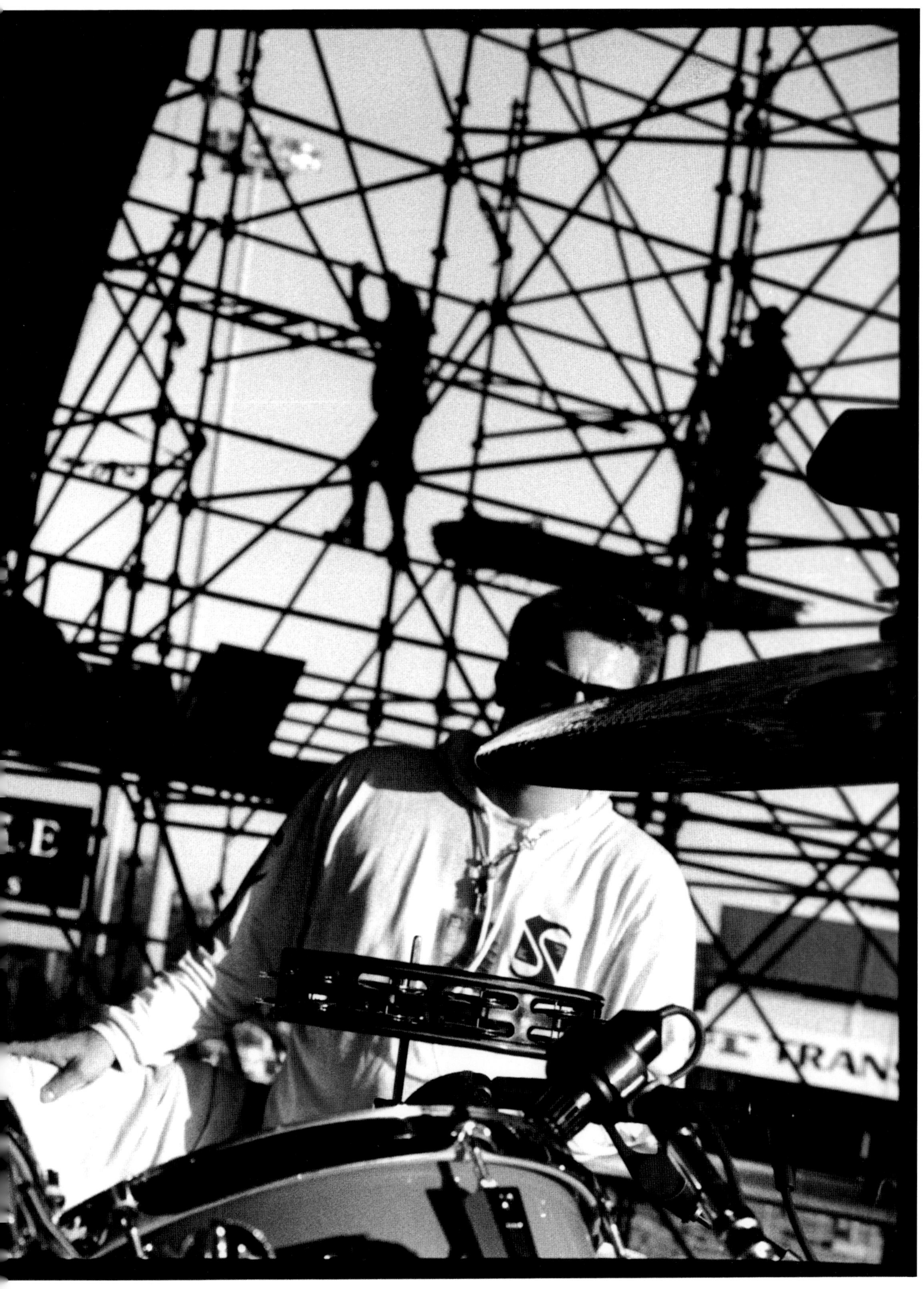

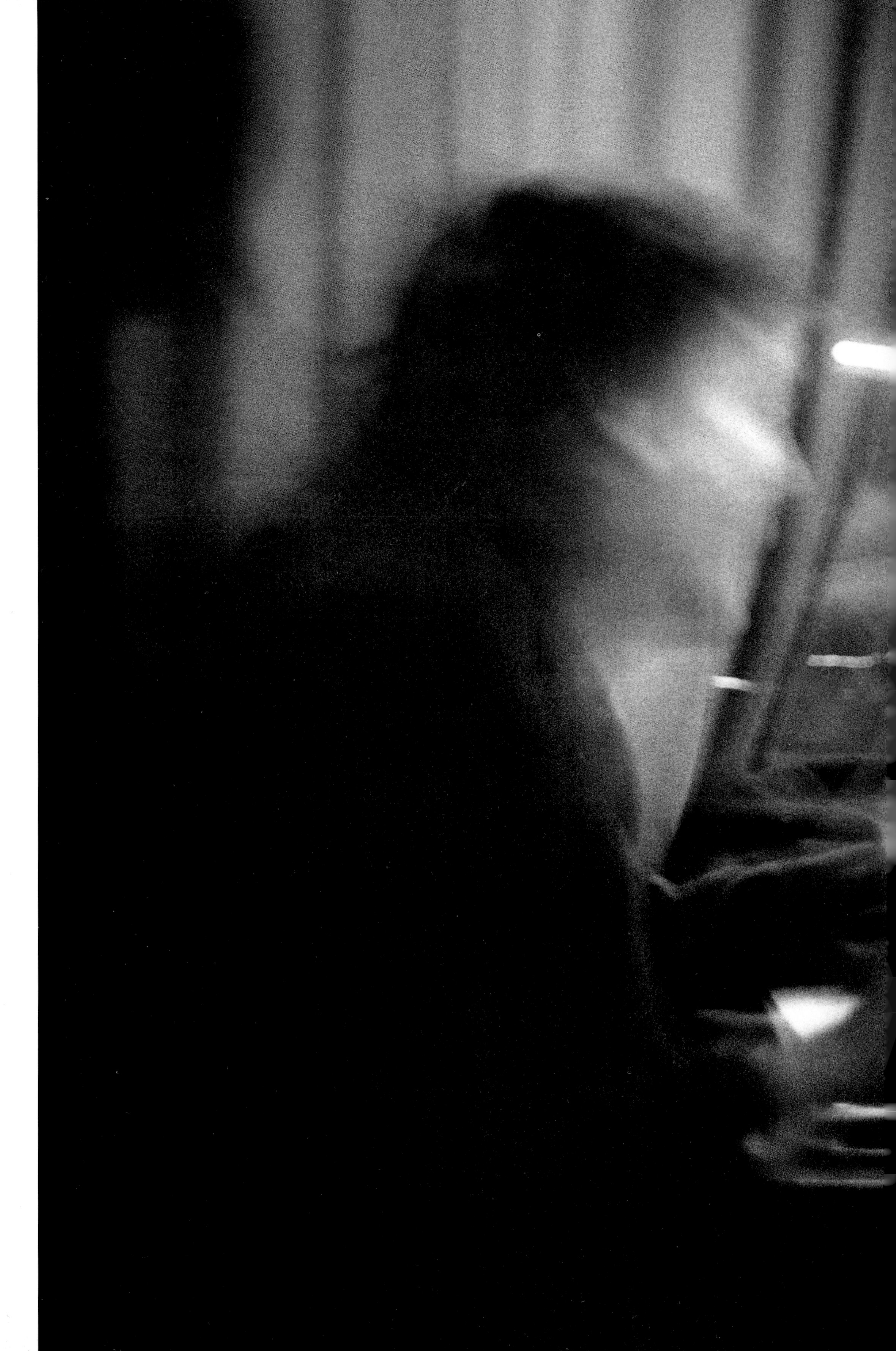

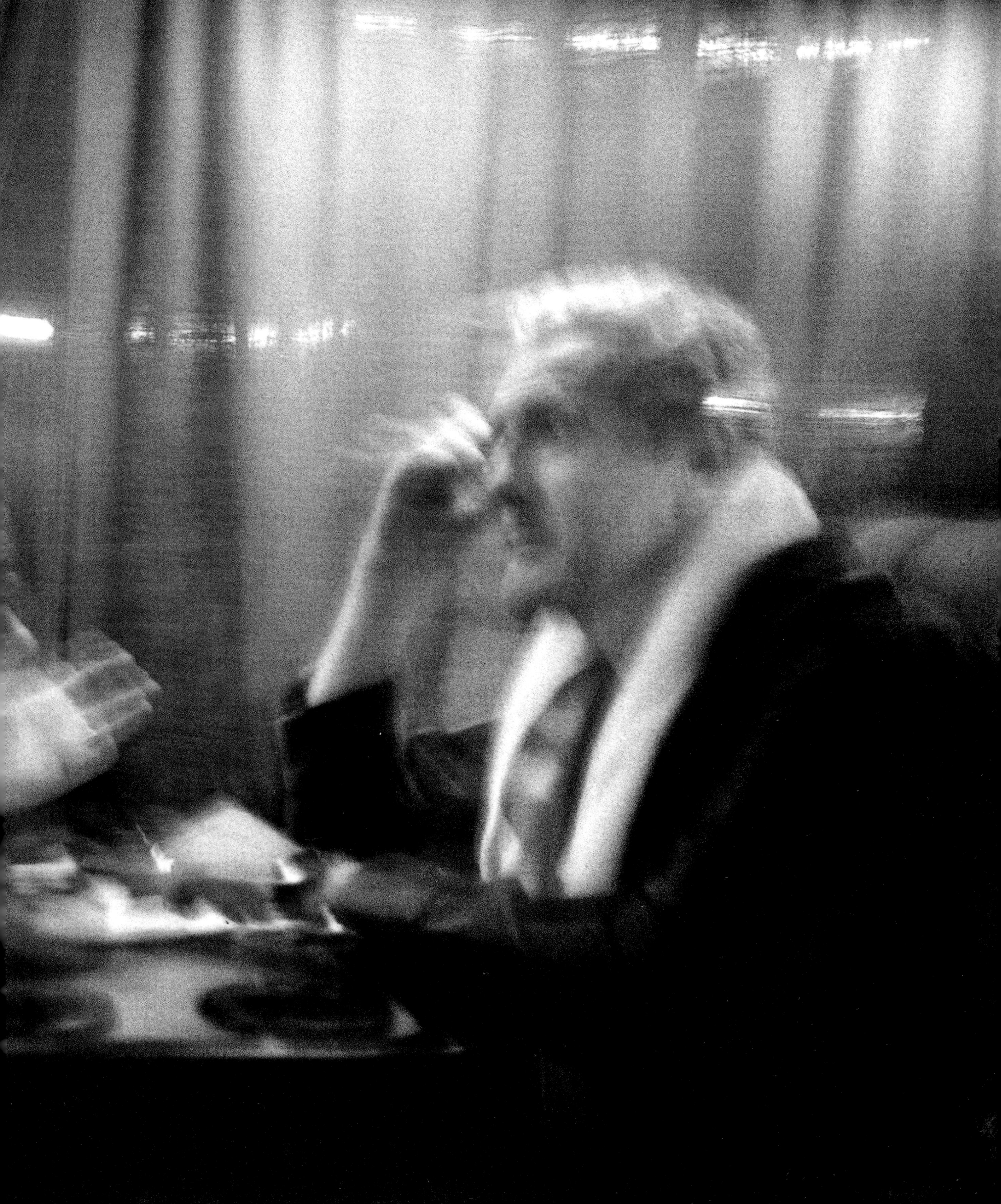

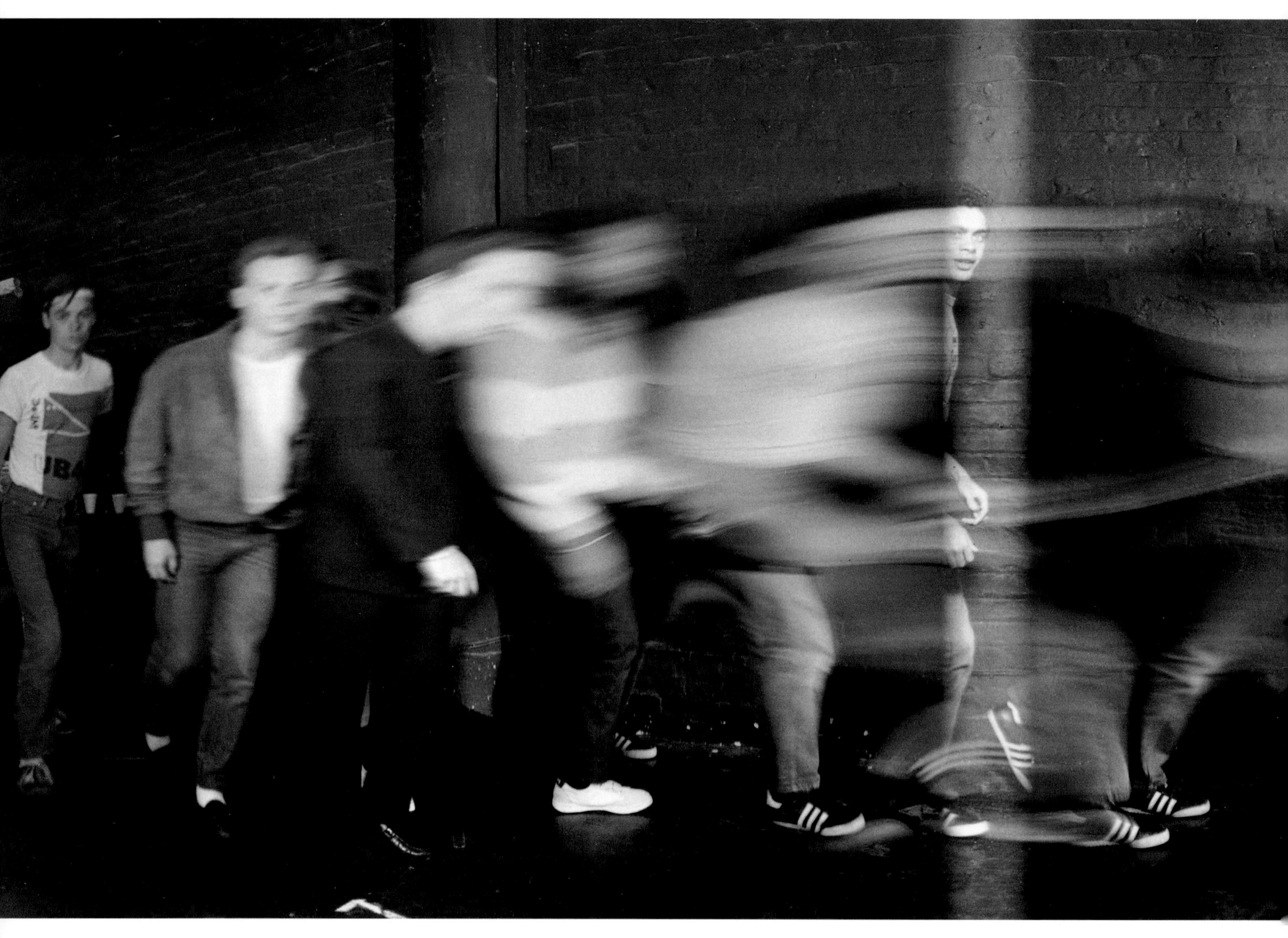

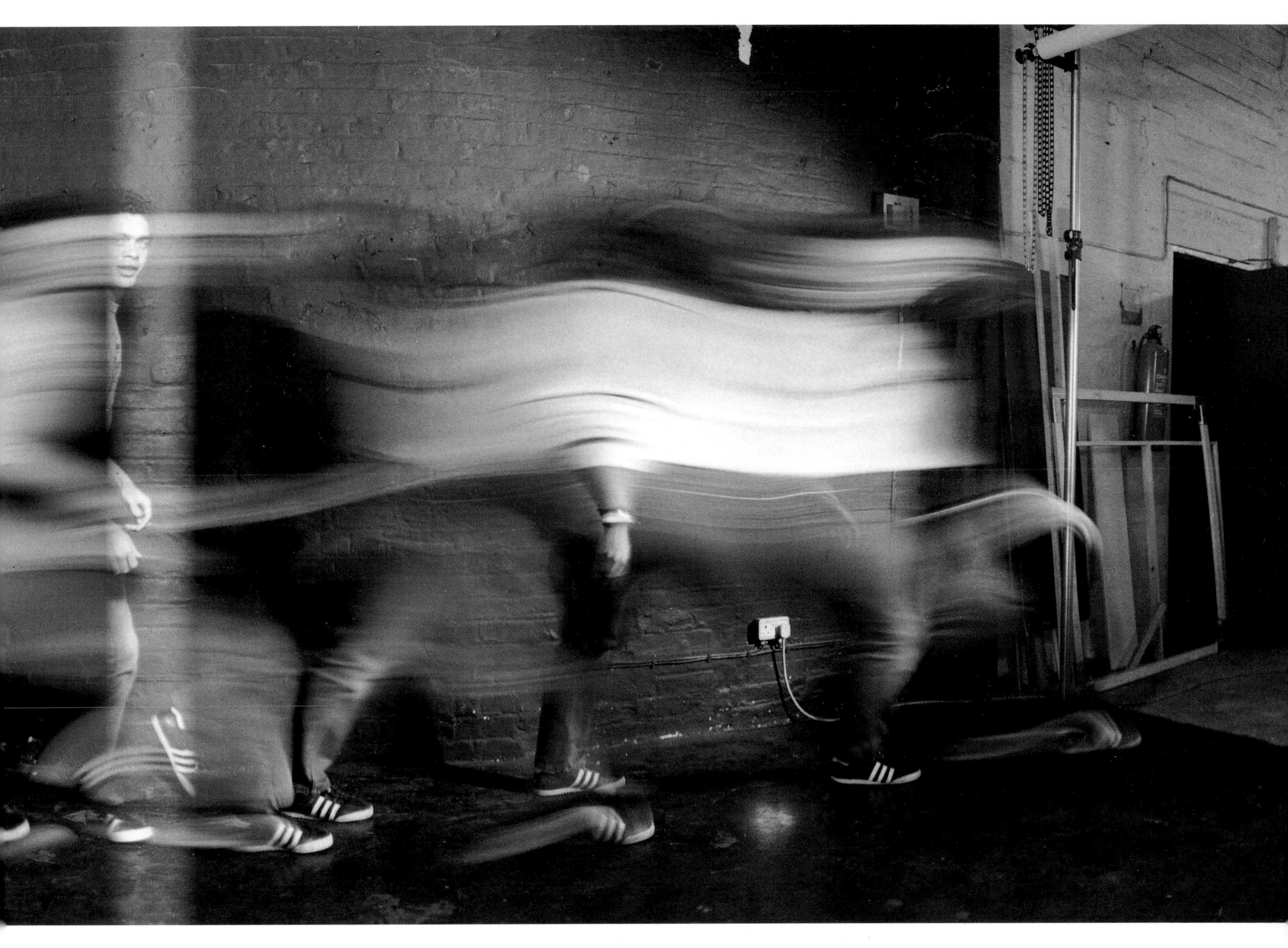

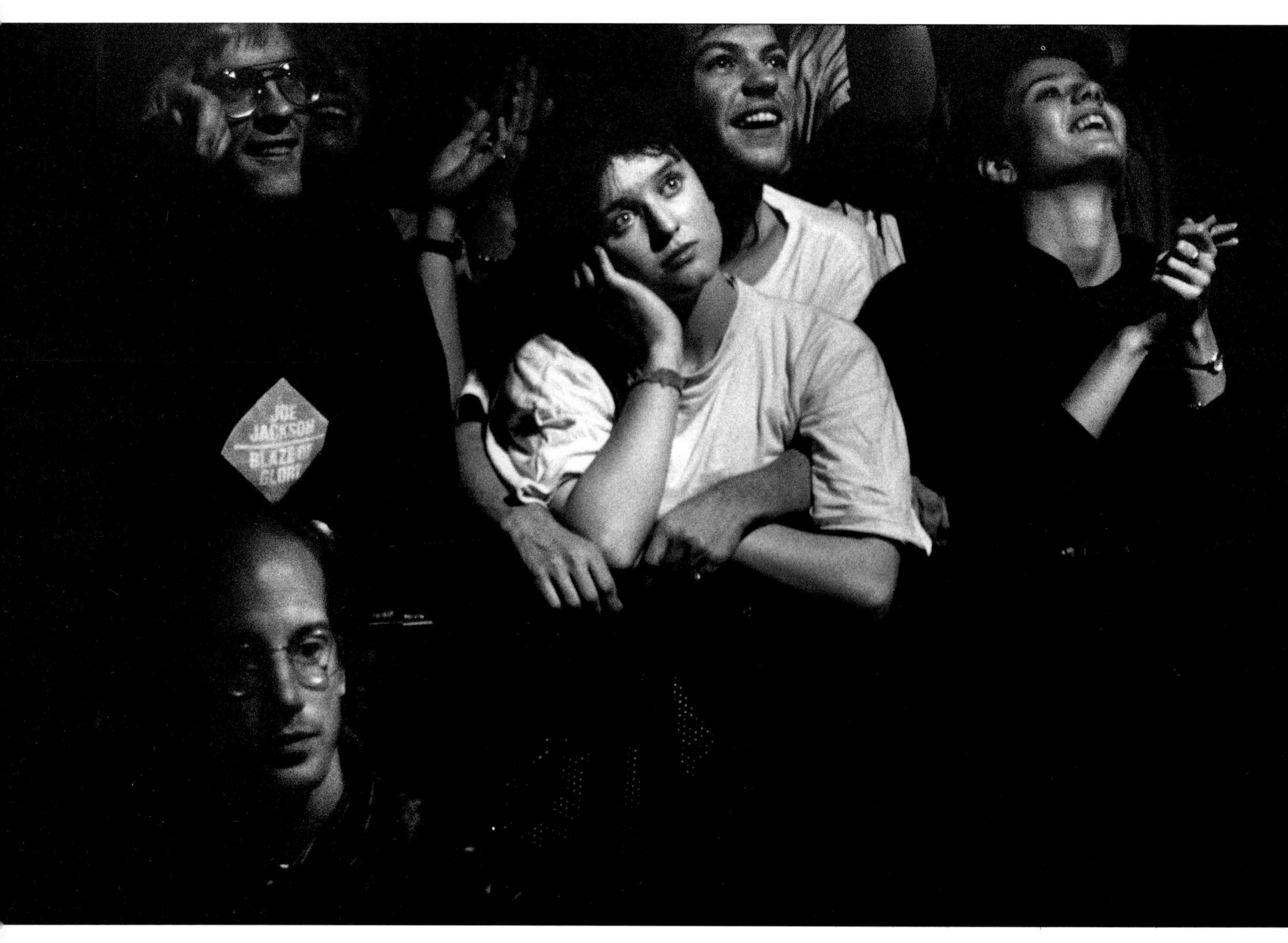
JOE
JACKSON

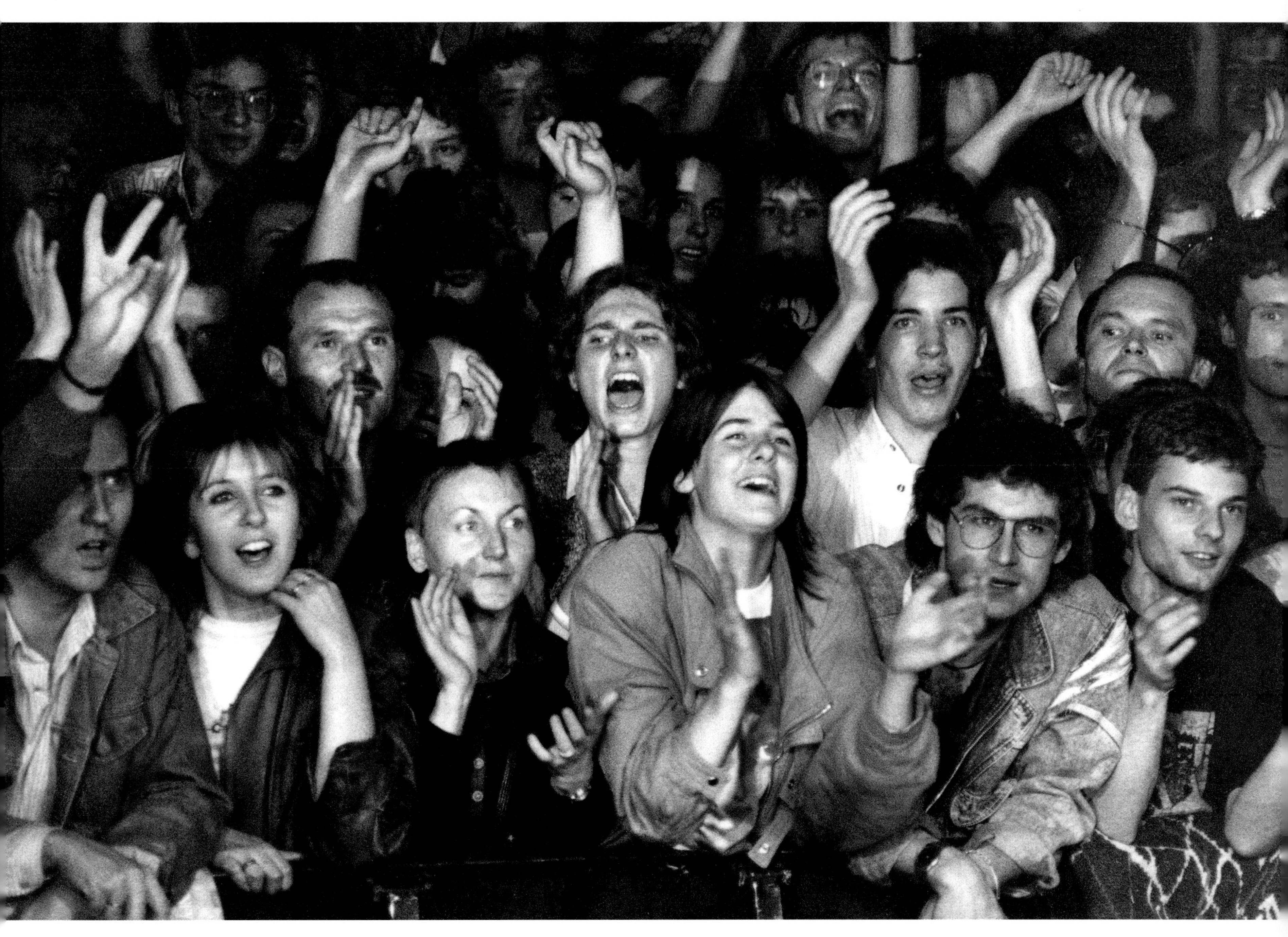

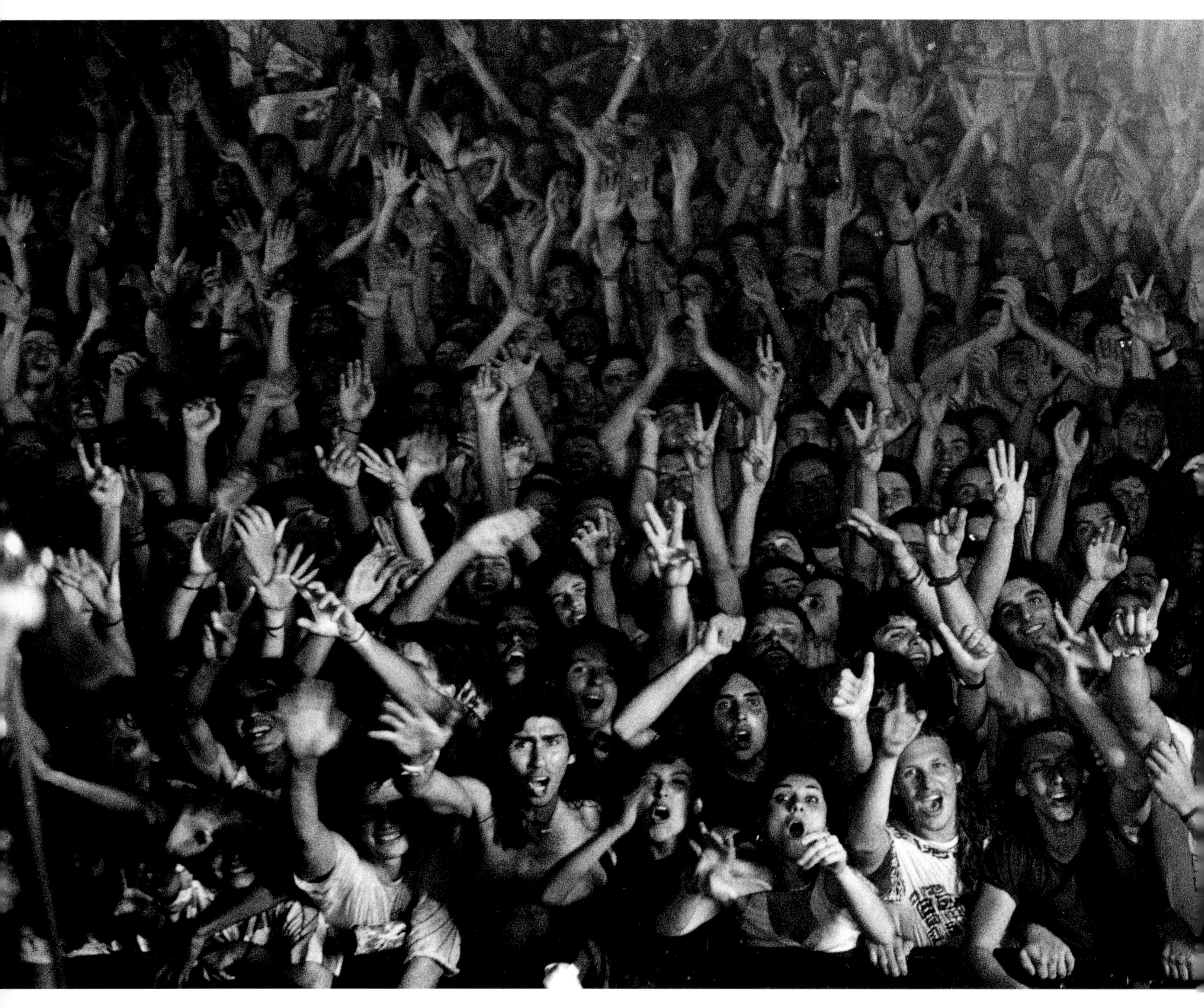

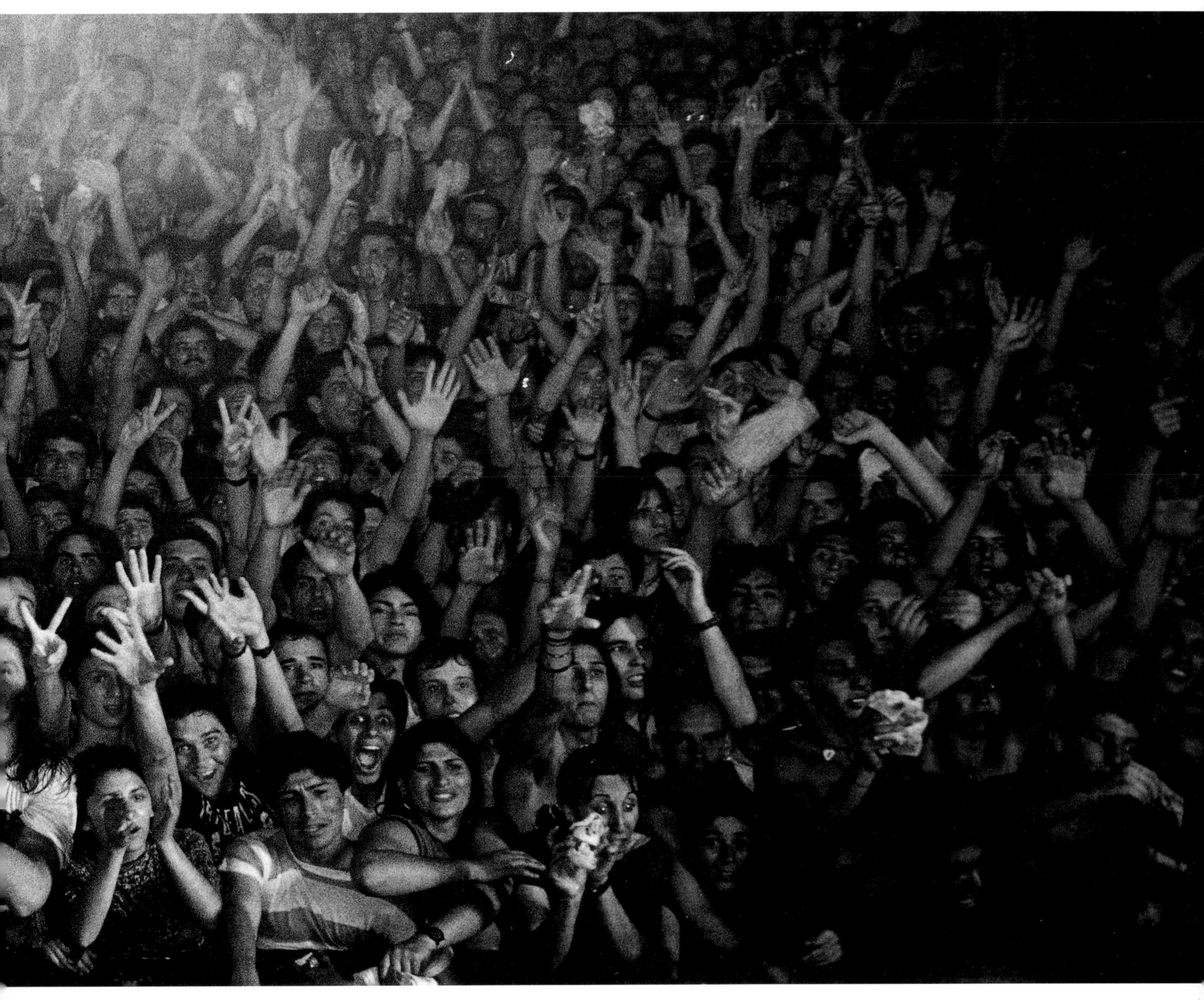

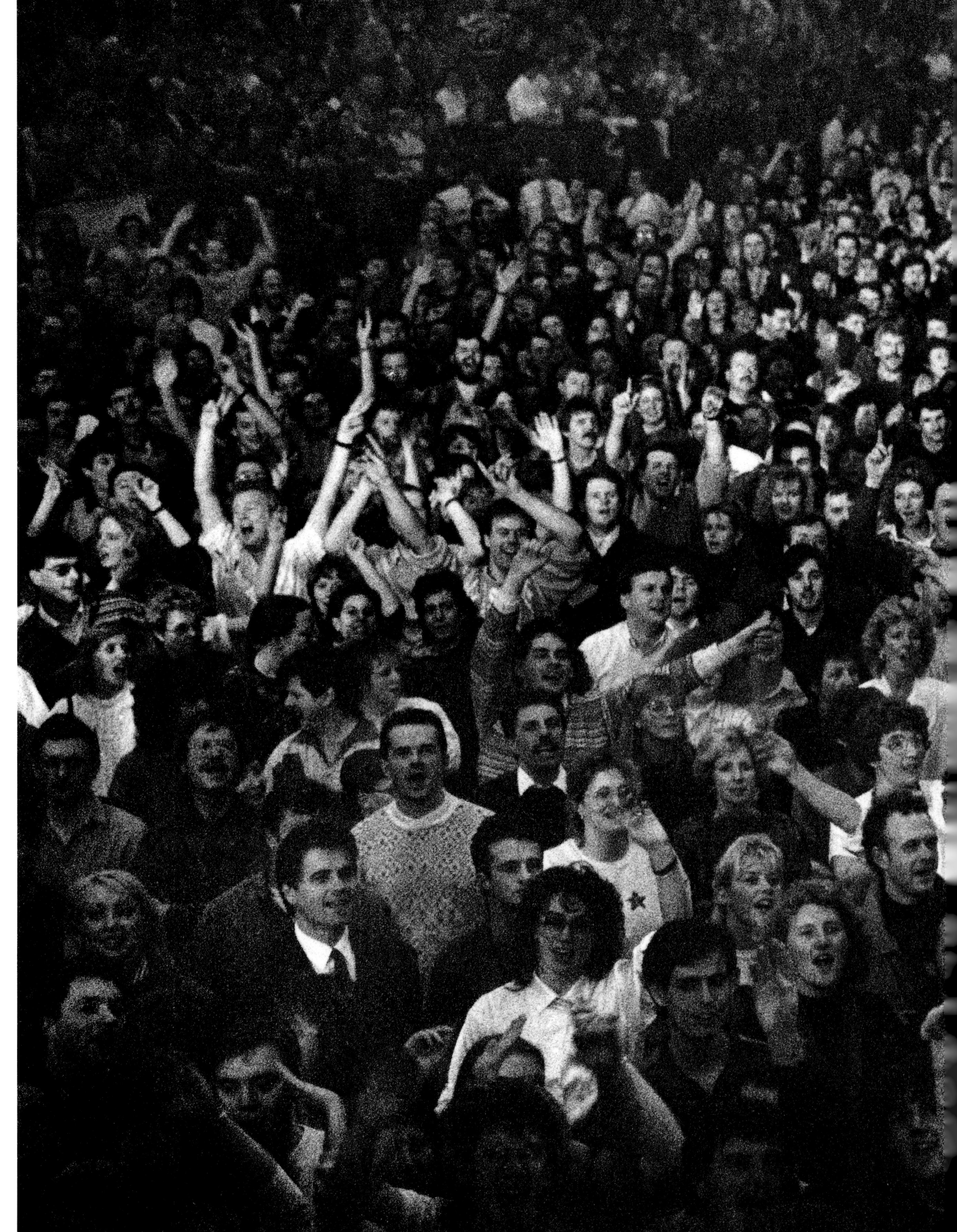

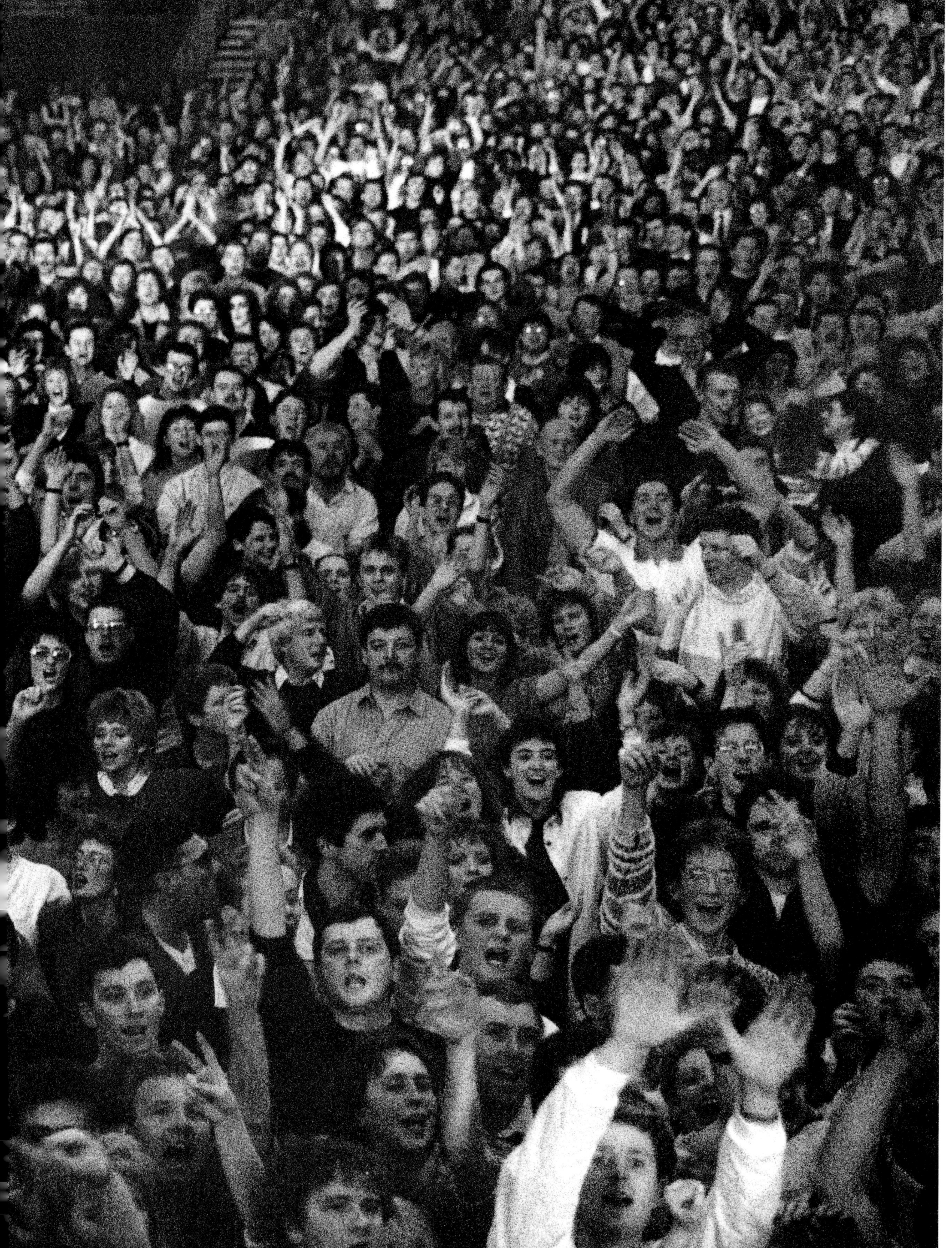

Looking out from deep below my eyes,

I capture moments in my life.

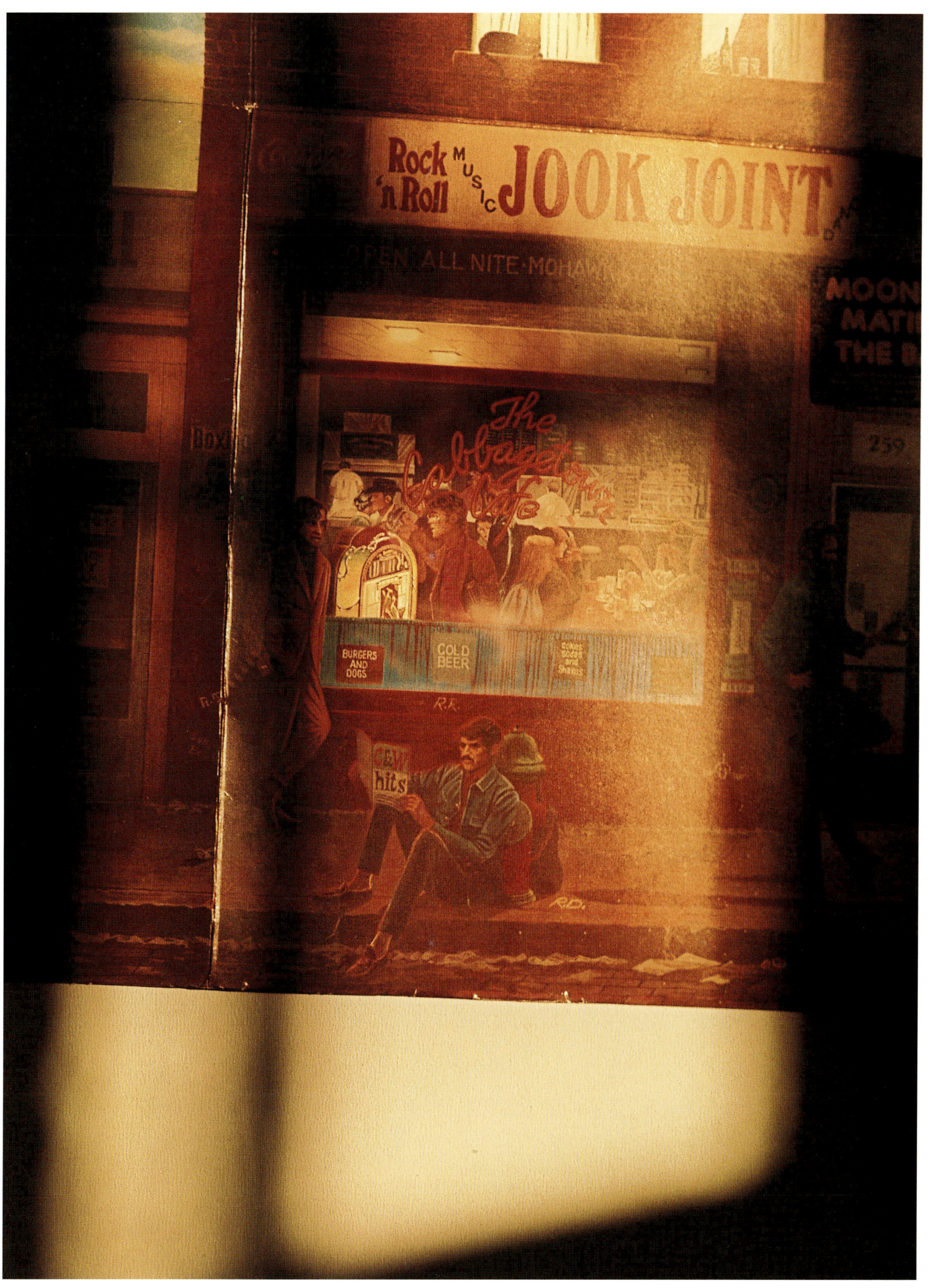
Rock 'n Roll
MUSIC
JOOK JOINT
The Cabbagetown Cafe
BURGERS AND DOGS
COLD BEER
259

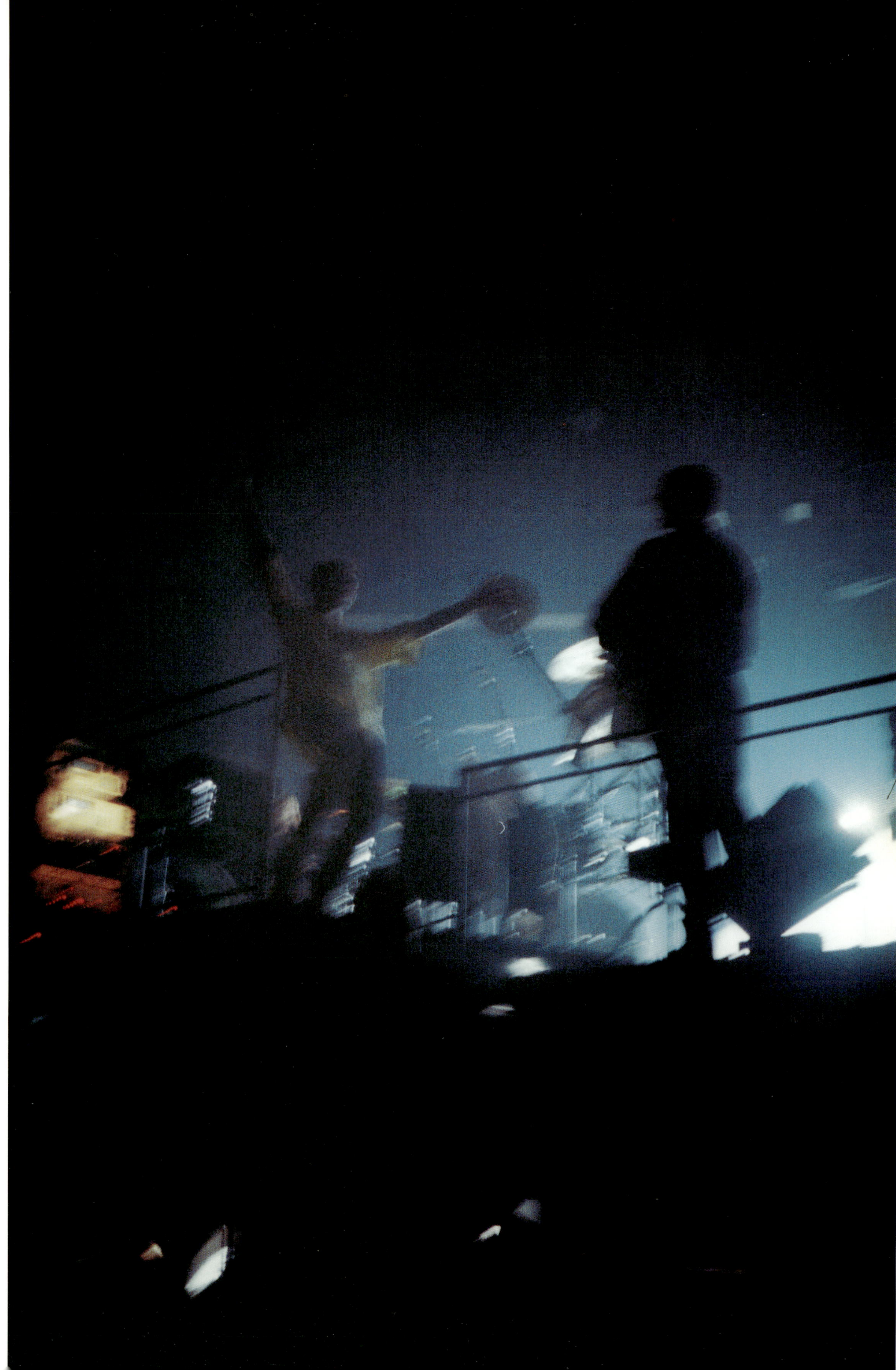

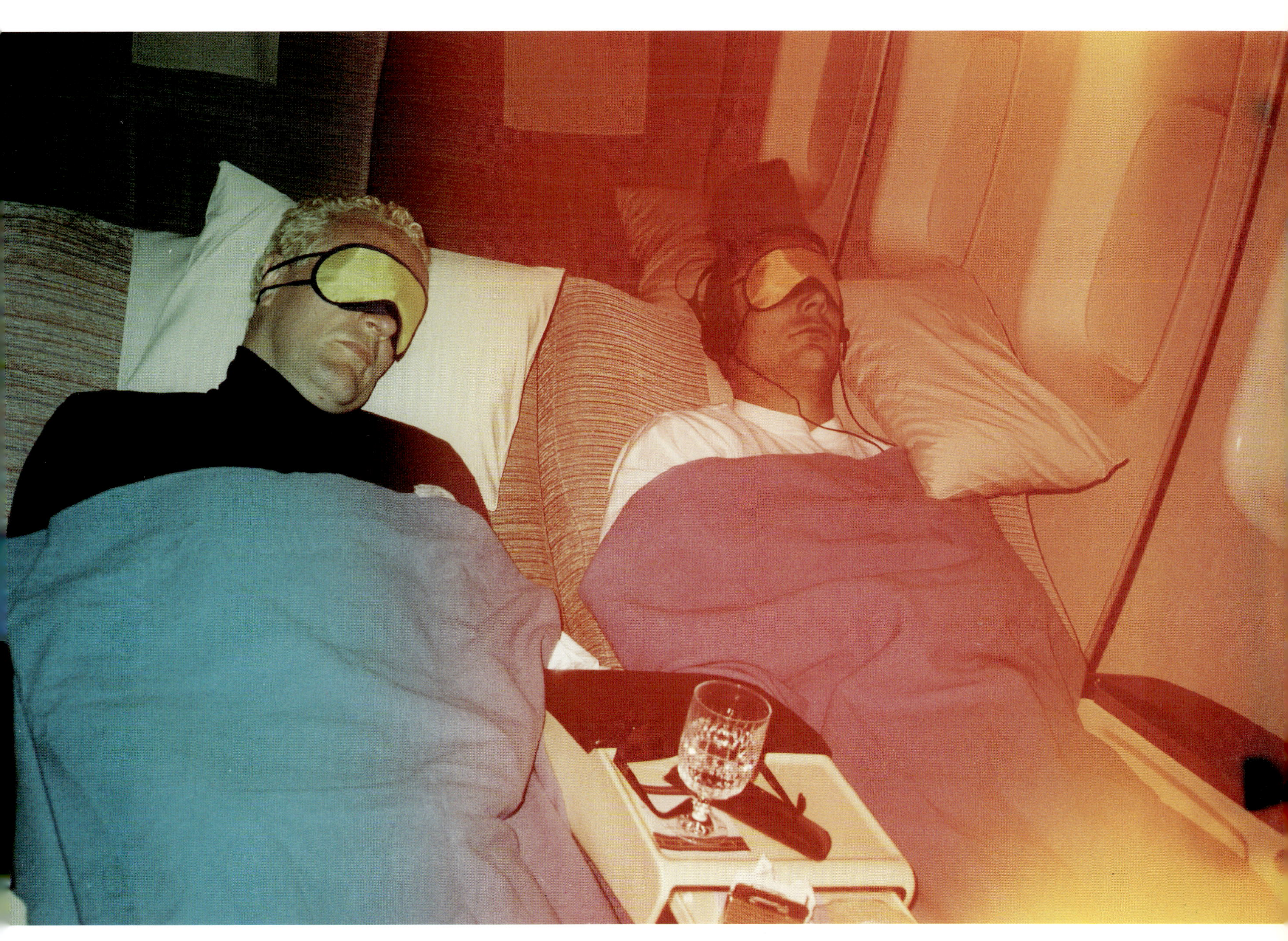

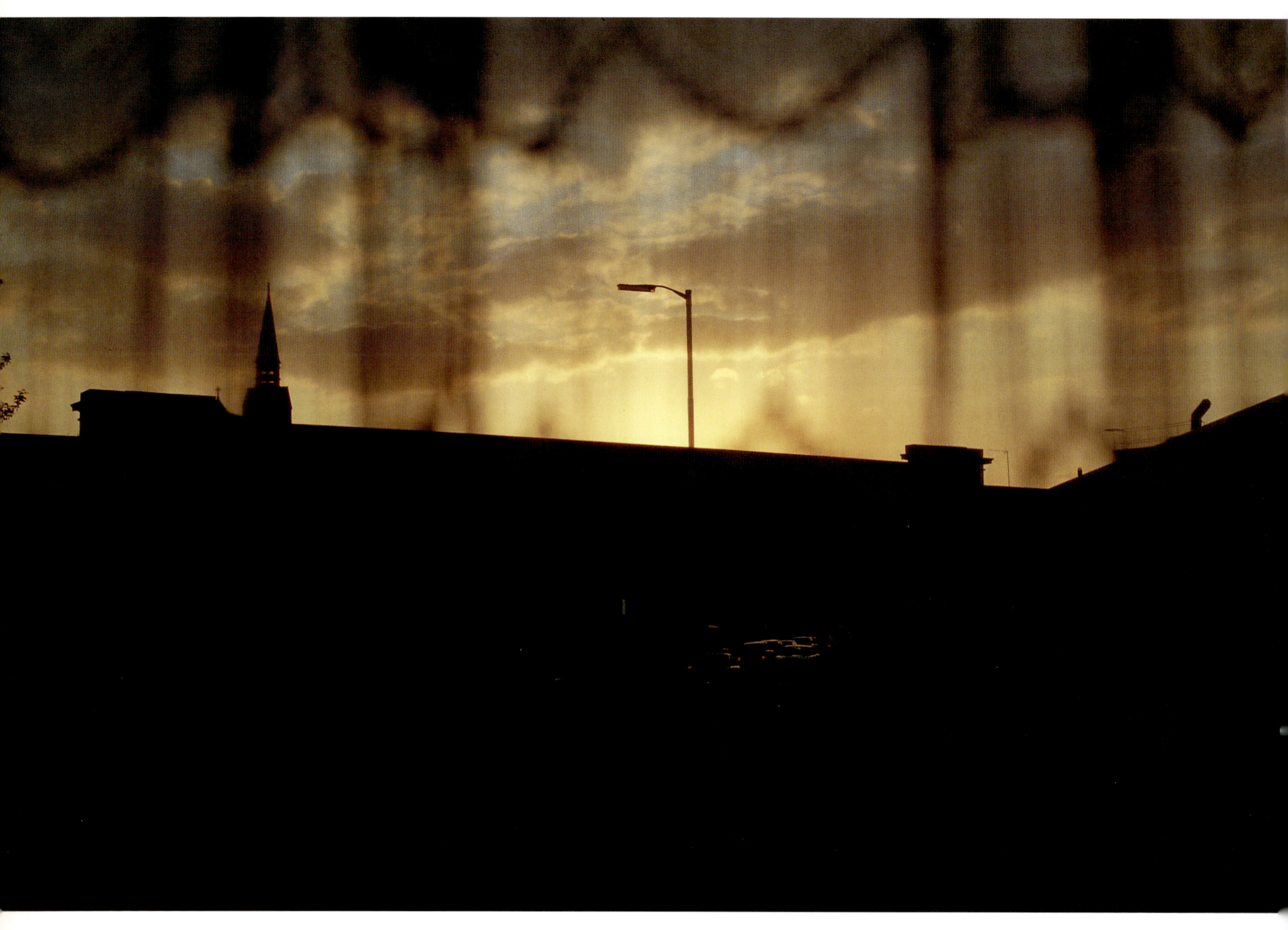

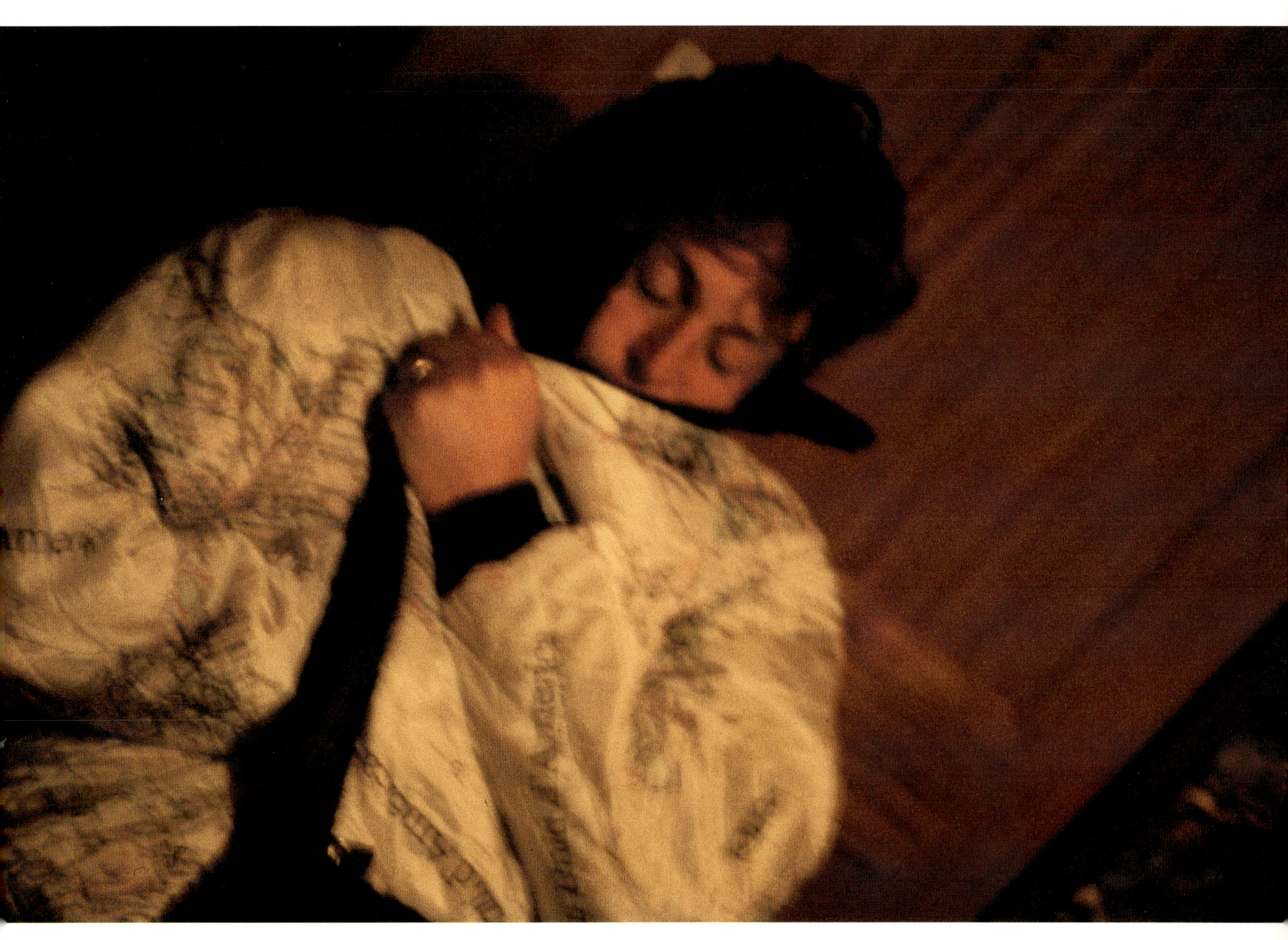

You can be anything you want to be if you're enthusiastic.

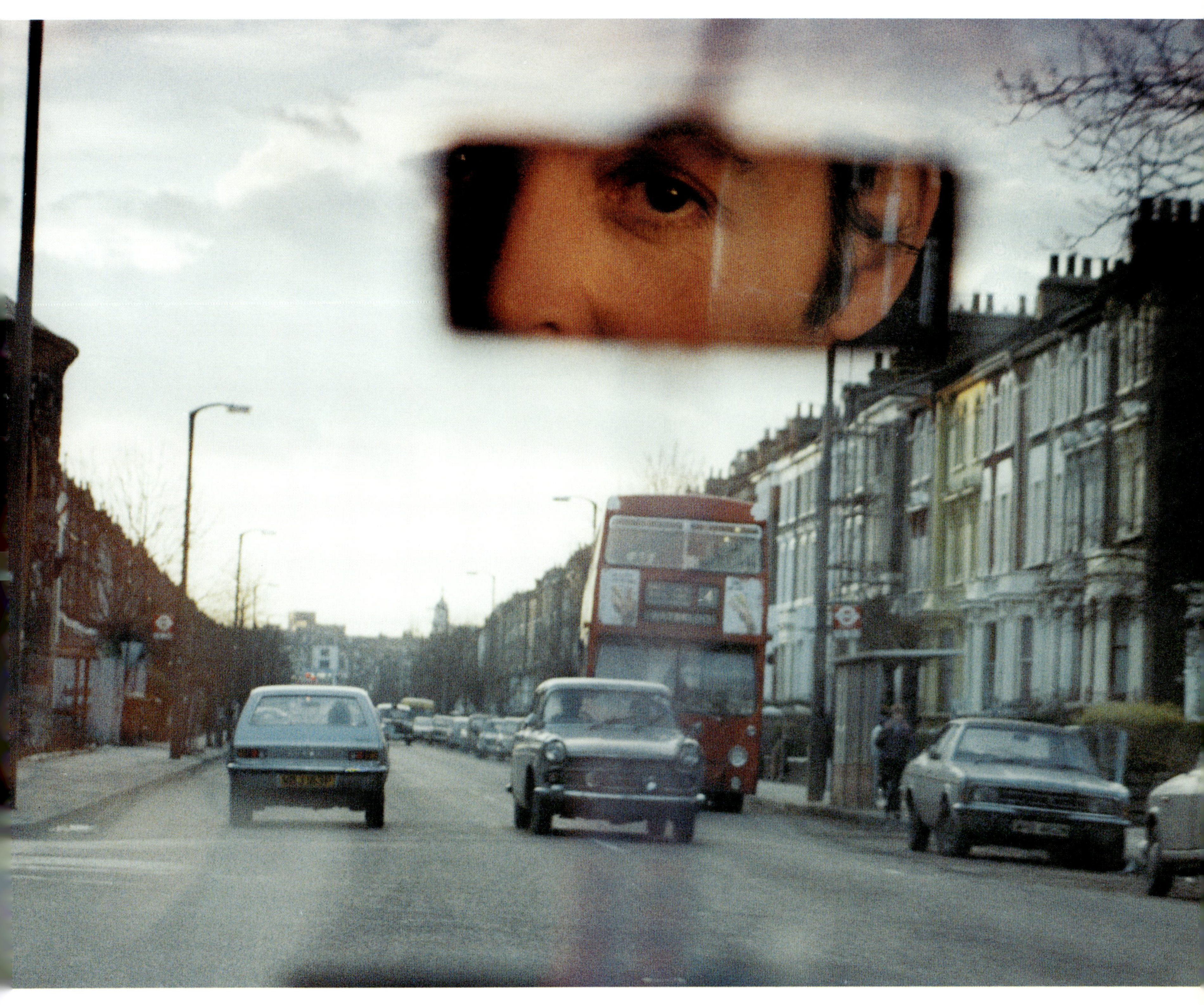

AFTERWORD

FEW OF THE PHOTOGRAPHS in this collection have been published before, and they might appear to represent a new aspect of Linda McCartney's work. In fact these rapid, intuitive glimpses have been at the core of her photography since the beginning of her career.

As a photographer she doesn't impose herself on situations – prefers to stay unseen, observing, with a keen eye for the transient moment. Quick, unobtrusive, somehow she doesn't miss a thing – I have noticed that, even when not taking pictures, she is one of those rare people able to concentrate on several different things at once. Uninhibited by formal training, she is a photographic free spirit, not afraid to break the rules, who works best from instinct.

In spite of Linda's early enthusiasm for the work of a wide range of photographers – from Edward Curtis and Dorothea Lange to Walker Evans and Edward Steichen – her own development was mostly outside of photography's mainstream. The photographs in *Roadworks,* for example, often have a filmic "from-the-hip" look, but she evolved this approach independently – before becoming really familiar with the 35mm work of New York School photographers like Robert Frank and Louis Faurer. Of course, something of the zeitgeist comes through in any period. What impresses about these vivid photographs, though, is that, like their author, they're completely natural, spontaneous – she sees modern life in an unusual but always truthful way.

MARTIN HARRISON

PHOTOGRAPHS

PAGE

2 Soul motorcycle. Arizona, 1993
7 Magic Robin. Kent, 1981
8/9 Wild truck. 1979
10 AC. Nashville, 1974
11 Pavilion. 1979
12 Slush. London, 1979
13 Jaywalkers. London, 1979
14 Waiting hungry. Arizona, 1993
16 Partial eclipse. London, 1984
17 Skip. London, 1984
18 Don't worry. London, 1984
19 Running with the ball. Scotland, 1969
20/21 Looking in. London, 1983
22 JH. Liverpool 1988
23 Vintage couple. Staffordshire, 1981
24 Thin pipe. London, 1984 *top*
Long pipe. London, 1984 *bottom*
25 Jogger. New York, 1978
26/27 Dead bears. London, 1988
28 Mannequins. London, 1982
29 Safe sex. London, 1982
30 Pocket pool. Liverpool, 1987
31 Totter. London, 1984
32 Stop. West Indies, 1981
33 Glare. London, 1989
34 Rock truck. 1969
35 Woven tires. 1969
36 Bus. 1985
37 Lollypop. Jamaica, 1991
38 Like father, like son. 1979
39 Number 28. London, 1969
41 Rag bag. Jamaica, 1972
42/3 Sunday best. West Indies, 1975
44 Gurner. 1971
45 Give. 1973
46 Corner. 1972
47 Watney. 1974
48 Red Dog. Arizona, 1992
49 Mother and child. Corfu, 1969
50/51 Sprites. Jamaica, 1978
52 Mourning. Portugal, 1969
53 Glance. Portugal, 1969
54 Check apron. Portugal, 1969
55 Prince Charles lookalike. Portugal, 1969
57 Heavy load. New Orleans, 1979
58/59 Boys on the beach. Barbados, 1969
60 Science fiction. California, 1982
61 Hook. 1991
62 Players. London, 1977
63 Portraits. London, 1977
64 Break. New York, 1968
65 Punter. London, 1979
66/67 Café. Denmark, 1971
68/69 Ace hi. 1972
70 Evelyn. Jamaica, 1977
71 Joy. Surrey, 1971
72 Silver beard on a red bus. London, 1995
73 After school. London, 1995
74 Hector. Scotland, 1970
75 Loco. Liverpool, 1991
77 End of the earth. 1989
78 Power lines. Liverpool, 1984
79 Power station. London, 1973
80 Gloved fear. Sussex, 1992
81 Dangerous drums. West Indies, 1982
82 Single engine. Scotland, 1980 *top*
Swallow line. Scotland, 1983 *bottom*
83 Tanks for nothing. Australia, 1979
84 Go veggie. 1981
85 JC. Barcelona, 1981
86 Hurry up. 1982
87 Escape. Tokyo, 1993

88 Trucking. New York, 1993
89 Mesh. Paris, 1971
90 Rendering. New York, 1989
91 Tipped. Chicago, 1989
92 Steam. New York, 1976
93 Cross. 1989
94 Going. London, 1974
95 Hopes. New York, 1990
97 Bellhop. Tokyo, 1989
98/9 Out here. California, 1975
100/1 Saga. 1978
102 Travelers. Surrey, 1989
103 Hands on. Sussex, 1969
104/5 Road signs. New York, 1988
106 Flare. Arizona, 1987
107 Rose. 1988
108 Roadworker. Scotland, 1975
109 Blue van. 1989
111 O'Malley. 1992
113 Wander. Sussex, 1978
114 The Sign Shop. 1988 *top left*
Lena. 1970 *center left*
Tops & Bottoms. 1979 *bottom left*
Please. 1990 *top right*
Psychic readings. 1990 *bottom right*
115 Liquors. 1991 *top left*
Palm reader. 1991 *bottom left*
Arrow. 1988 *top right*
Children crossing. 1978 *center right*
Sand in glove. 1992 *bottom right*
116 Fizz. 1989 *top left*
Fat burger. 1988 *center left*
Bert's dining. 1992 *bottom left*
Get It At Pages. 1987 *top right*
Uncultured pearls. 1988 *bottom right*
117 Once is all it takes. 1987 *top left*
Face painting. 1975 *bottom left*
After shaving. 1990 *top right*
Leather men. 1982 *center right*
Between Two Worlds. 1990 *bottom right*
118 14 bottles. 1962 *top*
12 motorcycles. 1962 *bottom*
119 Spark plugs. 1980 *top left*
Jawbreakers 1988 *bottom left*
Pigeonholes. 1991 *top right*
Bin. 1980 *center right*
Special offer. 1988 *bottom right*
121 Coalmen. Sussex, 1981
122 Hell's Kitchen. New York, 1990
123 Glaswegian. Scotland, 1969
124 Power. West Indies, 1970
125 The First of the Mohicans. 1981
126 Drac Hulk Billy. California, 1981
127 Put it there. London, 1975
128 Paper boy. Arizona, 1995
129 Wig. New York, 1989
130/1 Fur coats. London, 1990
132/3 Cocktails. New York, 1962
134 Rock-ola. London, 1982
135 Jive. London, 1982
137 Damp. Brazil, 1992
138 R&B van. 1986
139 Chrome truck. Tokyo, 1989
140/1 Cold set. 1982
142 Jacket and ties. Scotland, 1970 *left*
On the line. Scotland, 1970 *right*
143 Jacket. 1982 *left*
Keep music live. 1982 *right*
144 Dick's place. 1990
145 In makeup. London, 1982
146 Loaching and liming. Rio de Janeiro, 1993

147 Space. Rio de Janeiro 1993
148 Shaky. Kansas City, 1993
149 Intense. Kansas City, 1993
150 Duster. Surrey, 1989
151 Mark. 1990
152 Wix. 1992
153 Sea Saint. New Orleans, 1979
155 Carlucci. 1993
156/7 Sound check. 1993
158/9 After the gig. 1992
160/1 Wide UB. 1990
162 From the stage I. 1989
163 From the stage II. 1990
164/5 Uplift. 1993
166/7 Wings. 1990
169 Joint. 1990
170 The blast. 1992
171 Lights out. 1993
172 Curtain. 1988
173 Wrap. 1993
175 My love. London, 1985

Special thanx to

Martin "ML" Harrison, Mary McCartney, Zoë Norfolk, Robby "SA" Montgomery,
Paul McCartney, Pete Trew, Danny Pope, Roger Huggett, Allen Ginsberg,
Brian Clarke, Elaine and Bo Steer, Amanda Harrison,
CJ and all the Little, Brown people,
everyone at MPL, Stella, James, and Heather.

First Edition
Concept and layout by Martin Harrison
Designed and typeset by Roger Huggett
Jacket design by Steve Snider
ISBN 0-8212-2172-8
Library of Congress Catalog Card Number 95 - 83422
A CIP catalogue for this book is available from the British Library.

Published simultaneously in the United States of America by
Bulfinch Press, an imprint and trademark of
Little, Brown and Company (Inc.),
in Great Britain by Little, Brown and Company (UK),
and in Canada by Little, Brown & Company (Canada) Limited.

PRINTED IN ITALY